POLICE PISTOLCRAFT

The Reality-Based New Paradigm of Police Firearms Training

Michael E. Conti

SABER PRESS

North Reading, MA

A Subsidiary of Saber Group, Inc.

www.sabergroup.com

Police Pistolcraft:
The Reality-Based New Paradigm of Police Firearms Training
by Michael E. Conti

First Edition

Copyright © 2006 by Michael E. Conti

ISBN: 0-9772659-1-9
Printed in the United States of America

Published by Saber Press, a subsidiary of
Saber Group, Inc.
268 Main Street, PMB 138
North Reading, Massachusetts 01864, USA
Tel. (978) 749-3731
Fax: (978) 475-5420

Direct inquiries and/or orders to the above address or
contact us online at **www.sabergroup.com**

Copies of this book are available at special discounts for bulk
purchase. Special editions or book excerpts can also be created to
specifications. For details, contact the Special Sales Manager at Saber Press.

Cover photo by Al Pereira (www.advanced-photo.com). Courtesy Eagle-Tribune.

All photographs and illustrations by the author unless otherwise noted.

This book is dedicated to:

*The memory of Charley, Alje, Hanna, Bobby, Charbo,
and all our other brothers and sisters in blue
whose names grace the walls
of the Law Enforcement Officers Memorial.*

*And to the prayer
that no others will join them there.*

Other Books by Michael E. Conti

In the Line of Fire: A Working Cop's Guide to Pistolcraft

*Beyond Pepper Spray: The Complete Guide to Chemical
Agents, Delivery Systems, and Protective Masks*

Table of Contents

Table of Contents

....

SECTION TWO

WARNING
A Note on the Use of Lethal Force

The expressed purpose of this book is to present an overview of the New Paradigm Police Firearms Training Program to the trained police officer, military, or security professional. It is in no way meant to replace or contradict any department's or agency's current policies or procedures.

The justified use and employment of any type of weapon, regardless of its intended level of force, is a subject that must be addressed by each individual department or agency. Federal law, state law, departmental rules, regulations, policies and procedures must all be satisfied.

Today, in the United States, the use of deadly force by a law enforcement officer is generally only permissible as a last resort, when in the reasonable and considered opinion of the individual police officer there is an imminent threat of death or serious bodily injury to himself or someone else.

It is imperative that each officer operating in the field knows and understands both the meaning and the intent of all applicable standards regarding the use of any level of force option available to him. It is also imperative that he be able to clearly and reasonably articulate his actions, especially when those actions involve the employment of any level of force.

As civilian, military, and security professionals, we must also be familiar with various federal statutes and court rulings that have a direct impact on what actions we may take and how they may affect our liability exposure while performing our duties.

Your department, unit, or agency is responsible for your training in this area. Once properly trained, the onus of responsibility for adhering to this training is then placed squarely on the individual officer.

Neither the author nor the publisher is responsible for the use or misuse of any information contained in this book. It is presented for information purposes only.

Attention! Firearms training is a dangerous activity that can lead to serious injury or death if not properly and safely performed. All training must be conducted at approved ranges and under competent supervision.

Reviewer's Credentials

H. Anthony Semone, Ph. D.
Licensed Psychologist
8825 Patton Road, Wyndmoor, PA 19038
Tx: 215-836-7179 Fx: 215-836-0822 email: tonys05@bellatlantic.net

Dr. H. Anthony Semone has developed a rare blend of education, training, acquired skills, and experiences that make him uniquely qualified to review police firearms training programs such as that described in *Police Pistolcraft.*

A graduate of Kent State University, he holds an M. A. in Psychology and a Ph. D in Clinical Psychology. He is one of 11 psychologists in the country certified personally by Dr. Ralph M. Reitan to administer the Halstead-Reitan test batteries. His extensive experience in the field of Psychology includes service as an Internal Consultant for the Abraxas Foundation, Pittsburgh, PA; a Clinical Neuropsychologist at the Rehab Hospital of York, York, Pennsylvania; Clinical Director for The Child and Adolescent Unit, York Hospital, York, PA; Associate Professor of Psychology at Clarion State College; and independent Practice of Clinical Psychology and Forensic Psychology in Clarion, PA.

Dr. Semone has also evaluated and intervened on behalf of law enforcement officers suffering from the enduring effects of post-shooting trauma and post-traumatic stress disorder, and provided pro bono testimony in a Federal sentencing hearing during which he was qualified as an expert in post-shooting trauma and post-traumatic stress disorder. In addition to advanced studies and experience in forensic psychology, clinical neuropsychology, clinical psychology, and police psychology, Dr. Semone, a member of the Police Policy Studies Council and an Adjunct Instructor with Strategos International, has pursued both basic and advanced courses in the fields of professional firearms training and education.

To this end he has attended courses at many recognized police and private firearms training academies to include the Baltimore County (Maryland) Police Department, Chapman Academy, Defense Associates of Connecticut (Taylor Method), Defense Training International (Farnum Method), Lethal Force Institute, Smith & Wesson Academy, and Thunder Ranch. He has been awarded instructor-level status from the Lethal Force Institute, NRA, Pennsylvania State Police, Smith & Wesson Academy, and Strategos International.

Dr. Semone has relentlessly pursued the achievement of these specialized skill sets for more than four decades, with the determination and tenacity befitting his status as a former member of the United States Marine Corps.

These unique qualifications have enabled him to provide clinical and neuropsychological consultation in high-profile civil and criminal cases. As a result, he has testified in both federal and state courts in cases involving alleged terrorism, homicide, rape, and aggravated assault, and provided affidavits in cases involving serial murder, multiple murder, and arson, to include death penalty cases.

Dr. Semone has been in private practice since 1995 in Wyndmoor, Pennsylvania.

Foreword

Michael E. Conti has written the most objective and informative book I have ever read concerning police firearms training. I believe this book should be required reading for every law enforcement firearms instructor in the United States. I also believe that the training program described within it should be adopted by every law enforcement agency in the country.

As a former law enforcement officer and firearms instructor since 1961, I was personally involved both in academia as an instructor and in the field where I participated in many violent duty confrontations. During my law enforcement officer days, I quickly learned that in order to survive in the field, I needed to develop my own techniques, for what we were taught in traditional police firearms training classes was of little use in actual confrontations.

It was amazing to me as I read Michael's book, how his ideas and thoughts were parallel to those I had arrived at through my experiences as a member of the NYPD. This book is right on the mark.

Michael has great courage to address the inadequacy of the majority of the current fundamental law enforcement firearms training programs and approaches. His in-depth findings will no doubt be criticized by proponents of the current nationally recognized methods. However, the research, study and resultant training program Michael has presented in this book are vital to the safety of all police officers working in the field and should be adopted by all agencies responsible for police firearms training.

I congratulate Michael for producing a much needed study and contribution toward improving the training for all the members of our law enforcement community.

Jim Cirillo
Retired NYPD
NYPD Honor Legion
Former FLETC Law Enforcement Instructor
Author, *Guns, Bullets, and Gunfights: Lessons and Tales from a Modern-Day Gunfighter*

Foreword

This is a brilliant, seminal, groundbreaking work.

The debate between point shooting and sighted shooting advocates has been raging for years, and will no doubt continue to rage for centuries to come. For those who are interested in this vital debate, Mike Conti's book has clearly captured and defined the point shooting side of this issue. Even for those who are not "sold" on point shooting, there is MUCH that you can learn from this book.

I predict that this will be the definitive book on the topic of point shooting and handgun performance under stress, as well as handgun training in the point shooting school, for the foreseeable future. This is much more than just a training manual. Building on the true pioneers in this field, combined with the best available modern research, and powerful, extensive new research that the author himself has conducted, this book provides an invaluable insight into the psychology and the physiology of combat.

Mike Conti's scientific analysis and application of his many years of observations and training in the "House of Horrors" are simply brilliant. His assessment of the "puppy" or unconscious mind, and the application of operant and classical conditioning in firearms training represent the best writing and thinking that I have ever seen on the subject.

I am very proud and honored to observe the material drawn from own work, and I am honored by Mike's generous acknowledgment of my contribution to this seminal text. If this book had been available to me earlier, much of it would have been integrated into my own book, *On Combat*.

I highly recommend *Police Pistolcraft* to anyone interested in this vital field.

Lt. Col. Dave Grossman
U.S. Army, Retired
Former Professor of Military Science & Chair, Arkansas State University
Former Assistant Professor, Department of Behavioral Sciences and Leadership, USMA, West Point
Author, *On Killing: The Psychological Cost of Learning to Kill in War and Society*

Acknowledgements

It would be impossible to acknowledge and thank all of the individuals who have helped make this book possible. Years of dedicated research and hard work have been expended by countless men and women in the name of improving police firearms training and increasing officer safety awareness levels, all of which have contributed in ways big and small to the development of the New Paradigm.

Therefore I will limit myself to acknowledging those who have had a direct influence and affect on my work in this area, and who have contributed personally to the creation of the program and this book. If I have overlooked anyone, please be assured it was an unintentional oversight on my part.

On the home front, as always, my wife Kathy, and children Katie and Nick have proved infinitely patient and supportive of my efforts. One of my greatest hopes is that my children will come to understand when they are older what drove me to spend so many hours away from home working and training, as well as the many hours spent away at home, locked in the basement, researching and writing.

To my parents, Margie and Jim, brother Jim and sister Carol; for all the years of support and encouragement.

To one of my oldest friends and fellow police officer, Patrick McAdam, without whose influence I would never have followed the path that lead me to the most rewarding career I could have imagined.

To all the members of my department who have participated in and otherwise contributed to the development and administration of training programs, old and new.

Especially to the members of the Massachusetts State Police Firearms Training Unit (FTU), who continue to work hard every day in order to ensure their fellow officers receive the best possible training that can be provided. In particular, thanks to Donna Losardo, Paul Wosny, and Johanna Lawlor, stalwart souls all.

An additional thanks to Paul Wosny and Donna Losardo is also necessary, for they both generously consented to allow me to photograph them demonstrating the various techniques shown in the book. Their contributions were critical and I greatly appreciate their time and efforts.

To the original members of Saber Group: Paul Damery, Tim Donnelly, Tom Robbins, and the late Roger A. Ford. Many recognized the problem. A few attacked it. I am proud to be associated with each one of you.

To Colonel Rex Applegate, whose belief in the combat value of Point Shooting was like a bright flame that flickered in heavy winds for many years, but refused to be extinguished. His adamant insistence that there was a better way to train police officers to use their weapons continued up until the day he died. Thanks to his unwavering commitment to his beliefs, there is now a new generation of instructors who will carry on with the work.

To Bill Burroughs, one of the greatest influences on my teaching style and approach. Bill showed me that it was all right to believe in and teach your material with an almost religious zeal, as long as you did the research and truly understood what you were preaching, and just as important, to whom you were preaching and why.

To Jim Cirillo, one of the few men with the courage to remain true to the mission, regardless of who may be offended, or how many ivory towers may be shaken. In addition to being a true friend, Jim has also served as an inspiration for me, for whether he is aware of it or not, he has shown me much more than pistolcraft techniques. Jim Cirillo personifies the qualities of tenacity, loyalty, and dedication. I will always consider myself extremely fortunate to have had the opportunity to learn from him.

To Dr. H. Anthony Semone, who never hesitated when I asked for assistance with this project. This will surprise no one who has been helped by "Doc" over the years, for he is a good man whose kindness and patience run as deep as his commitment to providing comfort and aid to the members of the law enforcement community.

To Bert DuVernay and the training staff at the Smith & Wesson Academy, many of whom were released to the winds during the last acquisition; thank you all for your time, knowledge, and patience. I have no doubt that the pursuit of improved training will flourish wherever you take root.

To the members of the Heckler & Koch International Training Division, the SIGARMS Academy, and all the other institutions private and public dedicated to improving the art and science of police pistolcraft; even though there are occasionally differences of opinion and approach, it is good to know we are all striving to achieve the same goal–safer police officers and citizens through continuous, ongoing training.

To the many dedicated officers and trainers I have been privileged to have learned from and work among, thank you all for being what you are and doing what it is you do that makes you such a valuable–and limited–resource.

I believe Lt. Colonel Dave Grossman sums it up best when he accurately refers to members of this breed as the modern warrior trainers, or sensei.

It is to Dave Grossman that I extend my final heartfelt thanks, for it was while reading his groundbreaking book, *On Killing,* that the pieces of the puzzle truly came together before my eyes.

Founding members of the Massachusetts State Police Firearms Training Unit. From Left; Trooper Dana Pullman, Sergeant Bob Sheehan, Trooper Mike Conti, Trooper Kevin Ford, Trooper Johanna Lawlor, and Trooper Donna Losardo. (Not pictured, Trooper Jim Bretta. Photo courtesy Massachusetts State Police archives.)

Preface

What is the "New Paradigm" of Police Firearms Training?

Quite simply, the new paradigm, or model of police firearms training is a reality-based approach to firearms training for police officers. It was created because the currently entrenched sight-oriented, marksmanship-based approach hasn't been working.

This opinion is based upon the data regarding actual police-involved deadly force encounters that has been collected and analyzed for more than thirty years indicating that the average officer misses with more than 80% of the rounds he fires at threat subjects.

This poor performance record is compounded when you consider that the vast majority of police-involved shootings have always been, and continue to be, close-range affairs, with more than 80% occurring with the officer and offender twenty feet and closer, and more than half taking place within a distance of *five feet*. (FBI Uniform Crime Reports).

How New is New

While the reasoning behind its development is explained in detail on the following pages, in the interest of accuracy I am compelled to note here that the "New Paradigm" program is–in many ways–simply the latest rebirth of a system of combat pistol shooting and instruction that reached its apex more than sixty years ago! How can this be, you may ask?

In the review of the history of the development of police pistol training provided in Chapter Three, it will become apparent that two distinct approaches to this subject–one marksmanship-oriented, the other combat-oriented–have been struggling for dominance since the beginning of the twentieth century.

One of the main reasons the struggle has gone on for so long, I believe, is because like the two entwined snakes in the illustration, both approaches appear similar at first glance. Closer examination, however, reveals that one is better suited for mortal combat than the other.

Since the occupation of the law enforcement officer inevitably brings him or her into contact with dangerous situations and people, the need for a system of weapons training that allows officers to develop reliable, life-saving skills with their most commonly available firearm–the handgun–is imperative.

And, as these skills will overwhelmingly need to be employed against other human beings during terrifying instances of close quarter violence, logic demands that the combat-oriented training approach be embraced as the only sane choice.

Incredibly, this argument between marksmanship-oriented and combat-oriented training approaches has been fought and won in a repetitive cycle throughout the past century and into the new.

Each generation of police officers and trainers has had to relearn this simple truth–or deal with the consequences. For me, the process took many years and an incredible amount of frustration, research and labor, only to discover, at its conclusion, that my questions had all been asked decades before, and that the answers I so painstakingly arrived at had been discovered by others long ago.

One of the primary reasons for this constant struggle has been the fact that there has never truly been a system of pistol training designed exclusively for the members of the civilian police profession.

Police officers' training programs have always been derived from, or at least heavily influenced by, outside sources. Both military and non-police civilian influences, while well-meaning, have generated a great deal of confusion in this regard.

This confusion has also undoubtedly been compounded by the tremendous volumes of work produced by numerous authors, trainers, and pundits in the field, all extolling the universal virtues of their own particular brand of pistolcraft.

I would ask the reader to consider this, however: of all the books that have been published on the subject of pistolcraft over the years, this is *the first* to bear the simple and specific title, *Police* Pistolcraft.

In addition to providing an objective perspective to this particular body of knowledge, it is my sincere hope that *Police Pistolcraft* will help the members of the law enforcement profession untangle the symbolic snakes, recognizing and appreciating both for what they are, and realizing that while similar, they are as different as life and death.

Author's Notes Regarding Book Composition

Gender Consideration: Throughout this book I have avoided the use of compound gender references such as his/her, s/he, etc., and used the masculine references he, his, him. This has been done solely to simplify the text and make the reading easier. I trust my sister officers will understand I mean no disrespect in this, and will not feel excluded from the materials in any way.

Age Consideration: The size of the font used throughout the book has intentionally been selected to be easily read by those of us in the "over 40 years of age" category. A reduced font would have allowed the book to be produced in a smaller size and at less cost, but I understand the pleasure of being able to read a book while holding it a reasonable distance from the eyes and without the aid of the $9.95 pharmacy reading glasses. If you're laughing, you understand. If you're not, don't worry–you'll get it eventually.

Fiscal Consideration: The price of this book has been intentionally set much lower than the current market would indicate. I understand that funds for training materials of this type are usually in short supply, and more often than not are drawn from the police officer's own pocket. I wished to ensure that the information would be available at a reasonable price. That is one of the reasons why I have published *Police Pistolcraft* myself, under the Saber Group, Inc. banner.

Introduction

Order and simplification are the first steps towards the mastery of survival–the actual enemy is the unknown.

> – Thomas Mann
> *The Magic Mountain*

The New Paradigm

The New Paradigm Police Firearms Training Program has come about as the result of many years of work conducted by professional police officers, trainers, and researchers. Among these people are individuals such as Steve Barron, Clyde Beasley, Bill Burroughs, Lou Chiodo, Jim Cirillo, Paul Damery, the late Roger A. Ford, Dave Grossman, Donna Losardo, Gregory B. Morrison, and Bruce Siddle, to name but a few.

All have influenced my work in this area, both through their efforts in their own unique disciplines and by the personal examples of courage and tenacity they set.

The single greatest influence on my efforts however, has been the tremendous volume of work produced, and unwavering determination exhibited by one man, the late Colonel Rex Applegate, whose contributions are more fully noted in the text.

To their credit, most of the people involved in the work that led to the New Paradigm–including, incredibly, Rex Applegate–have been regarded by many within the professional firearms training community as iconoclasts. That is because their ideas and research methodologies are often in direct opposition to much of the dogma laid down by some of the highly regarded "gun gurus" who rose to prominence during the past few decades espousing the supremacy of the police firearms training methodology embodied in the system commonly referred to as the Modern Technique.

The Modern Technique, in fact, became so firmly established in the collective minds and culture of US law enforcement toward the end of the Twentieth Century that to challenge its viability was likely to get you branded as a heretic, or at the least, as one who was sadly ignorant and unenlightened.

I know this because I was once a firm believer in the Modern Technique, its highly stylized, Weaver-based stance and reliance on marksmanship-oriented, qualification type programs, and shared this view.

I can still recall the frustration I felt more than a dozen years ago during a firearms qualification program while trying to explain to a veteran state police officer why the Weaver stance was superior to the Isosceles. This veteran officer, initially trained to use the Isosceles position years before, argued that the Weaver didn't feel "natural."

My arguments, founded in pure Modern Technique doctrine, were obvious and predictable. As he listened politely on the 25-yard line, I patiently explained how the Weaver position provided better stability and control, worked off the bladed body interview position that keeps the holstered weapon away from suspects, allowed you faster acquisition of the sight picture and faster follow-up shots.

"But," the unenlightened veteran replied, "The few times I've had to pull my gun for real I know I didn't stand like that, and I know I probably won't in the future either–so why should I stand like that here while training?"

"Because it gives you the best chance of hitting the target, especially from this distance," was my reply.

And to this day, I do still believe that. The problem however, and one that I could not see at the time, was that should that officer need to pull his gun for real again in the future, he would probably not be standing 25 yards away from his target, and his target would not be paper, metal, cardboard or plastic, but flesh and blood, close and dangerous.

Motivations

> There are two levers which move men: fear and self-interest.
>
> – Napoleon Bonaparte

While many people have written about police firearms training for a variety of reasons, my own interest in this subject is purely selfish. As I acknowledged in an article published in *Guns & Ammo*, my motivations here are as base as Napoleon's description of what motivates men–fear and self-interest.[1]

My fear, I wrote at the time, is of attending more funerals of murdered police officers.

My self-interest lies in my desire to avoid having others attend mine.

While that basically sums it up, there are additional considerations involved here beyond funerals, however, that I would like to expand upon.

Like all members of the law enforcement profession, I depend upon my ability to properly handle a firearm under stressful conditions for both my life and livelihood.

As a member of the law enforcement community, I have also been exposed to the

reality of personal loss suffered when a brother or sister officer is taken by violence while performing their duty.

In addition, I have also been witness to the tremendous toll that is taken when an officer is forced to employ deadly force against a person perceived to be presenting an immediate threat–only to discover afterwards that the reality was different from the perception.

Finally, I have grown from being perplexed by the actions of officers who do not fire their weapons when faced with a person who presents an absolute immediate threat of death or bodily injury to the officer–but rather allow themselves to remain in the line of fire while ordering the subject to "Drop the gun, drop the gun, drop the gun…" over and over again–to a deeper understanding and respect of what makes the best of us sometime act that way, and why our training must enable us to overcome these "better angels of our nature".

All of these factors have contributed to my sincere belief as a trainer in the critical importance of properly preparing police officers to deal with the dangerous realities of the law enforcement profession.

Years of studying the data gathered about actual police-involved shootings combined with my personal experiences as a police officer and interviews with hundreds of other officers, however, convinced me that the Modern Technique-based training programs we employed–and I had embraced–were not filling the bill.

Enlightenment in a Darkened Hallway

One evening in the early 1990s I was participating in a stealth entry as a member of my department's tactical team. The covert entry had been successfully made well after dark into a two-story residence. Inside the house was a self-proclaimed suicidal individual armed with a shotgun. As he spoke with a police negotiator on

---

[1] In the Line of Fire, *Guns & Ammo* Magazine, February 2001.

the telephone upstairs in his bedroom, we positioned ourselves downstairs to ensure he could not exit the house and present a danger to other residents in the densely populated neighborhood.

After many hours the negotiator had succeeded in calming the distressed subject a bit, and we were instructed over the radio to prepare to take him into custody so he could be transported to a medical facility for further care.

Several of my teammates and I then quietly ascended the staircase, our presence in the house still unknown to the subject. The plan was to take him into custody as quickly and calmly as possible, so as not to unravel all the fine work the negotiator had accomplished.

As two of us rounded the corner in the upstairs hallway, the subject, still on the telephone speaking with the negotiator, suddenly walked out of his bedroom into the hallway and looked–very quickly and with a shocked expression–first at us, then at a 12-gauge shotgun propped against the wall next to him, then back to us.

Operating in an adrenaline-fueled heightened state of awareness and a bit startled at the sudden appearance of the subject in the hallway, my immediate reaction was to raise my pistol to eye-level and simultaneously focus on the front sight as it came into view between my eye and the subject's upper torso.

In that fleeting moment as the subject cast those seemingly desperate glances first at us, then the shotgun, and then back to us again, however, I experienced an epiphany of sorts as I felt my eyeball's focus literally RIPPED off that front sight and placed on the subject. It was an intense and uncontrollable physiological response that made a lasting and indelible impression on me. For even though I immediately *consciously* chose to lower the weapon and refocus on the subject to determine if he presented an immediate threat, my momentary startle-induced reaction allowed me

to personally experience something that ran directly contrary to my training and the Modern Technique doctrine.[2]

What it came down to was this: I had been thoroughly trained to hold my weapon below my line of sight until an immediate threat was identified. Once identified, the Modern Technique dictated, the weapon would be raised to eye level, the sights would be acquired, centered on the threat, and rounds would be delivered.

Yet, there in that hallway, facing a potential close quarter threat, my body reacted in a way that I believe would have not allowed me to focus on those sights at all should I have needed to fire. My training had been overridden by something more powerful and base.

This seemingly innocuous experience that undoubtedly occurred in less than a tenth of a second caused me to begin questioning not only the training I had received, but more important, the training I had provided to other officers as a departmental firearms instructor.

As I reflected on this incident over the next few months, many of the inconsistencies that had bothered me for years about both police firearms training methodologies and actual police performance began to make sense. The deeper I looked into the subject, the more I began to understand. Gradually, my experience in that hallway turned into a somewhat obsessive investigation into these matters, the culmination of which has resulted in a new police firearms training program that has been developed and successfully administered to over 2,500 police and military personnel as of this writing.

This book is intended to document the investigation and the results produced by it to date.

2 The subject was subsequently removed from the house without incident.

A Homicide Investigation

In January 2000, while working as a death investigator for the Suffolk County State Police Detective Unit, I was tasked by the Superintendent of the State Police at that time, Colonel John DiFava, to organize, staff, and train a new Firearms Training Unit (FTU) for the department.[3]

Up until this time, the department's part-time tactical team had been responsible for conducting yearly qualification courses of fire for department personnel.

Prior to accepting the assignment, I requested clarification from the Colonel on the overall mission of the FTU. In particular, I was concerned that the FTU's function would be relegated to administering the standard types of Modern Technique-based, marksmanship-oriented firearms qualification courses that were still overwhelmingly prevalent both within our own department and the vast majority of other agencies nation-wide–and which I had lost faith in as being the best means for improving officer performance and ensuring the best chance for officer survival.

Colonel DiFava replied that the mission was to build not just a new unit, but a new firearms training program that would, in his words, "meet or exceed all the national standards and provide the highest possible liability insulation for the members of the department and the organization itself."

Then came the hook. Colonel DiFava, known in law enforcement and community circles as someone who cares deeply not only about the mission but also the people who must carry it out, added, "But most of all, Mike, I want you to build a program that will make our people safe, make sure they get home at the end

of the shift. That's what I want."

After accepting the assignment, I set out to do two things. First, I began to gather and organize all the research and training materials I owned or could get my hands on. Three years earlier a basic police firearms training manual I had written called *In the Line of Fire: A Working Cop's Guide to Pistolcraft* had been published by Paladin Press. I had kept all the reference materials collected prior to writing the book, and those combined with what I'd acquired since it was published filled two bookcases, a large locker, and several file cabinets in my basement. More than gathering data, I was gathering evidence.

In the intervening years since I had written *In the Line of Fire*, I had been assigned to a detective unit and had been working with, and trained by, some of the finest investigators on the department. During the 2 ½ years I was assigned to the unit, Detective Lieutenant Billy Powers and Sergeant Paul Hennigan had taken me under their wing and taught me the basics of conducting a solid homicide investigation. I was still in the process of benefiting from their experience and guidance when I was given the FTU assignment.

As I cleaned out my desk and case files, amid the pangs of guilt for the cases I would not get a chance to see through to trial came an idea: perhaps the way to understanding exactly what was wrong with the police firearms training model we employed nationwide wasn't by approaching the problem through the eyes of a firearms instructor. Perhaps the answers could be found by approaching it through the eyes of a detective–by conducting an investigation, leaving all suppositions and pre-conceived ideas behind, and letting the evidence and a careful analysis of that evidence tell the tale. In essence, I decided at that point to open and conduct this investigation as if it were a homicide investigation.

Days later out at the State Police Academy in New Braintree, as I stood alone at the front of

---

[3] Colonel DiFava has since retired from the MSP and is currently serving as the Chief of the MIT Police Department. His retirement was postponed several weeks after the terrorist attacks on 9-11 while he served as interim Director of Aviation Security at Logan International Airport at the Governor's request.

the new range classroom looking over the empty tables and chairs, my eyes fell upon five brass plaques mounted on the rear wall of the room. Each of the plaques contained a portrait of a member of my department who had been murdered in the line of duty, and a short passage indicating the events that had led to their deaths.

As I looked at their faces, the data I had read many times in FBI reports and articles suddenly appeared before my eyes: *hundreds* of US police officers murdered in the line of duty in the past thirty years alone. More than fourteen thousand men's and women's names inscribed on the Law Enforcement Officers' Memorial in Washington, DC. That's when it truly hit me, perhaps for the first time.

It *was* a homicide investigation.

The FTU: A Team Effort

The second thing I needed to do was recruit a group of officers to form the nucleus of the FTU cadre. With over 2,000 sworn officers on the department, it might seem like this would be no problem. However, there were obstacles in the way.

First, the Academy was located in a somewhat remote area with no easy access from major roadways. This meant that for most officers, assignment to the Academy entailed a long commute, especially during the winter months when the volatile New England weather would often dump enough snow and ice on the ground to make the winding roadways treacherous and the commute more time-intensive.

Second, the previous firearms training program and its employment of up-range stress (see Chapter Four) had not been very popular with many members of the department, leaving some to view the very idea of firearms training in a less than positive light.[4]

Third, being a completely new entity, join-

ing the FTU was a risky proposition. How it would be structured, what its mission would be, and how it would be run were all unknown at the beginning. Naturally, there were also some members of the department who viewed the creation of the new unit with some skepticism, and others, still true believers of the Modern Technique-based model, who didn't agree with the need for a new approach to firearms training.

Finally, there was the natural resistance most people have to getting up in front of an audience and speaking–much less presenting a class to the toughest peer group in the world![5]

Trooper Donna Losardo, who would eventually become Assistant Director and then take my place as the Director of the FTU, was the first person I called. Without hesitation she signed on for the mission. Having known and worked with Donna in a training capacity in the past, I believed that she would not only be critical to ensuring the overall success of the new unit and program, but would be instrumental in bringing about greater significant change on an organizational-level through her talent, hard work and example. The fact that she was a female in a somewhat traditionally male-dominated role was not what qualified her for the assignment–but the fact that she was a highly motivated and extremely competent female police officer and trainer meant the positive impact she would have would be felt on many levels throughout the department. (This proved true.)

During the first few weeks, Donna and I began to assess and reorganize the new multi-million dollar firearms training complex that had been completed just prior to the creation of the FTU. At the same time, we continued to recruit other members of the department into the unit. Among the handful of officers who first signed

---

[4] Some reasons for this are detailed in the text.

[5] Several years ago a poll was taken that indicated that more people were afraid of public speaking than of dying. A comedian observed at the time, "That means that whenever you go to a wake, more people in the room would rather be in the coffin than giving the eulogy!"

on were Trooper Kevin Ford, Trooper Dana Pullman, Trooper Jim Bretta, and Sergeant Bob Sheehan. A few weeks later Trooper Johanna Lawlor joined us, and the unit began to take shape. Though there were only six of us in a unit designed to be staffed by eleven, we began the work that would consume most of our time and energy for the next two years. [6]

We had to move fast. We wanted to commence training as soon as possible. Countless hours were spent preparing, many on our own time. We organized the equipment we had, begged and borrowed the equipment we needed, and improvised the rest. The department armorers, Sergeant Marty Driggs and Trooper Mike Wilmot also pitched in, helping us secure additional equipment and supplies and volunteering to become adjunct instructors. Donna and I built a basic firearms instructor program to get the unit members on the same page, borrowing heavily from work that had been accomplished a few years earlier by another dedicated member of the department, Sergeant Paul Damery.[7] Outside trainers were brought in to teach other skills, and members were sent to a few training courses provided by outside agencies. As usual, the opportunity to attend outside agency training courses was limited by time and funding.

Meanwhile, I continued to analyze the evidence both while at work and–thanks to an understanding wife–at home. The investigation and the case book began to grow. I would periodically pose questions to the FTU staff to get their responses. Being intelligent individ-

uals, many of the answers they gave enlightened me and took the investigation in slightly different directions. Weeks passed. I began referring to the case book as the "manifesto". As the investigation unfolded, I became more convinced that this was the right approach. Ideas and training methodologies I had accepted for years fell by the wayside, knocked down by logic, common sense, and science. Myth, misperceptions, and blatant examples of historical revisionism were exposed. I was learning more about training through this simple investigative approach than I had learned while attending countless schools and instructor-level training programs.

Once the evidence was assembled and analyzed, the construction process began. I decided to use another investigative technique to help me figure out the best way to design the new program. Quite simply, I attacked the problem in reverse, starting with the "body" and working backwards.

The body in this case was the lethal force encounter. As far as I was concerned, any time an officer felt himself to be in enough danger to draw his firearm–regardless of whether he discharged the weapon–it qualified as a lethal force encounter. That was what a police firearms training program was ultimately intended to prepare the officer to deal with. So how do you prepare someone to deal with the typical law enforcement lethal force encounter?

We knew that the typical encounter occurred at close range, often in low or reduced light, and usually happened extremely fast. Should rounds be fired, statistics indicated they would probably be few in number and fired fairly rapidly, indicating a need for fast, first round hits. We also knew that one or all participants would more than likely be operating under the effects of some type of mind-altering chemical substance–whether drugs, alcohol, or the naturally-occurring dump of more than 40 organic chemicals into the bloodstream that would be initiated by the sympathetic nervous

---

[6] The grueling pace initially established combined with the long days and daily commute eventually took their toll: three of the original members left the FTU within fifteen months. Fortunately, other dedicated officers have stepped forward and joined the FTU on a full-time basis, including Tpr. Paul Wosny, the current Director. Other officers have also volunteered to serve with the FTU on a part-time basis, and interest in the unit and its mission appears to be growing within the organization at the time of this writing.

7 Sergeant Damery was the first officer to design and build a nationally-recognized and certified Basic Police Firearms Instructor Course for the MSP.

system in times of great stress.

Obviously, the best way to prepare a person to deal with these realities would be to have him experience them firsthand, under controlled conditions, so he could learn *through experience* how to deal with them both physically and psychologically.

Therefore, a structured and controlled course that allowed our people to experience these realities, overcome them and prevail became the ultimate level of the program.

The next step in our backward progression then became figuring out how to devise a course that would adequately prepare the officer to successfully deal with the ultimate level course that preceded it.

By moving backwards in a series of progressive and efficiently constructed courses, each designed to prepare the officer trainee to succeed at the one that followed it, the program basically unfolded before my eyes. All I had to do was follow the evidence-inspired logic and write it all down.

After the final individual course segment–centered on basic individual skills development–was formatted, the program was assembled. This final course of fire then became the first step in the program, the foundation on which the rest would be laid. If it worked as planned, participating officers would begin working on a basic level, then move up to the next level and the next, each level increasing in difficulty and complexity until finally, at the conclusion of the program, they would participate in a simulated lethal confrontation as real as we could make it without actually having them engage in gunfights with penetrating ammunition.

If the previous courses of fire were designed properly, the officers should be able to deal appropriately and effectively with the ultimate level of training. If the entire program was designed properly, then the officers should develop a true sense of confidence in their individual ability to engage in high-stress, dang-

erous encounters, giving them an edge should they become involved in an actual lethal force encounter in the world. That was the idea, anyway. It seemed to make sense. There were only three problems.

First, the entire program, encompassing all of the different levels of training, would have to be completed in a one-day stand-alone training program. This meant that time-efficiency and high training value were critical.

Second, the program had to be kept within a reasonable budget, for with more than 2,000 officers to train and limited funds available, huge expenditures would make the program cost-prohibitive and therefore impractical.

Finally, by following the evidence and the conclusions it led to, the program that resulted was unlike anything we had ever done. The methods of training and standards of proficiency indicated by the evidence also went against the vast majority of nationally accepted police firearms methods and training standards. What this meant was that as an agency, we would be rejecting not only the national norms, but the state norms as dictated by the Massachusetts Criminal Justice Training Council.

In effect, we would be standing alone, charting a new path in unchartered waters with a new, untested unit and a significantly different training approach and program.

Fortunately, we were backed by the members of our chain of command, from the newly-assigned, progressive commandant of the Academy, Lieutenant Tom Robbins, all the way through to the Superintendent.[8]

On May 3, 2000, Major Brad Hibbard advised me that the first version of the 240+ page New Paradigm Training Program had been officially approved by Colonel DiFava.

---

[8] After the 9-11 attacks, Robbins was assigned to Logan International Airport where he succeeded Colonel John DiFava as the Director of Aviation Security. In early 2004, Robbins (then a Major) was promoted to Colonel and appointed Superintendent of the Massachusetts State Police by Governor Mitt Romney.

On June 12, 2000, after working furiously to finish constructing the fourth level "House of Horrors" training course, the first officers reported to the range for training and we began to implement the program. We adjusted as we went, "tweaking and buffing" each segment. We proceeded as the investigation indicated we should.

Many segments and ideas we implemented were truly leaps of faith. We leaped.

Day after day our people came in for training. They responded. It made sense to them as well. The results astounded us. We were not only able to provide the best, most relevant police firearms training to the members of our extended law enforcement family that any of us had ever experienced, but we were able to do it while operating within the common law enforcement confines of small budgets and limited training time.

In order to better gauge its effectiveness, we have also let people from outside our agency attend the program. Police and military personnel from the US and abroad who have gone through the one-day program responded in the same positive manner.

More than a series of individual courses of fire, it's a process we've created, and it works.

As of this writing, our own mission continues, but it is well under way. The FTU has established itself and its reputation for hard work and relevant, professionally administered training programs, all designed with one goal in mind: *Saving Lives through Superior Training.*

Exposure through a series of articles I wrote for *Guns & Ammo* magazine detailing the program and its reasoning; a videotaped program about the New Paradigm produced by the Law Enforcement Training Network (LETN); and articles written by Joan Hopper for *Law & Order* magazine and Ralph Mroz for *Guns & Weapons for Law Enforcement* have piqued the interest of many in the field regarding

The MSP Firearms Training Unit (FTU) Insignia. This badge is authorized for wear only when the FTU-certified instructor has completed one full year of service with the unit.

our work and the program.[9]

I have received numerous requests from across the US for information about the program, and while I have tried to provide as much information as possible to individual trainers and officers, the numbers of requests have outstripped my ability to respond and perform my normal job functions.

The purpose of this book, therefore, is simply to get the word out to as many of our fellow law enforcement officers and trainers as possible, let them examine our investigation, understand our work, and use the results as they see fit.

All I ask is that the reader keep an open mind, and avoid the propensity people often have of resisting something simply because, "we've never done it like that before."

Note: While New Paradigm-based training courses have been formatted for weapons systems other than the duty handgun, this book's focus has been limited to the development of the original pistol training program.

---

[9] Portions of this chapter appeared previously in *Guns & Ammo* magazine. Used with permission.

May 12, 2004 Washington D.C.
FBI National Press Office

Preliminary Statistics for Law Enforcement Officers Killed in 2003

Washington, D.C. – According to preliminary statistics released today by the Federal Bureau of Investigation, 52 law enforcement officers across the Nation were feloniously killed in the line of duty in 2003. The number of slain officers is 4 fewer than the 56 officers killed in 2002.

Geographically, 29 officers were killed in the South, 12 in the West, 8 in the Midwest, and 3 in the Northeast.

By circumstance, 13 officers were killed during traffic pursuits/stops, 11 in arrest situations, 10 while responding to disturbance calls, 9 in ambush situations, 7 while investigating suspicious persons/circumstances, and 2 while handling and transporting prisoners.

A breakdown of the weapons involved in these slayings revealed that in 2003 firearms continued to be the weapon most frequently used in the killing of officers. Forty-five of the 52 officers were killed with a firearm. Of these 45 officers, 34 were killed with handguns, 10 with rifles, and 1 with a shotgun. Six officers were killed with vehicles, and 1 was slain with a police baton.

At the time they were slain, 35 officers were wearing body armor. Eleven of the 52 slain officers were killed with their own weapons. Eleven officers' weapons were stolen from the scene. Ten officers fired their weapons, and 9 officers attempted to fire their weapons during the 46 fatal incidents.

In addition to the officers feloniously killed in 2003, there were 81 separate incidents in which 82 law enforcement officers were accidently killed in the performance of their duties. This is 6 more than the 76 officers accidentally killed during the previous year.

The FBI will release final statistics and complete details in the Uniform Crime Reporting Program's publication Law Enforcement Officers Killed and Assaulted, 2003, in the fall of this year.

This press release is available on the FBI's Internet site at www.fbi.gov.

CHAPTER ONE
The New Paradigm: Why Now?

Our weakness lies in this - that we have never got down to an exact definition of what we are seeking. Failing that, we fall short in our attempt to formulate in training how best to obtain it, and our philosophy of discipline falters at the vital point of its practical, tactical application.
  – S.L.A. Marshall
  Men Against Fire
  1947

Police firearms training is a subject that has always engendered a great deal of emotion and controversy from those both within and without the law enforcement community. There are many reasons for this. The most obvious is because officers' and citizens' very lives often hang in the balance when a police officer has cause to introduce his firearm into any real-world situation.

Another aspect that must be considered is that the personal and professional reputations of the involved officers, departments, and organizations are greatly impacted by each individual officer's performance in the field, *especially* when involved in situations that require the use of any level of force, much less lethal force. For in addition to the physical, mental, and monetary toll that may be incurred as a result of an officer's involvement in a lethal force encounter, is the potential loss of trust and confidence in the police by those in the society we serve should the application of lethal force be determined to have been unwarranted.

Training Approaches

Another factor that has played a significant role in fanning the flames of discord in regard to this subject matter over the years is the tremendous impact that firearms trainers and and enthusiasts in the private sector have had on the way civilian law enforcement firearms training is both approached and conducted in this country and abroad.

It is generally acknowledged that many of the so-called "combat" shooting techniques taught in the US (and throughout the world) over the past thirty years were originally developed to assist individuals to compete in static-level, highly structured, marksmanship-type competitions.

While these stylized, marksmanship-oriented shooting techniques (perhaps best represented by the system commonly referred to as the "Modern Technique"[1]) may indeed enhance the average officer's ability to achieve hits on a stationary target under controlled conditions, experience has indicated that they cannot be reasonably expected to sufficiently prepare the average officer to engage and prevail in a spontaneous lethal force encounter against a moving, thinking aggressor under dynamic, close quarter, uncontrolled conditions.[2]

---

[1] Documented in *The Modern Technique of the Pistol* by Gregory B. Morrison, published by Gunsite Press 1991.

[2] Statistics consistently indicate that more than half (53%) of all police officers feloniously killed by assailants armed with firearms were within a distance of five feet or less from their assailant at the time of the attack; more than 73% were within 10 feet, and that 85% occurred within twenty feet or less. (FBI Uniform Crime Reports)

Training Failures

The above supposition would appear to be supported by logic when one considers that while the minimum passing score on most accepted, Modern Technique-based departmental qualification courses is 70 percent, studies consistently indicate that less than 20 percent (on average) of all rounds fired by police officers when engaged in a lethal force encounter *actually hit the adversary.*[3]

This disparity in performance would seem to speak for itself, especially when one considers that the vast majority (85%) of police-involved shootings occur at distances of *twenty feet and less.*[4]

Combining the two sets of data produces an inescapable conclusion: not only are we missing the threat with more than 80% of the rounds we fire in real life encounters, *but we are missing close-in where it happens!*

A common response from proponents of the Modern Technique when questioned about this disparity is to claim that either a) the officers involved in the shootings were not trained thoroughly enough in the Modern Technique to ingrain the many complicated positions and stylized weapon handling skills, or b) the officers involved in the shootings who *were* thoroughly trained in the Modern Technique failed to perform as they were trained. (This latter "failure to perform" response generally refers to the practice of training the shooter's eye to focus on the front sight while firing the weapon in training. Studies have indicated, however, that the body's natural physiological reactions, combined with the attendant psychological effects that occur during actual encounters, may preclude this ability in the vast majority of involved persons.[5])

Considering that the basic factors common to armed, close quarter engagements have changed little since human beings first began employing handguns against one another as offensive/defensive weapons, it would seem that the disparity illustrated above between what is achieved in training and what is achieved under actual civilian police combat conditions begs closer examination.[6]

Mental Preparation: Deficiencies

Preparing officers psychologically to deal with the realities of the police-involved deadly force encounter is another critical aspect of police firearms training that is too often ignored or misunderstood. Usually referred to as mental preparation or mental conditioning, this aspect of training is actually the foundation on which all other training components must be built. And like any foundation, it must be properly designed and constructed if the finished product is to be stable and strong.

More than just learning to shoot quickly and accurately in front of an audience, or to reload and fire while being timed or yelled at by an instructor, the mental conditioning aspects of police firearms training must be approached from a job-specific perspective. This means that while shooting paper, plastic, steel, or "running man" moving targets will help you develop your mechanical skills with the pistol, it is by no means preparing you to deal with the physical and psychological realities experienced when facing another human being who presents what you perceive to be an immediate deadly threat to you or others.

---

[3] NYPD S.O.P.#9 is one example of this type study. Results of this study indicated a 14.4% hit potential.

[4] FBI Uniform Crime Reports

[5] Reference Appendices B and V

[6] An examination of current "state of the art" training methods reveals that training practices used to prepare individuals for close quarter handgun engagements have also changed little. Consider the much vaunted (and warranted) acclaim for "Simunition" ammunition that allows one pistol-armed trainee to engage another with handguns that fire non-lethal training rounds. A version of this practice, while currently "revolutionizing" combat firearms training, was actually employed as early as 200 years ago by French dueling instructors.

While many people consider this to be obvious, the truth is that practicing the mechanical skills needed to draw, accurately fire, reload, clear stoppages, and move to cover with the pistol is usually as far as police firearms training is currently taken in the US. And while these skills are absolutely essential, they do not, by themselves, constitute a viable, reality-based, court-defensible firearms training program.

To provide that type of program, realistic training that simulates as closely as possible the actual sorts of situations and environments the officer will be operating in must be conducted.

Only through training of this sort can we learn to truly control ourselves, our weapons, and others.

Just how greatly this aspect of training is misunderstood by many people involved in firearms training was made clear to me years ago during a conversation with an IPSC competition shooter.[7] At the time, I was a member of my department's SWAT team. He had been practicing at a local range where several of my teammates and I were training. After watching us practice various close quarter battle (CQB) drills, he began to explain to us that we should compete in his pistol league because he believed it was the best way to prepare oneself psychologically to deal with stress.

In his words, "You don't have any idea what *real stress* is until you shoot competition in front of an audience!"

My teammates and I looked at one another, nodded and agreed politely, and returned to our drills. The reason we reacted this way was not because we were arrogant, but because the very night before we had responded to a call-out where an emotionally disturbed and violent individual had tried to kill his elderly parents with a shotgun. For several hours we had kept him contained in the darkened house with the large slug-holes in the front door, until negotiations became impossible and the decision was made to send a team in to apprehend him.

At one point during the stealth entry, the man's threatening voice floated down from the darkness saying, "Let me see that helmet again..."

The situation climaxed when the suspect, exposed to an application of shotgun-launched chemical agents and confronted by the entry team, dropped his own shotgun and drove his head through a glass-paned window screaming incoherently. He was then apprehended in the dark, a raving bloody mess.

Comparing the notion of "stress" generated by a situation like this as opposed to the type of stress induced while shooting paper for fun in the sun is probably the best way to illustrate just how confused the issue of mental preparation has become.

While I will concede that some benefit may be gained by participating in competition-focused shooting activities, I overwhelmingly believe that we can no more properly prepare police officers to deal with the realities of the statistically-likely pistol fight by having them exposed to competition or "stage-fright" induced stress, than we can by having them exclusively practice highly-stylized marksmanship skills from unrealistic positions and distances.

Before explaining some of the methods we have implemented to rectify these and other training deficiencies, I would like to offer a review of my own developmental history and experiences as a police firearms instructor, as well as an overview of police firearms training practices in general.

I believe both are necessary in order to fully understand how the Modern Technique evolved into the predominant civilian police firearms training model–and why it needs to be replaced.[8]

---

[7] International Practical Shooting Confederation

[8] Portions of this chapter appeared previously in *Guns & Ammo* magazine. Used with permission.

"Combat Shooting - Action Shooting - Practical Shooting - IPSC - USPSA." These terms and acronyms have been seen a lot in recent years. The big money matches, and indeed the many club matches from which they sprang all have one thing in common. They all have a common root. All developed from Practical Shooting, and the organization that developed that sport: the International Practical Shooting Confederation (IPSC).

IPSC's world and national championships are widely regarded as the "official" title bouts for shooters in all types of "action-speed-combat" disciplines...

The basic game originated in Southern California in the 1950s and were known as "Leatherslap" matches. Very little was standardized. As the game evolved it became an amalgam of many elements. Some old-west fast draw, sometimes an obstacle course to run around and through, some "street-smarts" challenges to decide what to shoot and what not to shoot, and more points were given to heavier calibers.

IPSC (pronounced "ipp-sick") was created as an organization in 1976 at Columbia, Missouri, by representatives from nine nations where the sport of "combat" shooting was becoming popular. This became known as the Columbia Conference. The term "practical" went into the name instead of "combat" in deference to public image and Jeff Cooper who was elected the first President. Jeff's writings and philosophy of "practical pistolcraft" were highly regarded and earned him the title of father of the sport.

> – Dick Metcalf
> Excerpted from the *Member's Handbook of the United States Practical Shooting Association, 5th Edition, May 1990*

(Reprinted with permission.)

CHAPTER TWO
Subjective View: One Instructor's Journey

On the instructional side of this work there have been two schools of thought, the first of which would cling steadfastly to target shooting methods which might be considered old fashioned and very much out of date in conditions of modern warfare and police work in Occupied Territories. The other school insists that only the very latest methods of close quarter work within limited boundaries, such as street fighting and raiding rooms, is necessary.

> – Major H. Grant-Taylor
> *The Palestine Police Force Close Quarter Battle Handbook*
> 1943

My sanctioned introduction to firearms began when I was about twelve years old, introduced to air rifles and pistols by my older brother Jim.[1] Twenty-two caliber rifles and eventually larger bore weapons followed. Most of my shooting activities at that time were limited to plinking cans and paper targets and the occasional small critter.

While I enjoyed shooting for fun, I was very much aware that guns were also used for serious business, as my father was a police officer and carried a Smith & Wesson revolver on his hip every day. It was during this time period that I developed what was to be a life-long fascination with firearms. While other kids were playing games, I was obsessed with learning how different types of guns worked and how they were used by the police and the military. Many hours were expended reading *Guns & Ammo* magazine and anything else related to the subject. Years later one of my relatives would jokingly tell people that I was "raised in a closet full of guns and badges," and, for better or worse, the truth is he was pretty close to the mark.

After graduating from high school I joined the US Army and began my professional association with firearms. During a three-year fulltime hitch and two years afterward in the Army National Guard serving as an infantryman, I became intimately familiar with all the standard light infantry firearms in use at the time. Among these were the 1911A1 .45 Caliber Service Pistol, the M16A1 5.56mm Service Rifle, and the M60 7.62mm General Purpose Machine Gun (GPMG).

The earlier training I had received from my brother apparently paid off during this time, as I felt comfortable with all the systems and was designated high scorer of my training company during the basic rifle marksmanship program.

Later, while stationed in Europe, in addition to familiarization training with Soviet Bloc weapons, I had an opportunity to train with members of the West German Army and subsequently qualified with light infantry weapons such as the 7.62mm G3 Service Rifle, 7.62mm MG3 Machine Gun, and 9mm Uzi Submachine Gun.

All of my firearms training experiences in the military were conducted in the traditional manner, on "cold" ranges. We loaded just prior to firing and unloaded immediately afterward. We were also not allowed to insert magazines or chamber a round while performing security functions in Europe, though we did carry loaded magazines in our pouches. Most of the firearms training I

---

[1] Refer to Appendix E regarding my unsanctioned introduction.

received in the service was dedicated to long guns. Pistol training was rare and usually relegated to firing very few rounds from stationary positions on static ranges.

After completing my regular army enlistment I returned home, took a job as a security officer, joined the National Guard, enrolled in state college, and took the entrance test for the Massachusetts State Police along with 13,000 other hopeful candidates. I passed the test with a grade high enough to be in the running for one of the coveted slots in a recruit class, and was placed on a waiting list.

Two years after being discharged from the Army, I found myself in boot camp once again, this time at the Massachusetts State Police Academy in Framingham. In 1986 the Massachusetts State Police carried .357 Magnum Smith & Wesson Model 65 revolvers.

While I had collected several semiautomatic pistols, a shotgun, and a few rifles of my own that I shot on a regular basis since getting out of the service, the only revolver I had ever employed extensively up till the Academy was a .44 Magnum S&W Model 29 with an 8³/₈" barrel that I had bought to hunt with. While I enjoyed shooting the big wheelgun made famous by Clint Eastwood in the *Dirty Harry* films, and felt comfortable taking it into the field for game, I always felt better equipped with a semi-automatic pistol for personal defense.

Training at the Academy changed that feeling quite a bit–though it didn't eliminate it completely–and after a few weeks of drills and instruction I had qualified expert, placing second overall during the basic pistol training program, and felt very confident with the well-balanced stainless revolver.

During firearms training at the Academy we were essentially trained in the Modern Technique (though no one referred to it as such), the "Weaver" position being the preferred stance. "Cold" ranges were also the norm. (In fact, the first time my classmates and I would be allowed to load and carry our duty pistols out-

side the range environment was the night we graduated from the Academy.)

In addition to the revolver, we also received basic familiarization fire training with the 12-gauge Remington Model 870 pump shotgun and the select-fire 5.56mm Ruger Mini-14 AC556 Rifle. The firearms instructors were very competent, several having been schooled similarly through nationally recognized training institutions such as the Smith & Wesson Academy in Springfield, MA, and all the members of the 67th Recruit Training Troop completed the two-week long firearms block, meeting the qualification standards one way or another.[2]

After graduating from the Academy in December 1986, my classmates and I were dispersed out into the Troops to learn the profession.[3] Approximately five years later, I was selected to join the MSP Special Tactics and Operations (STOP) Team, and would serve with the team over the next four years as an entry team member and departmental firearms instructor.

During this period I was issued and trained with the 9mm Heckler & Koch MP5 submachine gun, the 5.56mm Galil SAR Assault Rifle, the 12-gauge Remington 1187 semi-automatic shotgun, and various other weapons and equipment, to include chemical agent weapons.[4]

In addition to seeking out as much real world experience and professional instruction on all facets of close quarter defense/offense as I could get access to at this point, I also began to truly study the art and science of instructing people in the use of weapons and tactics. I was privileged to be taught by some of the best in the

---

[2] The "other" refers to the employment of "uprange stress" discussed in Chapter Four.

[3] The Massachusetts State Police divides the Commonwealth into "troops" to facilitate complete coverage and allow for a manageable command and control structure.

[4] The Galil SAR, being select-fire capable, is a true assault rifle, unlike the semi-automatic only versions that are often referred to as such.

business in these endeavors, including several of my department's own charismatic and highly-effective trainers. Officers like Paul Damery, Tom Robbins, and the late Roger A. Ford went out of their way to help me learn better ways both of "doing" as well as teaching others how to do.[5]

Lt. Colonel Bob Hunt who, after retiring from the Massachusetts State Police, went on to become the second Director of the prestigious Smith & Wesson Academy in Springfield, MA, allowed me access both to him and the very knowledgeable Smith & Wesson Academy cadre during this period. Bill Burroughs, then Assistant Director of Training at the SIG Arms Academy in Exeter, New Hampshire, is another first-rate thinker and teacher I learned a great deal from during that time.

I absorbed as much information as I could from all of them. My own studies led me in a variety of directions, most notably to Greg Morrison's book *The Modern Technique of the Pistol,* and anything related to it.

Know What You Know, and Know What You *Don't* Know

It was at this point in my development as a firearms instructor that I made a major error. To paraphrase General George S. Patton, Jr's quote above, I didn't know what I didn't know. Looking back on it, I can see why this might have happened; however, that it did still bothers me.

With my background and training in the military and state police, I had been conditioned to accept pretty much all of what I was taught without question, and to follow all lawful orders without hesitation. Having been exposed to this mind-set early on in organizations populated with and ruled by professional soldiers, police officers and trainers, I never really thought to challenge what was taught to me, though I did occasionally question various aspects of how the

techniques were taught.

After all, I reasoned, fulltime military and police institutions belonging to the greatest and most powerful country in the world must have devoted untold resources to the research and development of only the most advanced and effective training methods and techniques. Countless scores of people had been working on this stuff for decades, if not close to a century. It went without question, then, in my mind at least, that the best possible way to train police officers to use their firearms had been worked out years ago by the experts in the field. And the way we all did it at that point in time was through the Modern Technique of the Pistol.

Yet, even after all that had been accomplished, police officers, trainers and instructors nationwide were still arguing–in print and otherwise–about the best way to train people to use handguns to defend themselves and others.

Even though the proponents of the Modern Technique had apparently prevailed, people just kept tinkering with it, kept insisting that there were better ways. They wouldn't let it go. The question begged to be asked: Why?

Because there were still those pesky holes to contend with, that's why.

The Holes

In 1992, after having attended several firearms instructor certification courses and while continuing to serve as one of my department's firearms instructors, I started writing a series of articles for the *Trooper Newspaper*, the official publication of the State Police Association of Massachusetts.

The series was entitled *Interview Position*, and the idea behind it was to put out sound, use-

---

[5] My teachers instilled in me the belief that the saying, "Those who can, *do*. Those who can't, teach" was an unacceptable premise. You've no business trying to teach something you can't do. In my experience, the inverse is often just as problematic, for there are many people who can do but can't teach others effectively.

ful, tactical information to the troops in a format that was short on technical jargon and easy to understand. These articles eventually evolved into my first book, *In the Line of Fire: A Working Cop's Guide to Pistolcraft.*[6] The book was intended to provide a clearly-written, comprehensive overview of modern, accepted pistolcraft techniques for use by the recruit or working police officer who may not otherwise have a strong interest in, or much exposure to, the subject matter.

As I worked on the book, I researched what I deemed to be all the pertinent subject matter available to me, basically filtering it through my own approach and experiences and expressing it in my own words. The result was a book that received favorable reviews but broke no new ground.

For my own personal instructor development, however, the work itself was of immeasurable value. For it was while working on this book that I began to truly grasp that something was not quite right. I couldn't put my finger on it at the time, but I began to get the same feeling I'd had in the past while conducting an investigation, when something–a statement, a piece of evidence, a timeline, whatever–just didn't add up.

The deeper I dug, the stronger the feeling became: I was missing something.

Though I tried to address some of my concerns in the book, it wasn't until *In the Line of Fire* was finished and shipped to the publisher that I finally realized what it was that kept shouting at me from the corner of my brain. It was the damned holes.

The serious holes in the Modern Technique doctrine could not be ignored, especially when you forced yourself not to dismiss them, but really looked at them. One of the largest holes had been staring at me and my fellow instructors for years. The data indicating the great disparity between officer shooting performance in training and during actual gunfights had been known for decades. It wasn't exactly

news. More than once I had been involved in discussions with other officers when this fact would be brought up. And without fail the conclusion would be the same, generally expressed by one of us saying words to the effect, "Of course you don't hit as good in a gunfight as you do at the range, no one is shooting back at you on the range! That's only common sense." Then we'd nod and say, "We can only do the best we can," and we would avert our gaze from that dismal unblinking hole staring right at us and return to running the qualification course.

The other major hole for me was in regard to the front sight doctrine. The Modern Technique was unmoving on this issue. If you expect to hit the target, the doctrine espoused, you must always focus on the sights, at the very least using a "flash" front sight picture before you fired. Based on my own experiences and interviews with numerous other officers over the years, I had come to believe this might be less than achievable when faced with an actual threat at close range, even though articulating words to this effect could get you branded as weak or undisciplined, or worse.[7] Regardless, I had attempted to address this issue by including a chapter titled "Point Reflexive Shooting" in the book–a chapter, I might add, that I was advised by several people to omit, including a few professional firearms instructor I greatly respected.[8]

The reasons I was given for omitting a chapter describing how to "aim and shoot quickly and accurately without using the sights" are important, I believe, for now, looking back on them, I feel I can better understand the motivations of those who thought its inclusion–yes, even its acknowledgement–would be counterproductive.

---

[6] Published by Paladin Press, Boulder, Colorado, 1997.

[7] Over the years I have unofficially debriefed approximately 350 officers who have been involved in use of force encounters. More information regarding the information yielded and conclusions drawn are included later in the text.

[8] *In the Line of Fire*, Chapter 9.

Following are the three primary reasons I was told it should not be included.

First, the weapons were designed with sights for a reason, and if an operator does not use those sights when firing and hits someone or something they did not intend to hit, the operator is both negligent and liable.

Second, I was told that close-combat point shooting techniques should not be taught to police officers because even though they were accurate enough to allow you to hit a man-sized target at close ranges, they were obviously not as accurate as sighted-fire techniques, and fell apart at all but the closest distances.

The third and final reason I was given really confused me at first because outwardly it made sense and could be seen as reasonable justification for an instructor to exclude non-sighted fire training and techniques. Quite simply, I was told that these techniques were *too easily taught and learned*, and didn't require a great amount of time to master. This was bad, I was advised, because administrators could turn this against us to justify cuts in training time, budgets, and resources. We need to train more, not less, I was told emphatically, *that's* why point shooting was so largely discouraged.

Upon reflection, this last reason, more than any of the others, convinced me that there was some fatal flaw inherent in the logic of the entire systemic approach. For while I could understand the strong desire to promote more training as opposed to less, I could not see the logic in omitting a system that was designed to work close-in, especially when most of the gunfights *occurred* close-in.

In addition, having worked in the profession for more than a decade and been involved as a police firearms trainer for several years at that time, as well as being active in several law enforcement training associations, I believed I had a somewhat reasonable handle on the reality of police firearms training. And from what I had seen, the reality was that comprehensive, viable firearms training had never been considered a priority by the vast majority of law enforcement organizations throughout the country. This despite numerous precedent-setting cases that indicated it needed to be.

As a result, training time and budgets were fairly consistently limited across the boards, despite the hard work and admirable attempts by numerous dedicated instructors to change this.

Furthermore, a reasonable officer might presume, if this situation had already existed for decades (as a review of most US law enforcement firearms training practices indicated), barring any tremendous, unexpected events or nationally-dictated reversals, it probably would continue to exist for the duration of my career, at the least. [9]

And if that were the case, wouldn't it make more sense to try and fix the problem best as possible while working within the parameters of these perpetually-imposed limitations, making the absolute most of available training time, budgets and resources?

The alternative approach, based on national statistics, apparently hadn't been working. Those statistics indicated that officers tended to miss the person presenting a threat to them with more than 80% of the rounds they fired at him, and that 85% of the time the officer and suspect were closer than seven yards to one another! They also indicated that an officer died in the line of duty in the US approximately every 57 hours, many of them murdered while performing their duty.

How many more, I considered, would die over the course of my career alone? How many more families, departments and communities would suffer their losses?

One of the paradoxes that also became apparent to me at this time was that when we did

---

[9] Even a tremendous, devastating event such as the September 11, 2001 terrorist attack on US soil and subsequent war on terrorism has not brought about a major change in regular law enforcement firearms training standards and practices, at least as of this writing.

lose an officer, many people's understandable first reactions were to dig deep and contribute time, money and energy to the families of these fallen officers, and to consecrate their loss by traveling many miles to attend funerals, or participate in memorial races or tournaments. As admirable as these activities were, I reasoned, wouldn't it also be worthwhile to invest more time and energy to re-think the fundamental training issues, to at least try another approach to fill in those holes?

At that time in my development as an instructor, logic indicated to me that the answer *must* lie in the future. The Modern Technique had developed from all that had come before it, and was overwhelmingly considered the best way so far devised to accomplish the mission.

Therefore, I reasoned, if there was something lacking in the training methodology, then the Modern Technique would surely serve as the answer's foundation; would be the starting point from which to move forward and conquer the beast.

So that was where I started from when I began working on *In the Line of Fire*.

Blunder and Lightning

The four years spent working on *In the Line of Fire* in my spare time led me to learning a hard lesson about myself: as a police firearms instructor, I had blundered. I had failed to look beyond the apparently obvious, and had therefore missed what *should* have been obvious.

Disregarding the training and experiences I had had as a police officer, I had approached the entire firearms training subject from only one angle, moving forward from what I presumed was an already established point A, in this case, the Modern Technique. In effect, I failed to step back and look at the total picture objectively.

Obviously, when this is done, you're like-ly to end up with only part of the story, and that one part can lead you to the wrong conclusions.

Reminiscent of the story of the six blind men of Indostan describing an elephant by feel, each comes to believe that the entire creature is composed only of the particular part of the elephant they happen touch.[10] Much like the blind men in that story, the problem in my case was that it never occurred to me that I was missing anything.

Furthermore, I am now convinced that my ignorance about many aspects of police firearms training has been shared by the vast majority of professional police firearms instructors of the past thirty years or so, and that this ignorance has in effect been institutionalized for a number of reasons.

I realize this is a bold statement that raises at least three natural questions:

Q. *How could this be true, especially since there have been so many schools, so many well known and popular gun gurus espousing their various accepted Modern Technique-based methods and systems for more than thirty years?*

A. After much examination and experimentation, I've come to believe we took the wrong path up the right mountain about 50 years ago. The gurus who have developed so many of the systems, methods and techniques we use, and who have been guiding us since that time, either still don't realize a mistake was made, or cannot admit it now and must try to discredit or destroy any who question what they have done and where they have taken us.

Q. *Who am I to challenge the recognized masters of the Modern Technique-based discipline and the long-accepted police firearms training standards?*

A. I am a professional working police officer

---

[10] From the fable "The Blind Men and the Elephant" by John Godfrey Saxe. One describes the elephant as a wall, one as a spear, one as a snake, etc.

looking for answers that will help keep myself, my fellow police officers, and those we work around safe. Unlike many of the gurus who start out as military or non-police, civilian firearms instructors and eventually get involved in some type of police work to provide credibility to their resume, my interest in police firearms instruction grew out of my direct involvement with police work, my appreciation for the weapons we use, and my experiences in the field. For me, the training is not an end unto itself. It is simply a critical component of police work because it enables us to do *better and safer* police work.

Q. *Finally, why am I challenging the system and many of those who are recognized as the true experts in the field, if not to try and establish myself as some type of Gun Guru?*

A. The idea of establishing myself as any type of guru is not only absent from my agenda, but is repugnant to me. From what I have seen, gurus often tend to create an aura around them, a cult of personality that promotes blind acceptance of their methods and techniques by those who follow them. In addition to attracting people who possess follower or "disciple-type" personalities, the guru model also tends to produce an atmosphere lethal to ideas different from, or opposing in any way, the guru's espoused doctrine. This, in my opinion, is the kiss of death for progress in any field or discipline, for as General Patton famously noted, "When everyone is thinking alike, *no one is thinking."*

Regardless of their motivation, many of the gurus, while doing a lot of good for the various shooting sports and arts in many ways, have also done substantial harm to the one specific cause I am concerned about and that is the focus of this book–*police* firearms training.

And in regard to police firearms training, the person who has had the most influence on my training approach and the philosophy of the New Paradigm in particular, is the embodiment of the quintessential anti-guru–the late Colonel Rex Applegate.

For while I provided the blunder in my search for answers, Applegate, through his modest manner and years of unyielding dedication, provided the lightning.

Fifty of the World's Greatest Combat Competition Shooters Shoot this Way

In 1997, right after *In the Line of Fire* was published, I began working on a second book. This book would address another subject in the realm of police tactical sciences that interested me: chemical agents.[11] Working on the first book had given me the research bug, and I figured that writing a volume on chemical agents would let me learn more about them in depth as well as give me access to more training and gear. It was while discussing the feasibility of the chemical agent book with Jon Ford, Paladin Press's Editorial Director, that the subject of Colonel Rex Applegate came up.

Jon mentioned that the Colonel was working on a revised edition of his classic book, *Riot Control: Materiel and Techniques*. He then suggested I call Applegate. My first instinct was to decline, because I didn't want to bother him. I knew that Applegate, widely regarded as a legend in many circles, had to be in his 80s. I also had no idea as to the state of his health, and the thought of calling him out of the blue seemed a bit presumptuous to me. After being assured by Jon that the Colonel wouldn't consider my calling him intrusive, but rather that he welcomed contact from police and military personnel, I decided to make the call.[12]

After introducing myself, I told Colonel Applegate a bit about what I had been doing, and

---

[11] *Beyond Pepper Spray: The Complete Guide to Chemical Agents, Delivery Systems, and Protective Masks*, published by Paladin Press, 2002.

inquired about his progress with the revised issue of *Riot Control*. The conversation eventually turned to pistols and training. As I listened, I heard a change come into Applegate's voice. He had an old man's voice, and an easy chuckling laugh that punctuated many of his thoughts, but when he spoke of police firearms training a kind of solidness came into his voice.

He spoke from the heart. And he spoke like I had heard people speak from the witness stand, with a certain and determined manner that was grounded in the truth–or what he firmly believed to be the truth, anyway.

And then he told me a story.

After his World War II service, he had left the US and worked primarily out of the country. He was gone, pursuing various business activities in Latin America and other places for many years. Then in the mid-1990s, Applegate attended a lecture at a US law enforcement conference and heard a young police firearms instructor extolling the virtues of the Modern Technique to the audience. At the end of the class, according to Applegate, another police officer stood up and asked the instructor why he believed that the system he had just described was the best way to train police officers for the street.

"Because," replied the earnest instructor, "fifty of the world's greatest combat competition shooters shoot this way."

---

[12] Part of the reason I did was because of an experience I'd had several years earlier with another legend in the field, famed Border Patrolman Bill Jordan. After reading his tome, *No Second Place Winner* a number of times, I decided to call him on his birthday one year and wish him well. I was given his number by a member of the US Border Patrol I had taken a class with after inquiring as to Jordan's status. The officer, about my age, surprised me by telling me that not only was Jordan alive and well, but that he had his home telephone number in Linwood, Texas. When I asked why he had the number, he told me that Jordan really enjoyed hearing from the troops. "In fact," he added, "you should call him next week, it's his birthday and I know he'd get a kick out of hearing from a Mass State Trooper!" I did make that call, and spent an enjoyable half-hour discussing pistols and police work with Bill Jordan, the man Charles Askins once described as "the fastest man on the draw I have ever seen in action."

It was this exchange that made Applegate realize that the US approach to police firearms training had gone off track. To the chagrin of many, it was this realization that motivated Applegate to re-enter this particular arena.

"They've been doing the Weaver style of two-handed, sights-only shooting for so long that they don't realize that they're missing the point–we need to prepare the police to engage in *combat* with their pistols, *not competition*!"

We ended that first conversation with Applegate telling me to call anytime I wanted to discuss anything further, and me asking him if he'd consider reviewing a copy of my chemical book manuscript when it was completed. "I'd be happy to." he replied, "In fact, I'd appreciate it if you'd send me a copy of your pistolcraft book for my library."

Feeling a bit intimidated–this was the author of *Kill or Get Killed*, a combat instructional manual still being used by the US Marine Corps, after all–and after qualifying my book by referring to it as a first effort that I knew was far from perfect, I assured him I would.

After our initial conversation I thought about what Applegate had told me. I had called looking for advice and information about chemical agents, but I kept coming back to his comments about pistol work, in particular about the young firearms instructor's sincere belief in the Modern Technique. The reason I was drawn to this particular part of our conversation was because I could see myself as that young instructor, absolutely convinced of the viability of the system we had been taught–and had taught to others–to keep ourselves and those around us safe with a pistol in the real world.

What he said, and the way he said it–with no bluster or sense of self-importance–made sense to me. It also went against much of what I had believed for many years, and what–regardless of the "holes" I had long been aware of–still retained the power of mainstream acceptance.

Enter Jim Cirillo

In January 1998 I participated as a guest instructor at the annual American Society of Law Enforcement Trainers (ASLET) conference in Mobile, Alabama. On the first night of the conference, I attended a general meeting and sat in the audience. A panel of senior instructors, many of them noted experts in the field of firearms training, had been assembled. After addressing various issues–most of which endorsed the core training beliefs of the Modern Technique–the matter of the re-emergence of Applegate and the Point Shooting technique was raised by one of the moderators. This gentleman then expressed his views on the subject, which were less than favorable and not based entirely on the facts as I had begun to learn them straight from the Colonel.

As it was an open forum, I made a few comments in an attempt to clarify the salient points being discussed. The atmosphere in the room became a bit heated. A few other instructors in the audience then began to express their own dismay with the way we trained our officers and more specifically, with the apparent training failures that continued to surface on the street. In response to the exasperated looks on the faces of some of the experts on the panel, I then posed this question:

"If the data generated for the last thirty years overwhelmingly indicates that officers required to score a minimum of 70% hits in training only achieve hits of 20% and less in real world encounters, then does that data not indicate a serious training failure on our part? And," I continued, "if that is true, is it not our responsibility, our duty as professional police firearms trainers, to address this failure and fix the problem?"

After a few moments of uncomfortable silence from the members of the panel–during which I might add, more than a few members of the audience sat looking expectantly at the panel and nodding–the moderator finally said, "Well, I suppose what you're saying deserves some attention. Why don't we go down the panel and see what each member thinks."

Starting at one end of the panel, each member was polled. I was a bit dismayed when each either skirted the issue, or didn't respond at all! To say I was a bit disappointed–not truly surprised, but disappointed–is an understatement. The reason I wasn't really surprised was because the panel was comprised mostly of professional firearms instructors, *not* professional police officers. A few had some part-time experience in law enforcement, one had a military background and no law enforcement experience–the usual mix that is found whenever you examine the vast majority of the modern day firearms training experts and/or gun gurus.

Then, the question landed in the lap of the last member of the panel, Jim Cirillo. I had heard of Jim for years, but had never met him. A legendary member of the New York Police Department, Jim had served with the Stakeout Squad in the early 1970s. In a matter of a few short years, he had been involved in 17 documented close-quarter gunfights with armed criminals. Twelve men he faced had been permanently retired from a life of crime and taken up residence in a cemetery. Jim was the real deal. In addition, not only had Jim been operational, but he was a highly-regarded firearms trainer as well. Not only could he do, but he could teach.[13]

Jim, who had been fairly silent to this point, then boomed out in his New York accent, "Hey! Maybe the kid's right. If there is a problem, we need to look at it. We can't be afraid to consider these things, to look at other ways of doing our job as trainers and police officers. In fact we *have* to do it. It's what we're all about, right?"

---

[13] Jim Cirillo has produced a book, *Guns, Bullets, and Gun Fights: Lessons and Tales from a Modern-Day Gunfighte*r, as well as two videos on the subject. (Available from Paladin Press).

Again, nods from audience members, some uncomfortable silences and sideways glances from the other members of the panel, and then the discussion moved along to other matters.

This was my initial introduction to Jim Cirillo. I recognized him as a man unafraid to stand apart from the crowd and question the status quo regardless of who might be offended, because the mission–saving cops' lives–was most important to him. That first personal exposure to him cemented my opinion of Jim from that moment forward–good cop and good man. In the years since, having gotten to know the man behind the legend better both professionally and personally, this opinion has only been strengthened.

The Camel Has its Nose under the Tent

Over the next several months, I made a fairly regular nuisance of myself with Colonel Applegate. He reviewed my pistol book for me, and gingerly advised me that while he found most of it pretty well done, he had a problem with my chapter on point shooting.

"You're close, but not quite all the way there," was how he graciously put it. Having gone back over his material in his classic book, *Kill or Get Killed*, with a renewed interest and a now open mind, I had an idea of what he meant. By telephone he continued to offer me different advice, and through the mail he sent me videotapes and copies of written materials he had produced and collected over the years.[14]

It became apparent to me that the Colonel was once again on a mission–except this time it was a self-directed mission, and he was fighting an uphill battle against the thirty-year entrenched and established Modern Technique training system.

I also realized that while I was one of the people he was trying to educate, I was far from the only one. I was one of many who had found their way to him from a variety of different angles and backgrounds, but for the same reason–we were all aware that there was a serious training problem within our law enforcement community, and we were searching for answers.[15]

Around this time, I asked Applegate if he would consider coming to the East coast in order to speak at a seminar on the Point Shooting Technique. The old man, who now walked with a cane, agreed without missing a beat.

"If you can set it up, I'll be there. We need to get the word out, let people see what they're missing so they can judge for themselves and make up their own minds."

As he was to attend a similar seminar for the California Peace Officers Standards and Training (POST) Council in July, we decided to hold ours a few weeks later in August.

Through Saber Group, Inc., the small start-up company I had formed to facilitate just this type of program, I arranged for his flights and lodging, sent out brochures, and rented a conference room. I also arranged for Bill Burroughs, President of Talon Training & Development, to co-present at the seminar. This way, we all agreed, the Colonel could present his views on the importance of the subject matter and answer any specific questions, and Bill–who had sought out and been trained personally by Applegate a few years earlier–could present the bulk of the material on the Point Shooting Technique and its development, thereby minimizing the physical demands on the Colonel.

With the seminar set, all we had to do was wait until August. If all went well, by the end of the summer, the Colonel would have successful-

---

[14] Included in these materials was a copy of *Bullseyes Don't Shoot Back*, a book about the Point Shooting technique he had collaborated on with Michael Janich. (Paladin Press 1998.)

[15] Steve Barron and Clyde Beasley of Hocking College, Bill Burroughs, President of Talon Training & Development, author Gregory P. Morrison, and New York firearms instructor Matt Temkin were among those who had also sought out Applegate.

ly launched his campaign to once again get the word out on the Point Shooting Technique to instructors from both the West and East coasts; Bill would have had a chance to work with the Colonel, presenting material he knew cold and believed in; and I would have a chance to meet a man whom I had come to admire and respect greatly. A man who was not looking for fans or disciples, or to be held in awe by those around him, but rather a man who just wanted the opportunity to explain why he believed what he believed, and why it was so damned important.

Applegate was not only a good soldier. Like Cirillo, he was also a good cop.[16] Someone who could be counted upon to be there when you needed him; who would do the right thing regardless of the consequences; and who would not waver from his duty until either the job–or he–was finished.

As fate would have it, however, none of these things would come to pass. On July 7, 1998, the morning of the POST seminar in San Diego, the Colonel suffered a stroke. Days later, he developed pneumonia. On July 14, 1998, Colonel Rex Applegate succumbed to complications and passed away. He was 84 years old.

One of the last things he said to me prior to leaving Oregon for California made me laugh at the time, and influenced several key decisions later.

Just before hanging up, I mentioned that we'd had a great deal of interest in the East coast seminar we were putting together. He then told me that there was also a lot of interest on the West coast, and that more and more mainstream law enforcement instructors seemed to be opening up their minds a bit to the idea that there may be a better way to train police to stay alive on the street.

"I believe that the camel," he said chuckling, "has its nose under the tent."

Charlie Mike (Continue the Mission)

With Applegate's passing, a decision had to be made regarding the Point Shooting symposium we had scheduled for August. The California POST conference, already started, had continued without Applegate's presence after he had fallen ill and been taken to the hospital.

A few days after the Colonel's death, I spoke with Bill Burroughs. Together we came to the same conclusion: we must continue the mission. Anything less, and we would be betraying the Old Man, ourselves, and what we believed was an important mission–helping to get the word out to the law enforcement training community.

"Charlie Mike?" I asked Bill, using the military vernacular.

"Yes," he replied, "I don't see how we can do anything else." Then he added, "Besides, I don't want the Old Man mad at me for the rest of eternity!"

We ran the seminar. On August 17, 1998, Bill Burroughs presented the entire block of instruction on the Point Shooting Technique to a group of instructors from all over the Northeast. As usual, he presented a complete and professional program. It was a good show all way around and I believe the Colonel would have been proud. Dan Meany, on assignment for SWAT Magazine, covered the event, ensuring the word was passed to greater numbers of people.[17]

But it couldn't stop there–and it hasn't.

In the years since Applegate's death, a number of people have carried on with the inextricably-joined missions of improving police firearms training and saving lives.

Bill Burroughs in Texas, Steve Barron and Clyde Beasley in Ohio, Lou Chiodo in California, Bruce Siddle in Illinois, and many others across the US are still digging, still trying

---

[16] Applegate actually started out as a police officer, serving as a Lieutenant in the US Army Military Police Corps.

[17] "Carry On, Colonel Applegate", *SWAT* magazine, May '99.

to find a way to better fill those holes through hard work and open-minded research.

Here in Massachusetts, due to the efforts of many dedicated individuals, tremendous strides have also been made in furthering the mission of "saving lives through superior training".

Before presenting the results of our work, however, I believe that an objective review of the people and events that have influenced and shaped police firearms training practices in general is necessary to more fully understand not only where this path is leading, but also how we arrived at it.

Colonel Rex Applegate
1914-1998

CHAPTER THREE
Objective View: How Did We Arrive Here?

What can be more important to any community, city, state, or government organization than proper training for law enforcement officers? Who could have more urgent need for actual and practical training in fast, sure hitting, effective revolver shooting than our police and kindred law enforcement officers? Who are more deserving of and should receive more consideration and encouragement along such lines than our police officers? Do they, as a general rule, get it? I'll say not. Are they, as a rule, given any post-graduate training under conditions that are in any way similar to the actual conditions that usually arise, and under which their shooting must be done, when it is done? This is a very important question that is deserving of much consideration. How in the name of common sense can any officer be expected to develop into an alert, quick draw, rapid fire, sure hit, dead center shot, and bandit exterminator, under all conditions of excitement, surprise, traffic jams, and danger to himself, if he is forced to conduct his training under conditions that never did and never will arise, or are never in evidence, and could not exist at or during any of the actual happenings where his services of such an order may be required, when called on in line of duty to use his gun in protection of life and property?

> – Ed McGivern
> *Fast and Fancy Revolver Shooting*
> 1938

Police *Combat* Handgun Training, Historical Overview

Most of us have heard the old adage usually attributed to George Santayana, "Those who do not remember the past are doomed to repeat it." Understanding the origins and development of any human endeavor is necessary in order to fully grasp where we have come from and more important, where we need to go to in order to progress.

This is no less true in the matter of pistolcraft, the art of fighting with handguns.

The problem with applying this approach to combat pistol training in general, and police combat pistol training in particular, is because so much of the actual history of pistolfighting has been romanticized and distorted by gun writers and Hollywood movie makers for so long, that the often less-romantic–though truly effective–techniques are often perceived as too simple and even a bit of a letdown.

While the development and employment of the first handgun can be traced to the 1300s, and the combat use of this short weapon in its many variations has been documented through the ensuing centuries, the story of modern law enforcement employment of the handgun truly begins in the nineteenth century.

Not by coincidence, this time period also marks the beginning of the age of "pistolero mythology"–an age that, while dealt some blows, continues to exist.

The Wild, Wild West

He who can hit a four-inch circle at six paces will be master of the situation provided he is quick enough. But the aim, if aim it can be called, must be taken with the rapidity of thought; there must be no dallying to find the sights; no hesitation in the hope of bettering the aim. Delay, however occasioned, may cost us our life. Not that we would counsel hurry or want of coolness, for this will inevitably cause us to shoot wide of the mark. There is such a thing as being rapid, cool, and accurate, and this is what is needed. It is evident that in making shots of this kind we have no time to look along the barrel and bring the sights into line. The aim must be taken in the same way that the boy throws a stone, or the wood-chopper strikes the exact spot where it is necessary that the axe should fall. How is this done? Simply by steadily fixing the sight on the object (not on the weapon), bringing the pistol quickly up, and firing the moment hand and eye both tell us that it is in proper position. This requires practice, but it is an art that is not nearly so difficult to acquire as would first appear.

> – Author Unknown
> *The Pistol as a Weapon of Defence in the House and on the Road* [1]
> 1875

The American Civil War (1861-1865) that tore much of our nation apart also produced a new breed of gunman. Prior to this war, the long gun was the preferred primary personal weapon used to engage the enemy. Traditional long guns–both rifles and shotguns–had often been supplemented by short guns, commonly referred to as handguns. Handguns were primarily designed to be easily carried on the person and therefore readily available. They were most often employed as a weapon of last resort–just ahead of the edged weapon–and used at fairly close distances.

It wasn't until the advent of the Civil War

that several interconnected events converged to propel the handgun to prominence as a primary weapon. These events included the rise of horse-mounted guerrilla irregulars (such as the Union's "Jayhawkers" led by a former US Senator, James H. Lane and the Confederacy's "Bushwhackers" under command of Captain William Clark Quantrill[2]); the development of the lightning-fast, close-quarter form of mounted combat they employed; and most of all, the availability of the short, easily manipulated weapons they used that allowed them to perform as efficiently and effectively as they did.

After the war ended, these new methods and techniques of close quarter pistol fighting found their way to the western United States, as veterans from both sides sought out the possibilities of wealth and adventure offered by the quickly disappearing frontier.

One of the most well-known of these efficient horse-mounted pistol fighters had served as a scout for various federal units during the Civil War. He would later gain fame as a celebrated Indian fighter and lawman. His given name was James Butler Hickok, but he would be immortalized in American history and pistolero mythology as "Wild Bill." While there were many notable gunmen produced both during and after the Civil War, it is with Hickok that our particular examination begins.

It is also through Hickok's experiences and professional involvement with pistols and pistol fighting that the correlation between mental

---

[1] *The Pistol as a Weapon of Defence (sic) in the House and on the Road*, recently rediscovered and published by Paladin Press in 2004.

[2] Captain William Clark Quantrill led a band of wild young men into scores of guerrilla ambushes and operations during the war. Among these men were Frank and Jesse James, who would survive the war and later become infamous as gunmen and thieves. The guerrillas employed the pistol as their primary weapon, often carrying at least four pistols on their person, and more mounted on their horses' saddles. Their abilities with their weapons, especially when firing from horseback at full gallop, were legendary. Another of the more notorious Confederate guerrillas, William "Bloody Bill" Anderson, died while charging into - and through - an overwhelmingly superior force of Union militia troops, a pistol blazing in each hand. He was shot twice in the back of the head after breaking through the line.

preparation, pistolcraft skills, and performance during high stress lethal force encounters can be illustrated.

Profile of the Archetype Lawman/Gunfighter: James Butler Hickok

Hickok's place in the annals of American western mythology is well documented. Commonly referred to by monikers such as "The Magnificent," the "Prince of Pistoleers," and of course, "Wild Bill," Hickok has been the subject of countless books, articles, and Hollywood films.

Most of these tales, however, do not depend upon the factual accounts of his life. Complicating the matter is that the stories that do relate his many documented experiences usually embellish and edit the facts in order to present Hickok as the mythological American lawman and pistolero.[3]

None of this diminishes Hickok's remarkable and memorable life. He was both highly-valued and truly feared by citizens, soldiers, and gunmen alike during some of the most dangerous times and in some of the most harrowing environments imaginable.[4]

Yet many of the elements of his story, usually overlooked or downplayed, provide an invaluable insight into the realities he dealt with, and which the modern-day lawman must still face.

Hickok's comparatively short life–he was murdered at age 39–began in LaSalle County, Illinois on May 27, 1837. His life was unremarkable up until about the time he was 18 years old. That's when he made his way to

James Butler "Wild Bill" Hickok
(Archival photograph)

"bleeding Kansas" and served with General Lane. He also had his first experience as a lawman around this time, working for a while as a constable. During this time it is likely that Hickok was exposed to a good deal of violence, though no documented records exist of his direct involvement in any close quarter pistol fights.

A few years later while employed as a wagon driver on the Sante Fé Trail, Hickok was mauled by a grizzly bear. As he recuperated over the next several months, he became involved in an extended conflict with one of the managers of the company he worked for. The conflict quickly became personal in nature, and culminated in July 1861 with what is believed by some historians to be Hickok's first killing.

Reports surrounding this incident vary. In Eugene Cunningham's classic work, *Triggernometry: A Gallery of Gunfighters*, Hickok's first killing is described in great detail and–if the account is accurate–can best be characterized as an act of murder.[5] According to

---

[3] Contrary views and opinions of Hickok's life and deeds have been documented in Miller & Snell's book, *Great Gunfighters of the Kansas Cowtowns, 1867-1886.*

[4] The term "gunman" was originally used to describe someone who developed–and used–pistolcraft skills, regardless on which side of the badge they stood while employing them. It wasn't until the early Twentieth Century that the term became synonymous with criminal.

---

[5] *Triggernometry* was first published in 1941 by The Caxton Printers, Ltd., Caldwell, Idaho.

43

Cunningham, the most believable version of the story has the victim in this case, a man named David McCanles, arguing with Hickok about money owed to McCanles by Hickok's employer. The argument eventually moved indoors, where, it is alleged, Hickok shot the unarmed McCanles through the heart (possibly with a rifle), while Hickok stood concealed behind a curtain. Two men named Gordon and Woods (also possibly unarmed, though their reported actions would make more sense for armed men than not) who had accompanied McCanles were nearby and ran to the house after hearing the shot. As they approached they saw McCanles stumble from the house, fall to the ground, and apparently die.

Woods then entered the house and was immediately shot two times by Hickok who stood concealed again, this time behind the door, pistols in his hands. Woods then ran from the house and fell, seriously wounded, into some weeds.

Gordon, the second man, turned and ran after Hickok shot Woods. Hickok then allegedly emerged from the house and fired at Gordon on the run, hitting him twice and missing with the rest of the rounds he fired at him. This allowed Gordon to escape into the puckerbrush. Hickok–the bloodlust having apparently taken hold of him–then had to be dissuaded from killing a stableman who was on scene.

The encounter came to a conclusion with the coup de grace allegedly being administered to Woods by a woman who hacked him to pieces with a gardening tool, and by the hunting down and execution of Gordon with a pistol. Exactly who delivered the final shot into Gordon has never been clarified.

Hickok, the woman, and another man were arrested and charged with the murders. The informal proceedings held at the time ended when "no motive for the crime" could be introduced, and Hickok and the others walked.

If these accounts of Hickok's experiences up to this time are accurate, and assuming–based upon the historical evidence–that he was not an aggressive psychopath, one could postulate that his early and continued exposure to violence provided more than ample environmentally-induced stress inoculation, desensitization, and classical conditioning to allow him to engage in cold-blooded murder as described above.[6]

If the murder of McCanles was indeed his first direct killing, one can also imagine him finding it easier to overcome any final internal resistance to killing by firing his first fatal shot from a bit of a distance and a concealed position. Based upon current research into "Killology", it is also reasonable to surmise that once this barrier had been crossed, future killings would be easier for him to commit.[7]

However the incident went down, Hickok apparently cleared out immediately after being released and went to work as a wagon master for the Union Army in August of 1861. According to legend, it was during this time that he was christened "Wild Bill" by a resident in Independence, Kansas, after ending a brawl in a local saloon by convincing the participants to leave at gun point. No shots were fired.

Discounting numerous unconfirmed stories and tales, what is known about Hickok's activities during the war indicates that he served primarily as a scout for Union troops.

While he was undoubtedly involved in many actions during this time, there are few documented accounts of his performance with pistols.

After the Civil War came to an end, Hickok found his way to Springfield, Missouri. It was in Springfield that he engaged in his first documented pistolfight on July 21, 1865 at approximately 6 p.m. An argument over either a woman or a card game with a man named Dave Tutt eventually came to a head when Tutt, gunning for Hickok, refused Hickok's repeated

6 These terms are defined in Chapter Four.

7 Killology is the study of the act of killing pioneered by LTC Dave Grossman.

orders not to cross the town square toward him.

Hickok, Navy Colt in hand, reportedly challenged Tutt from a distance of about 75 yards. Tutt, ignoring Hickok's warning, then fired one round at him and missed.

According to eyewitness accounts, Hickok, Colt in his right hand, steadied the pistol on his left forearm, aimed carefully and returned fire, placing one round through Tutt's heart. This shooting was deemed self-defense and established Hickok's reputation as a deadly gunman.

Hickok then spent the next four years alternating his employment between lawman and Indian fighter. In February 1867, Hickok's life was drastically altered when he became a nationally-known "celebrity gunman" based upon a story that appeared in *Harper's New Monthly Magazine*. The romanticized article inspired both adulation and derision depending upon whether the reader was a fan or enemy of Hickok's.

By 1869, Hickok was a full time professional lawman, serving as Sheriff of rough and tumble Hays City, Kansas.

During his time in Hays, Hickok reportedly killed several more men in gunfights. Unlike the Hollywood versions, the gunfights of the old West were not much different from the gunfights of today, the primary difference being found in the hardware used.

With long distance encounters such as the Tutt shooting the rare exception, the vast majority of Hickok's confirmed gunfights occurred at fairly close ranges in low-light environments. They were overwhelmingly fast and furious events involving only a few rounds being fired, and usually involved one or more participants operating under the influence of some type of drug, usually alcohol. Based upon reports from the time, it would appear that one of the reasons Hickok generally prevailed in these encounters was because he was always armed and constantly aware of his surroundings. Maintaining this constant, almost hyper-vigilant

state insured that he would see trouble coming and have time to prepare himself to deal with it. Given the particular time and circumstances he lived in, this attitude was critical to his survival, for threats could come from anyone, anywhere, at any time.

As an example, in one notable incident, Hickok became embroiled in a bar fight with several members of the Seventh Calvary, during which he shot two of them, mortally wounding one. (The popular version of this story has Hickok being jumped in a saloon by a group of soldiers under the command of General George Custer's brother, Tom. However, official records of the time do not support this.[8])

Shortly after this, Hickok left Hays City and moved to Abilene. Abilene had been without a chief law enforcement officer since Marshall Tom Smith had been murdered in the line of duty on November 2, 1870.

On April 15, 1871, Hickok was hired and assumed the job of Marshal. Six months later in October, Hickok was involved in two more killings. Tragically similar to events that still occur in modern law enforcement, one of the people he killed was a close friend and fellow lawman.

While there are differing versions of this encounter, what is undisputed is that Hickok faced an armed man named Phil Coe one evening outside a saloon. What is also undisputed is that there had been bad blood of a personal nature between Hickok and Coe for some time. At some point during the encounter, rounds were exchanged between the two men from a reported distance of eight feet. Exactly who fired first or from what position is still a matter of contention.

Regardless, Coe was critically injured during the exchange while Hickok escaped unscathed. During the gunfight, a friend and fellow officer named Mike Williams reportedly ran up to the scene and was inadvertently shot and

---

[8] Miller & Snell.

killed by Hickok. (One version of the story has Williams running directly into Hickok's line of fire, while another has Williams running up from behind Hickok, who, hearing the noise, spun and fired at the sound, killing Williams instantly.)

According to some historians, Hickok, while physically unharmed, never completely recovered emotionally from this incident.

A month later he left Abilene and law enforcement, and spent some time touring the East. Short stints as an actor with Buffalo Bill's show, as a trail guide, and as a prospector followed. Eventually, Hickok arrived in Deadwood, South Dakota with a friend and settled in to work a prospecting claim. Though rumors began to circulate that Hickok would be offered the position of Marshal for Deadwood, he was not serving as a lawman on that fateful afternoon in August when he joined several of his friends in a saloon for a game of poker.

Foregoing his normal practice of sitting with his back to a wall facing the door, Hickok took a seat at the table with his back to the open door and began to play. For whatever reason, he compounded this tactical disadvantage by failing to pay attention to a local drunk who entered the saloon and sidled his way to a position directly behind Hickok. As Hickok contemplated the soon to be infamous hand of cards he held, the drunk, Jack McCall, fired one shot into the back of Hickok's head killing him instantly.[9] The date was August 2, 1876.

McCall, allegedly inspired to murder by enemies of Hickok, then ran out of the saloon but was captured by another colorful character of the time, "Calamity Jane" Cannary.

After either escaping or being released (supposedly aided by enemies of Hickok) a short time later, McCall was eventually arrested again and charged with the murder. He was convicted and sentenced to hang, which he did on March 1, 1877.

Now we leave Hickok, for a bit, and advance our story approximately 40 years ahead and 6,500 miles to the East to another town filled with gunmen and flying lead.

The Wild, Wild East

Shanghai, China during the 1920s and 1930s was not only equal to any of the American Western frontier towns of the late 1800s in regard to providing opportunities to engage in close quarter pistol combat, but was by many accounts vastly superior.

The forces of law and order in what has often been described as the toughest city in the world during that era were represented primarily by the Shanghai Municipal Police (SMP) Department.

Two British police officers assigned to the SMP would exploit the opportunities presented by the rampant lawlessness and numerous criminal elements to develop an unprecedented body of knowledge of effective close quarter combat methods and techniques. Chief among these skills would be the art and science of pistolfighting.

Profile of the Archetype
Lawman Gunfighter/Trainer:
Fairbairn and Sykes

The boss of the operation was SMP Assistant Commissioner William E. "Dan" Fairbairn. While a competent marksman, Fairbairn's primary interest and strengths lay in hand-to-hand combat skills, with a strong emphasis on edged weapon techniques.[10] A former Royal Marine, Fairbairn would also be instrumental in developing the prototypical versions of the modern riot control squad and police tactical

---

[9] Hickok held two pair–aces and eights–that would forever after be known as the "dead man's hand."

[10] Fairbairn and Sykes are also credited with designing the Fairbairn-Sykes (F-S) British Commando knife.

operations or SWAT team.

Working with Fairbairn was another Englishman named Eric A. Sykes. Sykes, originally a firearms and ammunition salesman, also served as a special police officer for the SMP and was in charge of the police sniper element. Sykes, having a greater interest and stronger skills with firearms than Fairbairn, complemented Fairbairn and insured that the training they provided as a team was equally balanced between armed and unarmed fighting techniques.

Together they trained all of the indigenous members of the SMP, as well as numerous American military personnel who were stationed in prewar Shanghai. During the time they served with the SMP, Fairbairn and Sykes were involved in more than two hundred violent incidents, many of them involving the use of handguns and close quarter combat.

They developed a no-nonsense attitude toward both the weapons they carried and the techniques they used to employ them.

Their systems were based on the experiences they had in the field while performing their jobs, and their jobs were quite simply to enforce the law while operating as police officers–not soldiers–and deal with often armed and dangerous criminals in heavily populated environments.[11] (The reason I make the distinction between police officer and soldier here is because the missions are markedly different even though some of the methods and techniques that are used to carry them out are sometimes similar–a fact that seems to be lost on many of those currently involved in civilian police firearms training.)

As a result of their personal experiences and observations, Fairbairn and Sykes developed a system for close quarter pistol fighting that incorporated the natural reactions exhibited by human beings when engaged in close quarter

pistol fights. The system was primarily designed to be used while armed with a semi-automatic pistol, but would be effective, according to Fairbairn, with any type of one-hand gun including a flintlock pistol.

The basic system, fully described and illustrated in their book *Shooting to Live*, consists of having the shooter standing square to the target, holding the pistol in the dominant hand. The shooting arm is then locked out to the front, the pistol held in line with the center of the body. By bending the wrist slightly toward the dominant side of the body, the bore of the pistol is directed straight out from the body's centerline.

Keeping both eyes open and the arm locked out, the pistol is then raised along the centerline of the body until it is at–or just below–eye level and in line with the target. As soon as the pistol is in line with the target, the hand is convulsed and the pistol is fired, with the shooter's focus being maintained on the target, not the sights.[12]

After firing the pistol, the arm, still locked out, is lowered down until the pistol is pointing approximately 45 degrees toward the deck, in the "ready position."

After mastering this technique–a process that was expected to require approximately one-hour's time dry-firing the pistol–the student would then be issued dummy ammunition and taught how to safely load and unload the pistol, as well as disassemble it for cleaning.

Next, the student would be provided with live ammunition, and placed in front of a life-size silhouette target at a distance of no more than two yards. The student would then fire a series of shots at the target using the

[11] It is believed that Fairbairn participated in and studied the results of more than 200 gunfights during his time with the SMP.

[12] The adoption of similar combat pistol techniques was also encouraged by other British officers in the early part of the Twentieth Century. One of these men, Captain Charles D. Tracy, cited the use of unsighted snap-shooting, the "whole hand squeeze," and the idea of sweeping the pistol up through the target, AKA the "vertical lift" in his 1916 manual, *Revolver Shooting in War.*

recommended technique at the instructor's command. This drill would be repeated until the student developed confidence in his ability to deliver rounds accurately into the human-shaped silhouette.

Total recommended time for this entire block of instruction was also one-hour.

Once the basic technique had been established, the student would be introduced to the advanced technique. This required the student to adopt a slightly modified stance. Referred to as the "three-quarter hip" position, this stance required the student to assume what Fairbairn and Sykes knew to be a "natural" body position that human beings would generally assume when faced with threats.

The main differences between the three-quarter hip position and the basic position are found in:
1) the way the dominant arm is held–still centered on the centerline of the body but with a slightly bent elbow;
2) the placement of the feet–body is still held square to the target but one foot is placed forward of the other;
3) the way the shooter stands slightly crouched.

Three-Quarter Hip Position
Excerpted from *Shooting to Live!*
(Courtesy of Paladin Press).

Also included in this segment of training were blocks of instruction on other close quarter and various shooting positions; engaging moving targets; and engaging targets while the shooter is on the move. In addition, methods for using the pistol to engage the occasional threat target at distances beyond the normal close ranges encountered in pistol fights–such as Hickok encountered when he exchanged one round with Dave Tutt in Springfield–were taught. These included the use of a two-handed grip and firing from behind cover while using the sights when time and distance permitted.

Practical, dynamic courses of fire were also included in the training, as was a course Fairbairn described as a "mystery shoot." The mystery shoot as employed by Fairbairn and Sykes required the student officers to navigate a course of fire on a range that had been modified by screening walls and various props to resemble real-world environments. Human looking dummy targets–both threat and non-threat types–would then be activated by the instructors as the student moved through the simulated environment, and the student would have to react to the target and take appropriate action.

The combination of the basic pistol training program that instilled safe handling skills and above all, *confidence* in the student officer's ability to use the pistol to hit a man-sized target, and the psychological training benefits generated by programs like the mystery shoot produced extraordinary and well documented results.

According to Fairbairn and Sykes, the members of the SMP–trained as indicated above–engaged in no less than 666 armed encounters with criminals over a twelve and a half year time period (approximately 53 encounters per year).

In the close quarter encounters where pistols were used by the police officers, more than 260 criminals were killed and 193 wounded, compared to 42 officers killed and 100 wounded.

Statistically, this means that the pistol-equipped members of the SMP suffered an average of 3 officers killed and 8 wounded per year during more than a decade of incredible street violence, compared to an average of 21 criminals killed and 15 wounded per year during this same time period. (It is interesting to note that police firearms training being conducted in the United States during this same time period primarily consisted of target-shooting style qualification courses of fire, utilizing highly-stylized marksmanship oriented positions and techniques as shown in the photo at right.)

Shortly after World War II began, both Fairbairn and Sykes were called home to England and immediately commissioned as Captains in the British Army. Their original mission was to train the poorly equipped British Home Guard to repel a German land invasion. Eventually they were tasked to train Allied commandos and intelligence personnel in their hard-learned techniques of close quarter combat.

In 1942, Fairbairn was sent to the United States to assist the newly formed Office of Strategic Services (OSS) in setting up a training program for guerrillas and intelligence operatives. It was there he would meet a young Army Lieutenant named Rex Applegate.

Colonel Rex Applegate, the COI, OSS, and MITC

The son of a pioneering Oregon family, Rex Applegate was commissioned a lieutenant in the U.S. Army's Military Police Corps after graduating from the University of Oregon in 1940. In 1942, he was assigned to the Coordinator of Information (COI), forerunner of the Office of Strategic Services (OSS), which would later evolve into the CIA.

One of the missions given him at the time by World War I Medal of Honor winner Colonel William J. "Wild Bill" Donovan, was to "learn everything there is to know about close

Massachusetts State Police officers training with their duty pistols, circa 1924. While various stances and stylizations have been employed over the years, the emphasis on this type of target-shooting oriented training has remained prevalent throughout the US. Not everyone has followed this formula, however. For example, a training course of fire designed for police officers by Ed McGivern during the 1920s required officers to fire from a variety of realistic positions, while running, using flashlights, and even from moving vehicles. It is also interesting to note that instructors of the time were well aware that "the evidence seemed to show that the majority of such affairs (gun fights between police and criminals) occur at distances that are less than thirty-five feet, and very many of them under fifteen feet." McGivern's police firearms courses of fire reflected these realities, 15 yards being the furthest distance normally engaged during training. (Photo courtesy Massachusetts State Police archives)

combat."

Applegate took the mission to heart.

While initially researching this broad topic, Applegate ended up in Deadwood, South Dakota, the place where another "Wild Bill"– James Butler Hickok–had met his end in 1876.

According to Applegate, he found a letter written by Hickok that had been stored for years in the basement of the Deadwood City Hall. In the letter, the accomplished western gunfighter reportedly explained how he had managed to defeat so many opponents in close quarter pistol combat.

In Hickok's words, "I raised my hand to eye level, like pointing a finger, and fired."

This basic description of Hickok's pistol fighting technique intrigued Applegate, but the method wasn't made completely clear to him until after meeting and training with Fairbairn, who arrived from Britain in 1942.

It was then that Applegate and Fairbairn met and worked together for more than a year. During this time, Applegate and Fairbairn polished not only what would become known as the Point Shooting Technique, but also how the system was taught.[13]

The mechanical movements of the technique were simplified and based on people's normal reactions to stress and fear–not highly stylized stances and marksmanship techniques that fell apart when true danger from an armed opponent was introduced into the equation.

The basic technique (illustrated at right) worked in training and was proven time and again in the field.

While the techniques themselves were effective, the job of truly preparing the students for real world encounters required another level of training that would address the mental conditioning aspects so often overlooked by conventional police firearms training programs.

This level was addressed by ramping up Fairbairn's "mystery shoot" program. Formally

---

[13]Among his many accomplishments, Applegate attended British Commando School in Scotland, participated in behind-the-lines operations in France and North Africa, tracked down the Thompson Submachine Gun-armed killer of an FBI agent, organized and commanded the Combat Section at the US Army Military Intelligence Training Center, served as the personal bodyguard for President Franklin Delano Roosevelt, toured war-time Korea and Vietnam as a non-combatant, served as a consultant for the US and other countries regarding less lethal methods for controlling civil disturbances, wrote several books and numerous articles, and went on to become the world's fore-most authority on riot control. His story is more fully told in *The Close Combat Files of Colonel Rex Applegate*, published by Paladin Press.

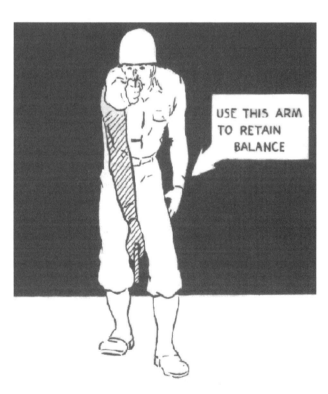

Point Shooting Illustrations excerpted from *Kill or Get Killed*. (Courtesy of Paladin Press)

renamed the "House of Horrors" program, the course, set up in the basement of a building, was designed to simulate experiences the students would most likely be encountering in the field.

This version of the program consisted of an instructor directing one student at a time through a lowlight, danger-fraught environment. The student would be armed with the basic tools of the trade, a firearm and a knife. As the student walked through darkened rooms and along hallways littered with debris, uneven surfaces–and in some cases, bodies–he would be confronted with various types of enemy and/or friendly figures in front of him.

The enemy, either a dummy or live role-player, would be dressed, equipped, and even speak like the known enemy. Often, blank-firing weapons were used to add to the sensory input.

Friendlies would be dressed like Allied soldiers or civilians. If the student reacted appropriately to the figure or scenario, either by shooting, knifing, or holding his fire, then the instructor would praise him with a simple and immediate, "Good boy, that's right, good job."

If the wrong choice was made, the student would experience a great deal of the emotional stress and disappointment such a mistake in an actual situation would generate. (While relating information about this program to me more than 50 years later, Applegate clearly recalled the effect this type of training had on the people who took part in it. According to him, they would consistently experience the type of excitement, adrenaline rush, and stress-induced effects as experienced by men in actual combat. The idea was to let them experience these effects for the first time in training, in a controlled environment, so they could learn from their mistakes and develop confidence in themselves and their ability to deal with these types of situations.)

Many of the students who were trained by these methods (as well as the OSS instructors themselves) used the Point Shooting technique successfully in behind-the-lines operations.[14]

The system–to include the "House of Horrors" program–continued to be taught at the Military Intelligence Training Center located at Camp Ritchie, Maryland throughout the end of the war.

Among the many government, military, and law enforcement personnel trained in this system during this time were members of the Federal Bureau of Investigation.

The FBI

One of Rex Applegate's assignments during his time with the OSS was to serve as President Franklin Delano Roosevelt's personal bodyguard. While working this assignment, Applegate became acquainted with Frank Baughman, a high-ranking official of the FBI.

Baughman, then in charge of the FBI's laboratories and training division, was especially interested in firearms training. He even designed a front sight for revolvers that was named after him and marketed by the Smith & Wesson Company.

After Applegate was transferred to Camp Ritchie in 1943, he invited Baughman to the MITC to observe the training they were administering. According to Applegate, Baughman was particularly impressed with the Point Shooting Technique and the methods used to teach it. After Baughman returned to Washington, he talked the matter over with his superiors and recommended adoption of the Point Shooting Technique and the training system being used to teach it, to include the House of Horrors program.

Shortly thereafter, a young FBI agent named Hank Sloan was sent to Applegate at Camp Ritchie for training. When he returned to Washington, Sloan, at the direction of Frank Baughman, instituted the Point Shooting

---

[14] Among the students was an OSS officer named Aaron Bank, who would later become Colonel Bank, the founding "father" of US Army Special Forces.

program–as taught by Applegate–into the FBI training curriculum.

According to Applegate, the Point Shooting Technique was an intrinsic component of the FBI's firearms training program until Baughman changed assignments approximately seven years later.[15] Hank Sloan, who would eventually become the officer in charge of firearms training at the FBI Academy in Quantico where he served for almost 30 years, reportedly eased out the Point Shooting system as taught by Applegate and replaced it with a firearms training "system" of his own shortly after Baughman left.

The bastardization of the Point Shooting Technique had begun.

It was during the period from 1950-1960 when the "FBI Crouch" and its attendant training methodologies appeared.

The FBI Crouch involved a variation of the Point Shooting technique that was more highly stylized than the Applegate version.

It also required more initial training time to learn, and a greater amount of practice time to become–and *stay*–proficient with. The result was a firearms training system that was not as easily taught, assimilated, or retained as was the Applegate version.[16] Since this version was also referred to as "point shooting," the very name began to be associated with a complicated and inefficient method of handgun deployment.

It was also during this time that the FBI became associated with the now famous "Hogan's Alley" training course. This course, similar to the House of Horrors and other earlier programs, was also modified by the FBI.

Basically, they altered this concept as well

The FBI Crouch. The non-dominant arm was held across the body in hopes that it would "catch" an incoming round and prevent it from going into the chest/torso area. Demonstrated by Sgt. Frank Hughes, MSP Gang Unit.

by taking the fear out of it and turning it primarily into a marksmanship course. Whereas the House of Horrors incorporated 3-dimensional targets and role players who would actually move and shoot (blanks) at the trainee, Hogan's Alley was populated only with two-dimensional plastic, paper, or cardboard targets.

The games had begun.[17]

---

[15] According to Applegate, the FBI consistently denied ever having used or taught the Point Shooting system in later years. Applegate, however, kept digging until he located a training film produced by the FBI that not only showed FBI agents using a somewhat bastardized form of Point Shooting, but actually extolled the virtues of this close-quarter fighting system. Applegate sent me a copy of this film which is exactly as he described, right down to J. Edgar Hoover's signature on the written introduction placard.

---

[16] To avoid confusion, the Point Shooting Technique as refined at the MITC will be referred to as either the "Applegate" version, style, or technique throughout the text.

[17] The FBI would later build an elaborate "Hogan's Alley" training facility at their Academy in Quantico. Opening in 1987, the new Hogan's Alley would employ the use of role players and live fire training/marking ammunition, effectively putting the fear and realism back into the program.

Going Hollywood

Have gun, will travel reads the card of a man. A knight without armor in a savage land.
— Johnny Western
The Ballad of Paladin
From the CBS television series,
Have Gun, Will Travel. (1957-1963)

At the same time this was occurring, a number of other factors came into play to further taint the whole concept of Point Shooting.

For years Hollywood had popularized the Western with numerous short movies and feature-length films. Then, during the late 1940s and early 1950s, as television found its way into more and more homes, Hollywood began recycling these films on the small screen. Soon, Western-themed television series were all the rage, and the public couldn't get enough of programs like *Gunsmoke, The Lone Ranger, Wild Bill Hickok, Wyatt Earp*, etc.

The star of the majority of these programs was Tinsel Town's incarnation of the sixgun-armed pistolero. Having more in common with the sensationalized dime novels of the late 1800s and early 1900s than with historical reality, these celluloid images captured the hearts and imaginations of much of the world.

Unfortunately, many of the people who would later find their way into US law enforcement were raised on images such as the hero gunslinger walking slowly toward the villain on a dusty town road, squinting into the high noon sun, drawing and firing his pistol–only after the bad guy made his move first of course–at hip level and defeating the black-clad desperado with a single dramatic shot.

Across the US the "sport" of fast-draw exploded along with the popularity of the Hollywood "screen slinger." Much time, money, and excitement were devoted to this game that required the participants to draw and fire a western-style single action revolver from a customized cowboy rig as fast as possible. Accuracy, like reality, had nothing to do with this activity. The guns were loaded with blanks.

Another contributing factor that helped destabilize the reputation of the Applegate Point Shooting Technique was found in a man who actually employed an accurate version of point shooting closer to the Hollywood ideal than the reality-based Applegate technique. This man, the legendary Border Patrolman Bill Jordan, was no celluloid gunslinger. In fact, he was a Marine veteran who saw action in World War II and Korea, as well as during numerous police encounters. What set Jordan apart was the fact that he devoted an enormous amount of time, energy, and natural talent to developing his drawing and point shooting abilities, to the point that his skills were almost beyond belief.[18]

This was a man who could place a ping pong ball on the back of his hand, hold this hand directly above his holstered pistol, and then draw his pistol so fast that the ping pong ball would fall into the empty holster. This was a showman who would stand with his revolver at hip level, point, shoot and hit an aspirin tablet with wax bullets on a table ten feet away–twice in a row.

The thing that must be taken into consideration about Bill Jordan is this: even though he was an actual field-experienced working police officer, the gunhandling and shooting skills he so arduously developed were *exceptional*. The average police officer could hardly be expected to develop the types of extraordinary skills that Jordan devoted himself to developing–and nor, in actuality, should they be.

Jordan did what he did because he *loved to do it*. He excelled at it and used his talents as a vehicle to further causes he believed in, like the preservation of the Second Amendment and NRA firearms safety and training programs.

---

18 Bill Jordan wrote the classic text, *No Second Place Winner*. First published in 1965. Available from Police Bookshelf. It is interesting to note that Jordan is shown on the book jacket holding his revolver in what appears to be the "three-quarter hip" position illustrated previously.

The problem came when many in the public viewed his unique skills–so similar to those displayed on the silver screen by the Hollywood gunslingers–as being truly representative of the Point Shooting Technique.

As a result, the very term "point shooting" began to be viewed synonymously with others like "hip shooting," "instinct shooting" and "trick shooting."[19]

The Modern Technique

Our experience demonstrates conclusively that quick, accurate fire is most reliably delivered through one's use of the sights, the goal being to land two hits in an area about the size of the open hand, from the holster, in less than two seconds. It takes no more time to bring the pistol to eye level with two hands than it does to thrust it straight out with one hand. In addition, the use of the sights increases measurably the odds for hits in those body areas most likely to incapacitate (areas not as large as you might hope). Even under adverse light conditions, we have found that properly programmed reflexes learned with the use of the sights carry over when the sights are less visible or not visible at all. But this is still sighted fire!

– Gregory Boyce Morrison
The Modern Technique of the Pistol
1991

Amid the national fever of fast-draw and shooting games during the 1950s emerged a loosely knit, southern California-based organization of sport shooting enthusiasts that called themselves the "Bear Valley Gunslingers."

Jeff Cooper, a Marine Corps veteran of World War II, headed this organization. Cooper and others in the club shunned the fast-draw games and focused on the development of live fire sporting competition courses that were conducted for fun.

When asked about this period of development, Cooper was once quoted saying, "We started with nothing. Just a bunch of guys enjoying themselves. We started having contests using the point shooting systems," but the courses were developed and expanded from there.[20]

One of the primary ways the courses were initially "developed and expanded" was by incorporating live fire "combat shooting courses" utilized at that time by various national and international law enforcement agencies. Among these courses was an adaptation of the FBI's Hogan's Alley reaction course–a watered down, marksmanship-oriented version of the House of Horrors training program.

A critical juncture in the development of police firearms training had been reached.

Competition "shoots" began to be held an average of once a month. A large number of police officers were drawn to these competitions in the San Bernardino Mountains. Courses of fire began to be developed that promoted–and rewarded–speed and accuracy more than tactical sensibility. Techniques and stylizations such as the one now commonly known as the "Weaver Stance", designed to allow the participant to efficiently employ a two-handed hold to better shoot at and hit non-threatening static and moving targets during these competitions, were adopted.

The games and the rules became more complicated. The firearms and carry gear followed suit, becoming more refined, expensive, and less practical. Cooper began to write extensively about the guns and techniques being employed.

The Bear Valley Gunslingers renamed their organization the "Southwest Combat Pistol

---

[19] Please note that the term "instinctive" is not an accurate description of Point Shooting, even though it does appear in *Shooting to Live!* by Fairbairn and Sykes. The fact is that pointing a handgun or your finger accurately at an object is not an instinct, it is a learned skill.

[20] Excerpted from *The Gun Digest of Combat Handgunnery* by Jack Lewis and Jack Mitchell. Published by DBI Books, Inc.

League." Big money, high-profile shooting contests like the Bianchi Cup, Steel Challenge, and Second Chance competition helped popularize the sport and established champion gamesmen as the new "combat handgun masters."

Cooper and other popular gun magazine writers of the time declared the birth of a "new technique of the combat pistol," consisting of the Weaver Stance, quick draw, quick sight picture, and surprise shot break.[21] Another bedrock component of the new technique was the preference for big bore 1911-type single-action, semi-automatic pistols, most notably in .45ACP caliber.

With the rejection of the fast-draw games and the "gunslinger" image also came an indiscriminate rejection of any technique even remotely related to, or described as, "instinct," "hip," or "point shooting."

Finally, within the course of a relatively few years, assisted by the establishment of popular shooting schools such as Cooper's American Pistol Institute (API) and the development of organizations like the International Practical Shooting Confederation (IPSC) and United States Practical Shooting Association (USPSA), the term "combat handgun shooting" became synonymous with the unrealistic, competition-based shooting games conducted at these types of matches.

The cart had been placed before the horse and the "new technique"–which has now become, for our purposes, the old paradigm– was firmly established.

While credited to California Sheriff Jack Weaver, the man who popularized it, the two-hand hold and bladed stance can actually be traced back to at least 1930 and a New Englander named John Henry Fitzgerald. "Fitz" as he was known, was an influential force in American pistol shooting for many years. Shown here from a photograph from his book, *Shooting* (G.F. Book Co., Hartford, CT., 1930), Fitz demonstrates a shooting position remarkably similar to the much later-dubbed "Weaver".

---

[21] Much like the "New Paradigm", Cooper's "New Technique" had its roots in earlier techniques and practices. The "Weaver" stance, as noted in the photo caption above right, can be accurately attributed to J.H. Fitzgerald, circa 1930. The quick draw, besides being desired for obvious reasons, had roots to the American West of the 1800s. As for the quick sight picture and surprise shot break, both of these elements can be traced back at least as far as World War I.

The New Paradigm

It is necessary to develop a new training paradigm to use as the vehicle of facilitation for the new research. Dynamic Encounter Training (DET) has been designed to provide the tools that enable trainers and administrators to work together to achieve specific goals. This approach requires that trainers develop skills beyond the competencies they currently possess to design and administer training.
– William E. Burroughs
  1998

For well over the next thirty years the vast majority of US law enforcement agencies in the US centered their handgun training programs on the highly-stylized, sight-oriented, marksmanship-based shooting techniques that were developed to assist gamesmen achieve victory during shooting competitions.

In essence, various types of stationary or moving targets were fired at from different distances to record the success or failure of the officer's ability to achieve hits on these targets.

In order to best achieve hits on these paper, plastic, or metal training targets, the emphasis was placed on using highly-stylized stances and the pistol's sights–*especially the front sight*–at all distances and under all conditions.

During these same thirty or so years, however, US law enforcement officers consistently averaged hit rates of less than 15% when engaged in actual real-world, predominantly close-quarter gunfights during which the targets not only shot back, but usually shot *first*.

Unbelievably, this situation was allowed to continue virtually unabated until the 1990s.

The first documented organizational challenge to the Modern Technique took root in early 1992, when two police firearms instructors at Hocking College in Nelsonville, Ohio, noticed a disturbing trend after they introduced Simunition training ammunition and dynamic simulation training into their firearms program.

Steve Barron and Clyde Beasley, both steadfast proponents of the Modern Technique, were at a loss to explain why their students' demonstrated abilities to hit their target during standardized qualification courses all but evaporated when they were faced with targets that shot back.

They were further dismayed as they observed their students' carefully taught and ingrained stances and techniques consistently disintegrate time and again while they participated in any type of dynamic interactive training simulations.

Like many other police firearms instructors across the US, however, Barron and Beasley were faced with an unyielding philosophy–the Modern Technique was the only acceptable way to train police officers, regardless of the fact that it only seemed to be effective when used on the training range firing line.

To their credit, instead of just shrugging their shoulders and saying, "Well, what can you do?", Barron and Beasley struggled privately with these issues for several more years. The first solution they tried was the one most often provided by the same people who had ushered in and reinforced the Modern Technique, namely, "If your students aren't hitting in dynamic encounters, real or simulated, then you're either not training them properly in the Modern Technique, or you're not training them *enough* in the Modern Technique!"

So they provided more training to their people, who became even more proficient on the static firing line–only to see these reinforced skills "crash and burn" as well during dynamic encounters.

After more than three years of trying to figure out a viable solution, their search led them to Rex Applegate.

Both Barron and Beasley established a solid working relationship with Applegate. In addition to providing them with written and video-taped information, Applegate personally trained them both in the Point Shooting Technique in 1995. This collaboration

56

eventually resulted in Hocking College officially adopting the Point Shooting Technique after approximately two years of study and experimentation by Barron and Beasley.

According to Barron, the results have been both dramatic and outstanding. He succinctly summed up his opinion regarding this matter in the book *Bullseyes Don't Shoot Back* with the following quote:

> Point Shooting was developed to win gunfights, not competitive games. It was developed for average people, not gun enthusiasts. Most importantly, it is combat proven. Simply put, it works! [22]

Around this same time, several other US police firearms instructors also found their way back to Applegate and the Point Shooting Technique.

On the West Coast, Lou Chiodo, a member of the California Highway Patrol, instituted the technique into his agency's firearms training program after years of research and study. Like Barron and Beasley, Chiodo also noted a dramatic improvement of his students' abilities on the firearms training range. In addition, numerous real-world police-involved gunfights have indicated an enormous turn-around in the abilities of CHP officers to hit suspects presenting an immediate threat during spontaneous, dynamic encounters. This turn-around, Chiodo believes, can be directly attributed to the training.

On the East Coast, my own personal journey (described in Chapter Two) also led me to Applegate and the Point Shooting Technique. Both were inspirational in the formation of the new Massachusetts State Police Firearms Training Unit and the designing of the New Paradigm Police Firearms Training Program that was officially adopted in May 2000.

While the basic Point Shooting Technique was incorporated in the new Massachusetts State Police program much as it had been in the Hocking College and CHP programs, we also took the emulation of the original MITC approach a step further by recreating and implementing a "House of Horrors" program based upon the original.

The combination of both the Point Shooting and the House of Horrors course is a powerful one, producing beneficial training and operational results the likes of which haven't been seen in the United States to my knowledge since 1945.

Of course, unlike the MITC Program, our program was formatted and designed to train the modern US law enforcement officer, not the soldier or commando. This factor is significant, and must obviously be considered by the members of civilian law enforcement agencies prior to implementing any type of firearms training program based on the MITC model.

After years of research and work, drawing from many of the resources described above, we have created an easily-reproduced, cost-efficient, customized training program that better serves the needs of our department and the citizens of Massachusetts.

In order to differentiate this particular program from the many others produced since that critical juncture took us in the wrong direction in the late 1950s, it has been christened the "New Paradigm".

The rest of this book documents the philosophy, design and implementation of the New Paradigm program as it has evolved to date.

Before concluding this chapter on the history of US police combat pistol training, however, I feel it necessary to include a few words about another organization that has played a role in this story–the NRA.

---

[22] *Bullseyes Don't Shoot Back* by Col. Rex Applegate & Michael D. Janich. Published by Paladin Press, Boulder, Colorado, 1998.

The National Rifle Association

The NRA, incorporated in 1871, has a long and proud history. Many of the most well known police trainers and instructors (such as Bill Jordan and Jim Cirillo) have fostered and maintained close ties with the organization. For its part, the NRA has been very supportive of law enforcement officers, and has encouraged training on many levels within the field.

In 1960, the NRA formally established the Police Training Department under its Education and Training Division. Through this entity the NRA began offering structured training courses for police officers. Gradually, the emphasis shifted from providing training for individual officers to the training of law enforcement firearms instructors.

In 1979, the Police Training Department was reorganized into a separate division called the Police Activities Division. Gaylord W. "Eliot" Ness, a retired US Army Lieutenant Colonel, was placed in charge. In 1981, under Ness's direction, the Police Activities Division began to offer training for security officers as well as sworn police officers. At this time, police pistol "combat" competitions were also incorporated into the programs, and the division's title was changed to the Law Enforcement Activities Division (LEAD). Rifle, submachine gun, and "tactical" handgun courses have also been added since that time. Many of these programs are available to members of law enforcement tuition-free, or at reduced-cost.

Currently, the organization also provides a valuable resource in its Technical Information Center, which provides a central database of firearm information available to US law enforcement firearms instructors.[23]

While the vast majority of programs conducted through the NRA LEAD programs is what we consider for the purposes of this book as Old Paradigm-based materials, both of Colonel Ness's successors, Craig D. Sandler and Ron Kirkland, share law enforcement backgrounds and will, I trust, be open to considering the New Paradigm approach as detailed on these pages.

---

[23] For more information contact the NRA LEAD. (www.nra.org)

Because this study revealed fundamental programmatic differences between departments' approaches, opportunities exist for identifying outcomes and impacts that could lead to an empirically-based foundation for building, modifying and advancing policies and programs. *Beliefs* about training currently predominate in this field, yet maximizing officer and public safety will require replacing many of these with credible knowledge about 'what works'.

– Gregory B. Morrison
Deadly Force Programs among larger US Police Departments
Police Quarterly 2006

CHAPTER FOUR
What We Actually Do With Our Pistols & How We've Been Preparing To Do It

The first business of every theory is to clear up conceptions and ideas which have been jumbled together, and, we may say, entangled and confused; and only when a right understanding is established, as to names and conceptions, can we hope to progress with clearness and facility, and be certain that author and reader will always see things from the same point of view.

> – Carl von Clausewitz
> *On War*
> 1832

What Do We Actually Do with Our Pistols?

As police officers, we use our pistols to assist us in controlling out of control behavior. That, after all, is the purpose of any level of force we employ. From our mere presence, through the use of verbal commands, empty hand techniques, chemical agent weapons, impact weapons, and finally, up to and including the employment of deadly force by means of our firearms or otherwise, it is all about control.

The level of force we employ is directly dependent upon the level of force we perceive being employed against us or others. Therefore, when we feel the need to draw, point, and/or fire our pistols, it is because we believe we are facing a serious immediate threat to ourselves or others that must be stopped.

We know from the data that has been developed over decades that in the vast majority of cases, we will be dealing with a close proximity threat, most often (85%) from about seven yards and closer. We also know that more than half the time (53%) the threat suspect will be five feet and closer to us when the lead starts to fly. As far as distance goes, that is only a step-and-a-grab away!

We also know that in the vast majority of cases we will be dealing with a spontaneous threat. That means that the suspect will more than likely make the first violent move, putting us behind the eight ball and the reactionary lag. (See Appendix L)

Common sense tells us that we may face a deadly threat at any time of day or night, from any-one or any direction. Statistics tell us that we're most likely to face an armed violent assault during the hours of darkness, or in low-light environments.

The typical police-involved deadly force encounter is usually over in a matter of seconds, with only a few critical rounds fired.

Situations like the much publicized North Hollywood bank robbery and shootout on February 28, 1997 may garner a lot of press, and be the subject of conversation, study, and analysis for years to come, but most officers will face their moment of truth and terror alone or with a partner, while performing their regular day-to-day patrol functions.

Aside from using our pistols to save our own life or someone else's life through the immediate employment of deadly force when faced with an immediate threat of deadly force, we may also draw our weapons in a number of other circumstances;

• when searching areas or locations where a deadly threat could be present;

• to assist us to control individuals who are displaying any type of behavior that would cause a reasonable officer to believe that the suspect could immediately present a threat of death or serious bodily injury to the officer or others;

• when we can reasonably articulate why we felt a need to take our weapon from the holster and have it ready in our hand;

• to stop the suffering of a seriously injured animal when other options are not feasible;

• when participating in firearms training, qualifications, and practice at approved locations.

With the exception of the last two, all these situations would obviously generate a great deal of stress on the average, normal human being, seeing as how they require (or could potentially require) the officer to recognize, deal with, and ultimately control at least one threatening human being during a potentially life threatening event.

More stress is also generated because officers do not operate in a vacuum. This means that in addition to dealing with a threatening suspect or suspects, they may also be required to make life and death decisions while simultaneously trying to process information regarding other people present on the scene or in the area.

Add to this mix that, as a result of the stress, the officer's own body will be pumping powerful, naturally occurring chemicals into his blood stream that will elevate his heart and respiration rates, induce perceptual narrowing, and basically take away varying degrees of his control over his own actions and thought processes, and you can understand why a quiet day on the range firing at targets that don't fire back would offer the least amount of stress from

all the selections above!

Yet, in many cases throughout the United States, officers also experience a great deal of stress while participating *in training*–training that often does not truly prepare them to do with the pistol the things that police work requires them to do with it.

Closer examination ultimately reveals that the reason for this disparity between need and training can be attributed to a classic case of the tail wagging the dog.

How Have We Been Preparing Our Police Officers to Use Their Pistols?

In this section we will examine the methods we have been using to prepare our police officers to use their pistols while performing their duties in the real world.

In order to facilitate this examination, an analysis of typical "old paradigm"-type firearms training programs must be performed.[1] This is necessary in order to determine in a logical manner the following factors:

1) the specific types of firearms training programs that are utilized (e.g. static, dynamic, or interactive) in the old paradigm training matrix;

2) what mechanisms these programs employ to achieve desired results, and

3) exactly what these desired results are, or are believed to be.

First, however, we need to break down the primary elements found in the majority of old paradigm police firearms training programs and analyze which mechanisms are being employed in each. This is necessary because many of these elements are routinely combined to produce individual, stand-alone training

---

[1] Please note that when this analysis was first conducted, the "New Paradigm" had not been developed. At the time, I used the term "current paradigm." For clarity's sake, the terms new paradigm and old paradigm are used throughout this work to distinguish between training models.

programs.

Make no mistake: a thorough analysis of these elements and mechanisms is critical. For should the exact purpose of the training program not be clear in the designer's mind, or should the designer improperly employ any of the various training methodologies outlined below, then not only might the training value of the program be overestimated, but participation in the program might produce results that actually run *counter* to the desired training objective.

Police Firearms Training Programs:
Levels of Training (Synopsis)

1) **Static Training:** This is the formative stage. The instructor first explains to the student what is desired. The instructor then demonstrates what is desired, modeling the activities for the student. The student then imitates what has been explained and demonstrated to him, slowly at first. Enough repetitions are then performed by the student to ingrain the activities and allow a baseline proficiency to be established.

2) **Dynamic Training:** This is the mid-level stage. Additional movements are added. The student continues to perform repetitions of the desired activities, increasing the speed of the movements as proficiency develops.

3) **Interactive Training:** The experiential learning stage. The student is introduced into a controlled, dynamic environment, where the newly-learned skills are employed. For this stage to be of benefit to the student, immediate feedback from the instructor must be given, proper employment rewarded, and improper employment corrected.

Police Firearms Training Programs:
Primary Elements

The primary elements found in the vast majority

of police firearms training programs can be effectively described as:
1) Marksmanship Training (MT)
2) Physical Skills Development (PSD)
3) Mental Conditioning (MC)

For the purposes of this work, the following definitions will be used when referring to these individual components:

1) **Marksmanship Training (MT):** This primarily static-level component, generally first introduced during entry level training, has two primary objectives: a) to enable the officer to achieve a good score on a stationary target, and b) to enable the officer to make an accurate shot by using the sights of the weapon (when possible) during a lethal-force encounter.

This component is generally implemented in the following manner:

New officers or recruits become familiar with the particular weapon system used and its attendant equipment and are instructed in acceptable methods to safely handle, clean, and store it. They are then introduced to, and instructed in, the basic fundamentals of marksmanship.

After demonstrating to the instructor's satisfaction an ability to safely handle and employ the weapon, the student then participates in a marksmanship test. This test's primary purpose is to allow the student to demonstrate to the instructor that he has acquired sufficient knowledge and developed enough physical skill so that he can utilize the weapon system in a safe manner to deliver an acceptable number of accurately placed rounds into a specific area on a stationary target.

Very often, time limits are established within which the officer must, after responding to a stimulus, complete firing the stipulated number of rounds during individual segments of the course of fire.

Upon completion of the entire course of fire, the number of holes that indicate the number of rounds that the officer was able to successfully place into the specific designated area of the stationary target are then counted. If the officer has successfully placed a sufficient number of rounds into this designated area, then he is deemed qualified with the weapon.

2) **Physical Skills Development (PSD)**: This primarily dynamic-level component, also generally first introduced during entry level training, is designed to assist the officer in developing the physical skills needed to safely and effectively employ the handgun while performing in the capacity of law enforcement officer.

These physical skills must take into consideration everything the officer needs to be able to do with the weapon while carrying and/or employing it in the field. Examples of the physical skills training that must be addressed include–but are not limited to–the presentation, reload, stoppage clearing drills, speed shooting drills, moving target drills, recovery to the holster, etc.

The ability to physically employ the weapon effectively while operating in varying degrees of illumination, in different physical environments, and within predicted physical and mental parameters must also be developed in this training segment. In addition, a comprehensive law enforcement firearms training program must also include weapon retention training, close quarter combat skills training, and weapon disarming technique development.

3) **Mental Conditioning (MC)**: This component, often neglected or misapplied in entry level firearms training programs, is critical to ensuring that the officer is truly prepared to employ the handgun safely and effectively while performing in the capacity of law enforcement officer. The development of a winning mind set, true confidence in his physical and mental abilities, the ability to employ sound judgment while engaged in a lethal force encounter, and the ability to cope with the mental and physical

toll that involvement in such an encounter may exact are the objectives of this training element.

Common interactive-level conditioning methodologies used to prepare subjects to achieve these objectives include:
1) Stress Inoculation Training (SIT)
2) Pavlovian Classical Conditioning (CC), and
3) Skinnerian Operant Conditioning (OC).

An outline describing these conditioning methodologies and the primary elements associated with their use (indicated by abbreviations) is provided here for consideration.

Police Firearms Training Programs:
Mental Conditioning Methodologies

1) **Stress Inoculation Training (SIT):** Stress Inoculation Training is recognized as a major component of Cognitive Behavior Therapy. Psychologists employ SIT as a means of helping people to become better observers and more accurately interpret incoming information. (Meichenbaum & Cameron, 1983; Meichenbaum, 1985). It is believed that controlled exposure to an anticipated frightening situation will gradually extinguish the intense fear response and cause the person to think more realistically about the situation. Research indicates that both exposure to the frightening situation and correcting an individual's faulty perceptions and conclusions about it are generally effective in reducing fears. It is also believed that in order for SIT to be optimally effective, the exposure to the stimulus situation should be controlled and gradually increased. It must also be experienced without distortion or defenses. (Epstein, 1983). The process can be broken down into the following components:

Phase I: Conceptualization of the stressor
● Anticipate the stressor (MT, PSD, MC)
● Understand the problems it will present to you (MT, PSD, MC)
● Assess your current skill level (MT, PSD, MC)

Phase II: Skills acquisition & rehearsal
- Mental preparation (MT, PSD, MC)
- Physical fitness (MT, PSD, MC)
- Tactical skills training (MT, PSD, MC)

Phase III: Application & follow-through
- Dynamic encounter training (MT, PSD, MC)
- Actual field work (MT, PSD, MC)
- Analyze & critique performance in constructive manner (MT, PSD, MC)

**Stress Inoculation Training (SIT):
Other considerations**

In his review of this work, Dr. H. Anthony Semone, commenting specifically on Stress Inoculation Training, noted,

> Stress Inoculation Training, in my view, should also take into account the (student's) history of exposure to stressing events... E.g., a (student) whose prior life history has been replete with exposure to and/or receipt of such stressors arguably may show a differential response not only to stress inoculation techniques, but also to the stressors themselves. E.g., (students) who have grown up in abusive/abusing families may well show, as a function of the classical conditioning of emotional responses, contemporaneous stress responses similar to those they displayed in their own family. E.g., when as troopers they are called to a domestic scene, they may be differentially affected by it in such a way as to call forth emotional responses similar to the ones they showed in their own history.

Accepting Dr. Semone's opinion, one can infer that there may also be residual effects from past exposure to other stressing events, such as a serious motor vehicle accident or lethal force encounter that would also drastically influence an officer's emotional responses to similar situations/stimuli.(This matter and one approach to addressing it are discussed in Chapter Five.)

2) (Pavlovian) Classical Conditioning (CC):

Historically, Classical Conditioning relates to the way(s) in which involuntary responses are elicited reflexively, by some unconditional or conditional stimulus. For example:
a) an eye blink as a function of presenting a puff of air to the eye, or b) a body alarm response-complex in an officer who sees a person who looks similar to a person who shot at him.

The most well known illustration used to explain how Classical Conditioning works is found in the experiments I.P. Pavlov conducted with canines.[2] Pavlov placed the dogs in controlled environments. Just before feeding the dogs, he would ring a bell. After a short period of time, simply ringing the bell would cause the dogs to salivate even when no food was present. In this manner, Pavlov proved that you could associate two unrelated things–in this case the ringing of the bell and food–and bring about a physiological response in an organism.

In training, Classical Conditioning is evident in its capacity to facilitate the following:
- Association of behavior with reward or penalty (MT, PSD, MC)
- Desensitization to stressor (MT, PSD, MC)

3) (Skinnerian) Operant Conditioning (OC):

Operant conditioning refers to behavior(s) which is (are) emitted in the context which calls them into activity.[3]

B. F. Skinner successfully illustrated the process of Operant Conditioning in the laboratory using rats.[4] The animals were placed into specially constructed cages. Within the cages were a small light, a lever, and a feed chute. The rats quickly learned that whenever

---

[2] Ivan Petrovich Pavlov, 1849 - 1936. Awarded the 1904 Nobel Prize in Medicine.

[3] S1 occurs in association with S2 setting the occasion for a Behavior or Response to occur which then occurs in association with a Consequent Event.

[4] Burrhus Frederic Skinner, 1904-1990, pioneered the process of "behavioral engineering."

the light came on–and *only* when the light came on–if they pressed down on the lever, a small piece of food would slide into the cage. The light served as the *stimulus*, pressing the lever was the desired behavior or *response*, and the food was the immediate *reward*. After a short period of exposure to this process, the rats would press the lever when the light was illuminated, regardless of whether food was delivered.

As noted by Colonel Dave Grossman, this process has also been applied very effectively to humans who serve in most modern military forces. If you have ever participated in a "pop-up" target course in the service, you have been exposed to an Operant Conditioning program specifically designed to make you an effective soldier, by conditioning you to shoot at and kill enemy personnel. In these programs, the human-shaped silhouette target that "pops up" in the field is the stimulus, shooting and hitting the silhouette is the desired behavior or response, the target falling and the positive reinforcement from authority figures and peers that follows (Good job!) is the reward.

In training, Operant Conditioning is employed in the following manner:
- Specific threat stimulus (discriminative or signaling cue or Sdelta) is presented (MT, PSD, MC)
- Response (target behavior) is displayed (MT, PSD, MC)
- Correct response or behavior is rewarded (positive reinforcement) (MT, PSD, MC)
- Efficiency is further rewarded with additional positive reinforcement (e.g. praise) and/or some form of "token economy" (e.g. trophies or badges)[5] (MC)

Classical and Operant Conditioning (CC / OC): Other considerations

In his review of this document, Dr. H. Anthony Semone, commenting specifically on Classical and Operant Conditioning, noted:

In the real world, in addition to many other principles of learning and behavior, classical and operant conditioning co-occur, occur in tandem, and in chained sequences. You can imagine… that a trooper who encounters a suspect who resembles someone who had shot at him/her, injured a trooper colleague, etc., can in fact experience, by way of classical conditioning principles broadly understood, body alarm reactions by the sheer presence of a deadly threat; operant conditioning principles can then account for his/her subsequent behavior in relationship to that threat. If the trooper freezes, it is likely that his/her history has conditioned him/her to freeze in response to threat; if the trooper runs or flees, he/she has had a prior history of escaping or avoiding threats; if the trooper takes cover, engages the threat with appropriate levels of force, that trooper will have had the experience of taking cover, engaging, etc., strongly rewarded.

Police Firearms Training Programs:
Mental Conditioning Methodologies, Summary

A review of the above outlines reveals that these powerful conditioning systems are present in what I have identified (for the purposes of this work) as the primary elements involved in common police firearms training programs.

In summary, I believe that in order to achieve the stated program objectives (the development of a winning mind set, true confidence in physical and mental abilities, ability to employ sound judgment while engaged in a lethal force encounter, and ability to cope with the attendant mental and physical toll), that

---

[5] The New Paradigm concept does not employ the use of gamesmen-inspired "marksmanship" qualification badges for token economy or other purposes. While many officers enjoy winning and displaying sharpshooter or expert qualification badges, I feel that they are inappropriate for civilian law enforcement firearms training purposes, and may even prove detrimental, i.e. should an officer involved in a real world shooting have to explain why a certified "expert" such as himself couldn't just have shot the gun out of the suspect's hand, etc.

these mechanisms must be intelligently and responsibly incorporated into any progressive police firearms training program. How we went about doing this in the New Paradigm is detailed in the following chapter. The incorporation of these mechanisms into many old paradigm training programs is discussed below.

The Old Firearms Training Paradigm: An Overview

In addition to the core, critical subjects of firearms safety and safe handling skills that are axiomatic to any competent training program, the old firearms training paradigm focuses primarily on the development of, and reinforcing the officer's skill in achieving, accurate shot placement onto stationary targets at varying distances under controlled conditions (MT, PSD).

While the development of individual judgmental skills has been addressed during recent years by many departments through the employment of Firearms Training Simulation devices such as the FATS and Range 2000/3000 systems, this technology has been limited to those departments able to afford the cost of these usually expensive, computer-based training tools.

Interactive, force on force simulation training utilizing duty weapons that have been modified to fire marker training ammunition (such as produced by Simunition®) has also been employed by many departments. This technology however, is also limited to departments that have funding available for both the equipment and instructor-level training courses.

While some improvements have been made in regard to educating officers as to the likely situational realities they may face when engaged in a lethal force encounter (SIT) through the production and distribution of training videos and literature, there has generally been very limited effort made nationally on

either the recruit or in-service levels to educate officers about the possible effects of stress they may experience while so engaged.[6]

In addition, while some progress has been made through different venues, on a national level there has been little or no effort made to formally educate officers about established techniques that may be used to overcome physiological and psychological obstacles (dissonance) and control the effects of stress.

While most officers do participate in various marksmanship (MT) and physical skills development (PSD) training programs that require them to utilize both physiological and psychological stress control techniques (to varying degrees) in order to successfully complete the exercises, techniques for accomplishing these levels of control are limited primarily to the physiological aspects.

There are also very few programs in place on the in-service level that require officers to participate in stress-inoculation training programs designed to mirror as closely as possible the realities they will face while operating in the field.

Regardless of the slight variations on this paradigm (as indicated above) that have been explored in some departmental firearms training iterations, an examination of common existing lesson plans and most police departmental training records indicates the following: in most cases, only *two* basic and specific types of courses of fire constitute the basis upon which the members of police departments are both trained and evaluated in regard to their abilities to safely handle, maintain, and employ their issued handguns.

Examples and a brief synopsis of both these types of programs are provided on the following pages.

---

[6] Videos illustrating various police-involved situations have become practically an industry-standard training tool over the past few decades, especially since the explosive rise of "reality-based" television programs that exhaustively feature police-involved situations.

Before examining the design and training value of these types of programs, however, I believe we must address what is without doubt one of the most critical aspects of the old paradigm, specifically, the way it is often administered. For in my opinion, an analysis of the methods often used to administer the old training paradigm programs would seem to indicate that a misapplication of the powerful conditioning systems described in the previous section has occurred.[7]

The Matter of Stress

The first inkling I had that this problem even existed occurred more than thirteen years ago, shortly after I had been assigned to the range as an instructor. A veteran officer that I knew and had a great deal of respect for showed up one fine clear morning to participate in the qualification courses. As I walked over to greet him, I couldn't help but notice that his face was pale, eyes bloodshot, and his hands were slightly shaking. He looked so obviously ill that the first thing I asked him was, "Are you OK?"

The officer, a great cop and investigator with a sterling reputation on the street–and who *hadn't* been drinking the night before–looked me straight in the eye and said, "I'm OK, I just haven't slept in about three days." Figuring he had either been working a case or was having some type of personal problem, I then asked if there was anything I could do to help. Looking at me a bit sheepishly, he then said, "No, it's nothing. I just always get like this before going to the range. Have since the Academy."

"What do you mean?" I asked, slightly baffled.

"It's nothing; I just get wound up before qual's, that's all. I'll be fine once I get this over with."

My first impulse when he told me this was

to laugh. Having always personally enjoyed shooting, and knowing the caliber of officer he was, I couldn't believe he was serious. This was an officer I had gone through doors with on high risk warrant services, a guy who was a fearless, dedicated professional. And here he was telling me that coming to the range to put holes in paper was stressing him out?! I just couldn't understand it.

But after that conversation, I started looking around more, to see if his was just a personal condition, some sort of anomaly that no one could really explain. And what I discovered as our people came to the range day after day, week after week, was that he was not the only person on my job who had that type of reaction to range training. Much to my surprise, quite a few of the officers I worked with, among, and around would experience stress from the moment their name appeared on the range assignment list.

Many of them would have trouble getting to sleep a few nights before their scheduled training date. And a few of them would even get physically ill.

The main reason I believe that I and my fellow instructors had a hard time understanding this was because we obviously all enjoyed training–after all, that's why we had gravitated towards being instructors. As far as any of us were concerned, there was no better way to spend a day or night, rain or shine, than at the range running and gunning, other than working in the field, where we could run and gun for real.

And then I remembered something from my own Academy days. As with any group of people, some within the group will have more of an aptitude for some activities than others. Shooting is no exception. Having grown up around firearms I was very comfortable and confident with them, and as a result I experienced little stress when working with them. I had also spent a few years in the Army where I had been trained with them, and all my experiences there had been positive as well.

---

[7] Refer to Police Firearms Training Programs: Mental Conditioning Methodologies

The State Police Academy experience had been more of the same. Like many of my classmates, I had looked forward to, and thoroughly enjoyed the firearms training program. But thinking back on it, I realized that the same could not be said for a few of my classmates. One in particular, a good natured, athletic guy, just couldn't do what the instructors wanted him to do with the pistol.

It wasn't that he wasn't intelligent, motivated, or willing; he just got balled up and then couldn't get himself unballed. The more the instructors worked with him, the more nervous he became, and the worse he did.

Finally, in an effort to get him squared away, the instructors decided to use a form of shock therapy. They unleashed the dogs of war, so to speak, and barked, bit, and chased him down to the ground. This was the Massachusetts State Police after all, and we were highly motivated, totally dedicated, rough, tough, Massachusetts State Police trainees. Now I am not saying that they beat him or hazed him or anything else–they simply put it on him in a direct, forceful manner, letting him know in no uncertain terms that he had better unball himself pretty damned fast unless he wanted to find himself traveling down Route 9 (the highway that ran east to west in front of the academy) that evening with all his "rotten civilian trash" stuffed in his seabag, to live out the rest of his life telling people how he "could've been a trooper if only it wasn't for that whole pistol shooting business…"

That evening, as the rest of us packed our gear onto the buses that would take us from the range back to the academy, the last view I had of my classmate was of him running up and down the buttes of the range, carrying one of the heavy wooden target stands over his head, dust flying, drill instructor nipping at his heels.

The epilogue to this story is that 1) he eventually did successfully complete the course, 2) to this day he experiences a great deal of stress whenever he has to attend any type of firearms training, and 3) as of this date he is one of only a handful of my classmates who has been involved in a deadly force situation where he was required to shoot a suspect. He fired one shot during the spontaneous encounter, hitting the suspect.

"See!" some will say, "this shows that type of high intensity training works!"

To this I would reply that yes, it is an option. An option I have also employed over the years, with varying levels of success. I know for a fact that–if you have enough time and truly know what you are doing–you can absolutely physically and mentally coerce someone into overcoming whatever internal confusion is balling them up, and get them to get a grip on themselves at least long enough to pass a marksmanship-based qualification course.

However, after looking at this objectively, I am forced to ask two questions:
1) is having our officers pass an unrealistic marksmanship course truly the critical goal we need to accomplish in firearms training? And
2) if it is not, has the price we have sometimes paid to achieve this goal been worth it?"

The Goal

The ultimate goal of any viable police firearms training program must be to prepare the officer to deal with extreme situations as he is likely to encounter while operating in the field. This means moving through populated environments while properly employing the firearm to control OUT OF CONTROL BEHAVIOR that is being exhibited by an individual or individuals. (See Figure 4-1 on following page.)

Achieving the Goal

The best way to properly prepare the officer to deal effectively and professionally with extreme situations and their attendant hazards, stressors, and stress-induced affects, is to have the officers

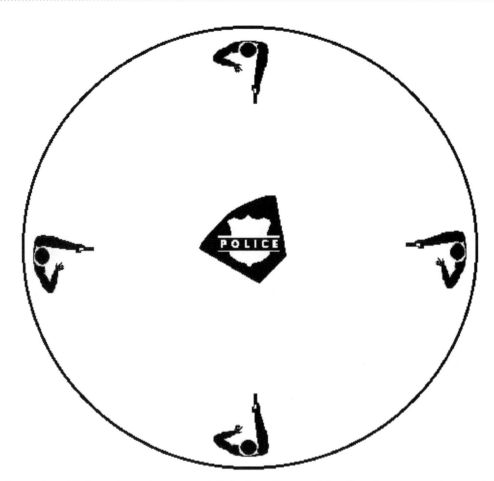

Fig. 4-1 In the real world, there is no down range! Both the officer and the threat can come from and move in ANY DIRECTION! (Police officer represented by badge symbol in center of circle. Threat subjects represented by silhouette gunmen on outer edge of perimeter).

participate in various Stress-Inoculation Training (SIT) programs designed to mirror as closely as possible the realities they will face while operating in the field. These programs should be developed in conjunction with foundation-building physical and mental skill development programs. Once established, the retention of these physical and mental skills can be verified while the officer participates in SIT-based programs.

The Methods We *Should* Use to Achieve the Goal

1. Officers must be educated as to the likely situational realities they may face when engaged in a lethal force encounter and as to the possible effects of stress they may experience when so engaged (SIT).

2. Officers must be educated in various ways to overcome physical and mental obstacles and control the effects of stress (SIT, CC, OC).

3. Officers must participate in various marksmanship (MT) and physical skills development (PSD) training programs that require them to utilize both physical and mental stress control techniques (SIT, CC, OC) in order to successfully complete the exercises while simultaneously developing the necessary physical skills.

4. Officers must participate in various stress-inoculation training (SIT) programs designed to mirror as closely as possible the realities they will face while operating in the field.

The Method We Often *Do* Use that Hinders Achievement of the Goal

The problem I have identified with the method we (and many other agencies) employed can best be summed up as an "improper application of the proper methodology."

It is found in the way that stress is often generated and directed during firearms training, and perhaps most important, what this stress is ultimately associated with.

To put it simply, what we need to be doing is conditioning the officer to deal with stress generated by a human being who is presenting a threat. In order to do this while training the officer within the confined borders of a typical firearms range, the threat stimulus/stress-generator should be coming from the target area that is *down*-range. (See Fig. 4-2)

In this way the officer will associate the threat stimulus with what is presented to him (threat-type target, muzzle flash, etc.), will respond in the appropriate manner, (taking cover, firing if justified), and be rewarded for performing properly (taking cover, hitting target, stopping threat, etc.) (CC, OC).

What I believe we have been inadvertently doing in many cases, however, is trying to condition the officer to deal with stress that will be generated by a human being who is presenting a threat *down*-range, by creating stress *UP*-range, both *behind and beside* the officer. (Fig. 4-3)

This counter-productive situation is created when instructors *behind* the officer generate negative stress directed *toward the officer* ("What's your problem?! If you can't hit the target by now you don't belong on the job!" etc.) in an effort to somehow produce beneficial stress in *front* of the officer. This effect is compounded should the officer have a history of long or short-term problems while trying to accurately place rounds onto the (in actuality) non-threatening target[8] downrange, especially if he feels that "everyone (peer group on line) is

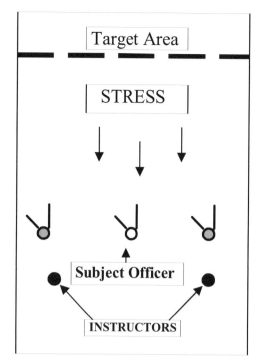

Fig. 4-2. The threat stimulus / stress generator needs to be presented to the officer from the target area or direction he is *facing*.

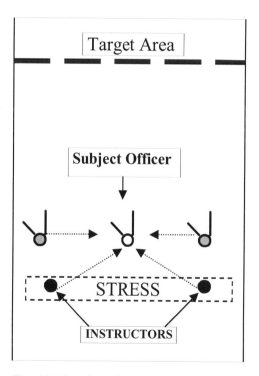

Fig. 4-3. Too often, the actual threat stimulus / stress generator is not to the front, but is instead decidedly *behind* the officer. Add to this stress the frustration of not being able to turn and deal directly with the stress generator, which in this case is the firearms instructor...

In this photo I am holding a "training aid" that was used in an old paradigm-style recruit firearms training program. Made of wood, the "big SIG" as it came to be known, was used to "motivate" recruits who either failed to perform up to standards during firearms training or did things such as accidentally dropping components of the disassembled weapon during cleaning. Recruits were often "encouraged" to hold the big SIG over their heads for extended periods in order to atone for their indiscretions, or to perform pushups over the dropped pistol component. In my opinion, regardless of the intent of the instructors, this is one glaring example of how to successfully create a long-lasting, negative association with a potentially life-saving piece of equipment during training.

watching me"[9] and "I can never hit the target with this gun."

After having spoken with many officers regarding this subject, I have also formed the opinion that officers who experience a long-term problem with the use and employment of their issued pistol during "qualification" training generally experience an increase in stress over

the years as the problem continues (if not worsens). Many of these officers report that they worry about their inability to perform *on the range during training*[10] a great deal of the time, and that many of them cannot sleep for a period of days prior to attending scheduled firearms training.

Given the training conditions outlined above, and applying what we know about the various mental conditioning methodologies present in these programs, we can surmise that what we have inadvertently achieved in many cases is a successful association between the generated stress with *the training*. More critically, a negative association is also created with the *pistol itself*–the very tool that the officer must depend upon and employ with confidence and skill to save lives should the need arise.[11]

To fully illustrate this point, let us again examine the training methodology outline presented in the previous section and compare it against the realities of the old training paradigm and the employment of up-range stress.

Stress Inoculation Training (SIT) and Old Paradigm Up-Range Stress

1. **Phase I:Conceptualization of the stressor**
● **Anticipate the stressor:** Human threat: downrange or uprange? Is the stressor the ability to stop a human threat or pass a marksmanship qualification test?
● **Understand the problems it will present to you:** Again, are we preparing to engage a human threat with deadly force if necessary or get a passing score on a marksmanship test?
● **Assess your current skill level:** Are skills being developed that are truly pertinent to potential real-world lethal-force encounters?

[8] Regardless of target used, if an active dynamic human threat is not perceived/presented downrange, the officer will be more inclined to focus on the active dynamic human threat uprange.

[9] Dr. Semone noted here in his review of this document that "Shame and humiliation are neurologically "hard-wired" to the same neural systems involved in "freeze, fight, flight…"

[10] During debriefing sessions with "problem shooters" I have rarely heard these officers express a concern about being able to employ their weapons efficiently in a lethal-force situation, indicating another training deficiency inherent in the Old Paradigm system, to wit, the primary focus is on range "qualification," not survival.

2. **Phase II: Skills acquisition & rehearsal**
• **Mental preparation:** Is the emphasis on dealing with a human threat or performing on the range?
• **Physical fitness:** Are truly relevant physical skills being developed?
• **Tactical skills training:** Are truly relevant tactical skills being taught, developed, and most important, conditioned in? Are we moving to cover or standing and drawing against a drawn gun?

3. **Phase III: Application & follow-through**
• **Dynamic encounter training:** Is it incorporated into the training program?
• **Actual field work:** Is the training based on field conditions/environments?
• **Analyze & critique performance in constructive manner:** Is this being done?

(Pavlovian) Classical Conditioning (CC) and the Old Paradigm

• **Association of behavior with reward:** What is being reflexively elicited in training? What unconditional and/or conditional stimulus is

presented? What involuntary responses are being reflexively elicited?
• **Desensitization to stressor:** What stressors are being presented, and from which direction?

(Skinnerian) Operant Conditioning (OC) and the Old Paradigm

A review of the Skinnerian Operant Conditioning methodology reveals yet another serious problem with the old training paradigm. Specifically, this type of problem occurs when the conditioning methodology is misapplied in any number of ways.

One glaring example of this problem is outlined here for consideration.

Upgrading Firearms Training Through the Employment of Realistic Targets

In an effort to make standardized range qualification training more beneficial and realistic, many departments have begun to use lifelike photo-targets depicting subjects presenting an immediate threat as the primary target/stimulus. (Example shown on following page).

Proponents of this practice generally believe that by doing this, they can employ marksmanship-based qualification courses (MT, PSD) to address mental conditioning (MC, SIT) training aspects as well.

While the intentions are commendable, an analysis of this practice would indicate that in reality, we are actually *decreasing* our officer's chances of survival. I realize this may seem counterintuitive at first. However, by using the Operant Conditioning template, the problem becomes immediately apparent.

1. Officer standing in front of a target is presented with a specific threat *stimulus* (discriminative or signaling cue): in this case, a

---

[11] Another aspect of the negative effects of this type of training was discovered while employing the "no up-range stress" approach. I actually had officers complain that they were not performing as well as usual, especially on the timed course. Several of these officers actually requested that I "yell at them just a little bit, in a motivational way." Curious to see the effect this would have, I complied, and "juiced them up" a bit by saying from behind them words to the effect, "Alright now, square yourself away, mister, focus, get ready, HIT 'EM, Yeah!!" The result was that they immediately locked themselves in and performed better. I could actually see them respond to the command prompts and tone of voice, focusing and smoothing out. Afterwards, the subjects stated that it had settled them down, helped them focus, and that they needed the up range stress. The problem with this is that in the real world, no one will be behind them telling them what to do, or prompting them to focus in the vast majority of cases! In addition, it is also likely that should the officers need to go for their pistols and fire, people will be shouting at them NOT to shoot. Obviously, police officers do not act as soldiers on a line. Rather, they usually act alone. As a result, the focus and decision-making abilities must be internally generated, and the up-range stress model works against that as well.

In an effort to make standardized range qualification training more beneficial and realistic, many departments have begun to use photorealistic targets depicting subjects presenting an immediate threat as the primary target/stimulus. (Target by Speedwell.)

lifelike photo-target of a subject presenting an immediate threat (as shown above).

2. The officer's *response* (target behavior) is emitted when the officer, *remaining stationary*, draws his pistol from his holster and fires at the immediate threat.

3. The officer's response/behavior is *rewarded* (positive reinforcement) both through the immediate feedback of achieving hits on the target and through the reactions of both the instructors and peers.

In many cases, the officer's efficient response/behavior would be further officially rewarded (token economy) through recognition in the form of the awarding of marksmanship badges for achievement of specified scores on qualification courses of fire.

The problem with this practice is found when you consider exactly what the officer has *actually been conditioned to do.*

In this case, the officer has been conditioned to *remain stationary and draw* against an adversary holding a firearm pointed at the officer.

In effect, the officer has been conditioned to try and outdraw a "trigger squeeze," a tactic that very obviously can–and has–proven fatal. This very situation was noted in an FBI study that was conducted regarding police officers feloniously assaulted and killed in the line of duty. It arose when one of the cop-killers asked the interviewer, "Why do cops have to be so macho?" When questioned further, the killer asked, "Why would a cop try to outdraw a trigger squeeze?" It turned out that this subject had gotten the drop on an officer, and ordered the officer not to move. According to the killer, the officer immediately went for his gun and was shot where he stood.

A first impulse to correcting this problem once it has been identified is to eliminate the use of these types of targets in training; however, it's imperative that we understand that the problem is *not* with the targets, but in the way they're being employed.

The approach we took to eliminating the improper application of Operant Conditioning is detailed in Chapter Five.

Synopses of Common Old Paradigm Individual Courses of Fire

The following synopses of individual "old paradigm" type courses of fire are provided to illustrate the types of training programs currently being used by many departments throughout the US. These and other similar marksmanship and physical skill development-based courses of fire constituted the basis of the Massachusetts State Police firearms training program for the last several decades, up until the development of the New Paradigm.

Program One:
Pistol Qualification Course

This typical qualification course required the participant to fire forty-four (44) rounds. It was primarily employed as a mechanism to evaluate each officer's safe weapon handling skills and marksmanship ability.

Of the forty-four rounds fired, at least 70% employed the use of sight-oriented, marksmanship shooting techniques.[12] One hundred percent of all rounds fired during this course were fired while the officers employed, (or were encouraged to employ), similar Modern Technique-based stylized shooting positions and fine motor skills.

Various silhouette-type paper-training targets were utilized to register the hits.

Presentation, reloading, stoppage clearing, unloading, and recovery skills were also evaluated during this course of fire. Time limits were used to both increase the level of stress and encourage the development of weapon handling speed and efficiency.

The qualification course required each officer to fire:
a) 5 rounds from the 25-yard line from the kneeling position, "strong"[13] hand, two hand hold, in 20 seconds or less.
b) 5 rounds each from the 17 yard line from the standing position, both "strong" hand and "weak" hand, two hand hold, in 12 and 15 seconds (respectively) or less.
c) 15 rounds total from the 12 yard line,
5 rounds kneeling "strong" hand, two hand hold,
5 rounds standing "strong" hand, two hand hold,
5 rounds kneeling "weak" hand, two hand hold, while employing a barricade, 45 seconds or less.
d) 6 rounds total from the 7 yard line, 2 rounds

(double tap) standing, "strong" hand, two hand hold, 2 seconds or less each double tap.
e) 6 rounds total from the 5 yard line, 2 rounds (double tap) standing, "strong" hand, one hand hold, 2 seconds or less each double tap.
f) 2 rounds total from the 2 yard line, 2 rounds (double tap) standing, "strong" hand, holster-to-hip, one hand hold, 2 seconds or less

Once the course had been completed, officers were generally instructed to make their individual weapon safe and re-holster. The number of holes that indicated the number of rounds the officer was able to successfully place into the designated "score" area of the stationary silhouette target were then counted. This designated score area , usually in the shape of an elongated oval, was 11 ¾ inches wide x 17 ¾ inches high at its widest points. (Approximately 208 square inches).[14]

According to the requirements, if the officer had successfully placed 30-34 (68%–77%) rounds into this designated target area within the prescribed time limits, he was considered to have displayed a skill level with the issued handgun sufficient to "qualify" him as a Marksman. A score of 35-38 (80%–86%) was considered sufficient to qualify the officer as a Sharpshooter, and a score of 39-44 (89%–100%) classified the officer as an Expert with the duty handgun. Should an officer have achieved 29 (66%) hits or less on the designated target area, then that officer was considered to have failed the qualification course and was deemed "unqualified" with the pistol.

Those officers who failed to qualify then received remedial training, and were given up to two (2) more attempts to achieve the minimum number of hits on the designated target area. At

---

12 Notation is made here for though officers were encouraged to employ a type of point shooting from the 7 and 5 yard lines, they were also encouraged to "look for the front sight", instead of focusing exclusively on the threat. In addition, many officers often intentionally focused on the sights in order to achieve a tighter shot group. If this occurred, then the percentage of sight-focused shots the officer actually fired was increased to 95%.

13 Notation is made here regarding terminology. Term "weak hand" is included here because it was incorporated into course lesson plan. Term is not recommended for use as it promotes negative connotation and may affect survival mindset. The terms "dominant" and "non-dominant" are recommended for use.

14 As represented by the Speedwell B-27 Massachusetts State Police-C target (target center).

one time, officers who did not achieve the minimum score during either (or both) of those two additional attempts were relieved of their handgun and cruiser (if issued) and assigned to participate in an additional course of Remedial Firearms Training.

Officers could also be deemed to be unsafe (and therefore unqualified) with the weapon based upon a demonstrated inability to handle the weapon in a safe manner while engaged in this marksmanship-oriented firearms course that was conducted under strictly controlled conditions. Permanent training records were also generated at that time indicating the officer's failure to achieve a minimum marksmanship score and/or to demonstrate acceptable safe firearms handling skills.

I believe it is also worth noting that officers who consistently achieved minimum qualifying scores were routinely classified as proficient under this system, and usually afforded no additional training unless they requested it.

Program Two: Commonly referred to as The Combat Stress Course

Courses such as this thirty-two (32) round live-fire iteration were commonly employed as a mechanism to evaluate each officer's safe weapon handling skills, marksmanship ability, and use of cover while the officer was operating under "stress." Typically, some type of physical exercise was required of the officer at the start of the program, in an effort to induce some degree of physical stress as may be experienced by the officer when engaged in a real-world, dynamic, lethal force encounter. Each segment of the course was also timed, in an attempt to both elevate the degree of mental stress as well as to induce the officer to fire quickly and accurately.

Of the thirty-two rounds fired during the course, at least 94 % employed the use of sight-oriented, marksmanship shooting techniques.

One hundred percent of all rounds fired during this course were fired while the officer employed (or was encouraged to employ) Modern Technique-based stylized shooting positions and fine motor skills.

Various silhouette-type paper-training targets were utilized to register the hits.

Presentation, reloading, stoppage clearing, unloading, and recovery skills were also evaluated during this course of fire. Firing while moving directly toward and away from the target was also incorporated into this course.

The Combat Stress Course required each officer to:
a) Sprint from 25-yard line, attach new paper target to target stand, return to start position and assume front leaning rest position.
b) On command, officer performed 5 pushups and stood up.
c) On command, officer sprinted downrange to a barricade at the 15-yard line. Pistol was secured in the holster.
d) On command, officer presented the weapon and assumed a kneeling position behind the barricade. The officer then fired 6 rounds from the 15-yard line from the kneeling position, "strong" hand, two hand hold, then switched hands and fired 6 more rounds from the kneeling position, "weak" hand, two hand hold. All 12 rounds were fired in 18 seconds or less.
e) On command, officer rose and performed a tactical reload. On command, officer then quick-walked to the next barricade located at the 10-yard line, while covering down on the target. Officer then assumed a speed kneeling position behind the barricade. On command, the officer then fired 6 rounds from the 15-yard line from the kneeling position, "strong" hand, two hand hold, then switched sides and fired 6 more rounds from the kneeling position, "strong" hand, two hand hold. All 12 rounds were fired in 18 seconds or less.
f) On command, officer then stood and performed a combat reload, and on command the officer walked to the 7-yard line at the low

74

ready position and prepared to fire failure drills.
g) On command, the officer fired a "failure drill" consisting of 3 rounds (2 to the body, 1 to the head) while walking forward directly toward the target. The officer then stopped at the 2-yard line and then, upon command, fired a second failure drill while walking backward directly away from the target.

h) The officer was then instructed to holster the weapon, and on command, walked to the 1-yard line.

i) On command, the officer then presented the weapon and fired 2 rounds (double tap), "strong" hand, one hand hold, "point directional" at the target while moving backward.

Once the course had been completed, officers were generally instructed to make their weapons safe and holster. The number of holes that indicated the number of rounds that the officer was able to successfully place into the designated "score" area of the stationary silhouette target were then counted. The designated score area was usually in the shape of an elongated oval and encompassed an area of approximately 208 square inches.

According to the stated requirements, if the officer had successfully placed 26 (81%) or more rounds into the designated target score area, he was considered to have displayed a skill level with the issued handgun sufficient to pass the course. Should the officer have achieved fewer than 26 hits on the designated target area, then that officer was considered to have failed the Combat Stress Course and was required to participate in remedial training and attempt to pass the course again. If the officer failed to attain the minimum score on the second attempt, the officer was assigned to participate in an additional course of Remedial Firearms Training.

Officers may also have been deemed to be unsafe (and therefore unqualified) with the weapon based upon a demonstrated inability to be able to handle the weapon in a safe manner

while engaged in this marksmanship-oriented, "Combat Stress" firearms course. Permanent training records were then generated indicating the officer's failure to achieve a minimum marksmanship score and/or demonstrate acceptable safe firearms handling skills.

Program Three:
FBI Stress/Reactive Shooting Course

This thirty (30) round live-fire course was employed as a mechanism to evaluate each officer's safe weapon handling skills and marksmanship ability, supposedly while the officer was operating under "stress." How this stress was believed to be induced is unclear. No physical exercise was required of the officer at the start of the program to induce simulated effects of stress, nor was any attempt made to induce a true high arousal state.

Officers were required to move laterally from target to target with their weapons drawn and then to fire at specified areas on the stationary target. This would not seem to be sufficient to induce any of the true effects of stress that would be experienced while engaged in a lethal force encounter.

The course was not timed. No score was recorded. Rather, a check mark was used on the individual officer's score sheet to indicate whether the officer completed the course. An asterisk was used on the score sheet to indicate that the officer did not complete the course, and a notation as to why the officer did not complete the course was to be made on the score sheet.

Of the thirty rounds fired during the course, 100% employed the use of sight-oriented, precision marksmanship shooting techniques.

One hundred percent of all rounds fired during this course were fired while the officer employed, (or was encouraged to employ), Modern Technique-based stylized shooting positions and fine motor skills.

Paper-training targets that displayed at least six (6) different geometric shapes in different colors were utilized to register the hits.

Presentation, reloading, stoppage clearing, unloading, and recovery skills were also evaluated during this course of fire. The course required each officer to fire his weapon dry. After firing the last round from the last magazine, the officers were not encouraged, instructed, or permitted to perform any further reloads, to access cover, or to explore any other options.

The FBI Stress/Reactive Shooting Course required each officer to:

a) Stand at the 12-yard line, weapon holstered. The weapon was loaded with a round in the chamber. Three 10-round magazines were in possession, one in the weapon, two in the magazine pouches.

b) On command, the officer presented the weapon and fired two rounds at designated colors/shapes on the target directly in front of him. If the indicated color/shape was not on the target directly to the officer's front, then the officer was required to cover down on the target but not to fire.

c) On command to move, officers were required to quick walk to next target to their immediate right, maintaining the weapon in a covering position. Once in front of the new target, the officer then fired at the designated color/shape if it was present on the new target.

d) When the officer reached the end of the target line, the officer was then required to holster his weapon and run behind the firing line to the far left target position. Once in front of this target, the officer then presented the weapon and repeated the exercise until his weapon ran out of ammunition.

e) Once all officers on the line had run out of ammunition, the line was considered safe and clear and the officers were instructed to remove the empty magazine, let the slide go forward, decock and holster.

Program Four:
Moving Target Firearms Course

This 8-10 round live-fire course was employed (when moving target equipment was available) as a mechanism to evaluate each officer's safe weapon handling skills and to familiarize the officer with the realities and difficulties of engaging a moving target. Course required the use of cover and one shooting position.

No physical exercise was required of the officer at the start of the program in an effort to induce some degree of physical stress as may be experienced by the officer when engaged in a real-world, dynamic, lethal force encounter. No attempt was made to induce a true high arousal state in the officer prior to beginning the course or during the course.

The course was not timed.

Of the 8-10 rounds fired during the course, 100% employed the use of sight-oriented, stylized marksmanship shooting techniques and fine motor skills.

Various paper-training targets (silhouette/realistic photo threat) were utilized.

The Moving Target Firearms Course required each officer to:

a) Position himself behind cover, weapon drawn and held at low ready position.

b) The target was then presented approximately 7-10 yards from the officer. When the officer observed the target, the officer was to issue challenge/command–"Police! Don't move!"

c) As the target moved (*stimulus*) the shooter was required to accurately fire as many rounds as possible at the target (conditioned *response*).

d) Should the target stop moving (*stimulus*), the officer was required to stop firing and cover down on the target (emitted *response*).

e) When so instructed or when out of ammunition, the officer was then required to make his weapon safe and clear and secure it in his holster.

Once the course had been completed, the number of holes that indicated the number of rounds the officer was able to successfully place into the target were counted and the officer's shooting skills were analyzed by the instructor.

No minimum scores were indicated for this course.

Per the lesson plan, all participants in this course were to be "advised that the existing circumstances for this drill provide that the use of force is necessary and that this training is not to teach the officers that all subjects who move after being told not to should be shot."

(Author's Note: In actuality, it would appear that this drill is operant conditioning-based. This would indicate that regardless of the rationalization presented to the participant, the officer was indeed being conditioned to shoot at a threat based on movement. Conversely, the officer was also being conditioned to STOP shooting at a subject presenting an overt threat when that threatening subject STOPPED MOV-ING. This becomes significant if you consider that most people–including threatening sub-jects–can fire and hit a target with greater ease and accuracy from a stationary position. If this precept is accepted as reasonable, then in effect, this drill would appear to be conditioning the officer to shoot at a threat target when it is mov-ing, and to stop shooting at the threat while it is stationary and presents the greatest degree of danger to the officer.)

The Old Paradigm: Summary

Upon attaining the minimum required scores for programs such as those outlined above, the officer is deemed to be sufficiently trained and qualified with the issued handgun to both safely carry and employ it while engaged in any and all law enforcement-specific activities.

It is apparent from a review of the above programs that the old paradigm training emphasis is overwhelmingly focused on the achievement of accurate shot placement on stationary targets from (primarily) stationary firing positions.[15] Complicated and highly stylized stances, grips, and fine motor skills are generally employed to achieve this end, as are specific tenants of basic marksmanship skills and a strong reliance upon the operator's ability to focus on the front sight under all conditions and at all firing distances.

It is important to note at this point that the programs outlined above represent typical static/dynamic-level police firearms training models currently in use throughout the United States and abroad. While training programs of this type are widely regarded as acceptable tools to both train officers and evaluate their ability to perform to acceptable levels with their issued weapons, upon direct examination, it becomes apparent that one of the main reasons for the continued use of these stylized, marksmanship-oriented, qualification-based training programs lies in the managerial approach most organizations have adopted in regard to police firearms training.

This approach dictates that the emphasis be placed on the conducting of mandatory train-ing courses (such as those outlined above) that emphasize uniformity in action on the range under controlled conditions, and that yield a quantifiable "score" that may be recorded and used to provide both a perceived level of training, weapon proficiency, and organizational liability insulation.

A review of several significant legal rulings and case law that have been established over the last few decades, however, indicate that the organizational tactic outlined above will not satisfy the judicially recognized need for relevant police firearms training, nor provide an effective level of liability insulation for the organization and/or municipality.

---

15 In fact, 100% of all rounds fired in the Pistol Qualification Courses and the FBI Stress/Reactive Shooting Course were fired from a stationary position. 75% of all rounds fired in the Stress Combat Course were fired from a stationary position. (25% of all rounds fired in the Stress Combat Course are fired while moving in a straight line directly toward or away from the sta-tionary target).

The terms *failure to train, deliberate indifference*,[16] and *negligent training practices* [17] have been successfully employed in the last decade to secure large settlements against municipalities and agencies, and all indicators reasonably lead us to believe that this tactic will only be exploited more thoroughly in the coming years.

More significant, if we do indeed accept that the old paradigm training model's dependence on stylized shooting techniques (as represented by the Modern Technique) and marksmanship-oriented, qualification-based training programs have apparently not been adequately preparing our personnel to employ their weapons while operating during periods of high stress,[18] then we clearly have an inexorable moral and ethical duty and obligation to both the members of our police forces and the public they serve to create and adopt a new paradigm that does.

Determining Training Value

One of the first things I decided to do while conducting my examination was to take a close look at what we were actually doing during each of the old paradigm training programs we used.

What I initially set out to do was to break down each course of fire to its bare essence in order to extrapolate data that would allow me to "see" exactly what we were accomplishing–or not accomplishing–with each course. The plan was to use this data to reasonably estimate the aggregate training value of each course through a comparison of the specific number of rounds fired, positions used, number of hands employed, equipment used, distances fired from, etc.

The mental conditioning value, I reasoned, could also be indicated based upon the type of targets used, initiating stimuli employed, and desired or acceptable responses of the participants to the stimuli.

Once the core "ingredients" of each course was listed, I could then streamline and increase the training efficiency of the training programs, giving the participants the most "bang for the buck" possible. I employed a simple graph system to isolate each of the components of each course.

Two examples of this analysis using the Pistol Qualification Course (Program One) and the Combat Stress Course (Program Two) outlined previously are presented on the following pages. (*Course Analysis 1* and *2*).

Additional examples are included in Appendix A.

As I dissected the courses of fire using the graph system, something immediately jumped out at me. Having basically memorized the data regarding actual police shootings, the discrepancy was so blatantly obvious that I had to check my figures a second time. Then I was sure.

The numbers were inverted.

While we knew that the vast majority of police involved shootings occurred at close range, the vast majority of training we were doing was from distances well outside this range. It was at this point that the following question occurred to me:

Have we (the police) been failing to consistently hit actual threat targets in the world

---

[16] **City of Canton, Ohio vs. Harris, 109S. Ct., 1197 (1989)** The Court held that failure to train can be a basis for municipal liability and for the first time established a standard for determining such liability. That standard is, "The inadequacy of police training may serve as the basis for S. Sec. 1983 liability only where the failure to train amounts to deliberate indifference to the rights of persons which whom the police come into contact".

[17] **Popow vs. City of Margate, 476 F Supp.1237(DNJ, 1979)** The Court held that firearms training received was inadequate for the circumstances officers had to operate under. More specifically, the Court said that training needs to include the following: shooting at moving targets, night shooting, and shooting in residential areas. The training must also include instruction on state law, city regulations, or policies on shooting and how they are applied in practice. They also held that firearms training must be given on a continual basis.

[18] Based upon actual field performance.

not only because we haven't been training for what we actually do, but also because we've been training primarily at the wrong distances?

That was when I decided to further test the actual training value of each course by comparing the training data against the statistical data gathered from actual shootings.

My goal in doing this was to help me ascertain just how much of a discrepancy existed between the training focus and the actual training *needs* as indicated by the statistically probable events and conditions those being trained would encounter.

Again, the results were more than a little disconcerting to me. (Two examples, again using Programs One and Two outlined previously, are provided at the end of this chapter.)

The following day, I showed my graphs and figures to the other members of the newly-created Firearms Training Unit.

"How could this have happened?" I asked. "Was it so obvious that we missed it?"

"Perhaps," responded Tpr. Johanna Lawlor, "the logic was that if you can hit from twenty-five yards away with a handgun, *of course* you can hit from five yards and closer. It kind of seems self-evident."

That's when I remembered standing on the range, behind the line, watching the troops performing holster-to-hip draw and fire drills from the two-yard line during the qualification course. The reason this picture stood out was because at the time I was slightly amazed at how many of our people missed the target when firing the double-tap from six feet away. And while the instructors offered advice on how best to achieve hits from this close quarter distance, it was often paid little heed–*because it didn't really matter!*

Of course! As the light bulb went on in my head it became clear–the reason it didn't really matter was because the purpose of the training course was *qualification*.

And if you could achieve enough hits from far away using the highly-stylized, marksmanship-oriented positions and sight-focused techniques, you could afford to throw away the few rounds you fired from close-in–even though that was where the actual gunfights would more than likely occur!

It was at that particular moment that I decided that I would let logic, statistics, and common sense dictate the development of the courses of fire that would comprise the New Paradigm.

While this seems obvious now, at that time it was tantamount to heresy. And to some people–including a few within my own department–it still is.

Course Analysis 1: DUTY PISTOL QUALIFICATION COURSE (OLD PARADIGM)   (MT/PSD)

# Rounds	Distance	Position	Hand	# Hands	Time
5 rounds	25 yards	kneeling	dominant	two	20 seconds
5 rounds	17 yards	standing	dominant	two	12 seconds
5 rounds	17 yards	standing	non-dominant	two	15 seconds
RELOAD					
5 rounds	12 yards	kneeling	dominant	two	
5 rounds	12 yards	standing	non-dominant	two	
5 rounds	12 yards	kneeling	non-dominant	two	45 seconds total
RELOAD					
2 rounds	7 yards	standing	dominant	two	2 seconds
2 rounds	7 yards	standing	dominant	two	2 seconds
2 rounds	7 yards	standing	dominant	two	2 seconds
2 rounds	5 yards	standing	dominant	one	2 seconds
2 rounds	5 yards	standing	dominant	one	2 seconds
2 rounds	5 yards	standing	dominant	one	2 seconds
2 rounds	2 yards	standing/hip	dominant	one	2 seconds

Total rounds fired	% Rounds per distance	% Rounds per position	% Hand used	% # Hands used	Average time per shot
44	25–11% 17–23% 12–34% 7–14% 5–14% 2– 5%	Stand–66% Kneel–34% Prone– 0% Other– 0%	Dom.–77% Non-Dom.–23%	one–18% two– 82%	25–4.0 seconds 17–2.7 seconds 12–3.0 seconds 7–1.0 seconds 5–1.0 seconds 2–1.0 seconds

Total # Presentations (and Recoveries)	# Presentations per distance	# Presentations per position	# Presentations per hand	Total % Pres. requiring shot
10	25–1 17–1 12–1 7–3 5–3 2–1	Stand–10 Kneel–0 Prone–0 Other–0	Dom.–10 Non-Dom.–0	100%

Total # Reloads	Type Reloads %	% Reloads per position	% Reloads per # hands
2	Admin–? Emergency–? Tactical–?	Stand–? Kneel–? Prone–0% Other–0%	one–0% two–100% (NOTE: ? = not specified)

Use of Cover per % rounds fired	Type of Cover per position	% Time cover used use per % rounds	Flashlight technique
34%	Barricade (upright)	Stand–33% Kneel–67% Other– 0%	0%

Course Analysis 2: COMBAT STRESS PISTOL COURSE (OLD PARADIGM) (MT/PSD/MC)

# Rounds	Distance	Position	Hand	# Hands	Time
6 rounds	15 yards	kneeling	dominant	two	
6 rounds	15 yards	kneeling	non-dominant	two	18 seconds total

TACTICAL RELOAD

6 rounds	10 yards	kneeling	dominant	two	
6 rounds	10 yards	kneeling	non-dominant	two	18 seconds total

COMBAT RELOAD

2 rounds	7 yards	standing	dominant	two	2 sec
2 rounds	7 yards	standing	dominant	two	2 sec
2 rounds	7 yards	standing	dominant	two	2 sec

(NOTE: All rounds fired from the low-ready position from the 7 yard line)

2 rounds	1 yard	standing	dominant	one	2 sec

(NOTE: 2 rounds fired "holster to hip" from 1 yard line)

Total rounds fired	% Rounds per distance	% Rounds per position	% Hand used	% # Hands used	Average time per shot
32	15–38% 10–38% 7–18% 1– 6%	Stand–25% Kneel–75% Prone– 0% Other– 0%	Dom.–63% Non-Dom.–37%	one–6% two–94%	15–1.5 10–1.5 7–1.0 1–1.0

Total # Presentations (and Recoveries)	# Presentations per distance	# Presentations per position	# Presentations per hand	Total % Pres. requiring shot
2	15–1 10–0 7–0 1–1	Stand–10 Kneel–0 Prone–0 Other–0	Dom.–2 Non-Dom.–0	100%

Total # Reloads	Type Reloads %	% Reloads per position	% Reloads per # hands	
2	Admin–0% Emergency–50% Tactical–50%	Stand–100% Kneel–0% Prone–0% Other–0%	one–0% two–100%	

Use of Cover per % rounds fired	Type of Cover per position	% Time cover used use per % rounds	Flashlight technique
75%	Barricade (upright)	Stand–0% Kneel–100% Other–0%	0%

81

Course Evaluation Summaries & Comparisons to Statistical Data (SD)

Course 1: DUTY PISTOL (OLD PARADIGM) QUALIFICATION COURSE (9mm)   (MT/PSD)

% Rounds fired per distance (ft.)	SD Encounter distances (ft.)	% Time flashlight used	SD Encounter Time of day
0–5.................0% 6–10............. 5% 11–20..........14% 21–50..........48% Over 50........34%	0–5..............53% 6–10............20% 11–20..........12% 21–50............8% Over 50.........6%	0%	6 P.M.–6 A.M........62% 6 A.M.–6 P.M........38% (All figures rounded up)

Total # Presentations	Total % Pres. requiring shot	Total % shots requiring judgement	Total % shots fired in high arousal state
10	100%	0%	0%

Total # Reloads/Unloads	Total # Stoppage Drills	Total # positions used	Use of cover per % rounds fired
2 / 0	0	2	34%

Course Evaluation Summaries & Comparisons to Statistical Data (SD)

Course 2: STRESS PISTOL (OLD PARADIGM) COURSE (.40 CAL)   (MT/PSD/MC)

% Rounds fired per distance (ft.)	SD Encounter distances (ft.)	% Time flashlight used	SD Encounter Time of day
0–5.................6% 6–10.................0% 11–20..............0% 21–50..........94% Over 50..........0%	0–5..............53% 6–10...........20% 11–20..........12% 21–50............8% Over 50..........6%	0%	6 P.M.–6 A.M........62% 6 A.M.–6 P.M........38% (All figures rounded up)

Total # Presentations	Total % Pres. requiring shot	Total % shots requiring judgement	Total % shots fired in high arousal state
2	100%	0%	0%

Total # Reloads/Unloads	Total # Stoppage Drills	Total # positions used	Use of cover per % rounds fired
2 / 0	0	2	75%

CHAPTER FIVE
What We Actually Do With Our Pistols &
How We Should Be Preparing To Do It

Fighting has determined everything appertaining to arms and equipment, and these in turn modify the mode of fighting; there is, therefore, a reciprocity of action between the two. Nevertheless, the fight itself remains still an entirely special activity, more particularly because it moves in an entirely special element, namely, in the element of danger.

> – Carl von Clausewitz
> *On War*
> 1832

What Do We Actually Do with Our Pistols?

To reiterate what was stated in the previous chapter, in the real world outside of the training arena, police officers use their pistols to assist them in controlling out of control behavior. This includes every aspect of the pistol's use, from the deterrent effect caused by its mere presence, to elevated levels of control achieved when the weapon is held and/or pointed at a subject in combination with verbal commands, to the ultimate use of the weapon to achieve control by firing projectiles into the body of a subject presenting an immediate threat.

Having established that assisting officers to achieve control of subjects exhibiting out-of-control behavior is the primary purpose for the pistol in law enforcement applications, it seemed logical to surmise that the best way to properly prepare officers to deal effectively and professionally with such extreme situations and their attendant hazards, stressors, and stress-induced effects, would be to have the officers participate in various Stress-Inoculation Training (SIT) programs designed to mirror as closely as possible the realities they would more than likely face while operating in the field.

Naturally, these programs would need to be developed in conjunction with foundation-building physical and mental skill development programs, the content of which would also need to be based upon the actual conditions and situations the officers would most likely be dealing with.

Once established, the viability and retention of these physical and mental skills could then be verified while the officers participated in the SIT-based programs.

To establish my goals and set my compass heading, I wrote down the following outline on a piece of paper:

How Should We Prepare Our Police Officers to Use Their Pistols?

1. Officers must be educated as to the likely situational realities they may face when engaged in a lethal force encounter and as to the possible effects of stress they may experience when so engaged (SIT).
2. Officers must be educated in various ways to overcome physical and mental obstacles and control the effects of stress (SIT, CC, OC).

3. Officers must participate in various marksmanship (MT) and physical skills development (PSD) training programs that require them to utilize both physical and mental stress control techniques (SIT, CC, OC) in order to successfully complete the exercises while simultaneously developing the necessary identified mission-specific physical skills.

4. Officers must participate in various stress-inoculation training (SIT) programs designed to mirror as closely as possible the realities they will face while operating in the field.

After looking at this outline for awhile, I still couldn't determine how best to structure the training program. Keep in mind that my focus at this point was on developing a program that could effectively achieve all of the above goals in a one-day long in-service training program—far from an easy task. The program would also have to be time and cost-efficient, because the reality of police firearms training demanded it be if it were to have any chance of succeeding and accomplishing the overall goals.

I decided to apply a technique I had been taught while assigned as a death investigator for the department. I started with the body—in this case, the police-involved lethal force encounter—and then worked backwards.

That meant that the Stress Inoculation Program would be developed first. For this segment I reached back to 1945 and dusted off Applegate's "House of Horrors" program. If it worked as well as Applegate had told me, it would address most of the goals in my outline.

The next step in my backward progression became figuring out how to devise a series of courses that would adequately prepare officers to successfully deal with the House of Horrors program.

By moving backwards in a series of progressive and efficiently constructed courses, each designed to prepare officers to succeed at the one that followed it, the program unfolded before my eyes.

By the time I had reached the final individual course segment (centered on the development of individual safe firearms handling skills), the four-level training program was completed.

I then reordered them, and tried to figure out what to call them. I decided to keep the designations simple, just like the approach, since "order and simplification were the first steps to survival." Since they were duty pistol training courses, I called them that, employing the shorthand version, DPTC. Since there were four levels of training in the program, I numbered them 1 through 4.

The New Paradigm now had a structure.

Police Firearms Training Programs: Mental Conditioning Methodologies

In addition to structure, a review of the identified mental conditioning methodologies–specifically, Stress Inoculation Training, Classical Conditioning, and Operant Conditioning–was employed to ensure they were incorporated properly into the program.

This was critical to ensuring that the stated program objectives–the development of a winning mind set, true confidence in physical and mental abilities, ability to employ sound judgment while engaged in a lethal force encounter, and ability to cope with the attendant mental and physical toll–were achieved.

A brief synopsis of approaches we have taken regarding these aspects of training is provided here.

1) Stress Inoculation Training (SIT)

Through simulation training programs such as the House of Horrors we have been able to provide our personnel with controlled exposures to frightening situations such as those they may reasonably be expected to encounter. We have had a great deal of success in this area. (See

Chapter Nine.) We have noted many of the benefits of SIT, such as a gradual reduction of the intense fear response, which allows the participant to think more realistically about the situation.

We have also noted an overall reduction of fear regarding officers' perceptions about the realities of lethal force situations and their self-doubts or performance fears. As it is believed that the exposure to the stimulus situations should be controlled and gradually increased in order for SIT to be optimally effective, we have structured the entire program to continually increase both the level of difficulty and the perceived danger to the participant.

In addition, we have attempted to keep the environments and the participant's role within the scenarios as realistic as possible to maximize the impact of the experience.

Stress Inoculation Training (SIT): Other considerations

As noted in Chapter Four, based upon Dr. Semone's observations regarding the effects of prior stressful events on participants, we have incorporated individual Professional Experience History Forms (Appendix C) to collect general information relating to past work-related, use of force experiences members of the department have had.

This has allowed us to format and adapt training segments to best aid individual officers who have been involved in actual lethal force encounters.

The purpose of this training is to allow the individuals to experience situations similar to those that they have been involved in, in order to ensure that they are able to identify and/or work through any residual effects of stress that were generated as a result of their involvement in the incident.

2) (Pavlovian) Classical Conditioning (CC)

The tenets of Classical Conditioning have been incorporated throughout the program in a variety of ways. In fact, the entire approach to the New Paradigm training program has been based upon the idea of producing positive associations and responses to the weapon, the training, and the employment of the weapon to control out of control individuals by associating positive rewards with the exhibited desired behaviors.

The first step taken to achieve these goals was the complete elimination of "up-range stress" and all of its attendant deleterious effects. In its place an atmosphere of positive reinforcement has been created by all the instructors whose primary goals are to 1) run a safe and beneficial program and 2) assist each officer to reach their individual potential and beyond in this arena.

In its simplest form, this entails nothing more complicated than an instructor literally patting someone on the back and saying, "Good job!" when they perform well during training.

Overall, positive association is accomplished throughout the entire program by the instructors' consistently reinforcing both the need and the importance of the training, the weapons, and the officer's abilities to act professionally, effectively, and *with great valor* when the need arises.

While these changes have made the training experience much more user-friendly and enjoyable for all concerned, it must be understood that the elements of fear and stress have not been eliminated from the training experience–they have only been moved from "up-range" to "down-range" through the development and implementation of Level Three and Level Four programs such as the House of Horrors course. By having officers participate in these types of programs, they literally learn how to cope with dangerous individuals and situations similar to those they will most likely face on the street while simultaneously being guided and positively rewarded for proper performance by an instructor–a person who also happens to be a fellow officer and ally, as opposed to a fellow officer and stress-inducing adversary.

3) (Skinnerian) Operant Conditioning (OC)

As indicated in Chapter Four, the improper application of Operant Conditioning can produce extremely negative results, regardless of the best intentions of the instructor/course designer.

    The solution I have found to both ferret out these types of problems in existing drills as well as to construct effective and positive new drills is to employ the Operant Conditioning model as both a litmus test and a structural blueprint. I can best explain the approach we have taken using the example presented in Chapter Four regarding the unintended problem created through the intended upgrading of firearms training through the employment of photo-realistic targets.

    After first determining that the drill is Operant Conditioning-based, the model is used to determine exactly what response is being conditioned into our people. Once we ascertain that the drill is producing a negative result–in this case, incorrectly responding to the specific threat of facing an adversary holding a drawn gun–we then use the blueprint to construct a drill that will produce positive results.

The Operant Conditioning Model

1. A specific threat *stimulus* is presented
2. *Response* (target behavior) is displayed
3. *Reward* is provided for correct response or behavior (positive reinforcement)
4. Efficiency is further rewarded with additional positive reinforcement (e.g. praise) and/or some form of "token economy" (e.g. trophies or badges)

Operant Conditioning Model, Example

1. First, identify the specific threat (**stimulus**): here, it's an adversary pointing a drawn gun at an officer whose own weapon is holstered.

2. Second, determine the appropriate desired **response** (target behavior). In this case, one appropriate response would be for the officer to move immediately to cover while accessing his own weapon, in order to achieve control through verbal commands and/or by shooting the threat suspect.

Operant Conditioning Model, continued

3. Finally, the officer's proper response/behavior is **reward**ed (positive reinforcement) both through the immediate feedback of achieving hits on the target and through the reactions of both the instructors and peers. Good Job!

Classical and Operant Conditioning (CC / OC): Other considerations

In Chapter Four, regarding the effects of Classical and Operant Conditioning on police officers, Dr. Semone notes:

If the trooper freezes, it is likely that his/her history has conditioned him/her to freeze in response to threat; if the trooper runs or flees, he/she has had a prior history of escaping or avoiding threats; if the trooper takes cover, engages the threat with appropriate levels of force, that trooper will have had the experience of taking cover, engaging, etc., strongly rewarded.

Dr. Semone's comments bring to mind another example of Operant Conditioning-based training I have been involved with.

In September 1999, while running a team of law enforcement special operations personnel through an old paradigm style "combat-type"

firearms training program, I observed many of them committing a common tactical error.

The program required the officers to traverse the range, moving from cover to cover, while engaging various targets with their handguns. The targets that were used included life-size, stationary paper targets that depicted subjects presenting a threat (or no threat) to satisfy judgmental firearms skills training requirements, several pepper poppers, and a moving paper target that also displayed a subject presenting a threat.

The error that I observed many of the officers commit was found in their use of the provided cover. Many of them would not fully employ the cover to their best advantage, leaving themselves exposed to the downrange "adversaries." Some of the officers stopped completely in the open while moving from cover to cover in order to get into a traditional shooting stance and engage the targets.

While obviously neither taught nor desired, this response was understandable, since most of the officers had been conditioned over the years to stand upright with their feet planted directly in front of the target while participating in commonly-encountered departmental qualification-type firearms courses.

It was at this point that I decided it would be worthwhile to try and develop a program that would not only encourage the participants to utilize cover, but would actually *condition them* to use it to the best of their ability by employing the proven principles of operant conditioning.

Breaking it down to its simplest formula by utilizing the Operant Conditioning Model, the program works like this:

1. As the officer makes his way across an area where various types of cover are present, Simunition FX Marking Rounds are fired at him (*stimulus*).
2. The officer must think, move, and utilize the provided cover to the best of his ability (*response*) to prevent himself from being hit.

3. If the officer is successful, he will limit the number of times he is hit, or will not be hit at all (immediate *reward*).

4. The immediate reward is then reinforced when the officer is recognized by the instructor and his peers as being successful. It can be further reinforced after all participating officers have completed the course, the scores are tallied, and the officers are again praised for what they did right while completing the program.

While the actual administration of the course is more complex than indicated above, that basically sums up the process employed to achieve the desired result.

Believe it or not, even though the officers are actually shot at and often hit with the "pain penalty" producing rounds during the course, the program has been extremely well received by those who have participated.

In a word, the troops *love* this course!

A complete description and explanation of the course is presented in Appendix P.

The New Firearms Training Paradigm: An Overview

The new firearms training paradigm focuses primarily on helping the officer to develop relevant and practical mental and physical skills so that he may respond effectively to life threatening spontaneous occurrences while armed.

It is critical that these skills be reproducible while the officer is operating under the effects of stress in a dynamic, interactive environment.

Techniques that exploit natural body alarm reactions, stances, grips, and gross motor skills are employed to achieve this end, as is the use of dynamic, interactive, scenario-based, scripted training simulations.

Safe weapon handling skills and marksmanship skills are also integral to this model,

and serve as the foundation upon which the new training paradigm has been built.

These training considerations are addressed on the recruit level during an (at the minimum) 80-hour basic police firearms immersion training program.

On an in-service level, these considerations are currently being addressed with a great deal of success during individual, 8-hour training iterations, each of which is a standalone program, yet also an intrinsic component of the overall training matrix.

The following chapters are dedicated to explaining what we did with our project, how we did it, what we've seen as a result so far, and where we hope to take it in the future.

Validating Training Value

As the core purpose of the New Paradigm program was to prepare police officers for the realities they would most likely face during their careers, I had decided to let logic, police-specific statistics, and common sense dictate the development of the courses of fire that would comprise the overall training matrix.

Since the core purpose of the program was no longer qualification as commonly understood in the police industry–that is, shoot enough holes into a piece of paper under unrealistic conditions to get your name checked off on a list–I decided to use the reverse approach yet again. In this case I used the data from actual shootings to determine where we should put the training emphasis.

All I did was determine the number of rounds that were to be fired during each course of fire, and then break those numbers down according to the data extrapolated from actual police-involved shootings.[1]

The result was a series of courses requiring the participants to shoot the vast majority of rounds from distances closer to the target than was common.

Both a Course Analysis and a Course Evaluation Summary & Comparison to Statistical Data (SD) for DPTC No. 2 are presented on the following pages to serve as an example of the results of this course design approach.

I must admit that when I first examined the courses of fire that resulted from this approach, I was more than a bit concerned. It appeared as if these courses would be practically impossible to fail! For example, DPTC No. 2–the closest thing in the program that resembled a standardized qualification-type course–only required 3 rounds total be fired from 25 yards.

Another 3 rounds would be fired from 17 yards, and then the rest (67%) would be fired from 7 yards and closer.

Obviously, even though the data and logic dictated that these closer distances were the most deserving of our focus and attention, the question remained: if the course of fire was so simple that no one would have any difficulty with it, did it actually have any training value?

Shortly after formatting the original versions of the DPTC's, I presented them to the members of the FTU. We all agreed they were different from what we were used to. Sgt. Bob Sheehan, a veteran officer and a good man who had been among the first to volunteer for duty with the new unit, in particular had his doubts. So we all suited up and moved out to the range to give the courses a shakeout cruise.

After completing DPTC No. 2 (outlined above) employing precision shooting from 17 yards and beyond and point shooting at the closer distances, we checked out the targets and counted up the holes.[2] The targets didn't reflect that well on our performance to say the least. Bob Sheehan shook his head, laughed, and said, "See, Mike? I never did that bad with the regular (old paradigm) courses. This program's not right."

At first slightly confused, I stared at the targets until the brain cloud lifted.

"No, Sarge," I responded, "it is right.

Of course we're not as good as usual–we've never worked close in this much before. It requires different skills–close combat pistol fighting skills. This is where we need to be training, close in where it happens."

What we saw that cold day on the range would turn out to be a snapshot of the bigger picture. More than 2,000 Modern Technique-trained police officers and soldiers have participated in these courses of fire since that day in early 2000. Most of these officers have gone through the new one-day in-service program at least twice, during which DPTC No. 2 is administered twice in a row–once untimed, once timed utilizing turning targets.

While the overall shooting performance of the vast majority of our people has dramatically improved, as of this writing only nine individuals have achieved perfect back-to-back scores (firing the course un-timed and then timed) on what initially appears to be an "easy" course of fire.[3] This includes all members of the department–including highly-trained and skilled SWAT Team personnel–members from other police agencies, and US and foreign military personnel who have participated in the training program.

---

[1] The number of rounds fired during the course was determined based upon the number of rounds each officer was issued and carried. As our officers are issued thirty-seven rounds of .40 S&W Caliber ammunition (loaded into three twelve-round magazines, with one round chambered) for their SIG P226 Pistols, the course was based on thirty-six rounds. In this way, if the officer experienced no stoppages during the course, the weapon remained "hot" (loaded) throughout the program.

[2] The reasoning behind the adoption of the Point Shooting technique and methods for teaching and employing it are described at length throughout the rest of this book. The vast majority of officers exposed to the technique have quickly adapted to it and have drastically improved their close combat pistol fighting skills–and scores on the DPTC No. 2 course–as a result.

[3] This number is derived only from the one-day in-service program. A few members of the 75th and 76th Recruit Training Troops who achieved perfect back-to-back scores are not included because of the greater exposure to the techniques prior to participating in DPTC No. 2 for record (recorded score).

Course Analysis 6: DUTY PISTOL TRAINING COURSE No. 2 (NEW PARADIGM) (MT/PSD)

# Rounds	Distance	Position	Hand	# Hands	Time
3 rounds	25 yards	prone/cover	2 Dom/1 NonDom	two	20 seconds
3 rounds	17 yards	kneeling/cover	2 Dom/1 NonDom	two	15 seconds
2 rounds	7 yards	standing	2 Dom	two	2 seconds
2 rounds	7 yards	standing	2 Dom	two	2 seconds
2 rounds	7 yards	kneeling	2 NonDom	two	6 seconds
COMBAT RELOAD (While remaining kneeling)					
2 rounds	4 yards	standing	2 Dom	one	2 seconds
2 rounds	4 yards	standing	2 Dom	one	2 seconds
2 rounds	4 yards	standing	2 Dom	one	2 seconds
2 rounds	2 yards	stand rdy w/light	2 Dom	one	2 seconds
2 rounds	2 yards	stand rdy w/light	2 Dom	one	2 seconds
2 rounds	2 yards	stand rdy w/light	2 Dom	one	2 seconds
TACTICAL RELOAD					
2 rounds	1.5 yards	standing/CPD	2 Dom	one	2 seconds
2 rounds	1.5 yards	standing/CPD	2 Dom	one	2 seconds
2 rounds	1.5 yards	standing/CPD	2 Dom	one	2 seconds
3 rounds	1.5–2 yards	standing/move	3 Dom (reactive drill)	one	4 seconds
3 rounds	1.5–2 yards	standing/move	3 Dom (reactive drill)	one	4 seconds
ADMINISTRATIVE RELOAD (Weapon remains in holster)					

Total rounds fired	% Rounds per distance	% Rounds per position	% Hand used	% # Hands used	Avg. Time per shot
36	25– 8%	Stand–78%	Dom.–89%	one–67%	25–6.6
	17– 8%	Kneel–14%	N.Dom.–11%	two–33%	17–5.0
	7–17%	Prone– 8%			7–1.6
	4–17%	Other– 0%			4–1.0
	2–22%				2–1.0
	1.5–28%				1.5–1.1

Total # Presentations (and Recoveries)	# Presentations per distance	# Presentations per position	# Presentations per hand	Total % Pres. requiring shot
16 / 16	25–1	Stand–15	Dominant–16	100%
	17–1	Kneel– 1	Non-Dom.– 0	
	7–4	Prone– 0		
	4–3	Other– 0		
	2–2			
	1.5–5			

Total # Reloads	Type Reloads %	% Reloads per position	% Reloads per # hands	
3	Admin–33.3%	Stand–66.6%	one–33.3%	
	Tactical–33.3%	Kneel–33.3%	two–66.6%	
	Combat–33.3%	Prone– 0%		
		Other– 0%		

Use of Cover per % rounds fired	Type of Cover	% Time cover used per position	Flashlight technique use per % rounds fired
17%	Barricade (modified)	Stand–0% Prone–100% Kneel–50% Other–0%	17%

Course Evaluation Summary & Comparisons to Statistical Data (SD)

Course: DUTY PISTOL (NEW PARADIGM) TRAINING COURSE No. 2 (.40 CAL)   (MT/PSD)

% Rounds fired per distance (ft.)	SD Encounter distances (ft.)	% Time flashlight used	SD Encounter Time of day
0–5..............28% 6–10...........22% 11–20..........17% 21–50..........17% Over 50........17%	0–5..............53% 6–10...........20% 11–20..........12% 21–50............8% Over 50..........6%	17%	6 P.M.–6 A.M........62% 6 A.M.–6 P.M........38% (All figures rounded up)

Total # Presentations	Total % Pres. requiring shot	Total % shots requiring judgement	Total % shots fired in high arousal state
16	100%	0%	0%

Total # Reloads/Unloads	Total # Stoppage Drills	Total # positions used	Use of cover per % rounds fired
3 / 0	unplanned	3	17%

One-Handed Shooting

As you can see by referencing the sample DPTC No. 2 Course Evaluation Summary & Comparison to Statistical Data form provided on the previous page, most of the drills comprising this course–67%–require the participant to draw, hold, and fire the weapon with one hand.

While there is no statistical data to compare against, the decision to favor one-handed shooting over the more popular two-handed holds was made based upon common sense and the review of numerous videos that captured actual police-involved shootings.

Common sense dictated that police officers must be extremely comfortable, competent, and confident in their ability to control the pistol and fire accurately while employing a one-hand hold, because when operating in the real world, we usually need our other hand to do something else. Holding flashlights and radios comes

immediately to mind, as do other activities not commonly performed on the range but required while moving through tactical environments; opening doors, moving and holding vegetation, draperies, or other such impedances aside, and defending yourself from close quarter physical attack.

The review of numerous videos capturing police-involved shootings also indicated that in the vast majority of cases, officers confronted with a surprise, close quarters spontaneous attack would not leap into a classic Weaver-like, bladed-away stance and present the weapon using a two-hand hold, but would rather spring into a low crouch, body squared to the threat, and extend and fire the weapon at the threat using one hand.

So while we do teach (and recommend) a two-hand hold (and the use of the sights) to allow greater stability and accuracy of the pistol when time, distance, cover, situation and/or

91

environment allow, our primary focus is on the development of one-handed point shooting skills, because these are the skills our people will most likely need while actually doing the job. 🔫

In this photo, we see Police Pistolcraft as commonly taught on the range during old paradigm training iterations while...

Recruits on the firing line participating in an old paradigm firearms qualification course. Note highly stylized body positions and stances. The officers' focus during these types of courses is overwhelmingly on the weapon's sights–regardless of distance from the target–and on producing enough holes in the paper so they can be deemed "qualified." As illustrated by the other two photos on this page, these techniques and skills are better suited to achieving passing scores on the range than to employing the duty pistol in the vast majority of real world, spontaneous police encounters.

...here and below we see Police Pistolcraft in the real world.

Lawrence, Massachusetts police officers employ their handguns in the real world while apprehending an armed suspect. Note both are employing one-hand holds on their pistols, as their non-dominant hands are otherwise occupied (one holds a radio, the other a flashlight). Also note the squared stances, lowered body positions, focus on the threat area, and fingers on the triggers. Training must be designed to ensure that officers are confident and proficient with their weapons when operating in the field as opposed to primarily while in the controlled environment of the training range. This photograph was chosen for the cover of this book because it so accurately depicts the realities of police firearms use in the real world: high stress, no down range, and potential danger from a number of directions. It is succeeding in *this* environment, as opposed to qualifying on unrealistic, marksmanship-based courses of fire, toward which we must direct our training efforts. (Photo by Al Pereira. Courtesy of the Eagle-Tribune.)

Officers approach a bank robber's vehicle after shots have been fired. It is safe to assume that their focus is locked onto the occupants within the vehicle as opposed to the sights of their own weapons. Note the one-hand holds on the pistols and crouched body positions. (Photo courtesy of Calibre Press. From the book, *The Tactical Edge: Surviving High-Risk Patrol*.)

CHAPTER SIX
Putting It All Together With Training

One must learn by doing the thing; though you think you know it, you have no certainty until you try.
– Sophocles
Trachinia

The Integrated Duty Pistol Training Course (DPTC) Concept

In my experience, individual police firearms training programs are usually designed to accomplish a number of goals simultaneously. Often, the actual stated purpose of the course is not achieved, in many cases because there is no clarity of purpose.

This is crucial. For without clarity of purpose, true goals cannot be defined. In the absence of defined goals, confusion, misunderstanding, personal preferences, prejudices, and ego enter.

When that happens, all bets are off. A desire to "wrap things up quickly and go home," the cult of personality (wherein preserving, enhancing, and admiring the instructor's persona becomes the primary objective), or worse then becomes the focus of the exercise.

In some cases, lack of clarity also results in training programs that actually produce negative results. One example of this type of program can be found in marksmanship-oriented courses of fire that utilize "reality-based" photo realistic threat targets as discussed in Chapter Four.

These types of considerations must be clear in the police firearms course designer's mind. In addition, in order to fully eliminate the possibility of confusion on the part of the designer or trainee, each level of training must first be identified, then isolated, then addressed. Examples of these types of goal-specific programs are presented in this chapter.

Level One: Skill Development

The primary stated goals and objectives of Level One training courses as provided in the official lesson plans are included here for consideration and use:

According to current statistics, the average police-involved gunfight will occur within 20 feet. In fact, 85% of these gunfights take place within this 20-foot distance. More significant, 73% will occur within a distance of 10 feet, and, most significant, approximately 53% of these engagements will occur while the officer and offender are *five feet or closer* to one another.

Our training during these courses of fire is designed to reflect these realities.

We, as law enforcement professionals, are aware that we must understand the application of tactics and force as they pertain to our occupation, and thoroughly understand how and when they should be employed.

We must also be capable of employing tactics and our weapons in the most professional, expeditious, and efficient manner possible. This in turn not only assures us the greatest chance of survival in a life-threatening encounter, but also increases the safety margin for any innocent bystanders or other involved persons.

Therefore, during these courses of fire, we will utilize a series of exercises designed to assist us in developing and improving our individual skills with the pistol.

An example of a Level One training program is provided here. Instructors are encouraged to design their own courses of fire taking into account the design characteristics of the pistols and attendant equipment used, as well as individual departmental policies and procedures.

Skill building programs of this sort should be directed to assisting the individual officer to develop and polish critical skills that he will most likely need while operating in the field in real situations, under extreme circumstances. Choose the drills carefully, keep them simple, and allow the students enough repetitions to develop a solid mental and physical grasp of the techniques.

NOTE: Since the target itself will serve only as a diagnostic tool that will allow the instructor to gauge the ability of the participating officer to successfully deliver rounds to a specified target area, it is recommended that only neutral-stimulus (no-threat) types of targets (such as shown in the photo at right) be employed.

Example of a neutral-stimulus target. (Courtesy of JTA Corporation, Exeter, NH.)

DPTC 1: Overall Subject Objectives

Upon successful completion of a Level One course of fire, the participant will have been exposed to a series of training exercises designed to assist him in developing his individual, mission-specific pistol handling and manipulation skills to their fullest potential.

The original Level One course of fire we have been using consists of five separate drills, performed one after another.

The **first** of these is the **Reset Drill** (MT/PSD). This drill is intended to assist the officer in precision shooting skill development utilizing the weapon's sights. This exercise also assists the officer in developing proper trigger control and follow-through, two vital components required for accurate shooting. (See Appendix J.)

Second is the **Point Shooting Exercise**

(MT/ PSD). This exercise is intended to assist the officer in developing the critical skills needed to respond to a close proximity threat stimulus and efficiently deliver aimed rounds to it while focusing on the threat. Human startle responses and body alarm reactions dictate that the development of this skill must be provided for in training, for chances are great that when involved in actual close quarter combat, the average shooter will not use his sights but will focus on the threat instead.

Furthermore, when faced with an imminent threat, the body's natural physiological reactions will cause most people to crouch, body squared to the threat, and will also interfere with fine motor-skill movements. If officers are not afforded an opportunity to develop skills based upon the effects they will most likely experience when these reactions kick in, then they will be forced to "improvise" which usually results in poor shot placement. (See Appendix K.)

The **third drill** in this course of fire is designed to allow the officer to develop and improve his ability to recognize that a stoppage has occurred during firing and to clear it quickly and efficiently (MT/PSD). For this drill we employ dummy rounds mixed in with live rounds. For efficiency's sake, only the *TIRR Clear* **stoppage-clearing drill** and the *double-feed* stoppage drill are used, as these two drills have not failed to clear any normally-occurring stoppage during our training programs. (See Appendix H.)

The **fourth drill** is designed to allow the officer to practice a dynamic technique that combines both defensive tactics and **close proximity firearms skill development** (MT/PSD/MC). Depending upon the type of target used, this exercise may also be used to address some mental conditioning and stress inoculation training concerns. (See Appendix K.)

The **fifth and final exercise** also incorporates an **integrated use-of-force element**, and allows the participant to accomplish several things very effectively. This drill requires the participant to:
1) present his Aerosol Subject Restraint Spray (ASR) and deliver a ½ second burst to the head/face area of the target approximately two yards away. This simple act allows the participant to practice delivery of the agent, as well as to ensure that the propellant has not leached from the canister rendering the ASR useless (MT/PSD).
2) practice presenting the ASR and assuming a ready position while verbalizing commands (PSD/MC).
3) practice transitioning from one level of force (ASR) to another (firearm) while verbalizing commands (PSD/MC). (See Appendix M.)

In addition to assisting the individual officer to analyze/develop and improve his own tactical pistol skills, these exercises also allow the instructor to gauge the ability of the participating officer to successfully deliver rounds to a specified target area, employ verbalization, and manipulate the weapon while performing multiple separate and linked actions.

The incorporation of the various positions, tactics, and techniques that are employed during the course of fire are intended to provide the participating officer with an opportunity to employ them safely under controlled conditions so they may best be learned and assimilated.

Trained and experienced instructors must also be able to evaluate the participant's ability to properly and safely perform these techniques under controlled conditions, and assist the participants in the improvement of marksmanship, safe handling skills, and additional techniques as needed.

Level One Duty Pistol Training Course Evaluation

Given a pistol, support equipment and ammunition, the officer will participate in Level One Duty Pistol Training Courses using approved targets and equipment.

The following situations will result in the individual officer not successfully completing the course:
● Violation of safety rules
● Inability to perform techniques in a safe, efficient, and professional manner.

As the Level One programs are designed to aid each participant to develop their individual skills, I highly recommend that no documented "score" be sought or desired for these specific iterations.

By announcing that "holes in the target will not be counted" at the start of this course, I have found that the participant's stress levels decrease and their desire to learn and improve as opposed to "shoot and compute" (trying to count holes in paper during course) increases sharply.

COURSE OF FIRE: 36 ROUNDS (Originally designed for .40 Cal. SIG P226)

NOTE: Fully loaded #1 magazine is inserted in weapon. Round is chambered. Magazine #1 topped off and reinserted. Fully loaded magazine #2 is secured in pouch #1. Load 6 LIVE + 6 DUMMY ROUNDS in #3 magazine, place magazine #3 in pouch #2. Place an extra 7 LIVE ROUNDS IN POCKET.

SAMPLE DUTY PISTOL TRAINING COURSE (DPTC) No. 1
(Skill Development, Individual)

1.) RESET DRILL/PRECISION SHOOTING (Magazine #1)

(Any Neutral Stimulus Target) (Instructor explains and live-fire demonstrates Reset Drill)

Distance	Position	# Hands	Total # Rounds	Number Rounds Fired per Hand	Suggested Time Limit
3 Yards	Standing	2 Hand hold	3 rounds	3 Dominant	N/A
3 Yards	Standing	2 Hand hold	3 rounds	3 Non-Dominant	N/A
3 Yards	Standing	1 Hand hold	3 rounds	3 Dominant	N/A
3 Yards	Standing	1 Hand hold	3 rounds	3 Non-Dominant	N/A

DEMONSTRATE *COMBAT RELOAD* (Load Magazine #2) & RECOVER TO HOLSTER

2.) POINT SHOOTING EXERCISE, FULL EXTENSION

(Silhouette Target, Neutral Stimulus)

Distance	Position	# Hands	Total # Rounds	Number Rounds Fired per Hand	Suggested Time Limit
3 Yards	Standing (From holster)	1 Hand hold	1 round	1 Dominant	N/A
3 Yards	Standing (From holster)	1 Hand hold	1 round	1 Dominant	N/A
3 Yards	Standing (From holster)	1 Hand hold	2 rounds	2 Dominant	N/A
3 Yards	Standing (From holster)	1 Hand hold	2 rounds	2 Dominant	N/A
5 Yards	Standing (Low Ready)	1 Hand hold	1 round	1 Dominant	N/A
5 Yards	Standing (Low Ready)	1 Hand hold	1 round	1 Dominant	N/A
5 Yards	Standing (Low Ready)	1 Hand hold	2 rounds	2 Dominant	N/A
5 Yards	Standing (Low Ready)	1 Hand hold	2 rounds	2 Dominant	N/A

DEMONSTRATE *TACTICAL RELOAD* (Load Magazine #3) & RECOVER TO HOLSTER

3.) STOPPAGE CLEARING EXERCISE (Same Silhouette Target, Neutral Stimulus. One live round must be fired on each command of "UP", clearing stoppages as required until slide locks to rear. When completed, instructor checks and clears all weapons. Students recover to holster, load 1 magazine with 7 rounds from pocket, place magazine in pocket until told to "load and make ready.")

Distance	Position	# Hands	Total # Rounds	Number Rounds Fired per Hand	Suggested Time Limit
7 Yards	Standing (Low Ready)	2 Hand hold	6 rounds	6 Dominant	N/A

4.) CLOSE QUARTER ENGAGEMENT DRILL, REACTIVE, BODY POINT

(3-D Humanoid Target. Have participants perform DRY FIRE FIRST, by the numbers, several times! Then have them load 7 rounds into Magazine #3, chamber 1 round and perform drill LIVE-FIRE. Instructor MUST maintain a calm, professional manner and environment in order to ensure safety.)

Distance	Position	# Hands	Total # Rounds	Number Rounds Fired per Hand	Suggested Time Limit
1-2 Yards	Standing/Strike/Step/CPD	1 Hand hold	2 rounds	2 Dominant	SLOW
1-2 Yards	Standing/Strike/Step/CPD	1 Hand hold	2 rounds	2 Dominant	½ SPEED
1-2 Yards	Standing/Strike/Step/CPD	1 Hand hold	2 rounds	2 Dominant	¾ SPEED

5.) TRANSITION DRILL, ASR TO PISTOL

(Silhouette Target, Neutral Stimulus.) **NOTE! Weapons ARE STILL LOADED when performing this drill! ENSURE SAFETY!** Make it clear to all participants that their pistols are loaded but that they are not to fire during this drill. Rather, they are to practice covering down on a potential threat after transitioning from a lower level of force (ASR). Participants should also be instructed to practice verbalization skills during this course. Verbalization should be along the lines of "Police! Get down! Hands out! palms up! Don't move!"

Distance	Position	# Hands	Total # Rounds	Spray? Yes/No	Suggested Time Limit
2 Yards	Standing, present ASR	1 Hand hold	0 rounds	YES	SLOW
2 Yards	Standing, present ASR, verbalize, transition, verbalize again	1 Hand hold	0 rounds	NO	½ SPEED
2 Yards	Standing, present ASR, verbalize, transition, verbalize again	1 Hand hold	0 rounds	NO	¾ SPEED
2 Yards	Standing, present ASR, verbalize, transition, verbalize again	1 Hand hold	0 rounds	NO	FULL SPEED

DPTC No. 1-series: Analysis, Notes and Observations

Each relay of this course of fire can be expected to take from approximately twenty to thirty minutes to complete, depending upon the student's familiarity with the exercises and the instructor's teaching style.

While first formatting this course, I must admit that I had my concerns regarding how it would be received. This was, after all, being presented to seasoned, veteran officers, and I imagined some might object to being put through what might be seen as "basic" training drills. The stoppage clearing exercises in particular I thought might evoke some "What, are you kidding me?" type responses.

But to my surprise, the opposite occurred. This course was overwhelmingly appreciated by all who participated. The stoppage clearing exercises in particular were a big favorite across the boards.

Just being able to practice the various techniques while under no pressure to "qualify" seemed to breathe new life into many of the participants' appreciation both for their service pistols and the training.

In regard to training officers previously immersed in the Modern Technique, the ability to practice firing at close range while employing the Point Shooting Technique proved to be an interesting experience. From an instructor's point of view, it was interesting watching these officers establish an otherwise easily-learned skill while fighting their prior conditioning and old paradigm training dogma. Many would use the sights regardless of the instructions being given, as evidenced by the tight groups and slower firing rates. Usually, they would overcome this normal resistance to trying something different when reminded that they would be involved in a gunfight later in the day and would need the ability to hit quickly at close range–while facing a threat who *shoots back*–in order to save themselves a "pain penalty."

Using only one hand to draw and fire the pistol was also a skill that had been previously all but ignored in the overwhelmingly two-hand hold, Weaver-based world of police pistolcraft, and this deficiency was also apparent in their performance.

While at first uncomfortable using what many considered to be an "advanced" skill, officers quickly achieved a satisfactory level of proficiency shooting one-handed. The most common correction needed to be made by the majority of officers concerned the angle at which the pistol was held in relation to the location of center-mass of the target.

This one point in particular is of extreme interest, both in regard to validation of the training approach and more important, in regard to fulfilling the primary objective of saving lives. For time after time, we have witnessed officers previously trained in the Modern Technique consistently place bullets into the extreme lower areas of the target at distances as close as three yards when point shooting.

The reason is simple. Most modern manufactured pistols have a sharp bore-to-grip angle, usually closer to 90 degrees than a more optimum angle of (for instance), the 134 degree angle found in the German P-08 Luger.

When held in the hand and thrust directly at the target, people often tend to dip the muzzle of the sharper-angled pistols *down*.

Now combine this natural tendency to dip the muzzle when the arm is fully extended with a training program that is overwhelmingly based upon the shooter being required to use the sights in order to verify the muzzle is pointing at the paper target, and you can see the recipe for disaster taking shape.

For when the shooter is responding to an actual immediate, spontaneous threat, and the pistol is thrust *forcefully at that threat*, the shooter's eyes will more than likely be locked *on that threat*, making the sights–for all intents and purposes–non-existent.

Without the sights to verify alignment, the

pistol is thrust out, the muzzle pointed on a downward angle, and any fired shots will land exactly where logic would indicate–low.

This simple fact helps explain the mystery of the numerous reports of police-involved, close quarter gunfights during which the bad guy is shot in the legs or feet–*or missed entirely*–from distances that would seem impossible to miss from.

The solution is simply to allow the officers to ingrain the specific gross motor skills necessary to draw, point, and fire the pistol at close range, *primarily with one hand*, while the focus is on the threat.

Level Two: Marksmanship & Safe Handling Skills Assessment Tests

The primary stated goals and objectives of Level Two training courses as provided in the official lesson plans are included here for consideration and use:

According to current statistics, the average police-involved gunfight will occur at night (or in dim light) and within 20 feet. These encounters generally tend to be over within seconds. Seventy-three percent of these gunfights take place within 10 feet. *Fifty-three percent of these engagements take place within 5 feet.* At least 40% of the time there will be a potential secondary threat.

Most of these gunfights occur outdoors. The handgun is the weapon most often encountered. The average offender is male, young (average age 29), white, single, high school educated. Approximately 41% of the offenders are using drugs or alcohol at the time of the incident. Approximately 56% of offenders are diagnosed as possessing anti-social personality disorders.

Our training during these courses of fire is designed to reflect these realities.

We, as law enforcement professionals, are aware that we must understand the application of tactics and force as they pertain to our occupation, and thoroughly understand how and when they should be employed.

The SIG Sauer P-226 (.40 S&W) being held above has a bore-to-grip angle of approximately 105.5 degrees. Muzzle-dip such as this is extremely common when most semiautomatic pistols are "punched out" or shoved at the target without using the sights–*especially* when the majority of training time is devoted to sighted-only fire. Mission-specific training as described in this chapter can help overcome this.

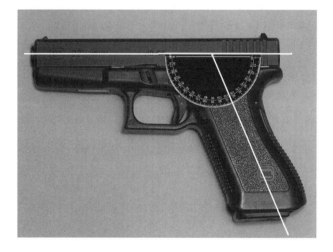

The .40 S&W Caliber Glock Model 22 has a bore-to-grip angle of approximately 112 degrees. As a result, muzzle-dip is much less severe when this pistol is "punched out" or shoved at the target without using the sights. When training, you should consistently employ the same pistol you will carry, for the internal "calibration" you will achieve with one pistol will not automatically correct itself for another with a different bore-to-grip angle. As an example, when I point shoot with the Glock 22, the rounds tend to go high, because the SIG P-226 I train with extensively has a sharper bore-to-grip angle. Thus, the compensation I automatically add when gripping and pointing the SIG causes me to over-elevate the Glock.

We must also be capable of employing our weapons and tactics in the most professional, expeditious, and efficient manner possible. This in turn not only assures us the greatest chance of survival in a life-threatening encounter, but also increases the safety margin for any innocent bystanders or other involved persons.

Therefore, during these courses of fire, we will fire a specified number of rounds from several different positions at various distances from the target. The distances and the number of rounds fired have been determined based upon statistics to better reflect the realities of police-involved gunfights.

The target itself will serve as a diagnostic tool that will allow the instructor to gauge the ability of the participating officer to successfully deliver rounds to a specified target area.

The incorporation of the various positions, tactics, and techniques that are employed during the courses of fire are intended to provide the participating officer with an opportunity to employ them safely, under controlled conditions, so they may best be learned and assimilated. Trained and experienced instructors will also be able to evaluate the participant's ability to properly and safely perform these techniques under controlled conditions, and assist the participants in the improvement of marksmanship, safe handling skills, and additional techniques as needed.

An example of a Level Two training program is provided here. Instructors are encouraged to design their own courses of fire taking into account the design characteristics of the pistols and attendant equipment used, amount of ammunition carried in the field, and departmental policies and procedures.

A specific number of rounds fired from the various distances has been calculated to more accurately reflect the percentages indicated by actual police-involved shooting situations.

NOTE: Since the target itself will serve only as a diagnostic tool that will allow the instructor to gauge the ability of the participating officer to successfully deliver rounds to a specified target area, it is recommended that only neutral-stimulus (no-threat) types of targets be used.

DPTC No. 2-series, Overall Subject Objectives

Upon successful completion of a Level Two course of fire the participant will have demonstrated an ability to accurately deliver rounds to a specified target area in a safe and proficient manner using the duty pistol.

The original Level Two course of fire we have been using consists of **eight separate drills**, performed one after another.

The **first** of these drills requires the officer to: 1) present the pistol and assume a prone position in a safe manner while holding and controlling a loaded pistol, 2) use cover properly, 3) employ the dominant hand to deliver two precision-fired rounds utilizing the sights from behind cover, 4) safely transition the pistol from the dominant hand to the non-dominant hand while behind cover, 5) employ the non-dominant hand to deliver one precision-fired round utilizing the sights from behind cover, 6) safely transition from the non-dominant hand to the dominant hand from behind cover, 7) safely recover to a kneeling position from the prone position while controlling a loaded pistol, and 8) safely recover the pistol to the holster while observing the threat area down-range (MT/PSD). (See Appendix N.)

The **second** drill requires the officer to: 1) present the pistol and assume a kneeling position in a safe manner while holding and controlling a loaded pistol, 2) use cover properly, 3) employ the dominant hand to deliver two precision-fired rounds utilizing the sights from behind cover, 4) safely transition the pistol from the dominant hand to the non-dominant hand while behind cover, 5) employ the non-dominant hand to deliver one precision-fired round utilizing the sights from behind cover, 6) safely transition from the non-dominant hand to the dominant hand from behind cover, 7) safely recover the pistol to the holster while observing the threat area down-range (MT/PSD). (See Appendix N)

The **third** drill requires the officer to: 1) present the pistol in a safe and efficient manner, 2) employ a two-hand hold, dominant hand on the pistol, to deliver two aimed-fired rounds utilizing the Point Shooting Technique, and 4) safely recover the pistol to the holster while observing 360 degrees around his position (MT/PSD). (See Appendix K.)

The **fourth** drill requires the officer to: 1) present the pistol and assume a kneeling position in a safe manner while holding and controlling a loaded pistol, 2) safely transition the pistol from the dominant hand to the non-dominant hand, 3) employ the non-dominant hand to deliver two aimed-fired rounds utilizing the Point Shooting Technique, 4) safely perform a Combat Reload while holding the pistol in the non-dominant hand, 5) safely transition from the non-dominant hand to the dominant hand, and 6) safely recover the pistol to the holster while observing 360 degrees around his position (MT/PSD). (See Appendix N.)

The **fifth** drill requires the officer to: 1) present the pistol in a safe and efficient manner, 2) employ a one-hand hold, dominant hand on the pistol, to deliver two aimed-fired rounds utilizing the Point Shooting Technique, and 3) safely recover the pistol to the holster while observing 360 degrees around his position (MT/PSD). (See Appendix K.)

The **sixth** drill requires the officer to: 1) present the pistol in a safe and efficient manner, 2) access and present the flashlight while controlling the pistol, 3) safely assume a flashlight-assisted shooting position, 4) employ a one-hand hold, dominant hand on the pistol, to deliver two aimed-fired rounds utilizing the Point Shooting Technique, 5) safely secure the flashlight while controlling the pistol, 6) perform a Tactical Reload while holding the pistol in the dominant hand, 7) safely recover the pistol to the holster while observing 360 degrees around his position (MT/PSD). (See Appendix N.)

The **seventh** drill requires the officer to: 1) present the pistol in a safe and efficient manner, 2) employ a one-hand hold, dominant hand on the pistol, to deliver two aimed-fired rounds utilizing the Body Point shooting technique, 3) utilize the non-dominant hand in a defensive/offensive posture, and 4) safely recover the pistol to the holster while observing 360 degrees around his position (MT/PSD). (See Appendix K.)

The **eighth** drill requires the officer to: 1) present the pistol in a safe and efficient manner, 2) employ a one-hand hold, dominant hand on the pistol, to deliver two aimed-fired rounds utilizing the Body Point shooting technique while utilizing the non-dominant hand in a defensive/offensive posture, 4) safely take one step back while transitioning to the one-hand Point Shooting position, 5) deliver one aimed-fired round to an alternate target area within the silhouette, and 6) recover the pistol to the holster while observing 360 degrees around his position (MT/PSD). (See Appendix K.)

In addition to assisting the individual officer to analyze, develop and improve his own tactical pistol skills, these exercises also allow the instructor to gauge the ability of the participating officer to successfully deliver rounds to a specified target area and manipulate the weapon while performing multiple separate and linked actions.

The incorporation of the various positions, tactics, and techniques that are employed during the course of fire are intended to provide the participating officer with an opportunity to employ them safely under controlled conditions so they may best be learned and assimilated.

Trained and experienced instructors must also be able to evaluate the participant's ability to properly and safely perform these techniques under controlled conditions, and assist the participants in the improvement of marksmanship, safe handling skills, and additional techniques as needed.

COURSE OF FIRE: 36 ROUNDS (Originally designed for .40 Cal. SIG P226)
NOTE: Pistol is holstered. Round is chambered. All three magazine are fully loaded. Magazine #1 in pistol. Magazines #2 & 3 in pouches. Neutral Stimulus Target Only.

SAMPLE DUTY PISTOL TRAINING COURSE (DPTC) No. 2
(Marksmanship & Safe Handling Skills Assessment)

1.) PRONE POSITION, USING COVER, SIGHTED FIRE

Distance	Position	# Hands	Total # Rounds	Number Rounds Fired per Hand	Suggested Time Limit
25 Yards	Prone/cover	2 Hand hold	3 rounds	2 Dom/1 Non-Dom	20 Seconds

(Begin prone segment from two-knees kneeling position. Draw pistol. Non-dominant hand on ground. Anchor weapon arm to ground, muzzle down-range. Student goes prone without moving weapon arm. When firing, keep to same side of barricade. Reference Appendix N.)

2.) KNEELING POSITION, USING COVER, SIGHTED FIRE

Distance	Position	# Hands	Total # Rounds	Number Rounds Fired per Hand	Suggested Time Limit
17 Yards	Kneeling/cover	2 Hand hold	3 rounds	2 Dom/1 Non-Dom	15 Seconds

3.) STANDING POSITION, POINT SHOOTING, AIMED FIRE

Distance	Position	# Hands	Total # Rounds	Number Rounds Fired per Hand	Suggested Time Limit
7 Yards	Standing	2 Hand hold	2 rounds	2 Dominant	2 Seconds
7 Yards	Standing	2 Hand hold	2 rounds	2 Dominant	2 Seconds

4.) KNEELING POSITION, POINT SHOOTING, AIMED FIRE

Distance	Position	# Hands	Total # Rounds	Number Rounds Fired per Hand	Suggested Time Limit
7 Yards	Kneeling	2 Hand hold	2 rounds	2 Non-Dominant	6 Seconds

DEMONSTRATE COMBAT RELOAD

5.) <u>STANDING POSITION, POINT SHOOTING, AIMED FIRE</u>

Distance	Position	# Hands	Total # Rounds	Number Rounds Fired per Hand	Suggested Time Limit
4 Yards	Standing	1 Hand hold	2 rounds	2 Dominant	2 Seconds
4 Yards	Standing	1 Hand hold	2 rounds	2 Dominant	2 Seconds
4 Yards	Standing	1 Hand hold	2 rounds	2 Dominant	2 Seconds

6.) <u>STANDING POSITION, FLASHLIGHT-ASSISTED, POINT SHOOTING, AIMED FIRE</u>
<u>ASSUME STAND-READY POSITION WITH FLASHLIGHT</u>
(Harries, Chapman, FBI Technique are all acceptable. Student should use their regular flashlight.)

Distance	Position	# Hands	Total # Rounds	Number Rounds Fired per Hand	Suggested Time Limit
2 Yards	Standing w/light	1 Hand hold	2 rounds	2 Dominant	2 Seconds
2 Yards	Standing w/light	1 Hand hold	2 rounds	2 Dominant	2 Seconds
2 Yards	Standing w/light	1 Hand hold	2 rounds	2 Dominant	2 Seconds

WHILE KEEPING TARGET COVERED, SECURE FLASHLIGHT AND DEMONSTRATE <u>TACTICAL RELOAD</u>

7.) <u>STANDING POSITION, CLOSE PROXIMITY DRILL (CPD), POINT SHOOTING, AIMED FIRE</u>

Distance	Position	# Hands	Total # Rounds	Number Rounds Fired per Hand	Suggested Time Limit
1.5 Yards	Standing /CPD *	1 Hand hold	2 rounds	2 Dom (Body Point)	2 Seconds
1.5 Yards	Standing /CPD	1 Hand hold	2 rounds	2 Dom (Body Point)	2 Seconds
1.5 Yards	Standing /CPD	1 Hand hold	2 rounds	2 Dom (Body Point)	2 Seconds

8.) <u>STANDING POSITION, REACTIVE MOVEMENT DRILL, POINT SHOOTING, AIMED FIRE</u>
(Execute CPD firing 2 shots, take 1 step back, extend arm and fire 1 additional shot to alternate target area)

Distance	Position	# Hands	Total # Rounds	Number Rounds Fired per Hand	Suggested Time Limit
1-2 Yards	Standing/movement	1 Hand hold	3 rounds	3 Dominant	4 Seconds
1-2 Yards	Standing/movement	1 Hand hold	3 rounds	3 Dominant	4 Seconds

DEMONSTRATE <u>ADMINISTRATIVE RELOAD</u> (Weapon stays in holster.)

---

* CLOSE PROXIMITY DRILL: Weapon presented to Body Point Position, non-dominant hand up in defensive position. (Reference Appendix K)

Level Two Duty Pistol Training Course Evaluation

Given a pistol, flashlight, support equipment and ammunition, the officer will fire an 80% or better score on the Duty Pistol Training Course (No. 2) using an approved target.

Suggested completion times are based upon Uniformed Track requirements, accessing and presenting weapon from an exposed holster.

Shots must be in the preferred area of the target to obtain a score for the shot.

SCORING BREAKDOWN (36 Rounds Total)

36–100%	24–67%	12–33%
35–97%	23–64%	11–31%
34–94%	22–61%	10–28%
33–92%	21–58%	9–25%
32–89%	20–56%	8–22%
31–86%	19–53%	7–19%
30–83%	18–50%	6–17%
29–81%	17–47%	5–14%
28–78%	16–44%	4–11%
27–75%	15–42%	3–8%
26–72%	14–39%	2–6%
25–69%	13–36%	1–3%

The following situations will result in the individual officer not successfully completing the course:

● Lack of passing marksmanship and handling skills assessment test score on both attempts for record (timed and not timed).

● Violation of safety rules.

DPTC No. 2-SERIES: Marksmanship & Safe Handling Skills Assessment Test Procedure

The officer will participate in the course of fire two times. Suggested time limits will not be applied during the first attempt. Suggested time limits will be applied during the second attempt. (Time limits are employed in order to assist the individual officer to achieve greater personal skill development and efficiency.)

Should an officer achieve an 80% score on either attempt at record, in conjunction with a positive instructor's evaluation of the officer's safe weapon handling skills and a score of not less than 70% on the other attempt, then the officer will be deemed to have successfully completed the course of fire.

Extra shots fired will result in the deduction of one hit each.

Shots over time (during timed attempt) will result in the deduction of one hit each, except as previously noted

A maximum 2 attempts for record will be permitted during the proficiency testing session.

If an 80% score is not achieved, one additional session will be arranged, which will consist of:
1. A maximum 30 minutes of preparatory exercises (Fast Track Program).
2. Two attempts for record.

If an 80% score is not achieved after the second attempt during the second session, the officer will be scheduled for a remedial program or make other arrangements for testing with the Director of the Firearms Training Unit / Range Master.

DPTC No. 2: Analysis, Notes and Observations

This course of fire can be expected to take from approximately fifteen to thirty minutes to complete per relay, depending upon the student's familiarity with the exercises and the instructor's teaching style.

This course of fire most closely resembles a traditional old paradigm, marksmanship-based "qualification" type course.

Keeping to our clarity of purpose, the

express focus of this program has been placed on safe and efficient manipulation of the pistol and flashlight, safe and efficient positioning of the body and pistol in relation to the environment and cover, and the effective employment of the pistol from these various positions to deliver aimed rounds to a specific target area, while the officer is operating in a controlled environment and under the effects of minimum induced stress.

One of the first aspects of this course of fire that causes a great deal of consternation among old paradigm proponents is the relative sparsity of rounds fired from the twenty-five and seventeen yard lines. This is understandable seeing as how the old paradigm programs placed a premium on precision-aimed sighted fire from these statistically-unlikely distances.

Another approach we have taken in regard to firing from any distance–*especially* when able to take advantage of available time, distance, cover, and employment of the sights–is to not only allow, but encourage our officers to exploit the inherent advantage of pistols such as the SIG Sauer P226 that allows you to manually cock the hammer to allow the pistol to be fired from single-action mode. The reasoning for this practice–it allows you to deliver a more precision-aimed round than if firing double-action–outweighs the potential negative consequences of having a few of your officers adopt the practice of cocking the hammer whenever the pistol is drawn. We strive to ensure that officers do not adopt this potentially dangerous practice by explaining that it is intended for use *only when the situation dictates it*, such as when preparing to make a critical, precision-aimed shot when time, distance, and cover allow.

While as an instructor I realize that one of our officers may not heed this instruction and cock his pistol when it may not be appropriate, I defend this practice because I firmly believe in two things: first, if you select, train, equip, and send people out into the world armed with weapons to do a dangerous job, then you must also trust them to do what is right–otherwise, you've no business sending them out in the first place. Second, we owe it to our officers (and those they may need to defend under dire circumstances) to provide them with as much knowledge and as many options as possible, so they may discover what works best for them and take full advantage when it counts most.

Another advantage we provide for our people is found in the linking of all the DPTC courses of fire. As an example, in DPTC 1 we introduce and allow our officers to practice the Re-set Drill at close range. Once they are back at the twenty-five yard line while participating in DPTC 2, we remind them to use the Re-set Drill as it will improve their ability to hit accurately regardless of the distances involved.

As further examination of DPTC 2 reveals, the majority of training is dedicated to developing the close-quarter point shooting skills that we know need to be focused upon, as well as developing and increasing the familiarity and safe handling skills of the officers involved. Leaving the weapon drawn and covering the target while securing the flashlight and performing the Tactical Reload is one example of training that encourages officers to learn and practice multiple linked motor skills while operating under controlled conditions.

One interesting observation I have noted since beginning administration of this course is that there is an almost equal delineation between those officers who perform better during this course when the targets are stationary, and those who perform better when the targets are turning within prescribed time limits. The breakdown has consistently been close to 50/50. My personal opinion regarding those people who perform better when the targets are turning is that they probably overthink and/or try too hard when the targets are stationary, and that this inhibits their ability to hit effectively. Then, when the targets are turning, they stop thinking and just "do," allowing their subconscious to take over and perform as trained.

On the flip side, I believe that those who hit better when the course is first administered un-timed with stationary targets, are more than likely trying to take advantage of the situation by using their sights (old paradigm approach) from all distances. Then, when the targets start spinning, the luxury of time and sight acquisition is gone and they're firing too late to achieve hits.

Regardless, once the participants have participated in DPTC 4 (House of Horrors), they tend to realize that the focus of the training has changed from achieving perfect shot groupings and high scores on paper to surviving and winning gunfights in the real world. Their future participation and performance during training greatly reflects this conversion, and scores on DPTC 2 tend to go up while obsession–and its related stress–with the paper score decreases.

Why? Because once the targets actually shoot back, putting holes in paper becomes a practically stress-free activity both up-range and down-range.

In terms of old paradigm vs. New Paradigm, what has occurred is that the old paradigm's "end"–a passing score on a marksmanship-based course–has become the New Paradigm's "means" to a redefined, *reality-based end*–skills development that will ultimately help you handle yourself, your pistol, and dangerous situations should the need arise.

The games have ended.

The Fast Track

I borrowed the term "fast track" and the idea from the FBI Firearms Training Unit. "Fast tracking" an officer who has not met the DPTC 2 standards as defined above basically involves having a trained and experienced instructor work one-on-one with the officer to diagnose the cause of the difficulty. Occasionally, the problem is simply one of

accommodation, such as when the pistol is too large for the officer's hand (See Appendix F).

Once the problem has been identified, the instructor provides equipment and/or technique options that the officer may experiment with in order to eliminate the difficulty. The officer is then immediately re-tested.

In the vast majority of instances, this stress-free, one-on-one instruction session is all that is needed in order to enable the officer to perform to standard–and not just during that particular training iteration. For by taking this immediate and positive hands-on approach, we have been able to dramatically reduce the number of so-called "problem shooters" that every department can lay claim to. Our success has been so great, in fact, that it has convinced me to agree with those who claim that while some students absolutely may provide more of a challenge to the instructor than others, the responsibility for a student's failure to perform up to standard belongs, in the majority of cases, to the instructor.

Paul Damery, one of my department's finest instructors, has always preached that "it is

Sgt. Paul Damery, founder of the MSP Bomb Squad (EOD Unit), also designed the first nationally-recognized police firearms instructor course for the Massachusetts State Police.

the instructor's job to turn the light on for the student." And, as Paul has demonstrated to me many times, it is also the instructor's job to be secure enough in himself to realize that if he cannot reach a student with his particular approach, then he must allow another trained and qualified instructor to work with the student, in the hope that this instructor can succeed where he has failed.

Given the normal human egos we are born with, and the often abnormal egos firearms instructors sometimes develop, this philosophy takes more strength of character to implement than it might appear.

**Level Three: Combination Drills
(Movement, Cover, Judgment, Verbalization, & Safe Handling Skills Assessment Tests)**

The primary stated goals and objectives of Level Three training courses as provided in the official lesson plans are included here for consideration and use:

These courses of fire are designed to expose the student to some of the physical (and to a lesser degree, psychological) realities that may be encountered during a dynamic, real-world, police-involved encounter. The scenario outlined in Section C, Sub-section 1, of the DPTC No. 3 sample lesson plan (Set-up) closely replicates police-involved situations that have occurred in the past, and that also have a high likelihood of occurring again.

Of course, this does not mean or imply that the learned behavior, skills, tactics, and techniques that will be used in any of these particular scenarios are applicable only to situations that precisely mirror these specific scenarios. For during the administration of all these focused and intense courses of fire, the student will have demonstrated an understanding of, and ability to do many, if not all of the following:
1) emerge quickly and efficiently from the cruiser
2) properly move to a position of cover
3) use available cover in an efficient manner
4) employ verbal commands

5) recognize an immediate threat based on visual cues
6) use good judgment while employing deadly force
7) effectively engage a moving target

Obviously, these learned behaviors, skills, tactics, and techniques are broadly relevant to any law enforcement professional, and must be addressed in training so that each officer will be exposed to, and gain a better understanding of, the proper application of tactics and force as they pertain to our occupation.

In addition, these courses of fire are designed to assist the student to develop a better understanding of both how and when these skills, tactics, and techniques should be employed.

That is the primary purpose of these courses of fire.

For it is believed that by exposing the students to scenario-based, dynamic training programs such as these, that we better prepare them to employ tactics and their weapons in the most professional, expeditious, and efficient manner possible when the threat is for real and the stakes are extremely high.

This in turn not only assures each of us the greatest chance of survival in a life-threatening encounter, but also increases the safety margin for any innocent bystanders or other involved persons.

An example of a Level Three training program is provided here. Instructors are encouraged to design their own courses of fire taking into account their departmental policies and procedures and the specific types of activities/situations their department members are most likely to be involved with.

A specific number of rounds fired from the various distances has been calculated to reflect the percentages indicated by actual police-involved shooting situations.

NOTE: In addition to serving as diagnostic tools that will allow the instructor to gauge the ability of the participating officer to successfully deliver rounds to a specified target area, Level Three training program targets also serve to present specific visual stimuli to the participant. For this reason, it is recommended that realistic threat-type and no-threat type targets be employed.

DPTC No. 3-series, Overall Subject Objectives

Upon successful completion of these courses of fire, the participant will have demonstrated the ability to adeptly exit the cruiser, properly move to a position of cover, to use cover in an efficient manner, to recognize an immediate threat, to employ verbal commands, to use good judgment while employing deadly force, to engage a moving target, or to fire effectively while on the move.

The original Level Three course of fire we have been using is outlined on the following pages.

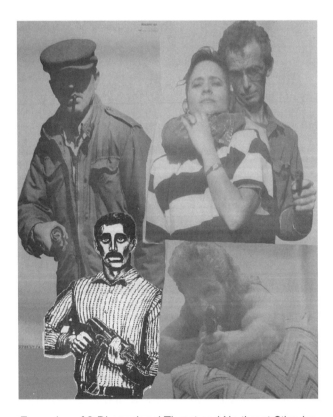

Examples of 2-Dimensional Threat and No-threat Stimulus targets. (Courtesy of Law Enforcement Targets and Speedwell Targets.)

DPTC No. 3-series: Analysis, Notes and Observations

This course of fire–from start to finish, including the debriefing–can be completed in under three minutes. While it is extremely time-efficient, it also yields significant results.

While at first blush this exercise may appear to be nothing more than a common moving target type of course, a closer examination reveals that it actually addresses critical components of each of the Primary Police Training Elements:
1) efficient vehicle (cruiser) escape technique (PSD)
2) tactical movement while controlling a pistol (PSD/MC)
3) use of cover (PSD/MC)
4) use of verbalization while controlling representations of both threats and no-threats (PSD/MC)
5) scanning / observation of environment while controlling representations of both threats and no-threats (PSD/MC)
6) engaging a threat from behind cover while the threat is moving through a less than sterile environment (PSD/MC/MT)
7) decision making skills regarding the if, when, and how of employing deadly force during a spontaneous, high-risk situation while trying to control representations of both threats and no-threats (MC)

Prior to administration, all aspects of the course–from explaining the scenario, to describing exactly what will occur and what is expected of the participants–should be detailed to the participants.

They should also be advised that in similar circumstances, many officers have failed to see anything but the threat, and have shot innocent bystanders as a result. The inclusion of 3D no-threat representations both in front of and behind the area where the threat target passes will allow the participants to see how easy it is

DPTC Level Three Course of Fire, Example

1. On signal, student puts vehicle into Park, releases seatbelt, opens door and exits vehicle.

2. As student runs downrange toward suspect vehicle mock-up, the instructor stays close behind to ensure safety. Another instructor oversees the exercise in the capacity of Safety Officer. (Photos courtesy MSP archives.)

3. After ensuring there are no immediate threats around suspect vehicle (mock-up), student uses the vehicle for cover as he observes the area where suspect was last seen. Verbalized warnings to both threat and no-threat targets are encouraged. Here the student engages the immediate threat presented by the 2-D photorealistic target on the "running man" system. Note the 3-D no-

threat stimulus targets to the left. They are situated so the path of the threat target running man passes in front of one and behind the other. The no-threats behind the threat target are more likely to be shot than those in front. NOTE: Regardless of the availability of actual vehicles, I strongly recommend that only plywood vehicle mock-ups be employed for these types of courses. The all wood mock-ups greatly reduce the risk of ricochet during training. Obviously, the mock-ups are also easier to maintain and move around than real vehicles while still providing high training value. This is because while operating under even low levels of stress, the simplest suggestion of reality will allow the subconscious mind to fill in the rest. Here, the general vehicle shape, "tail lights" (simple reflectors) and registration plate provide sufficient reference points to allow the mock-up to serve as an adequate representation of a vehicle during this training course. The mock-up was built as simple box to provide stability. Rear "window" and trunk dimensions were taken from an actual vehicle.

COURSE OF FIRE: 0-12 ROUNDS (Originally designed for .40 Cal. SIG P226)

SAMPLE DUTY PISTOL TRAINING COURSE (DPTC) No. 3
(Combination Drill: Movement, Cover, Judgment, Verbalization, Moving Target)

1. DPTC 3: SET-UP

STUDENT: Student is seated in cruiser, seat belt fastened, approximately 50 yards from target area. Student's pistol is holstered, snaps on. Student's pistol is fully loaded with a round in the chamber. Student is advised that he has just been involved in a motor vehicle pursuit of a suspect. The suspect is believed to be armed with some type of handgun, and was reported to have attempted to rob a convenience store just prior to the pursuit. The pursuit has just ended. The suspect stopped his vehicle in the middle of the road directly in front of the pursuing cruiser. The suspect was observed to flee from his motor vehicle and run behind a wall. The officer knows the area behind this wall to be a dead-end, a small alcove with no means of escape. The wall is at one end of a small shopping plaza. There are uninvolved people in the area.

2. DPTC 3: INITIATION

Instructor will initiate the course by verbal command, "READY, BEGIN!"

3. DPTC 3: PERFORMANCE OBJECTIVES

Student will ensure gear-shift lever is in PARK, release seat belt, open door, and exit cruiser as quickly and safely as possible. Student will move to the cover as presented by the suspect's abandoned vehicle, safely drawing his pistol to the low ready position. As the student approaches the vehicle, he should VISUALLY CLEAR INTERIOR OF VEHICLE through back window to ensure no secondary threat exists. Student should then use the vehicle for cover as he observes the area where suspect was last seen. Should the student observe the suspect, the student should determine if the suspect presents an immediate threat, use verbal commands (if feasible) to control the suspect and/or others in the vicinity, and engage the suspect with fire - if warranted and when, in the student's judgment, it is prudent to do so. The exercise is not terminated until the instructor advises the student that the situation has been brought under control. At this time the student will perform an administrative unload or a tactical recovery to the holster, dependent upon instructor's directions.

4. DPTC 3: POST-EXERCISE PROCEDURE

An immediate debriefing will then be conducted by the instructor and student. Since the instructor-to-student ratio is one-to-one, the student's individual performance and tactical choices will be reviewed in a way that is not possible when training is formatted for multiple participants or "line training." This police training "luxury" of individualized instruction and performance-based critiquing, even when limited to a few intense focused minutes, yields extremely positive results both in terms of morale and increased proficiency. During the debriefing the use of cover, movement, verbalization, and weapon handling skills will be discussed. The threat and no-threat targets will be checked for hits. The student will be asked if his perceptions were impaired, i.e. "Did you lose track of the friendlies at any point?" The student will be given the opportunity to ask any questions he may have.

After the debriefing is completed, the student will be instructed to perform a safety check of his weapon to verify it is SAFE, CLEAR, and EMPTY. The weapon will then be verified to be SAFE, CLEAR and EMPTY by the instructor. Any ammunition on the student's person will be collected. The student may then be directed to proceed to the weapon cleaning area to clean his individual weapon/s or prepare for additional training or other activities as directed.

5.) DPTC 3: MOVING TARGET EXERCISE (Moving Target, Threat Stimulus)

Distance	Position	# Hands	Total # Rounds	# Rounds Fired per Hand	Suggested Time Limit
12 Yards	Student's choice	1 or 2 Hand hold	0-12 rounds	Student's choice	N/A

DEMONSTRATE ADMINISTRATIVE UNLOAD

6.) DPTC 3: DIAGRAM

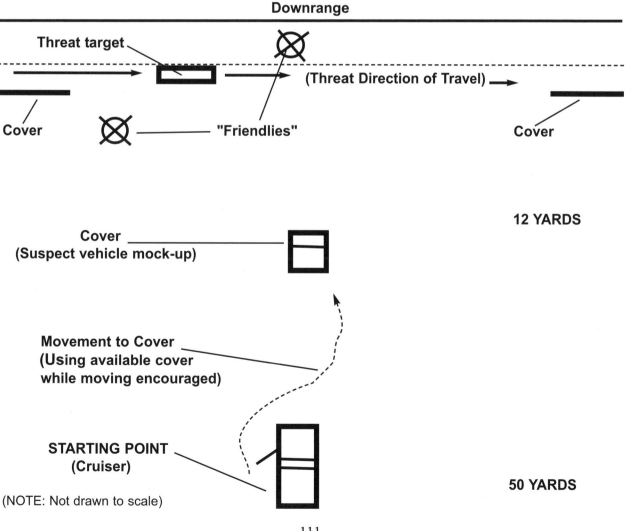

Downrange

Threat target

(Threat Direction of Travel) →

Cover

"Friendlies"

Cover

Cover
(Suspect vehicle mock-up)

12 YARDS

Movement to Cover
(Using available cover while moving encouraged)

STARTING POINT
(Cruiser)

50 YARDS

(NOTE: Not drawn to scale)

111

for this to occur, and will provide an experience under controlled conditions that they may learn from.

This particular exercise has generated a great amount of positive feedback from officers working in the field.

In many cases, officers report that while holding suspects at gunpoint, or otherwise operating in extreme situations with their weapons drawn and ready, they suddenly recall this exercise and the memory prompts them to scan the area more thoroughly for other personnel. In several of these cases, officers have stated that as a direct result of this, they have suddenly "discovered" that other people were standing directly behind the suspects or very close by, and this allowed them to adjust their position and actions accordingly to ensure the highest possible safety margins for everyone involved.

As for the gravity of these considerations, I usually explain to officers prior to their participation in the exercise that the "friendly" representations down-range are representations of members of my family–or their own. I then ask the question, "If it was your mother, father, son, daughter, etc. standing there when something like this happened, how would you want the responding officers to perform?"

How would *you*?

Level Four: Scenario-based, Dynamic Interactive Experiential Learning / Diminished Light Training

The primary stated goals and objectives of Level Four training courses as provided in the official lesson plans are included here for consideration and use:

These courses of fire will allow the participants to experience extreme situations under controlled conditions in a training environment, where trained instructors will be available to provide information, guidance and assistance to them as needed or requested.

These courses will also provide instructors and students with an excellent means of verifying the officer's individual skill retention levels, while allowing for the identification and reinforcement of strengths, the identification and improvement of weaknesses, and for the immediate identification and correction of any observed operating errors.

In addition, when formatted and administered correctly, these courses will allow the student to see, through his own eyes, exactly what the effects of stress are and how they may affect the individual. The degree of success attainable in this regard will be directly dependent upon the training, knowledge and observation skills of the instructor, as well as upon the instructor's ability to properly debrief the students immediately upon completion of the course.

Finally, by allowing students to experience the effects of stress as they employ the actual equipment, tactics, and techniques they will use while operating under conditions similar to those they are preparing for, we are able to educate them as never before and simultaneously inoculate them against these same, often debilitating effects.

The specific desired result of this type of training is to produce officers who can and will operate at a higher level of efficiency in the real world. This becomes possible as officers develop improved cognitive and judgmental abilities, which in turn will serve to improve their physical performance levels.

The end result is a more confident, efficient, effective, and above all, safer police officer.

An example of a Level Four training program is provided on the following pages. Instructors are encouraged to design their own courses taking into account their departmental policies and procedures and the specific types of activities and situations their department members are most likely to be involved with. Simulated environments, situations, and circumstances need to be tailored to reflect the statistically-likely realities officers may face.

NOTE: In addition to serving as diagnostic tools that will allow the instructor to gauge the ability of the participating officer to successfully deliver rounds to a specified target area, Level

Four training program targets also serve to present specific visual stimuli to the participant. For this reason, it is recommended that realistic 3D threat-type and no-threat type targets be employed.

DPTC 4: Overall Subject Objectives

Upon successful completion of this course of fire, the student will have been exposed to various reality-based, interactive and dynamic training scenarios, similar to those that may most likely be encountered while operating in actual working environments.

Interactive Dynamic training programs utilizing role players, dedicated training weapons and ammunition, scripted scenarios, safety officers, and trained instructors are perhaps the best possible way to train officers for the realities they may face while operating in the real world.

Unfortunately, the resources necessary to conduct these types of operations are often not available. There is, however, an alternative available that is not only time, manpower, and cost-efficient, but also produces positive, consistent results.

The type of program I am referring to is a powerful tool that incorporates elements of

Operant and Classical Conditioning as well as Stress Inoculation. We have named our version of this tool the "House of Horrors" training program, in honor of an earlier version last officially seen in the US in 1945.

The design, construction, and administration of a House of Horrors program similar to the one detailed here is described in App. Q.

The original Level Four course of fire is outlined here for consideration.

NOTE: In addition to providing specific visual, auditory, and pain penalty stimuli to the participant, House of Horrors threat-type targets also serve as diagnostic tools that will allow the instructor to gauge the ability of the participating officer to successfully deliver rounds to a specified target area. For this reason, target clothing should be changed or cleaned often when employing Simunition® or other marking-type cartridges, so officers may receive immediate feedback on their performance during the debriefing.

While the House of Horrors program has been intentionally designed to allow its safe administration by a single instructor, the option of integrating other instructors into the scenarios as role-players is available and serves to enhance the training impact.

For more information refer to Appendix Q.

House of Horrors animated 3-Dimensional Threat-stimulus (left) and No-threat stimulus (right) targets. Threat mannequin raises pistol, no-threat mannequin ducks behind dumpster. Both are manually operated by wires.

COURSE OF FIRE: 0-37 ROUNDS (Originally designed for .40 Cal. SIG P226)

NOTE: Fully loaded #1 magazine is inserted in weapon. Round is chambered. Magazine #1 topped off and reinserted. Fully loaded magazine #2 is secured in pouch #1. Fully loaded magazine #3 is secured in pouch #2.

SAMPLE DUTY PISTOL TRAINING COURSE (DPTC) No.42
(Scenario-based, Interactive Dynamic, Experiential Learning Training Exercise)

NOTE: This course incorporates moving targets, threat stimulus, no-threat stimulus, low-light environments, judgment training, skill development, stress inoculation training, operant and classical conditioning. Each station can be set up with Threat Representations, No-Threat Representations, or combinations of both. One possible set-up is described in detail here. (SC = Student's Choice)

EXTERIOR, DAYLIGHT / ALLEYWAY

1.) THREAT SUBJECT IN MOTORVEHICLE
(Threat Stimulus Moving Target)

Distance	Position	# Hands	Total # Rounds	Number Rounds Fired per Hand	Suggested Time Limit
0-5 Yards	Student's choice (SC)	SC	SC	SC	N/A

2.) NO-THREAT SUBJECT (HIDING MAN)
(No-Threat Stimulus Moving Target w/ Auditory Stimulus)

Distance	Position	# Hands	Total # Rounds	Number Rounds Fired per Hand	Suggested Time Limit
0-7 Yards	Student's choice (SC) Cover available	SC	SC	SC	N/A

3.) THREAT SUBJECT WITH NO-THREAT HOSTAGE
(Combined Threat and No-Threat Stimulus Targets)

Distance	Position	# Hands	Total # Rounds	Number Rounds Fired per Hand	Suggested Time Limit
4-7 Yards	Student's choice (SC) Cover available	SC	SC	SC	N/A

4.) NO-THREAT SUBJECT IN WINDOW
(No-Threat Stimulus Target w/ Movement and Auditory Stimulus)

Distance	Position	# Hands	Total # Rounds	Number Rounds Fired per Hand	Suggested Time Limit
0-5 Yards	Student's choice (SC) Cover available	SC	SC	SC	N/A

PERFORM TACTICAL ENTRY INTO HOUSE OF HORRORS

INTERIOR, LOW-LIGHT / HOUSE OF HORRORS

5.) NEGOTIATE NO-THREAT STAIRWAY
(No-Threat Stimulus Target w/ Auditory Stimulus)

Distance	Position	# Hands	Total # Rounds	Number Rounds Fired per Hand	Suggested Time Limit
0-1 Yard	Student's choice (SC)	SC	SC	SC	N/A

6.) THREAT SUBJECT (SHOOTING MAN)
(Threat Stimulus Target w/ Auditory Stimulus and Pain Stimulus)

Distance	Position	# Hands	Total # Rounds	Number Rounds Fired per Hand	Suggested Time Limit
0-5 Yards	Student's choice (SC) Cover available	SC	SC	SC	N/A

7.) NO-THREAT REFLECTED IMAGE
(No-Threat Stimulus Target)

Distance	Position	# Hands	Total # Rounds	Number Rounds Fired per Hand	Suggested Time Limit
0-2 Yards	Student's choice (SC)	SC	SC	SC	N/A

8.) NEGOTIATE HALLWAY, NO-THREAT SUBJECT (TURNING MAN)
(No-Threat Stimulus Moving Target)

Distance	Position	# Hands	Total # Rounds	Number Rounds Fired per Hand	Suggested Time Limit
4 Yards	Student's choice (SC)	SC	SC	SC	N/A

9.) NO-THREAT AND THREAT SUBJECTS (KNIFING MAN & VICTIM)
(Threat Stimulus Moving Target w/ Auditory Stimulus and No-Threat Stimulus Target)

Distance	Position	# Hands	Total # Rounds	Number Rounds Fired per Hand	Suggested Time Limit
6-1 Yards	Student's choice (SC)	SC	SC	SC	N/A

*** ADMINISTRATIVE UNLOAD ***

115

COURSE OF FIRE: 0-37 ROUNDS (Originally designed for .40 Cal. SIG P226)

SAMPLE DUTY PISTOL TRAINING COURSE (DPTC) No. 4
(Scenario-based, Interactive Dynamic, Experiential Learning Training Exercise)

1. DPTC 4: SET-UP

a) All individual weapons will be made safe and secured in the appropriate designated area before any scenario-based training is conducted. This includes firearms, ammunition, chemical agent weapons, impact weapons, and edged weapons. None of these items will be permitted in the designated training area. The instructor is responsible for ensuring that the training area remains absolutely free and clear of unauthorized weapons and personnel during the administration of the program.

b) All students will read a written safety and scenario briefing (such as shown in Appendix Q) prior to reporting to the instructor for training.

c) All students will be issued a Performance Evaluation Form. (See Appendix U). The students will fill out their personal information where indicated. The form will be given to the instructor immediately prior to the student's participation in the course.

d) After receiving the form from the student and visually checking to see if any weapons are visible on the student's person, the instructor will ask the student to physically check to ensure the student has no weapons of any kind on his/her person. The instructor may then perform a cursory physical pat-down of the student's outer garments to further ensure against the possibility of an unauthorized weapon being introduced into the sterile training environment.

e) Once the safety check has been completed, the instructor will physically load the Simunition-equipped training pistol in front of the student. The weapon will then be placed into tactical carry configuration (per department policy, i.e. magazine fully loaded, round in chamber, hammer safely lowered by decocking) and issued to the student. The student will then safely holster the pistol and secure the holster per department policy. Additional magazines loaded with Simunition® FX Marking ammunition may also be provided to the student at this time. Depending upon the scenario objectives and composition, inert training ASRs and /or batons may also be issued for use during the course.

f) The instructor will then issue the student the appropriate protective equipment required to safely participate in the course and assist the student to prepare as needed.

g) A verbal safety and scenario training briefing will then be administered by the instructor. The following information must be explained to each student:
    1) You are working and you've been dispatched to this location. A police officer is believed to possibly be injured somewhere within this area. His last radio transmission was a garbled cry for help. This area is known to harbor violent and desperate types. There may also be other police officers in the area, as well as uninvolved citizens. Your mission is to check this alley, working your way to the building at the end. Once there, you will need to check within the building. Time is critical as we may have an officer seriously injured, or possibly bleeding out somewhere in this area.

2) Once we begin, any decisions that need to be made will be yours to make. I (instructor) will be behind you all the way through, simply to guide you from station to station. Any and all threats, situations, and encounters will occur directly to your front, to your left, or to your right - never to the rear, I've got your back covered. Anything you say or do, any level of force you choose to use or not use while dealing with each situation, is up to you. From verbal commands to drawing and firing your pistol, to taking cover or advancing, it's all up to you. Once that particular station has been dealt with, I will direct you to the next. We continue on until the mission is completed. Do you understand?

3) Last thing before we begin. There are no tricks in the House of Horrors, no booby traps, collapsible stairs, or blood baths to slip on in the darkness. Simply deal with what you see and hear and do what you believe is right. And remember, even though the House of Horrors is populated with mannequins, these mannequins move, and some of them are armed with real clubs, bottles, knives, pipes, and in some cases, guns that fire Simunitions just like the pistol you're holding. Some of them respond to verbal commands. Some won't. Immediate deadly threats can be stopped by firing and hitting the offender center of mass. If you don't fire when you need to, or don't hit the threat enough to shut it down, then it may keep attacking until you do.

2. DPTC 4: INITIATION

Instructor will initiate the course verbally, stating: "Are you ready? Begin."

3. DPTC 4: PERFORMANCE OBJECTIVES

Student will negotiate each station while operating within the parameters of the overall scenario. The primary objectives are:
   a) to safely, efficiently, and professionally check and clear each individual station while exercising good judgment and employing proper tactics.
   b) to use verbal commands as needed.
   c) to employ reasonable levels of force as the officer believes they are needed.
   d) to locate the missing officer and assist him/her as needed.

Each station within the overall training scenario is terminated when the instructor advises the student that that particular situation has been brought under control. The entire training course will be terminated when the instructor advises the student that the program is completed. At this time the student will perform an administrative unload or a tactical recovery to the holster, dependent upon the instructor's directions.

4. DPTC 4: POST-EXERCISE PROCEDURE

An immediate debriefing will then be conducted by the instructor and student. The student will be asked to recall the events in reverse order, starting with the most recently completed station and working backwards to the first station.

The student's performance and tactical choices made at each station will be reviewed. The use of cover will be discussed. The threat and no-threat targets will be checked for hits. Any physiological and/or psychological stress-induced effects (i.e. shaking, sweating, perceptual narrowing, memory gaps, etc.) experienced by the student will be discussed.

4. DPTC 4: POST-EXERCISE PROCEDURE, Continued

After the debriefing is completed, the student will be instructed to perform an administrative unload and a safety check of his/her weapon to verify it is SAFE, CLEAR, and EMPTY. The weapon will then be verified to be SAFE, CLEAR and EMPTY by the instructor. Any ammunition, inert ASRs, or batons on the student's person will be collected.

Instructor will then fill out the student's Performance Evaluation Form. After the student has had an opportunity to review the form, it will be signed by the student (and subsequently placed into the student's training record jacket to be kept permanently on file). The student may then be directed to proceed to the weapon cleaning area to clean his individual weapon/s or prepare for additional training or other activities as directed.

5. DPTC 4: DIAGRAM

NOTE: The diagram provided here was created based upon the available space we had to work with. Any type of environment/location can be used to set up and administer House of Horrors type training programs as long as reasonable preparations are made and precautions taken. Because only Simunition® FX Marking type, non-penetrating ammunition is used, many of the limitations normally associated with the administration of firearms training courses that employ penetrating ammunition are not applicable. Safety rules must be clearly stated, understood, observed and enforced by all participants at all times.

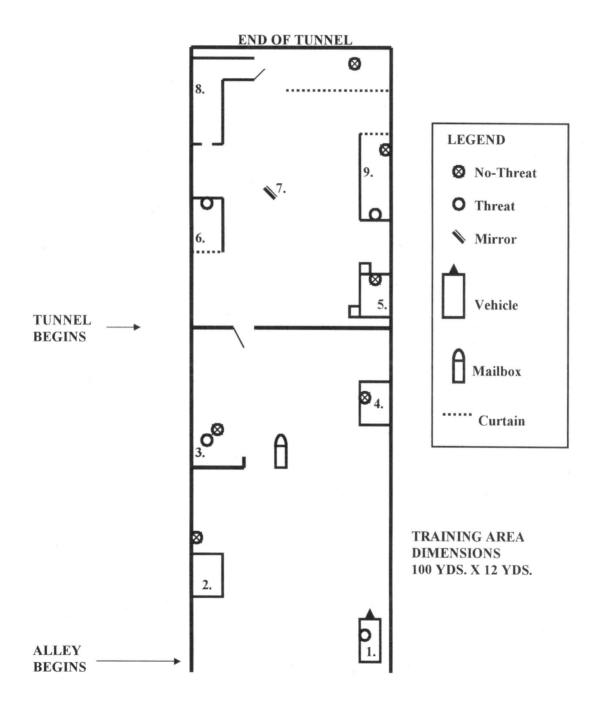

6. DPTC 4: SAFETY - FIRST, LAST, ALWAYS

ATTENTION! DUE TO THE VERY NATURE OF THESE TYPES OF TRAINING OPERATIONS, THE DANGER AWARENESS LEVELS OF ALL INVOLVED PERSONNEL MUST BE MAINTAINED AT THE HIGHEST POSSIBLE DEGREE AT ALL TIMES!

It is the responsibility of each individual agency/department to develop and adhere to a comprehensive series of safety protocols regarding the design and administration of all firearms training programs prior to their administration. This is especially critical in regard to those programs that employ dynamic interactive force-on-force, scenario-based experiential learning elements such as the House of Horrors program.

The following safety protocols are provided for informational purposes only.

SAFETY IS EVERYONE'S RESPONSIBILITY, ALL OF THE TIME!

1) SAFETY: Safety is the primary consideration when conducting Dynamic Interactive scenario-based use-of-force training.
　　All safe weapon handling rules apply.
　　Violations of any of these safe weapon handling rules will result in immediate removal from the training program.
　　A written report will then be generated and forwarded to the appropriate supervisory personnel.

2) WEAPONS: All weapons will be checked and re-checked prior to training, during training, and upon completion of training to ensure that there are no live firearms, ammunition, ASRs, or knives in the training area or accessible to any of the participants or instructors.

3) PROTECTIVE EQUIPMENT: Proper protective equipment must be worn by all persons present at all times while interactive scenarios are in progress.

4) EXCLUSION OF UNINVOLVED PERSONS: All persons who are not directly involved in the ongoing training scenario must remain in the designated holding area.

5) SAFETY BRIEFING AND REVIEW/DEBRIEFING: A verbal and written safety briefing will be conducted by the instructor prior to starting each individual segment of training. A verbal debriefing will be conducted by the instructor immediately upon the conclusion of the training segment.

7. DPTC 4: ADDITIONAL TRAINING CONSIDERATIONS

1) THREAT IDENTIFICATION: Threat identification is relatively simple on a static range during a training exercise. Difficulty in recognizing an overt threat (much less subtle threat-cues) increases, however, when additional sensory input is present.
　　Some degree of difficulty in threat identification/target determination will usually be noted when the training involves computer generated scenarios produced by Firearms Training Simulators such as FATs and RANGE 2000/3000 systems.
　　A greater degree of difficulty will usually be noted when the levels of sensory input are increased again when officers participate in dynamic interactive scenarios replete with role players/ mannequins, actual threats, and environmental impediments.

As difficult as the identification of the threat might be, more difficulty will likely be experienced in determining *whether to fire*. This is NORMAL. The purpose of this training, therefore, is to expose the officer to simulated, stressful situations similar to those he may encounter while working, in order to let each officer learn through experience in a controlled training environment, rather than during actual situations where mistakes can–too often–only be made once.

2) FACTORS THAT INFLUENCE SPEED AND CORRECTNESS OF RESPONSE: There are five basic factors that tend to influence the speed and correctness of an officer's response.

a) COLOR: Bright colors tend to draw our attention more than drab colors. The more colors and contrasts present, the longer it will take for the brain to determine what is being perceived. This process may produce confusion and/or hesitation on the part of the officer.

b) DEPTH PERCEPTION: An officer's perception of three dimensional objects can degrade during periods of extreme stress. The level of degradation will also be dramatically increased depending upon the level of darkness present in the environment.

c) MOVEMENT: An officer's ability to determine specific threats present when confronted with an individual moving in any direction may be severely limited. The myriad effects of stress and the resultant perceptual narrowing may inhibit the ability to focus on specific areas such as the subject's hands or face. Because the angles of view and the surrounding environment itself are also changing while the moving subject is tracked through it, additional sensory input (e.g. colors, obstacles, other people, etc.) will add to the confusion, increasing the level of difficulty for the officer in regard to his ability to discern exactly what is happening.

d) SOUND: Sounds can be easily misinterpreted, especially when an officer is operating under stress. Unexpected sounds may cause an officer to perceive an immediate threat and react accordingly, even if the sound is not actually associated with threatening behavior or activities. Stress-related perceptual narrowing also applies to auditory input. Depending upon the degree of stress, an officer may not hear extremely loud sounds, may hear faint sounds as though they were greatly amplified, and may not be able to discern or immediately recall even the most distinctive sounds.

e) EXPERIENCE: Officers who have previously experienced stressful situations similar to one they may currently be involved in may find themselves reacting emotionally and/or physically to the current situation based upon their experience with the previous situation. While making a motor vehicle stop, for instance, if the officer observes a number of similarities (time of day, location, vehicle type and color, activity and description of subjects within the vehicle) to a previous situation during which a violent attack occurred against him, he may experience stress-induced physiological effects (i.e. shaking, sweating, increased respiration and heart rates) as he pulls the vehicle over. These effects may be greatly magnified as he makes his approach, and in fact, it is very possible that he may respond to a non-threatening action from the occupants within this vehicle as if they were the threatening actions exhibited by the occupants during the previous stop. Based upon my observations while conducting training programs, it is also possible that the officer may actually "see" a weapon similar to that previously used against him under these circumstances, even though there may be no actual weapon present during the current encounter.

DPTC No. 4: Analysis, Notes and Observations

This course of fire is the most intense and critically productive segment of the entire New Paradigm program. In essence, it is the defining component of the approach we have taken.

As explained in Chapter Five, this segment was developed first because the entire point of the training from inception was to best prepare officers to employ their weapons under realistic conditions while dealing with reality-based threats.

Since all the other training levels were developed to prepare the officers to succeed during this final segment, what we actually accomplished can best be described as "putting the horse back in front of the cart."

In other words, our people performed well during Level Four because we prepared them during the first part of the day using training exercises developed based upon how people actually–and naturally–react when dealing with real world environments and threats.

This is directly contrary to the Old Paradigm approach, wherein officers were expected to overcome their innate, human startle and survival responses when facing a deadly threat by participating primarily in unrealistic marksmanship-based courses of fire, while employing highly-stylized stances and complicated techniques and operating in sterile environments under controlled conditions.

After more than four years of training operations and better than five-thousand successful trips through the House of Horrors, I can state unequivocally that the concept works as effectively today as it did back in Fairbairn and Sykes' Shanghai of the 1930's and during World War II under Rex Applegate's watchful and astute training eye.

As with each segment of the training program, specific goals were established prior to designing the Level Four course, and all were met.

In addition, we discovered while conducting training operations that the House of Horrors yields greater benefits to police officers–and consequently, those whom we serve–than we had ever imagined.

The following overview is provided to explain the specific process we've employed and the results we have documented so far during House of Horrors training iterations. (For information regarding the construction of a House of Horrors program, including the low-cost customized target systems we've fabricated, see Appendix Q.)

The House of Horrors Program

From start to finish, including the briefing and a complete debriefing, the course can be completed, on average, in approximately twelve minutes. Most of this time is spent during the debriefing. The amount of time spent actually dealing with the various stations from start to finish for this particular set-up is approximately three-to-four minutes.

When the course is set up with the manually-operated stimulus-response target systems we have designed, it only requires one instructor to run the program. Since only one student participates at a time, that yields an instructor-to-student ratio of one-to-one.

That means that similarly to the Level Three course, each and every member of the department participating in the Level Four course receives individualized instruction while participating in high-yield critical skills training that satisfies practically all of the current requirements and meets all of the standards mandated by statute and case law such as:
a) Moving targets
b) Reduced light training
c) Judgmental/decisional training
d) Use of cover
e) Realistic environments
f) Policy reinforcement

g) Force level integration and transition

h) Relevance to assignment (patrol, investigations, undercover, etc.)

Specific Goals

The primary purpose of our House of Horrors training program was originally to assist each officer in attaining, developing, and reinforcing their individual tactical thinking and operational skills and abilities thereby producing a more competent, confident, and safer police officer. As a result, we reasoned, more lives–law enforcement, victim, bystander, and suspect–would inevitably be positively impacted.

In addition, as the psychological conditioning methodologies we had previously identified as being present in programs of this type, i.e. Stress Inoculation, Operant and Classical Conditioning had been recognized and configured within the program to produce positive results, we anticipated that the program would also provide us the ability to:

- inoculate officers against the effects of stress and body alarm reaction
- assess officer behavior in realistic situations
- remediate such behavior as necessary
- uncover areas of training deficiency, both individual officers' and departmental, and correct them
- reinforce the use of good tactics and techniques
- decrease the use of poor tactics and techniques
- develop and assess judgmental / decisional skills
- test new tactics
- increase morale and confidence
- increase liability insulation for all department personnel

With these goals in mind and after weeks of preparation, we put the finishing touches on the House of Horrors course and prepared to begin training operations. Even though I had spoken with Colonel Applegate personally and been told by him that the House of Horrors format "had an unbelievable affect on the people who'd been through it" during the war years, as I walked through the narrowly configured rifle range we had converted for use during the course and gave the somewhat cheesy looking robot-mannequins (or the "range puppets" as Tpr. Johanna Lawlor would later christen them) a final test run, I couldn't help but have a moment of self-doubt.

"Now come on," the cynical cop-part of my brain taunted, "I mean, you can see the wires hanging there, and the puppets are so obviously, well, puppets! They're going to laugh you right out of the Academy, you screwball!"

The sheepish look on my face must have been apparent, because as I looked around at the other members of the fledgling FTU I saw it reflected in their faces.

Little did we realize that we were about to give thousands of police and military professionals a powerful experience that would alter the way they viewed their jobs, their weapons, and in some cases, their lives.

Because the real power, the well-hidden secret behind the House of Horrors had very little to do with what was actually in it.

It was really all about what was within the people who went through it.

The Theory in Practice

Before delving into some of the specific explanations and observations made during House of Horrors iterations, I need to explain the theory behind the program. I will do so to the best of my abilities, and strictly in layman's terms, as I am in no way, shape, or form any kind of psychologist, psychiatrist, mental health professional, or scientist, nor do I claim or pretend to be.

While I have taken courses in psychology, my understanding of these theories comes primarily from the study of works produced by highly-trained and skilled professionals like Col. Dave Grossman and Dr. Alexis Artwohl, and from conversations with other true experts in the field such as Dr. Anthony Semone.

My belief in the application of these theories comes from my years of training thousands of people while employing them and directly observing the results.

First, the equipment.

We are all issued a brain and a body at birth. Unfortunately, we are not issued an owner's manual for either one at that time. While many people do study and learn about how their bodies work, most of us go through our entire lives never truly understanding the theories pertaining to how our brains work, how our brains and bodies work–or don't work–together, or even why we do many of the things we do.

In regard to survival, using the Triune Brain Model as described by Colonel Grossman, the process can be explained like this:

While the human brain is an extraordinarily complex organ, for our purposes we will reduce it to three generalized components; the medulla (brain stem), the midbrain (mammalian brain), and the cerebrum (forebrain). It has been noted that the human brain, divided into these three sub-categories, can be seen as a model of evolution.[1] The medulla for instance–the relatively small tissue that serves to connect the spinal cord to the brain–can be likened to a reptilian brain in that it is only responsible for carrying out parasympathetic bodily activities such as maintaining heart and respiration rates.

For these reasons I refer to the medulla as the lizard when explaining this process.

Next on the upward evolutionary scale is the midbrain. The midbrain, comprised of a number of various complicated interrelating components, is where our subconscious mind lives, and can best be described for our purposes as the "animal brain." The midbrain's primary function is to keep the organism which within it resides alive–period.

The midbrain can best be described as the "puppy," because in many ways it is similar to a K-9 in that it can either be left alone to run wild or can be trained to respond to various stimuli in a number of different ways.

Finally, we arrive at the forebrain. The forebrain is the "human" component, if you will, the place where our conscious mind and all the unique parts of our personality that define us as individuals reside.

When facing a threat, what essentially occurs is this:

- the forebrain (you) takes in information / stimulus indicating imminent danger
- the midbrain (puppy) is immediately alert, and, based primarily upon its perception of the danger and prior experience, gets aroused to various degrees
- the puppy sends arousal signals to the medulla (lizard), which, being a lizard, simply responds to these arousal signals without thought, and activates various glands that in turn dump a number of powerful, naturally-occurring chemicals into the blood stream. These chemicals then elevate heart and respiration rates in direct correlation to the intensity of the puppy's arousal signals. In addition, these chemicals may produce a number of physiological side-effects, such as dry mouth, tremors, sweating, etc.
- the forebrain (you), already facing an immediate threat, suddenly experiences these physiological side-effects, and, if it doesn't understand what is happening and why, may become more fearful, triggering a stronger response from the puppy, which in turn triggers a stronger response from the lizard…

Now, what it most interesting here about all

these goings-on as far as we are concerned is that the puppy–our subconscious–will generally only respond to the threat based upon what it knows will work to save you. Furthermore, since the puppy–when startled into a fear state–is governed by what psychologist refer to as "biological imperatives" (i.e. Freeze, Flight, Fight, and Dissociate), it usually will try to plug one of these powerful survival-based response drives into the equation to try and save you.

In matters of survival based upon responding to an immediate severe physical threat from a member of its own species, the puppy will generally tend to want to fight or take flight. (Should the threat not be perceived as either immediately life-threatening and/or severe, other behaviors may be exhibited. The first of these, "posturing," may take the form of shouted commands or threats. The second, "submitting," may be expressed by the subject by holding up the hands, palms out, indicating submission to the threatening opponent.)

Since the puppy best learns how to respond through experience, that means if running away or submitting has saved the day in the past, the urge to flee or surrender may be overwhelming. If, however, fighting or posturing has been used successfully to control a threat in the past, then that will probably be the emitted response.

Obviously, for our purposes, we want the officer to do the latter in the vast majority of situations.

The remaining two behaviors, freeze and dissociate, may also occur, especially if the puppy has not been properly trained and/or prepared properly. While these behaviors may prove useful under certain limited circumstances (consider the potential victim who freezes in

place and is therefore overlooked by the predator) they are generally considered undesirable for our purposes.

As far as utilizing the House of Horrors program to train the puppy to respond reasonably and appropriately to a variety of situations, there is one other consideration that must be understood. According to many of the experts, the subconscious mind cannot differentiate between real memory and imagined memory. This indicates that any number of experiences / circumstances–if made real enough to the subconscious mind–can be stored in the subconscious, being effectively "filed away" for future reference.

While primarily associated with "imaging" techniques as used by many professional athletes (during which an individual visualizes himself performing some physical activity in a specific manner in order to aid actual performance), we have verified that this acceptance of imagined memory as real not only occurs during simulation training when there is enough stimuli to achieve a high arousal state in the participant, but is greatly *enhanced*.

This is the secret behind the powerful effectiveness of the House of Horrors program–while predicated upon simulated experiences, it is fueled by actual fear and adrenaline, resulting in stored memories that are nearly as vivid as any generated by real experiences.

Because officers are advised that there is actual potential danger to them in the form of mannequins armed with pain-penalty producing weapons; and because the officers know ahead of time that they will be required to make life or death decisions in a matter of milliseconds just like in real life; and, perhaps most important, because they are dealing with the unknown, they enter the course in a heightened state of stress and awareness. (In one experiment we did, an officer wearing a heart monitor reported an immediate increase in his resting heart rate from 77 to 84 just because he was advised he was the

---

[1] The Triune Brain Model, cited by Colonel Grossman in his work, was developed by Dr. Paul MacLean, Chief of the Laboratory of Brain Evolution and Behavior at the National Institute of Mental Health in Bethesda, Maryland. The model is being used in this work for educational purposes only and is not meant to be a literal analysis of the exact neurological processes involved in the activity.

next participant.)[2]

As soon as they begin the course, this heightened state of awareness is increased to the point where a true high arousal state is achieved. Once that happens, as far as the subconscious mind is concerned, everything in the House of Horrors is actually happening in real time!

Because the puppy believes it is real, several things occur. First, the puppy stimulates the lizard to start producing the chemical milkshake and injecting it into the officer's system.

Second, the body reacts to the chemical dump and brings about the physiological changes we would expect under the circumstances.

Third, based upon what we condition the puppy to do when faced with various threat stimuli, and how we reward it when it performs correctly and correct it when it does not, the puppy is trained and learns how to respond in ways we consider reasonable and appropriate. (Operant Conditioning)

Fourth, by providing these types of experiences to the puppy while in a high arousal state, we have allowed it to produce and store actual performance-based memories that it will draw from in the future when faced with similar situations, thereby allowing it to learn—in a controlled environment—both through its successes and mistakes (Stress Inoculation).

In addition to the benefits gained through the Stress Inoculation process, I believe this last element is also very important due to the fact that time and again officers have reported "remembering" entire accounts of similar real-world situations while responding to an individual House of Horrors event lasting no more than a few seconds, and will often base their present actions on their past experiences (see next section). Following this train of thought, it would only seem logical that the opposite would also occur, wherein officers would remember House of Horrors experiences during similar actual real-world events.

Finally, by having the puppy experience

(what it perceives to be) actual dangerous situations and allowing it the opportunity to successfully defend itself and others, we foster true confidence in its abilities to do so, as well as create a positive association with the techniques and tools (pistol, ASR, baton, etc.) it uses to accomplish its goals. (Classical Conditioning).

Regarding the very powerful Classical and Operant Conditioning methodologies that are such obvious and intrinsic components of the modern House of Horrors course, it must be noted that we did not simply add this into the mix—it was there from the beginning. And I do mean the very beginning. Early film footage showing W.E. Fairbairn guiding a soldier through the WWII version House of Horrors was used initially to format our modern version.

In essence, Fairbairn directed the soldier from station to station from behind, offering subdued guidance and support in the form of whispered directions and advice, i.e. "Go up those stairs, careful! Watch that door," etc.

At various stages throughout the course the soldier would be presented with a shoot/ no shoot/ or knife/no knife stimulus. If the soldier's response was correct (i.e. shooting when it was justified), then Fairbairn would reward him by immediately patting him on the back and whispering, "Good boy! That's the way!"

If the response was incorrect (i.e. shooting a no threat or "friendly"), then the student was corrected with an immediate verbal reprimand and the positive reinforcement pat-on-the back was withheld.

It is not known if Fairbairn and Applegate realized that the processes they were using were the subjects of experiments started during the first part of the Twentieth Century by researchers such as Pavlov and Skinner, even though Behaviorism came to be widely accepted among psychologists and the general public from the 1920s through the 1960s.

Regardless of whether they realized it or not, both processes were present and administered in the right way to produce positive results, a practice we have striven to continue.

The following "walk through the House of Horrors" is included to provide an overview of some of the things we have observed and learned while taking more than 4,000 trips through the course as presented, one instructor and one student at a time.

While results will vary depending upon course design and administration, a simple set-up as described in this section will enable normative behaviors to be quickly discerned allowing the instructors to immediately recognize problem behaviors that need to be addressed.

A Walk through the House of Horrors

Station 1: Threat Subject in Motor Vehicle

"Ready? Begin."

The words were spoken normally, almost subdued. The officer began walking down the alleyway toward a car parked on the right side, the instructor following from a respectful distance.

"Okay, check out the car first, then we'll move along. Remember, we may have an officer down somewhere around here, we need to find him."

The sun was high overhead, casting tight shadows on the ground. The car was too close to the wall to allow a passenger-side approach, so the officer angled himself slightly to the left, making the approach from the driver's side, slowly and carefully. A lone figure could be seen behind the steering wheel. The windows were up, glare from the sun making it difficult to see

---

[2] There has been a great deal of research into the effect of stress-induced increased heart rate levels on performance. While we did experiment using heart rate monitors, the equipment and resources available were such that I do not feel the inclusion of our results is warranted. For more detailed information regarding this facet of study, the reader should reference the work of Siddle, Grossman, Pomerleau and Lazzarini.

clearly within. The officer, right hand on his holstered pistol, body angled away from the center window post, rapped on the window with his left hand.

"Police! I want to talk to you. Show me your hands!"

When he received no response, the officer moved cautiously forward to get a better look within the car and rapped again. That's when he saw the gun being raised up from the subject's lap, muzzle pointed toward him...

For this station we used an old unmarked cruiser that was headed for the junk yard. Our friends at Fleet Section delivered it to the range; I built a range puppet to do what we needed it to do, and then simply figured out how to alter both to make it work. (See Appendix Q)

The responses to this one station were very enlightening. While the vast majority of our personnel reacted within normal parameters to this station, either by drawing and firing, drawing and falling back and then covering down or firing–"Good job!"–some responded in ways that I couldn't have predicted. In fact, we had more people injured while dealing with this first station than all the others combined.

While this was obviously never our goal, it was extremely telling. Because, as shown in Appendix Q, this range puppet did nothing other than raise his right arm while holding a replica pistol in his hand.

The injuries all occurred when the officer overreacted to this visual stimulus and fell, tripped, or stumbled, often crashing to the ground in a heap. Young and in great shape, or older with the former great shape all behind them, it made no difference.

Why would this occur? While some would probably guess that it was a result of inexperience, bad experience, or improper training, closer examination revealed otherwise.

The crash and burn response has not often been seen when training recruits, or new officers with just a short time on the job. It has most often been seen when training veteran officers who have worked primarily in uniform on the road, making numerous vehicle stops daily.

Among this group, no officer who had been involved in an actual road stop where a suspect displayed or fired a gun had exhibited the behavior. So what is the connection between the self-injured officers?

While I do not allow myself the indulgence of playing armchair psychologist, I am not averse to hazarding an informed opinion regarding this matter based upon my own experiences making road stops, all the activities and behaviors I have personally observed during years of training and operations, and after debriefing several of the officers immediately after the incident.

That being said, for what it's worth, the opinion I have formed is that this response occurred in these specific individuals with similar backgrounds and experience as a result of a combination of apparent conscious complacency and subconscious fear.

My belief is that, like all new police officers, these people began their careers making car stops while on break-in and then continued making them for years thereafter while performing patrol functions. Based upon my own experience, those first few car stops made right out of the academy are nerve-racking events, because you have been trained to watch for (and in many ways, expect) the suspect's gun to be raised–and so you do. However, after making a number of vehicle stops and not facing the raised pistol, I believe that many police officers begin to allow themselves to put that fear aside, and begin to construct their own "personal fable" regarding it actually occurring, i.e. "It hasn't happened, and *it's not going to happen.*"

Years go by. Thousands of car stops are conducted. The unthinkable hasn't happened. The approaches to the vast majority of vehicles are done in a "routine" manner. The conscious mind has in many ways rejected the very idea

Station 1: Threat subject in motor vehicle

instilled at the academy that danger lurks in every stop.

The subconscious mind however, the "puppy" whose only purpose is to keep us alive, has never forgotten.

And now the officer, perhaps a bit apprehensive because of the possibility of danger, begins to make yet another approach to a vehicle (this time during the training course), personal fable in tact, and suddenly–unbelievably!–there it is! The thing the puppy has been quietly fearing all these years is actually right there and BOOM! The survival response crashes into the personal fable and we have an officer down on the deck.

Again, obviously, we don't want any of our people injured during training. However, if this time-bomb is inside them, waiting to go off given that specific and very possible stimulus, then how much better to have it go off while in training–thereby diffusing it and recalibrating the officer's perception of danger–than on the highway where the badguys actually do shoot and traffic passes all too fast and close to the side of the road.

Other responses to this station also bear noting. Some officers saw the weapon come up and point at them and they just sort of gasped and froze, then looked awkwardly at the instructor and said things such as, "I should have shot there, or moved, or done something…"

These types of responses were handled by having the officer immediately do the station over, this time reacting in an appropriate manner. (Operant Conditioning)

Most of the officers who did respond appropriately by moving and/or firing exhibited a very strong sense of relief and accomplishment, having performed as they had obviously preplanned and expected they would–"Good job!"

Many officers who responded appropriately by moving back and drawing and firing into the threat subject often had a look on their face that indicated that while they knew they performed correctly under the circumstances, the action of firing into the human-looking mannequin in the car had been a bit unsettling. I usually commented at these times, "You did great, here, but it's a little strange shooting into something that looks so real, isn't it?" The normal replies were knowing looks and nodding heads, as they digested what they had just practiced–shooting another person in defense of their own life. (Stress Inoculation)

Station 2: No-Threat Subject (Hiding Man) behind Dumpster

The "Hiding Man" station had the officer check around a dumpster for possible threats while moving down the alleyway. The way it was set up, you could see the mannequin's feet sticking out around the far side of the dumpster, indicating it was in a sitting position, back against the wall, facing toward the alley.

Officers were advised on how to best approach, using the "slice-the-pie" technique to reveal more and more of the subject, while still being able to keep their distance from the subject and using the dumpster for cover.

Occasionally, an officer would decide to charge directly up to the dumpster, sidling around it and then jumping out to "surprise" and "get the drop" on the mannequin. (This "decision" may also be simply a subconscious reaction based upon past activities. A common exchange during the debriefing consisted of the question, "Why did you run up to the dumpster like that?" and an answer of, "I don't know!")

Most officers had already drawn their weapons while dealing with the Car Stop, and usually they would keep them out for the duration of the course given the specifics of the overall scenario, i.e. searching for possible downed-officer in a known dangerous area. (Note was made of how they held and oriented the weapon, as well as where they kept their trigger finger while dealing with all stations).

Regardless of the officer's distance from the mannequin, once the officer was in position to get a visual on at least part of the subject's body, the instructor pulled a wire and the mannequin pivoted from the waist, ducking toward the dumpster and out of the officer's view. When the mannequin moved, a series of tin cans with rocks inside them were also activated, adding an auditory stimulus as well as movement.

In the vast majority of cases, officers who had closed the distance between themselves and the mannequin tended to fire when the mannequin moved even though there were no weapons in the mannequin's hands or within its lunge area.

Close proximity seemed to produce a feeling of "not enough to time to respond" in the officers, and often resulted in an inappropriate discharge.

In many cases when officers had maintained their distance but had also placed their fingers on the trigger while covering/challenging the subject, inappropriate (startle) discharges would also occur when the mannequin moved and the noise stimulus was activated. In many other instances, officers who had their finger on the trigger but did not fire did exert enough pressure on the trigger to cause the hammer to visibly move slightly to the rear, indicating that they were able to maintain enough control to override the startle impulse.

As expected, the vast majority of officers

Station 2: The "Hiding Man"

who did not fire when the dual stimuli were activated tended to be those who:

- maintained a reasonable distance from the potential threat
- made use of the available cover and "pie-slicing" technique while issuing verbal commands and maintained trigger finger placement off the trigger and along the frame
- had some experience dealing with displaced/homeless persons while on patrol

Officers who did not fire were issued the physical pat-on-the back and the verbal positive reinforcement "Good job!" and were advised to move on down the alleyway.

Officers who did fire were asked to explain why they fired, to which they often stated, "because he moved." They were then asked if they saw a threat, to which most replied, "No." They were then asked if they were justified in firing at the movement, to which they responded, "No."

In several cases, when asked why they fired, officers replied, "Because he's a badguy."

When asked "What makes him a badguy?" one common response was, "Because he *looks* like a badguy."

In both instances officers were told to continue on down the alleyway, and to only shoot at immediate deadly threats.

Station 3: Threat Subject with Hostage

The next station the officers were presented with illustrated a scenario that is greatly feared and often portrayed in Hollywood productions.

This was the hostage scenario, wherein an offender is typically holding an innocent in front of him while holding a gun to the head of the hostage.

In this first version of our House of Horrors, this scenario was comprised of two stationary mannequins. While a real-world hostage situation would be much more dynamic, we used this station primarily to challenge the officer's perceptions of danger and to illuminate the difference between reality and the Hollywood ideal.

To this end, we first allowed the officer to deal with the situation as he saw fit.

Occasionally, the responding officer would take cover and verbally challenge and/or deliver a precision-fired round at the hostage taker ("Good job!"). The vast majority of the time, however, the officer would remain standing in the open–even though cover was available–and begin talking to the hostage-taker, using verbal commands to order him to drop the gun, or trying to reason with him and convince him to let the hostage go.

Quite often, the officer would do this while slowly advancing toward the threat.

At this point, the instructor would interrupt the scenario and ask the officer, "Out of the three of you involved in this scenario, who is in the most danger?"

The common answer was usually, "The hostage."

The reality of this type of situation was then either explained to the officer on the spot, or the officer was told that the threat had ended and was then instructed to continue on down the alleyway, the situation being revisited during the debriefing.

As for discerning the reality of who is in the most danger during this type of situation, the

Station 3: Threat subject with hostage. Though the hostage seems to be in the most danger, it is actually the responding police officer who faces the most immediate peril if proper tactics and cover are not employed.

following conversation would be conducted with the officer (with the most common responses following):

Q. "In this situation, if the hostage-taker shoots the hostage, what would your response probably be?"
A. "I'd shoot the hostage-taker."
Q. "Knowing this, do you think the *hostage-taker* would be inclined to shoot the hostage or keep him alive to use for barter and cover?"
A. "Probably he'd want to keep him alive."
Q. "Okay. Seeing this situation in front of you, especially if the hostage-taker was moving the hostage around in front of him as you would expect, do you think *you* would be fast to fire or slow to fire?"
A. "I'd probably be slow to fire out of fear of hitting the hostage."
Q. "That's a normal concern. Next question–if the hostage-taker decided to turn his gun *from the hostage towards you* and fire, would you be able to respond in time to fire first?"
A. "No. He'd more than likely be able to get off the first shots before I could respond."
Q. "So once again, out of the three of you

involved in this scenario, *who* is in the most danger?"
A. The common–and common sense–answer then given by officers to this previously unconsidered question was invariably, *"I am."*

Station 4: No-Threat Subject in Window

The officer was then instructed to proceed to the door leading into the House of Horrors proper. As the officer passed by the next station (a facade portraying a window with a curtain), the instructor pulled a wire which caused the curtain to open and an auditory stimulus to sound (in this case a wooden block attaching the curtain and the wire struck the side of the window frame emitting a loud knock), revealing a non-threatening mannequin we referred to as "Mr. Popow" due to the similarity of the case Popow v City of Margate.

In the vast majority of cases, the officer would whirl on Mr. Popow, but would not fire regardless of the movement/noise stimuli, even if the officer had fired at the Hiding Man (Station 2). When this occurred, the officer was rewarded with the positive reinforcement protocol (pat-on-the back, "Good job!").

Had the officer fired, he would then be asked to explain why he'd fired, to which officers often stated words to the effect of "because he startled me."

The officer would then be then asked if he saw a threat, to which most replied "No." He would then be asked if he was justified in firing at the noise and movement, to which the response would be "No."

The officers were then advised to only shoot at immediate deadly threats. Once they acknowledged this, they were told to proceed to the entrance to the House of Horrors interior and prepare to make entry. (Interestingly, most of the officers I have observed who shot at "Mr. Popow" whirled and fired very quickly, apparently at the sound, one hand on the pistol. This usually resulted in them striking the mannequin in the chest or face from distances of four-to-five yards.)

In regard to verbalization, while some officers did verbalize when exposed to this station, most did not, or more accurately *could not*. I say could not because I have observed more than one-thousand officers attempt to speak after the stimulus was given, only to hear guttural noises emanating from deep in their throats.

This inability to speak while under stress and involved in the heat of action is extremely common. Most officers reported that their "throat just closed up." Others actually recalled speaking, not aware that the words they thought they had formed and issued from their mouths never made it past their vocal cords.

S.L.A. Marshall noted this same phenomenon in his book, *Men Against Fire: The Problem of Battle Command in Future War.*

Commenting on the importance of communication between individual soldiers during the heat of battle, Marshall noted; "A chief fault in our men is that they do not talk. They are not communicative. In combat they are almost tongue-tied."

My belief regarding this phenomenon (based upon my observations) is that the tongue-tied state is a direct result of stress and the body's desire to channel all physical energy and efforts to ensuring its own survival.

However, since we know that the ability to communicate with others during high-stress encounters is vital to both the officer's and other's survival, we can and must continue to try and modify this behavior through training. By doing so, we accomplish the following:

● We assist the officer in being able to verbalize in order to identify himself in a professional manner (i.e. "Police officer!") to achieve better and faster control of individuals and situations.

● We ensure that officers will be able to communicate with one another during critical situations, allowing them to gain a psychological and tactical advantage over any adversaries

Station 4: No-Threat subject in window

present.

● We assist them in achieving a further psychological advantage as their apparent cohesiveness, tactical training and superiority as evidenced by their strong, vigorous, and professional communications with one another should prove demoralizing to any adversaries they are attempting to locate / apprehend.

Station 5: Negotiate No-Threat Stairway

Once the officer was prepared to make entry into the House of Horrors interior, the instructor gave him/her final instructions; "Okay, you're going inside now, be careful and stay alert. Once inside, head for the staircase on the right."

Once the officer acknowledged the instructions, the instructor would place his hand on the officer's back and say, "Ready? Go." (Usually, when placing my hand on the participant's back at this point, I could feel his heartbeat pounding in the chest cavity, even through the ballistic panels of the body armor).

The officer then opened the door and quickly entered the building, leaving the bright sunlight behind and entering a world of darkness and danger. (The officer was advised to keep moving should he freeze in the doorway, as occasionally happened).

In order to intensify the stress levels, this version of the program required the instructor to provide illumination for the student while inside the darkened interior. We used small but powerful Streamlight Stingers or Surefire flashlights with red lenses for the job. In this way, we could control the amount of visual sensory input, increasing or decreasing the stress levels as warranted, depending upon the student's responses. What we tried to achieve was a balance that kept the student in a high arousal state without inducing a panic state.

The student was then directed to proceed carefully up the staircase. At the top of the staircase the student had to turn left and cross a deck. Railings and walls kept the student from falling off the deck, and moving in the preferred direction.

The entire structure was painted black. As the student reached the end of the deck, the instructor flashed the beam of the light across (in this case) a motion-activated Halloween decoration hanging on the wall at head level. This particular decoration consisted of a small ghost with red eyes. When activated, the ghost's eyes flashed and a recorded voice repeated "HAPPY HALLOWEEN, HAHAHAHA" three times, loud enough to be heard over 100 yards away.

In the vast majority of cases the officers pointed their pistol at the ghost but did not fire. (A few officers have fired, apparently as a result of startle.)

The instructor then illuminated an old oil-on-felt painting of a tiger's head, which, again, in many cases, stimulated the student to point the weapon but not fire. (In fact, in all my experiences conducting this course, only two people ever fired at the picture. When asked later why they fired, they could not explain. On a related note, several officers have reported feeling uneasy when seeing tiger paintings similar to the one in the House of Horrors, not remembering until much later–or when reminded–that they were exposed to it while under stress during the course. (Classical Conditioning)

The instructor then illuminated the stairs leading down from the deck to the floor, whispering very quietly, "Okay, down the stairs. Careful, careful on the stairs."

Once at the bottom of the staircase, the student was instructed to move to the left, the instructor then directing him to a small room shielded by a curtain.

One of the first interesting discoveries I made regarding perceptual narrowing while running this program involved Station 5. Time and again during debriefings I would ask officers if they saw or heard anything on the stairs just minutes before, and the following answers quickly became established as the norm:
1. No, there was nothing.
2. There was some sort of ghost / demon / devil making some kind of weird noise.
3. There was some kind of animal on the stairs.

Those students who remembered the ghost /demon/devil were always asked to describe the noise or sounds it made. Very few ever remembered that it spoke words. Even fewer could recall exactly what it said. Most reported it made some unintelligible sounds.

I always asked them to replicate the noise for me, both because it was enlightening as well as entertaining for me. (I did spend a lot of time in that tunnel.) The noises they made were always nonsensical. Afterwards I would let them

Station 5: The Ghost greeting visitors

hear it again and they would usually recall right away that it said "Happy Halloween."

What I found most interesting about this particular station however was not simply that this information was lost or scrambled for them, but that other information was not. As I noted above, I always issued them whispered instructions about being careful on the staircase, while at the same time the ghost was loudly and repetitively yelling in their ear.

Therefore, my natural follow-up question regarding seeing or hearing anything on the staircase was, "Did you hear me say or do anything while you were on the stairs?" The answer that quickly established itself as the norm for this question was, "Oh yes! You were yelling at me to be careful on the stairs, and then you told me to go to the left once I was off the stairs."

Obviously, to my layman's mind at least, this bit of selective hearing was a prime example of the brain's survival mechanism functioning, excluding information it deemed unimportant while amplifying information it considered critical for its success. (More on this later).

As for the "animal on the stairs," very few recalled the painting at all, even fewer ever identified it as a tiger. (In these cases, for whatever reasons, people would remember it as a picture or stuffed animal in the form of a giraffe, cat, dog, wolf, elephant, etc.)

In regard to verbalization skills observed at this station, the following was noted:
- the vast majority of officers observed did not verbalize upon entry, nor while negotiating the staircase
- the few officers who did verbalize while entering and negotiating the staircase identified themselves in similar ways, in almost ritual form, i.e. "State Police, search warrant, State Police, search warrant..."

Not surprisingly, the officers verbalizing in this manner all had experience participating in narcotic / major crime entries, searches and

seizures. A smaller number of officers within this group actually verbalized in a natural, self-controlled and aware manner, speaking slowly and clearly while engaging each station, responding to what they saw and using their verbalization skills to help them achieve and/or maintain control (i.e. "Hey Joe"–referencing missing police officer being searched for–"where are you, buddy? We're here to help you..." "Okay, sir"–while speaking with man behind dumpster–"I'm a police officer, everything's all right, just show me your hands nice and slow..." etc.)

These officers tended to be highly-experienced, mature street cops who had seen a lot of action during their careers.

Station 6: Threat-Subject (Shooting Man) behind Curtain

The next station on the walk through the House of Horrors represented another common threat police officers may face at any time, a person pointing a gun directly at him.

The station was set-up with the stationary Shooting Mannequin (See Appendix Q) placed at the back of a small make-shift room.

A wooden chair was placed in front of the mannequin, a common low-wattage nightlight was hung to provide enough illumination to discern the pistol held at waist level, and a light-colored cloth was hung off to the side to add sensory input.

The mannequin itself was dressed in a dark T-shirt and baseball cap (see photo at right).

At the entrance to the room, a floor-length curtain concealed the interior of the space. The curtain was secured in such a manner that it had to be pulled aside from the right to the left and *then physically held open by the student* in order to deal with the scenario inside.

Upon approaching the station, the instructor would whisper instructions to the student, telling him that, "You've got to clear this small room in front of you. The curtain opens from the

134

right to left. Open the curtain and deal with what you find."

The student (left or right handed) would then generally grasp the curtain with one hand, hold it to the side, point his pistol into the room (holding it with one hand), and almost invariably immediately identify the threat as such.

The reactions from this point varied. In order of frequency, some officers:
1. immediately pointed their pistol and fired at the threat.
2. pointed the pistol and ordered the suspect to drop the weapon and then fired at the threat.
3. pointed the pistol and repeatedly ordered the suspect to drop the weapon without firing.
4. pointed the pistol and said nothing and did not fire.
5. dropped the curtain and moved back without firing.
6. dropped the curtain, moved back and fired through the curtain.

(Note: The number of rounds fired varied. While the majority of officers fired two or more rounds, many also fired a single round.)

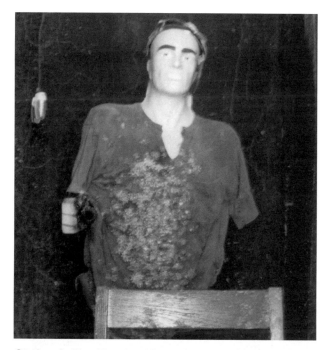

Station 6: The Shooting Man. Note overwhelming majority of Simunition hits in the center mass area.

If the officer took immediate action to effectively control the threat (reactions 1-2), he was given the positive reinforcement protocol (physical pat-on-the back and verbal "Good job!") and directed to the next station.

If the officer did not take immediate action to effectively control the threat (reactions 3-4), he was given additional threat stimulus in the form of shots being fired at him by the instructor-activated mannequin. When this occurred (approximately 3 seconds after threat had been identified) the following responses, in order of frequency, were observed:
1. The officer would immediately return fire.
2. The officer would immediately return fire and move away.
3. The officer would immediately move away and return fire.
4. The officer would drop the curtain and move back without firing.
5. The officer would drop the curtain, move back, and then fire through the curtain.
6. The officer would drop the curtain, move to the side, and then fire through the side curtain.

(Note: the number of rounds fired by the mannequin was usually one, though occasionally it would produce a double-tap. As in the case of firing at the visual threat only (prior to mannequin firing), the number of rounds fired by the officers after being fired upon was usually two or more, though there were many instances when the officer would only fire one round. In many cases where more than two rounds were fired, a string of five-to-seven shots were the norm. Instances of officers firing their weapons until empty were extremely rare.)

Again, if the officer took immediate action to effectively control the threat (reactions 1-3), he was given the positive reinforcement protocol (physical pat-on-the back and verbal "Good job!") and directed to the next station.

If the officer did not take immediate action

to effectively control the threat (reaction 4), he was advised to either take immediate cover or re-engage from a position of cover and take control of the situation, especially since the suspect's rounds would not be stopped by the flimsy barrier separating them. (This one consideration is significant in that most human beings, unless trained otherwise, tend to consider any type of barrier that blocks the view of the threat as sufficient to stop rounds from passing through and striking them. Conversely– and just as significant–unless educated regarding the matter, most people will also not consider shooting through barriers of any type in order to strike an adversary on the other side.)[3]

If the officer responded immediately after identifying the threat or after being fired upon by moving back or to the side and firing at the threat through the curtain, he would be administered the positive reinforcement protocol and directed to move on.

Personnel who responded in this manner would also receive additional instruction during the debrief regarding this option and the limitations that would need be considered as it pertains to police work. Given the specific scenario the officer was exposed to, (one suspect visually identified to be armed and alone in a small room presenting an immediate ongoing threat) this reaction would be seen as a reasonable response. However, officers were advised to consider the possibility of other uninvolved persons being present anytime the threat / threat area cannot be clearly seen.

Additional points of interest observed at this station have been identified and document-ed. They are presented here for consideration.

- While approaching the curtained room, everyone walked in a **low crouch**. In fact, while moving throughout the entire course, practically everyone crouched, especially upon entering the darkened interior environment.
- After pulling aside the curtain and seeing the threat, people overwhelmingly

squared their bodies to the threat.

- With rare exception, everyone extended and/ or fired the **pistol** at the threat while hold-ing it **in one hand**. (The station had been intentionally set-up to induce this behavior. Very rarely a participant would hold the gun even with the curtain while employing a two hand hold and push the curtain aside while canting the weapon, observing over the pistol into the room.)

Later, during the debriefing, the vast majority of participants reported that they held and fired the pistol at this station while employing a two-hand hold.

Most people reporting this were adamant about it, stating, when asked, that they would swear to this fact in a court of law. The partici-pants were then asked by the instructor to demonstrate the way they fired at the threat. Usually, one of two responses were observed:

1. The student assumed a two-handed grip on the weapon and pointed it at the closed curtain. The student was then asked if he fired through the curtain, to which (in all but a few rare instances as noted above) the answer was "no." The student was then again asked to demonstrate how he had fired at the threat. The student then opened the curtain and held it to the side while extending the pistol toward the threat with one hand. If the student let the curtain go to re-establish a two-hand hold, the view was blocked. The student then realized that he did, in fact, hold, fire–and hit the threat–with the pistol grasped in one hand.

2. The student pulled the curtain aside with one hand and extended the pistol toward the threat with one hand, momentarily confused, then stated, "Oh, yes, I guess I did only use one hand…"

I have been using the term "training memory" to explain this phenomenon. What I believe happens is this: since the vast majority of firearms training our officers have done over the past decades has required them to hold and fire their pistols almost exclusively while employing two hands, when exposed to any level of stress during which they are required to hold and fire their pistols, they tend to remember what they have *always done* as opposed to what they *actually did.*

- **THE SIGHTS ARE NOT USED.** Of the thousands of individuals (police and military) who have participated in the course, 99.8% have stated that they did not use, see, or think of the sights when engaging any of the threats in the program, with the exception of the Station 3 hostage scenario. (See Appendix B for more information regarding this subject). When asked why they did not use the sights, the answers given in order of frequency were:

1. **There was not enough time:** As for there not being enough time, as I stated earlier, there was a delay of approximately three seconds from the time the threat was observed/identified until the mannequin fired. The officer's pistol was already out, held and pointed toward the life-size threat that was located no more than fifteen feet away. Obviously, there was enough time given these conditions to raise the pistol, acquire the sights, and fire at the threat. The question of actual time, however, was not the issue. The true issue when dealing with dangerous situations under stressful conditions is the individual's *feeling* that there is not enough time to do anything but raise the pistol and fire. This is the human element that cannot be countermanded by the type and amount of firearms training police officers have always, and will most

certainly continue to receive barring significant unforeseen and unexpected changes in our society.

2. **I was looking at *him* (the threat):** My standard response to this answer was "Of course you were." You are facing an unknown potential threat alone in a darkened environment when you see a figure holding a pistol pointed at your body. Every fiber of your being is screaming out for more information and trying to decide what to do during what you feel to your very soul are the last few fleeting moments of your life–What the hell else would you be looking at?! As police officers in particular, our eyes not only will naturally be glued on the person we are trying to decide needs shooting or not, but they *must be trained to be there* as a matter of course so we can have as much information as possible in order to see exactly what that person has or is reaching for. Is it a pistol? A wallet? A badge? In turn, this fact demands we train our people to be able to fire their pistols and hit an immediate threat at reasonably-anticipated distances while staring at that threat and not at those sights that they won't see anyway!

3. **It was too dark to see the sights:** Well, actually, our pistols have Tritium night sights installed. They glow in the dark. A quick look at the pistol during the debriefing usually refreshed the memory in that regard.

Finally, regarding this contentious, hot-button issue of employing the pistol's sights at close combat distances while dealing with spontaneous threats, the majority of the .2% who claimed to use the sights recanted when asked to describe what they saw from the point they opened the curtain until they fired, their answers revealing that all they saw throughout the scenario was threat, threat, and more threat–no sights.

That leaves us with probably two individuals out of thousands who steadfastly insist they saw and identified the immediate threat at this station, raised the weapon, acquired the sights,

---

[3] Jim Cirillo provides one vivid account of this propensity when he relates the story of a police officer who had been knocked to the ground and had his pistol taken by one of the felons who had just assaulted him. As the felon pointed the pistol at the downed officer, the officer instinctively held his hand, palm up, in front of the muzzle. Each time the felon moved the pistol to get the muzzle clear of the upraised hand, the officer moved his hand, again "blocking" the shot. Thankfully, despite the felon's partner's inducements to shoot, the gunman gave up trying to get a clear shot and fled the scene.

and fired.[4]

My opinion regarding these individuals is... maybe they did. While I tend to accrue most of the claims of using the sights to the "training memory" phenomenon, I also believe that there are no absolutes when it comes to any form of human behavior / capabilities.

I know there are people out there in the world who can absolutely do things that the vast majority of people cannot. Why should this be any different? I also believe, however, that we must tailor our training to serve those in the vast majority, and not chortle on about how all "true professionals" must be able to perform contrary to the dictates of human nature, and that anything less is unacceptable. (I've always found it telling that statements such as these are uttered primarily by instructors who have never worked in the police trenches, or have only worn the uniform "part-time" because the actual business of police work interfered with their real job of selling their personas and their training courses!)

Station 7: Reflected Image

The next station encountered during this version of the House of Horrors program was a full-length mirror of the sort commonly attached to a bedroom door. The idea for employing the mirror was based on several factors:

- mirrors are commonly found in the environments police move through
- I and several officers I know have had the bejesus startled out of us on different occasions when coming face to face with our reflected images while clearing rooms during actual operations
- if World War II hero Audie Murphy could be startled enough to fire at his own image reflected in a mirror, then anyone could![5]

Responses to this station were as you would expect. The vast majority of people

Station 7: Reflected Image

exhibited the following reactions when encountering the mirror:

- sharp intake of breath
- immediate squatting down and squaring of body to the image
- immediate raising and pointing of pistol at reflected image (usually one-handed)

Occasionally, someone would fire at their reflected image, especially when operating in reduced-light environments.

Usually, there was some hesitation as the officer tried to process the familiar image, usually followed quickly by recognition.

During this momentary process the instructor would quietly confirm that, "It's all right, it's only a mirror, gets me every time too..." and then advise the student to move on.

---

[4] While debriefing dozens of officers over the years prior to the establishment of the New Paradigm program, I encountered a few occasions when officers would relate a bit reluctantly about how they acquired their sights while engaged in real-world close quarter spontaneous encounters. Usually these claims were made hesitantly, causing me to pursue the matter further, primarily through questioning that reconstructed the event step-by-step. It was only after ascertaining that the officer had not used the sights, but had focused on the threat instead, that the truth would be divulged by the embarrassed officer. The bottom line was, the officers claimed to use their sights even though they hadn't because they thought they had screwed-up by not using them as they had been taught.

[5] *To Hell and Back* by Audie Murphy

Station 8: Negotiate Hallway, No-Threat Subject (Turning Man)

After leaving the mirror, the officer was directed to a narrow hallway and told to enter. A common response was an unenthusiastic and concerned, "Go in here?"

"Yes," was always the answer, after which the student usually tended to crouch lower, walk slower, and hold the gun a little tighter in one hand while using the other hand to feel his way along the wall as he maneuvered down the "tunnel of doom."

Occasionally–especially on their maiden voyage through the program–a reluctant officer had to be encouraged to enter the hallway by a firm hand on the back and a steady push. On a few occasions, officers recoiled so vehemently at the very notion of entering the hallway that they needed to be ordered quietly but fervently by the instructor using the words, "We might have an officer down in here–Get in there!" (While some might argue that this would constitute "up-range stress," I disagree. While the order inducing the officer to move forward might be coming from behind, it was coming from an allied source. In addition, the order required the officer to deal with an unknown down-range stressor significantly more intense than the known up-range allied stressor embodied by the instructor. In this way, this situation actually mirrored real-world scenarios in a very realistic fashion, for officers are occasionally required to "encourage" other officers to move–or keep moving–into dangerous areas / situations while working).

At the end of the hallway, we had engineered a slight angle to the right. It was just beyond this turn that the hallway ended and the officer faced a closed door. As everything was painted black in the hallway including the door, officers first become aware of the door's presence when the shiny brass door knob was illuminated by the instructor's flashlight. At this point several common responses were observed:

- officers visibly regained greater degrees of composure once they realized that there was no immediate threat in the confined space of the hallway with them.
- officers tended to settle and regroup internally, bracing themselves for the next stressor–dealing with the unknown behind the door.
- occasionally, officers failed to observe the door knob, possibly due to perceptual narrowing.

This failure to see the door knob was most often evident in officers who initially balked at the idea of entering the hallway (causing me to suspect they may have had past negative experiences or reactions relating to close and/or dark environments).

When this occurred, it was not unusual for the officer to continue forward until he collided with the door. Finding himself in an apparent enclosure, it was not unusual for an officer–especially one already experiencing an arousal state high enough to induce the perceptual narrowing that caused him to miss the door knob–to exhibit signs of panic.

Occasionally in these instances officers would suddenly, desperately begin seeking a way out, eyes momentarily wide and vacant, pistol clenched tightly in the hand as it was banged against the surrounding walls. It was at this point that the instructor's trusted, calming voice and guiding hand was essential to maintaining safety as well as providing stress-control conditioning.

"Relax, take a deep breath, let it out slowly, look around, look around, what do you see?"

Within moments the doorknob would be spotted and a degree of composure restored.

The next stressor the student had to deal with was the unknown behind the closed door. The student was told to get ready *to open*–not kick in–the door. This was done for three reasons:
1) we want our officers to maintain the presence

Station 8: The Turning Man. Approximately 20% of all participants shot this this unarmed "officer".

of mind necessary for controlled action. Having them quietly turn the knob to see if it is unlocked, and then opening the door either slowly or quickly depending upon the circumstances helps them achieve this self-control.

2) we want our officers to consider other ways of entering a room rather than have them simply kick-in any doorway they encounter, for in the real world there are often uninvolved persons–sometimes very young, sometimes very old–on the other side of the door.

3) we initially spent an inordinate amount of time repairing and replacing doors on this station, which cut drastically into our training efficiency and supply of doors. (In one memorable instance, I watched as a rather tightly-wound officer booted the wooden door clean off its hinges, sending it flying more than thirty feet across the room.)

Once the door was open enough to reveal the "Turning Man" mannequin on the other side, the instructor illuminated the mannequin for one second and then, keeping the light on, pulled a wire (that was accessed through the wall inside the tunnel from behind the student) causing the mannequin to turn slightly more than 90 degrees, facing the student. The turn itself was completed in one second or less.

The Turning Man in this case was a 3D

molded sculpture equipped with no weapons. Both hands were plainly visible. In one hand at chest level a real police badge had been secured.

At this station the following responses, in order of frequency, were observed:

1. The officer, if not already in a very low crouch or even a kneeling position, would assume one, squaring the torso and **pointing the pistol** (overwhelmingly in a one-hand grip) at the mannequin, **and not fire**. **No verbalization** would be employed.

2. The officer, if not already in a very low crouch or even a kneeling position, would assume one, squaring the torso and **pointing the pistol** (overwhelmingly in a one-hand grip) at the mannequin, **and not fire**, **employing some type of verbalization** (even nonsensical noises made in an attempt to verbalize are included in this grouping). Verbalizations ranged from guttural stutters to "Police!" to "Easy brother, I'm a police officer, what's going on?"

3. The officer, if not already in a very low crouch or even a kneeling position, would assume one, squaring the torso and **pointing the pistol** (overwhelmingly in a one-hand grip) at the mannequin, **and fire** (usually no more than one to two rounds, one being the most common). **No verbalization** would be employed.

4. The officer, if not already in a very low crouch or even a kneeling position, would assume one, squaring the torso and **pointing the pistol** (overwhelmingly in a one-hand grip) at the mannequin, **and fire**, (usually no more than one to two rounds, one being the most common) employing some type of verbalization (even nonsensical noises made in an attempt to verbalize are included in this grouping).

If the officer did not fire, regardless of whether he verbalized, he would receive the positive reinforcement protocol–"Good job!"

If the officer did verbalize, he would be further rewarded with an additional pat on the back and the words, "Great verbalization, that's the way to do it!"

If the officer did fire–approximately 20%

of all participants did–the positive reinforcement reward would be withheld. In addition, the instructor would let out a quiet disappointed sigh that would often trigger a slumped shoulders, disappointed effect in the officer, who was usually already aware that he had fired inappropriately.

Later during the debriefing, questioning would reveal the following perceptions, actions and experiences shared by officers at this station. In order of frequency they were:

1. Most officers who shot would report that as the mannequin began turning, they could see a shiny object in his hand that they first interpreted as a threat. It was at this point that the decision was consciously made to fire. As the mannequin continued turning but *before the trigger had been pressed*, the officer consciously recognized that the shiny object was a police badge and not a gun. It was frequently reported that *at this very moment of realization the weapon would be fired.* Officers who fired stated that it was like the decision had been made and could not be called back–they could *not stop themselves from firing*. Since the mannequin completed the turn in less than one second the accelerated rate of cognitive thought can be seen through the detailed description of the event.
2. When asked why they did not shoot, the predominant reason given was, not surprisingly, either "because he had a badge" or "because I saw the badge."
3. One officer who went through the program was Gilbert DuVernay, the former Director of the Smith & Wesson Academy in Springfield, Massachusetts. Bert, a very experienced trainer, related the following regarding this station;

> "As I came through the door, I saw the subject begin to turn, and the light flashed off the side of the shiny object in his hand. At that moment, I recalled, very vividly and in great detail, a situation I had been involved in a few years prior. In that case, I was on patrol investigating a car parked in a secluded area. As I approached in uniform from behind the vehicle, two subjects, a male and a female, were visible in the front interior section of the car. It struck me as slightly unusual that the female was in the driver's seat, the male in the passenger seat. Suddenly, the male looked back at me with a startled expression, and began to turn in the seat toward me, raising his left arm. In his left hand I saw something both dark and shiny. In my mind I believed I was about to be fired upon. Part of my brain responded with *"THIS IS IT!"* as the other part reverted to my training. As I drew my pistol and brought it up to fire at the subject, I simultaneously realized he was displaying a wallet with a police badge. Luckily, I didn't fire. And that entire incident went through my mind as that mannequin turned on me, and that was one of the reasons I didn't fire here, because of that past experience. It made me look a little harder to see what it was."

Other observations:

Many officers reported that the mannequin did not move, but was already facing them when they opened the door. Others reported that the mannequin stood or jumped up from behind cover. Some officers stated that the mannequin walked or rushed towards them. Most recalled what actually occurred when the mannequin was turned for them during the debriefing.

Many officers had no recollection of this event at all, especially those that fired.

The majority of officers who did fire felt extremely bad about the situation, some deeply shaken. These officers were reminded that the reason for the training was to allow them to learn and make mistakes here, so they would be less likely to make them in the real world.

Once this station was completed, the officer would be directed to make a right turn, and then move to the left where a curtained room awaited.

As the officer moved toward the designated area, the instructor would slam the door to the tunnel behind him, adding more sensory input that would unfailingly induce varying degrees of startle response from the student, spiking the stress level.

Station 9: Threat Subject (Knifing Man) and No-Threat Subject (Victim)

The next station on the walk through this version of the House of Horrors would be the last, though the involved and often exhausted student wouldn't know this until it was completed.

This station was also set-up as a curtained off room. As the student approached it, the instructor would whisper these instructions: "Okay, you've got to check this room now. The curtain opens from the right." In addition to telling the student where the curtain opening could be found, the instructor would also illuminate the opening with the red beam from the flashlight. As the student located the opening and prepared to clear the room, the instructor would access a control wire located on the wall behind the student.

Almost without exception, the students would crouch as they prepared to open the curtain with their non-dominant hand, the pistol held firmly in the dominant hand. Most students opened the curtain quickly, immediately dominating the room and scanning. Some opened the curtain very slowly, trying to peek inside. Regardless of the method used to reveal what the room contained, as soon as the curtain was opened enough to see what was inside, the instructor would illuminate the interior of the room with the flashlight.

Inside the room were two mannequins. The first was lying on the floor immediately inside the room. This full-size, three-dimensional stationary dummy was dressed in the familiar uniform of a state police officer. Simulated wounds and blood were plainly visible on the face and torso. A pistol (plastic Redman training pistol painted black) was also lying on the floor next to the body. A common low-wattage night-light placed approximately two feet off the ground provided enough illumination to discern the badge, blood, pistol, and the rest of the area to the rear of the room.

Standing at the rear of the room directly in front of the student was the second mannequin. This mannequin, also a full-body, three-dimensional type, was dressed in dark pants and a sweater. In its right hand it held a shiny silver steel knife with a blade approximately four-inches long.

Approximately two-to-three seconds after the contents of the room were revealed to the student, the instructor would pull the wire slowly and steadily backward causing the standing mannequin to advance approximately 8-9 feet toward the student at about four feet-per-second. As the mannequin moved across the concrete floor on a wooden base with plastic wheels mounted to it, a rather loud trolley-like noise would be emitted.

At this station the following responses, in order of frequency, were observed:

If, upon opening the curtain, the <u>student saw the victim mannequin first:</u>

1. The student would **point his weapon at the victim mannequin** until the identity became apparent, and **not shoot the victim mannequin**. The student would maintain his focus on the victim mannequin and **employ some type of verbalization** (even nonsensical noises made in an attempt to verbalize are included in this grouping). Verbalizations ranged from guttural stutters to "Police!" to "Don't move" to "Police, I'm here to help you, buddy." In addition to verbalizing their desire to assist the wounded officer, some students would move toward the victim mannequin to attempt to physically aid it.
2. The student would **point his weapon at the victim mannequin** until the identity became apparent, and **not shoot the victim mannequin**. The student would maintain his focus on the victim mannequin and **employ no verbalization**. Some students would move toward the victim mannequin to attempt to physically aid it.

Station 9: The Knifing Man and Victim

3. The student would **point his weapon at the victim mannequin** until the identity became apparent, and **not shoot the victim mannequin**. The student would then scan the rest of the room and locate/identify the second threat mannequin, and take immediate action (as described below).

4. The student would **point his weapon at the victim mannequin and fire**. This response was rare, only observed approximately 1/3 of 1% of the time. Startle was usually the reason given during the debrief.

Again, each of the responses noted above occurred in the approximately two-to-three seconds *before the Knifing Man began to advance*.

Once the Knifing Man began to move toward the student, the student would redirect his focus to this threat mannequin, and:

a) if not already in a very low crouch or even a kneeling position, would assume one, squaring the torso and **pointing the pistol** (overwhelmingly in a one-hand grip) **at the moving mannequin, and fire. No verbalization** would be employed.

b) if not already in a very low crouch or even a kneeling position, would assume one, squaring the torso and **pointing the pistol** (overwhelmingly in a one-hand grip) **at the mannequin, and fire, employing some type of**

verbalization (even nonsensical noises made in an attempt to verbalize are included in this grouping). Verbalizations ranged from guttural stutters to "Police!" to "Stop!" to "Drop the knife!" to "Police! Don't make me shoot you!"

c) if not already in a very low crouch or even a kneeling position, would assume one, squaring the torso and **pointing the pistol** (overwhelmingly in a one-hand grip) **at the mannequin, fire, and then back out of the room. No verbalization** would be employed.

d) if not already in a very low crouch or even a kneeling position, would assume one, squaring the torso and **pointing the pistol** (overwhelmingly in a one-hand grip) **at the mannequin, and not fire, employing some type of verbalization** (even nonsensical noises made in an attempt to verbalize are included in this grouping).

e) if not already in a very low crouch or even a kneeling position, would assume one, squaring the torso and **pointing the pistol** (overwhelmingly in a one-hand grip) **at the mannequin, and not fire, employing no type of verbalization**.

f) if not already in a very low crouch position, would assume one while **backing out of the room** and **moving quickly away** from the station. **No verbalization**. (This obviously panic-induced response, rarely observed while training veteran officers, was most often observed in recruits or other persons with little or no police/military training. According to the tenets of operant and classical conditioning, this response would indicate that these persons had, up to this point, not been sufficiently trained to respond appropriately to these types of stimuli, or had at some time during their lives escaped injury/danger by fleeing, or both).

If the student did fire at the Knifing Man threat mannequin, regardless of whether he verbalized, he would receive the positive reinforcement protocol–"Good job!" If the student did verbalize, he would be further rewarded with an additional pat on the back and the words, "Great verbalization, that's the way to do it!"

If the student did not fire at the Knifing Man threat mannequin–approximately ½ of 1% of all participants did not–the positive reinforcement reward would be withheld. If, however, the officer continued to point his weapon at the Knifing Man mannequin while verbalizing for it to stop until the mannequin reached the end of its track and did in fact stop (usually approximately three feet from the student), then the reward would be given. This was done because the student *did* verbalize while keeping the threat covered, and *did* observe the threat stop advancing toward him.

While this course of action resulted in the student placing himself in greater danger than was prudent, the student did exercise extreme self-control (as evidenced by the continuing verbalizations), and did bring the situation (temporarily at least) under partial control, which could have led to full control in a real-world situation. While the action-reaction principle was discussed during the pre-briefing, students who performed in this manner–and could articulate *why*–were rewarded with the positive reinforcement protocol.

If, upon opening the curtain, the <u>student saw the threat mannequin first</u>:

1. the student, if not already in a very low crouch or even a kneeling position, would assume one, squaring the torso and **pointing the pistol** (overwhelmingly in a one-hand grip) **at the stationary threat mannequin** until the immediate threat / weapon became apparent, **did not fire**, and **did clearly verbalize** for the mannequin to drop the weapon.

2. the student, if not already in a very low crouch or even a kneeling position, would assume one, squaring the torso and **pointing the pistol** (overwhelmingly in a one-hand grip) **at the stationary threat mannequin** until the immediate threat / weapon became apparent, **did**

not fire, and **did not verbalize.**

3. the student, if not already in a very low crouch or even a kneeling position, would assume one, squaring the torso and **pointing the pistol** (overwhelmingly in a one-hand grip) **at the stationary threat mannequin** until the immediate threat / weapon became apparent, and **did verbalize** for the mannequin to drop the weapon, and **did fire** (usually one to several rounds).

4. the student, if not already in a very low crouch or even a kneeling position, would assume one, squaring the torso and **pointing the pistol** (overwhelmingly in a one-hand grip) **at the stationary threat mannequin** until the immediate threat / weapon became apparent, and **did fire** (usually one to two rounds), and then **did verbalize** for the mannequin to drop the weapon.

5. the student, if not already in a very low crouch or even a kneeling position, would assume one, squaring the torso and **pointing the pistol** (overwhelmingly in a one-hand grip) **at the stationary threat mannequin** until the immediate threat / weapon became apparent, and **did fire**, (usually one to several rounds), and **did not verbalize**.

6. the student, if not already in a very low crouch or even a kneeling position, would assume one, squaring the torso and **pointing the pistol** (overwhelmingly in a one-hand grip) **at the stationary threat mannequin** until the immediate threat / weapon became apparent, and **did fire** (usually one to two rounds), then **did verbalize** for the mannequin to drop the weapon, then **scanned** the room, **discovering the victim mannequin, pointed the weapon at it, did not fire** at it and **did not verbalize** to it.

7. the student, if not already in a very low crouch or even a kneeling position, would assume one, squaring the torso and **pointing the pistol** (overwhelmingly in a one-hand grip) **at the stationary threat mannequin** until the immediate threat / weapon became apparent, and **did fire** (usually one to two rounds), then

did verbalize for the mannequin to drop the weapon, then **scanned** the room, **discovering the victim mannequin, pointed the weapon at it, did not fire** at it and **did verbalize** to it, often identifying himself as "Police! I'm here to help you!" and occasionally adding "Are there any more badguys here?"

Again, all the responses noted above occurred in the approximately two-to-three seconds *before the Knifing Man began to advance.*

If the student, based upon the totality of the circumstances, identified the immediate Knifing Man threat mannequin and fired effectively (hitting it), he would receive the positive reinforcement protocol–"Good job!"

If the student verbalized, he would be further rewarded with an additional pat on the back and the words, "Great verbalization, that's the way to do it!"

If the student fired but did not verbalize, he would be asked to explain his actions during the debriefing. If he could articulate why, based upon the totality of the circumstances, he believed he was justified in shooting, then he was rewarded with the positive reinforcement protocol.

If the student did not fire within two-to-three seconds, regardless of whether he verbalized, then the **knifing man threat mannequin would** be activated and **begin to advance, knife raised, toward the student**. In these cases, the following responses, in order of frequency, were observed.

The student:
a) if not already in a very low crouch or even a kneeling position, would assume one, squaring the torso and **pointing the pistol** (overwhelmingly in a one-hand grip) **at the moving mannequin, and fire. No verbalization** would be employed.
b) if not already in a very low crouch or even a kneeling position, would assume one, squaring the torso and **pointing the pistol** (overwhelmingly in a one-hand grip) **at the moving man-**

nequin, and fire, employing** some type of **verbalization** (even nonsensical noises made in an attempt to verbalize are included in this grouping). Verbalizations ranged from guttural stutters to "Police!" to "Stop!" to "Drop the knife!" to "Police! Don't make me shoot you!"
c) if not already in a very low crouch or even a kneeling position, would assume one, squaring the torso and **pointing the pistol** (overwhelmingly in a one-hand grip) **at the moving mannequin, fire,** and then **back out** of the room. **No verbalization** would be employed.
d) if not already in a very low crouch or even a kneeling position, would assume one, squaring the torso and **pointing the pistol** (overwhelmingly in a one-hand grip) **at the moving mannequin, and fire**, employing some type of **verbalization** (even nonsensical noises made in an attempt to verbalize are included in this grouping).
e) if not already in a very low crouch or even a kneeling position, would assume one, squaring the torso and **pointing the pistol** (overwhelmingly in a one-hand grip) **at the moving mannequin, and not fire**, employing **no type of verbalization.**
f) if not already in a very low crouch position, would assume one while **backing out of the room** and **moving quickly away** from the station. **No verbalization.**

Again, if the student did fire at the Knifing Man threat mannequin, regardless of whether he verbalized, he would receive the positive reinforcement protocol–"Good job!" If the student did verbalize, he would be further rewarded with an additional pat on the back and the words, "Great verbalization, that's the way to do it!"

If the student *did not* fire at the Knifing Man threat mannequin–approximately ½ of 1% of all participants did not–the positive reinforcement reward would be withheld, unless the student continued to point the weapon at the Knifing Man mannequin while verbalizing for the mannequin to stop until the mannequin reached the end of its track and did in fact stop. (See above).

At this point of the course, the instructor would observe the student for a moment. The student's stress and adrenaline levels were usually quite high by this time. Students would commonly be observed to be breathing fast and hard, sweating, and scanning about for additional threats. Their pistols were usually held in one hand. The instructor would look to see if the trigger finger was in the proper position and if the weapon had been decocked. If not, the instructor would quietly advise the student to "Look around, look around, okay, you've brought it under control, lower the weapon now, decock, decock, decock, your finger's off the trigger now, along the frame, good job, you've completed the course, recover the pistol to the holster."

Upon hearing these words it was very common for the student to recover the pistol to the holster, look quickly around, then at the instructor, and ask, "It's over?"

Upon being told, "Yes, it's over, you did good…" it was also not uncommon to have the keyed-up student say, "Okay, thanks!" and then turn and begin to walk smartly off into the darkness, having no idea where he was going.

It was the juice at work in their bodies. The same juice that courses through our bodies when involved in real-world encounters.

By this point in the course, the primary objectives had been reached. The students had been exposed to a series of dynamic, high-stress situations that required them to make quick decisions and take immediate–and possibly life-altering–actions based upon those decisions. They did this while facing both danger and the unknown, pistols in hand, like they will be required to in the field, while stress-induced adrenaline coursed through their bodies, changing their perceptions and altering their body's physiological responses.

While in this state of high arousal, their proper responses were rewarded, their improper responses identified and corrected. They learned through experience how to better control themselves and their weapons while moving through dangerous, unknown areas and dealing with a variety of situations, environments, and individuals.

"What could possibly be better than this?" I thought after running the first officer, a veteran of my department, through the new House of Horrors course. The discovery came almost immediately.

I had intended to include a quick, immediate debriefing in the course from the outset. Initially I intended to question students primarily about mistakes that had been made, in order to provide immediate feedback, remediation and correction.

The very first questions I asked, however, would permanently alter the way we conducted the House of Horrors program from that moment forward.

Starting from the last station (Knifing Man and Victim) and working backwards, I asked the officer to simply, "Tell me what you saw and what you did here one minute ago." (The curtain had been closed again, and he was not allowed to see in the room while he recounted his experience).

A. Okay, I opened the curtain, and I saw a man lying on the ground.
Q. What did he look like?
A. He was hurt.
Q. How do you know?
A. There was blood.
Q. What did he look like?
A. I don't know.
Q. Did you shoot him?
A. No. Of course not. He was a cop.
Q. How did you know he was a cop?
A. Well, I don't know for sure, I mean he was dressed like a cop. I saw a badge.[6]
Q. Could you tell what department he was from?

A. No, I think he was wearing a uniform, but I don't know what uniform it was. I just remember seeing a badge. I think it was one of our badges, actually.

Q. What did his face look like.

A. I have no idea. I wasn't looking at his face.

Q. Did you say anything to him?

A. I think I asked him if he was all right. (He had not verbalized).

Q. Then what happened?

A. Then another guy who I didn't see at first started coming at me from the back of the room. (The officer's voice tempo and pitch increased at this point, body appeared to tighten slightly).

Q. What did he look like?

A. I don't know. But he had a knife.

Q. Can you describe what the knife looked like?

A. Yes. It was silver, had a long, shiny blade, and a dark handle, I believe.

Q. Where did he have the knife?

A. In his hand, his right hand I believe. (Holding his left hand up, then physically mirroring his body, as it were, until he reversed the image in his mind and held his right hand up.)

Q. Can you describe how he was holding it?

A. Yes, (holding his clenched right hand up near his head), he was holding it up, the blade out to the side, like this.

Q. Next to his head, like that?

A. Yes.

Q. Then what happened?

A. He came at me–I think I told him to drop the weapon, (he did not verbalize), then I fired.

Q. How many times did you fire at him?

A. I'm not sure, maybe twice, three times…?

Q. Where were you looking when you fired at him?

A. At his chest, you know, center mass.

Q. Did you hit him?

A. I don't know, I think so, did I?

Q. Yes you did. You fired three times and hit him three times center mass. You did good. (The instructor can generally see where the rounds hit because of the angle and especially because the instructor, who is not in a true high arousal state, suffers no perceptual narrowing.) Then what happened?

A. Then he stopped and you told me it was over.

Q. Let me ask you this, did you use your sights at all, you know, the sights on the pistol?

A. (Strongly) NO! What are you kidding me? There wasn't enough time. He was coming right at me. I just pointed it out at him like we were training earlier and fired.

Q. Okay. Now you've described what the knife looked like, right?

A. Yes.

Q. And you told me he was holding it up next to his head, like this (demonstrating), right?

A. Yes.

Q. Okay, good. Then tell me what his face looks like. Describe him to me.

A. (Looking sheepish) I can't. I have no idea.

Q. (Instructor, gently encouraging) Come on, was he white, black, Asian, Latino?

A. I think maybe white, but I'm not sure.

Q. Did he have facial hair, or was he clean shaven?

A. I believe he had facial hair.

Q. Excellent! Describe it please. You know, was it a mustache, beard, goatee, what?

A. Yes, I believe he had a goatee (indicating with his hand on his own face).

Q. Okay. And is there anything else you can tell me about the guy with the knife?

A. No–well, I think he looked angry.

Q. Okay. Now, getting back to the first guy you saw in here, can you describe what the injured officer's face looks like?

---

6 Many officers are wary of being "tricked" by instructors during training. That is one reason we make it clear before the course begins that there are "no tricks in the House of Horrors, everything is what it appears to be." In order to have an effective program, the students must believe that the instructors have the student's best interest at heart. Establishing–and keeping–this trust is a core consideration that requires a great deal of work and commitment by the instructors.

A. No, not at all. I'd be guessing. (I revisited this because both mannequins at this station, while dressed differently, were identical.)

At this point, I opened the curtain and showed the officer the scene again. The officer remarked that it looked quite different from how he had remembered it just moments before.

He was surprised to see that the Knifing Man was clean shaven and extremely pale. (In fact, these types of mannequins practically glow, even in low light, due to the plastic resin used to make them.) He also commented that the Victim Officer mannequin was much closer and much larger than he remembered, and that he couldn't believe he hadn't recognized his own department's uniform.

I suddenly realized that the House of Horrors program we had created–or recreated, to be accurate–was in actuality nothing less than a machine, a sort of combination "Pavlovian-Skinner Box" if you would. A machine that would not only allow us to better train our people how to react, but also show them *first hand* how this type of stress affected human beings both physically and psychologically! I then proceeded to debrief the officer on each and

Station 9: The Knifing Man. Officers could describe the knife in great detail, but not the face.

every station.

While this did significantly increase the amount of time required to put each officer through the program, I felt then, as I do now, that it is a must-do, at least for the first time an officer participates in the course.

The training value of the full debriefing is just too high to omit it.

In addition, as you'll see in the following section, many of the individual officer's perceptions pertaining to their actions and the actual circumstances presented at the various stations are faulty. By omitting the debriefing, these faulty perceptions are left intact. At best, this lowers the training value and results in confusion. At worst, the false memories and misperceptions become accepted as true memories, possibly adversely affecting the officer's future decisions and actions.

In order to more fully explain why I believe this so strongly, the following synopsis of general observations made during the thousands of debriefings we have conducted is provided.

Psychological Manifestations of Stress

Common Perceptual Distortions

All of the well-known perceptual distortions have been observed and documented while conducting the House of Horrors program.

As noted in the previous sections, participants have consistently reported and/or described experiencing:
1) *auditory exclusion* (not hearing or remembering what was heard)
2) *auditory magnification* (intensified sounds)
3) *tunnel vision* (only seeing or remembering seeing specific components of the total visual tableau)
4) *heightened visual clarity* (seeing specific components of the total visual tableau in high resolution / great detail)

148

5) *dissociation* (feeling detached from the events as they occurred)
6) *intrusive thoughts* (while some reported thoughts that were distracting, many reported thoughts that related to similar past experiences and were in fact helpful in determining action)
7) *time distortions* (time seems to be passing in either slow motion or fast motion)
8) *automatic behavior* (or "auto pilot," often linked with dissociation and memory distortions)
9) *temporary paralysis* ("freezing up"), and
10) *memory distortions* (including memory loss. See below).

Since most of these distortions are familiar to those with an interest in this material and covered in great detail in much of the current available literature, I will not delve into a comprehensive explanation of each of them here.[7]

I would like to offer the following information regarding some of these distortions, however, based upon personal experiences I've had both while working actively in the field and while conducting training operations.

Time Distortions

Time distortions, during which people and events seem to be moving faster or slower than they actually are, are a well known by-product of the type of stress induced during critical situations.

Many officers have described this distortion, most commonly relating how they and subjects they were dealing with suddenly appeared to be moving "in slow motion" during

the height of the action.[8]

A generally smaller percentage of officers report the opposite type of time distortion, during which people and events seemed to speed up.

The reason I am going into detail here regarding this common distortion is to add two observations I have made over the past few years I believe are relevant. Both observations, incidentally, indicate to me that the time distortion effect is experienced much more frequently, and recognized much less often than reported. If true, this factor both could and should influence training approaches in a variety of ways.

First, regarding the **fast motion perception**: our studies and experiences in the House of Horrors indicate that the vast majority of people facing what they perceive to be an immediate deadly threat *to them personally* will experience a feeling not so much of events speeding up, but rather of their own reaction time being too slow, making them feel as though they need to hurry or rush. I base this subtle distinction primarily on student's responses to the question, "Why didn't you use the pistol's sights?" when facing the immediate simulated threats, and the overwhelmingly adamant and common response, "Because there wasn't enough time!"–even though there actually was. (See "Station 6: Threat Subject (Shooting Man) Behind Curtain" in previous section).

Second, regarding the **slow motion perception**: during House of Horrors iterations it was extremely common for participants to describe events occurring in extreme slow motion–even though they *also* expressed the feeling of "not having enough time." (See "Station 8: Negotiate Hallway, No-Threat Subject (Turning Man)"). This description was identical to that of officers who had experienced and reported this distortion during actual encounters.

What I would like to relate here, however, is an (obviously subjective) observation based upon an experience I had while working in the

[7] *Deadly Force Encounters* by Dr. Alexis Artwohl and Loren W. Christensen is one such source that provides a good overview of these distortions.

[8] On a related note, researchers have hypothesized that this effect could trigger temporary paralysis if the officer experiencing it misinterpreted the implications of his perceptions, i.e. "Oh my God, I'm freezing up," causing him to then do just that.

field that strongly indicated to me that the slow motion effect is probably experienced much more frequently than realized.

Just prior to being assigned to the State Police Academy, I was working with a detective unit assigned to Suffolk County. One afternoon, I and several other officers were assisting the members of a local drug task force with a controlled narcotics purchase and arrest (buy-bust) operation.

The location where the buy-bust was going to occur was a house that had been equipped with hidden cameras in order to record the activities for prosecution purposes. As part of the takedown (arrest) team, I was to wait with my fellow officers upstairs in a room set-up with video monitors while the undercover officer made the deal with the suspect. Our job was to watch the monitors to ensure the undercover officer's safety, and, once the money and narcotics had been exchanged, to come down the stairs and take the suspect into custody.

Though it was the type of operation we had all participated in many times, we still prepared ourselves by assigning roles to each officer and practiced coming down the stairs and fanning out to secure the room. For while none of us had any information that would lead us to believe the suspect, an Hispanic male, would be carrying a weapon or would put up a fight, we realized only too well that you must always prepare for the worst case scenario.

And, contrary to the way these types of "war stories" usually unfold, as oftentimes happened, all the preparations and the investigator's opinions regarding this suspect proved to be–correct!

The buy, orchestrated by the experienced task force members and carried out by a highly skilled and competent undercover officer, went exactly as planned.

Upon being given the signal, the takedown team left the observation room and quickly made our way downstairs, around the corner, and took the suspect into custody without

incident. No weapons were found on the suspect, no injuries to anyone, drugs and money both safely in the good guy's custody, and the whole transaction caught on a videotape that was sure to ruin some defense attorney's day.

So what's the point of my recounting this incident? Simply this: about one week later, the head of the drug task force, the MSP's legendary Sgt. Mike Grassia, brought in a copy of the videotape, saying, "Hey, watch this when you get a chance, it went pretty good and we got the whole thing (transaction and takedown) on tape."

Naturally curious to see how the operation had looked from outside my own perspective, I played the video and watched the buy unfold.

Everything was exactly as I had remembered it from observing the monitor while the events had occurred that day in real time, one floor below us.

It was while watching myself come around the corner from the staircase and confront the suspect that I first realized that something had occurred that I never would have realized if not for the tape.

For I had experienced the incident and remembered it in the following way: I had come down the stairs quickly, first in line, pistol held at the low ready out in front of me. As I came around the corner, the seated suspect had looked up at me, a bit startled. Pointing my pistol at him, I slowly and calmly said, in Spanish, "Police! Don't move!"

The suspect, eyes locked onto mine, nodded slowly and said quietly, "Okay."

Keeping my pistol trained on him, I moved around in front of him so as to completely eliminate the undercover officer from my angle of fire, just in case the situation changed. As I did so, I could see the undercover officer get up and move away from the suspect in my peripheral vision.

Still locked eyes-on with the suspect, I then told him, again in Spanish, to put his hands on top of his head. Again he nodded slowly, said,

"Okay" a second time, and complied with my instructions. As I lowered my weapon but continued to cover the suspect, the contact officer moved in and handcuffed him. Once the suspect was safely handcuffed and searched, I recovered my pistol to the holster and we began to process the scene.

Again, while all this was business as usual, what had captured my attention so forcefully was that at no time during the activities described above had I been aware of any type of perceptual distortion, time-related or otherwise. The entire operation had occurred in "normal time" for me, neither faster nor slower than usual.

Yet on the tape, I was amazed to see that I had actually been moving, talking, and taking in information at a much faster rate than I had realized. Nearly double the speed I had perceived, as close as I can estimate it.

While many people might say, "So what?", for me this was quite the revelation. Suddenly a lot of loose ends were tied up. The old gunfighter saying, for example, quoted by Bill Jordan as "If you get in a gunfight, don't let yourself feel rushed. Take your time, fast." suddenly had a deeper meaning for me.

For if we, as trained and experienced police officers, could be reasonably sure that while engaged in dangerous or potentially dangerous situations, we were probably going to be moving *faster than we actually perceived*, yet with the same amount of control and skill possible at normal speeds, then this would mean that our chances of taking the right actions and being able to get there the "fastest with the mostest" was much higher than commonly believed.

And if this were true, then 1) our confidence levels in our skills and abilities could be realistically strengthened, resulting in us 2) being less likely to make the kind of mistakes often induced when we rush ourselves through the action because we feel like we "don't have enough time", even though we more than likely do. So take your time, *fast*.

Memory Gaps

The entire subject of memory gaps, or "critical incident amnesia" as Colonel Grossman and Bruce Siddle christened them, is truly fascinating.[9] It is even more fascinating when you experience one yourself, especially under controlled conditions so you can fully appreciate the magnitude of this effect. Approximately 85-90% of the students who have gone through the first version of our House of Horrors know this first hand, for this is the average percentage of people who experience at least one stone-cold memory gap during the four-minute long course.

It must be understood that I am not talking about a state of confusion, I am talking about highly educated, trained, and experienced people experiencing *lost time*–that is, not being able to recall anything about a dramatic albeit simulated incident they had participated in just moments before.

Although many studies have been conducted on this phenomenon and its existence is widely accepted, the intense reality of a memory gap must be experienced first hand to truly be understood. For even though someone can describe the effects to you, and you can grasp the concept intellectually, it doesn't become a concrete part of your reality until it happens to you.

Another problem with trying to study the phenomenon "in the wild," so to speak, by conducting interviews with people who have been through traumatic situations, is the fact that memory gaps are exactly that–*gaps*. Lost memory. In other words, I believe that many people do not report that they experienced memory gaps in the field, because they don't remember what they don't remember!

For these reasons, I strongly believe that a properly constructed and administered House of Horrors program can provide an extremely

---

9 Journal of the International Association of Law Enforcement Firearms Instructors, August 2001.

effective method for scientists and researchers to study the causes and effects of memory gaps and other perceptual distortions in human beings. For unlike in the real world, the environment, stimuli, and methods of administration can be kept consistent in this type of program. That means the only variables will be found in the individuals being put through the course, providing a degree of control during the experiments that is unattainable elsewhere.

In addition, it would also allow for immediate debriefings with the participants by a non-stress-affected, trained observer/researcher who would also be a witness to the events, and able to confirm or deny the participant's perceptions in a professional, constructive manner.

While I and my fellow FTU trainers have been doing just this for several years now, since I am not a trained researcher, I offer the following observations and opinions simply as that–my own, for whatever they are worth. The reason I feel such a disclaimer is warranted is because the things I have observed have led me to form some definite opinions–a few of which may be considered controversial.

It is my sincere desire that the publication of these observations and opinions are neither accepted as dogma nor simply dismissed as "junk science" by my peers and colleagues, but that they inspire further research and study by those more highly qualified than myself.

Memory Gap Theory

Why do people experience memory gaps during violent, stressful encounters? This is my simplistic layman's theory.

The forebrain (you) perceives danger. The mid-brain (puppy) activates, and then activates the medulla (lizard).

The lizard begins pumping chemicals into the organism (body). The body reacts as expected. High arousal state is achieved.

As the situation escalates, more chemicals are produced, and perceptual narrowing occurs. Tunnel vision, auditory exclusion, etc., are experienced, but for the most part the forebrain retains control and command of the total organism.

Then the event crescendo is reached–the immediate deadly threat (whether perceived or actual is of no consequence) is presented and at that precise moment the adrenaline spikes and the puppy pushes you out of the way and takes action, doing what it has been trained to do or what experience has taught it will best serve to save the organism. (I've been referring to this effect as "mid-brain override.")

Shortly after the immediate deadly threat has been eliminated or otherwise removed, the chemical levels subside enough to allow the forebrain to regain control of the organism. As the midbrain had been in control during those few critical moments however, and as the lines of communication between the midbrain and forebrain are rarely clear to us under even the best of circumstances, those few moments–including any actions we may have taken–are temporarily or even permanently lost to the forebrain.[10]

I arrived at this theory one afternoon shortly after commencing the new program. As I debriefed one of the officers I had just put through the House of Horrors, I asked about the noise the Ghost on the staircase had made.

As I had come to expect, the officer, who had experienced no memory gaps to this point, told me that the ghost had made unintelligible sounds that he paid no attention too, while I, on the other hand, continued to talk to him loudly and clearly as I directed him through the course.

Naturally, I had been whispering to him, as we had observed Fairbairn do in the old OSS training tape, but this selective hearing phenomenon was familiar to me by then.

---

[10] Memory Gaps induced in the House of Horrors often tended to partially "clear" either during the debriefing or shortly thereafter. It was not unusual for pieces of the events to be lost for longer durations, including permanently.

It was at this point, looking for some feedback from him about the reward protocol I had been using, that I asked him to tell me what I had said immediately after he had dealt with the "Shooting Man" station. As we had already debriefed that station, and he had recalled what had happened there (he had identified the threat, fired and hit it immediately), I was expecting him to tell me that I had patted him on the back and whispered, "Good job! Good job!," as I had done with every student from the first.

Instead, I received a blank look, and a suspicious, "What do you mean?"

Thinking he had misunderstood the question, I asked again, because there was no way he wouldn't recall me actively patting him on the back and telling him "good job" if he remembered me whispering throughout the rest of the course as well as what had happened at each of the stations.

But he didn't. In fact, he actually said, "You didn't say anything right away, but then you told me to move on down to the hallway."

Intrigued by this, I decided to try an experiment. The very next student (we trained up to twenty people per day, five days a week, for months at a time) I put through the course was treated exactly as the others with one exception. This time, when issuing the reward protocol, I didn't whisper. I yelled, "GOOD JOB!!!, GOOD JOB!!" and I aggressively patted him on the back at the same time.

Surprisingly, he didn't demonstrate any reaction to this, but then immediately responded to my whispered instructions to proceed.

During the debriefing, I asked the same question I had asked the prior student—"What did I say or do when you shot the man with the gun?" and received the same blank look.

No one remembered.

Eventually, when explaining to classrooms full of officers who were about to go through the House of Horrors for the second time, I would ask if anyone remembered what I said the moment immediately following their facing the Shooting Man or any other station inside the House. Generally, I'd get a room full of blank looks in return. Then one day, a K-9 officer said, "I think you said something like, 'Good boy! Good boy! ...' I remembered because I thought at the time that you were talking to me in the exact same way I reward my dog when he performs right!"

To this day, our instructors direct people through the House of Horrors quietly, and reward their correct actions loudly and proudly, with a pat on the back and a resounding, "GOOD JOB!," because that's how we train the "inner puppy."

As a final note to this aspect of the course, many officers have reported feeling a new and deep sense of calm within themselves after completing the House of Horrors course. While most express this feeling by stating words to the effect that they "finally feel like they could actually protect themselves with the pistol if they had to," many others can only say that the course has "changed them somehow," made them "feel different in a good way," "better."

After giving it some thought, I've come to believe that this can be explained by again employing the midbrain/puppy analogy.

Simply put, the midbrain (puppy) is cognizant of the types of dangers the organism (body) is exposed to at the direction of the forebrain (you).

Since the puppy's primary function is too preserve the life of the total organism, a great deal of stress is generated by this realization, especially if the puppy has not experienced and successfully dealt with these specific types of dangers before.

In a word, the puppy is afraid.

Naturally, this fear is conveyed to the forebrain, which only increases the amount of stress experienced by the total organism when faced with danger.

When enough fear and stress is experienced during a dangerous situation, and midbrain override occurs, then the puppy will take over and do what it knows from past experience (including training experiences) will control the danger and save the body. If there have been no similar past experiences, then the puppy will improvise, following whichever of the four biological imperatives seems most appropriate.

Should the biological imperative "flight" be seen as most likely to save the body, then the officer may break and run.

If "fight" is opted for, then the officer will more than likely fight as he has done successfully in the past–even if that method of fighting is not appropriate in this particular circumstance.[11]

If the officer has never engaged in any type of fight even remotely similar to the one he now finds himself in, then both the fight and flight response options may be activated simultaneously, possibly resulting in a "freeze" or "dissociate" response.

Now we take the officer and have him participate in the House of Horrors course. In a few brief but intense minutes he is exposed to a number of dangerous situations that closely replicate those he is most likely to face while working. Because a true high arousal state is induced at this time, midbrain override is allowed to occur, during which the puppy assumes complete control and takes action to save the organism.

Should it perform as desired and success-fully accomplish its mission, it is instantly praised and rewarded.

Should it not perform as desired, it is instantly corrected and allowed to perform the action again immediately, again being praised as it learns how it is expected to perform to save the organism.

Later, after the course has been completed, the puppy becomes more and more confident about being able to fulfill its primary objective as the simulated events are thought about and analyzed, their successful resolutions filed away deep in the subconscious.

The puppy is calmed.

Eventually (oftentimes immediately) this deep-seated feeling of confidence and calm is conveyed throughout the organism, inducing an overall feeling of having achieved more control of one's self, one's environment, and therefore, one's life.

The Power of Suggestion & False Memories

The brain hates a memory gap. I reached this conclusion after countless debriefings during which a disturbing side effect of the high arousal state was observed. In the great prepon-derance of instances during which memory gaps occurred, students could be fed very subtle suggestions as to what had happened or who might have been involved, and their minds would grab onto this information and fill in the gap. Male mannequins would be described as female, white as black, and so on.

Our intent during these debriefings was never to trick the students, only to see how sus-ceptible people could be to suggestion immedi-ately after experiencing a high arousal state. Simply saying, "Can you describe her–I mean, can you describe *who* you saw at this station?" would usually evoke a memory of a female when the mannequin appeared unmistakably male.

By having the student close his eyes and visualize the figure, we could lead them to a full but completely erroneous description: "Was she white or black?"

"White."

"Blonde or brunette?"

---

11   i.e. Occasionally we have observed officers reach out to grab or otherwise physically control threat mannequins armed with firearms, when the officer's own pistol was both available and the more appropriate choice. Usually, these officers have had a great many successful experiences controlling offenders physically. As a result, they often go on "automatic pilot" and take action in this manner regardless of the presence of a firearm, placing themselves at a huge disadvantage and more danger than is warranted or appropriate. Naturally, the opposite may also occur with inexperienced officers, whose first impulse when facing any level of threatening behavior may be to draw and or fire their duty pistol.

"Brunette."

"Heavy makeup or no makeup?"

"Heavy makeup."

"Can you see her clearly in your mind's eye now?"

"Yes."

The curtain would then be opened to reveal a bald male mannequin with a grey mustache.

Often the suggested memory was so strong that students would insist on looking behind the window frame to be sure we hadn't replaced one mannequin with another.

Another consistent pattern we noted indicated that in the absence of suggestions from an outside source, the brain tends to fill-in the memory gaps with whatever piece of loose memory may be available.

This was especially evident when asking students to describe mannequins that had presented an immediate threat to them. In these cases, it was extremely common to have students describe a no-threat mannequin from another station when providing their description. These descriptions were often very detailed, leaving no doubt as to the specific mannequin being described.

This often occurred even in cases where the student had good recall of the threat station. One of the reasons I believe this may happen is because the eyes are inexorably drawn to the specific areas it believes the information it needs to survive will be found. Since the actual threat will not be coming from the face area, the eyes quickly scan and generally seek out the hands, focusing intently there while looking for the gun, the knife, whatever.

So while enough of the image is taken in to form a complete mental picture (man holding a gun), there is a drastic disparity in the amount of information relating to what was deemed the vital components and the non-vital components of that image.

Long story short: in our mind's eye we've got a crystal clear picture of a small black pistol clenched in a hairy hand, an overall fuzzy image of a person holding that pistol, and a big gap where the face goes within that image.

The conscious mind, very uncomfortable with that gap, casts about within, searching for the rest of that picture. Now let's say that just prior to, during, or even immediately after that threat had been faced, there had been another person present, someone we had looked at but hadn't deemed to be a threat–allowing us to focus on their face for a moment.

Suddenly, this exact face surfaces from the internal ether of our subconscious minds, and the conscious mind grabs onto it and plugs it in to the unfinished portrait of our pistol-armed assailant.

Voila! We have a solid description, possibly even a positive identification if the true assailant has escaped, and our uninvolved face-donor is now deep in the jackpot.

What is truly unsettling here is that what we are then dealing with is not a lie, not a deception on the part of the person giving the description, or making the ID.

It is *The Truth* as they remember it. No way to dissuade them of this truth. No way to trip them up. It has become a true memory for them, and *though they are mistaken*, they are *not lying* when they point their finger at the face-donor and say, "It was him."

Perceptual Sets

Perceptual Sets can be described as perceptions or expectations that are established *prior* to an encounter that influence perceptions *during* that encounter.

If, say, you go into a situation strongly believing that someone has a gun, you may indeed see a gun during that encounter, *even if there actually is no gun present*. It is even possible that you may see and/or hear the gun being fired at you, rounds whistling by your head.

Oftentimes, all that is needed is something

to *suggest* what it is you are expecting to see, and your brain fills in the rest of the image. This image then becomes a mental "Kodak moment," filed away as true memory. This is, I believe, one reason officers are often incredulous when they have the opportunity to see what was actually there, especially when their true memory is so drastically different from the reality.

One common and less dramatic example of this we observed was found in student's perceptions of the interior layout of the House of Horrors. Set-up inside a one-room, enclosed rifle range, the space inside this area was actually long, narrow, and open. Inside this area we had built a small staircase and platform, a number of small curtained-off rooms, and a long, freestanding plywood hallway with a door at one end.

Time after time, while debriefing students and leading them out of the training area, they would look around quite stunned and say things like, "This is where we were? I thought we had gone through a couple of buildings, at least," or, "It's so much smaller than I thought it was, I can't believe this is the same place we just went through."

Another type of perceptual set was observed when students would fire at mannequins who moved but presented no threat, because they perceived the movement as threatening based upon the way the mannequin appeared: "He *looked* like a badguy!"

Other perceptual sets were also observed, such as students remembering seeing a specific mannequin they had encountered earlier in the day, when in actuality it was a completely different mannequin they had observed at the station just moments before.

The most profound examples of this type of perceptual distortion I observed, however, occurred only two times, but left a lasting impression on me. The first time I observed it in the House of Horrors was with a student who had been severely wounded by a knife-armed

Inside layout of the original FTU (2000) House of Horrors. Appears unremarkable until the lights are turned off and the "juice" is turned on. Any open space can be used for this type of training. Barns, basements, and unoccupied houses are ideal.

assailant in an actual police encounter. As we reached the final station, the Knifing Man and Victim, I carefully observed the student, for knowing his history I was concerned about how this station may have affected him.

Much to my relief, he performed outstandingly, actually challenging the threat-mannequin to "STOP! POLICE!" before aggressively firing and hitting it center-mass several times as it emerged from the shadows and came towards him, knife raised.

It wasn't until the debriefing a few moments later that I realized that something had occurred which I had not been able to see. For when I asked him to describe the weapon that the assailant had been holding, he described in great detail how the assailant had come at him while holding a double-barreled sawed-off shotgun.

After having him repeat the description, I readied him and then opened the curtain to reveal the scene. He was as confused as I was. For while a very few students had misidentified the knife as a stick or comb, never before had anyone mistaken the knife for anything so drastically different.

At the time I offered the following suggestion to him, to possibly explain this particular distortion. Perhaps, I reasoned, because he had been so grievously injured by such a weapon as actually held by the mannequin, his subconscious mind had translated the image into one that better represented the horrific damage the weapon was capable of inflicting–hence the double-barreled sawed-off shotgun.

Both he and I agreed that this was a reasonable explanation, and I filed it away in the back of my mind for further study.

Approximately six months later, I would observe this particular distortion for the second time.

Again, while running a student through the course who had been seriously injured by a real assailant with a knife, everything had gone as usual until the debriefing. This student, like the first, had performed extremely well, including at the final Knifing Man station. When asked to describe the weapon the assailant had been holding, however, the student responded by describing a "large machete" (holding his hands approximately two-feet apart to indicate length) that the assailant had been "holding up over his head."

While I can offer no concrete conclusions, I believe these two instances share too many similarities to be ignored. The implications are substantial, especially in regard to the possibility of an officer's previous experiences directly influencing their perceptions–and subsequent actions–during other unrelated situations.

The Johari Window

The Johari Window is a model used to illustrate how people can learn about themselves and others based upon the premise that people's identities can be divided into four sub-categories. These four categories are referred to as: 1) the **open self**, the part of yourself you are aware of and choose to show to others, 2) the

hidden self, the secret part of yourself that you are aware of and choose to hide from others, 3) the **blind self**, the part of yourself that you are not aware of but that others can see, and 4) the **undiscovered** or **subconscious self**, the part of yourself that neither you nor anyone else is aware of.

One of the first things I discovered while conducting House of Horrors training programs was that the once a high arousal state had been achieved, the Johari Window would be thrown wide open.

Simply put, you cannot hide what is inside of you, when you are inside the House of Horrors.

Many people who participated in the course performed in ways that surprised both me and them. Some individuals with reputations or personas as "high speed, low drag" types would fall apart while going through the course.

Others, who had very little actual operational experience would cruise through the course, making correct decisions and taking action instantly, oftentimes to their complete surprise.

In this latter category, a specific subgroup was identified that not only performed consistently well through the course, but also exhibited the highest degree of memory and recall compared to any other group during the debriefings.

The subgroup in question? While the first inclination might be to assume that the members of a tactical unit or narcotics unit would achieve this distinction due to the frequency with which they were involved in high stress entries and takedowns, the actual subgroup we identified as the most proficient and with the clearest recall were members of the Crime Scene Services (CSS) Section.

I remember being quite dismayed during the first debriefing with a member of this unit, for I was quite certain that the individual had possessed a great deal of operational experience based upon his performance and near perfect recall of events during the debrief.

"Narcotics work?" I inquired.

"No."

"Tactical team experience?"

"No. Never," came the reply. "I've been in Crime Scene Services for thirteen years, spent a short time working the road before that."

After several more members of the same unit (with similar backgrounds) came through the program and performed equally well, I came to see it as a definite pattern, not an aberration. Having worked in investigations of major crimes, I also began to form an opinion as to why this might occur.

Each scene the CSS officers respond to shares common characteristics. Usually, the scene is static, the actual crime having already been committed, with only the fruits of the crime being left. In the overwhelming majority of instances, these fruits will include the remains of a human being or two who has been beaten, tortured, shot, stabbed, burned, strangled, raped–or a combination of the above–to death.

Men, women, and children. Hundreds upon hundreds of crime scenes. Day after day, case after case, the CSS officers respond, take their photographs, fingerprint the corpses, collect their evidence, attend and document the autopsies, all in a methodical, regimented, professional manner, while suppressing the natural human feelings of revulsion, horror, and fear that these scenes provoke.

Put into this context and employing the inner puppy analogy again, one possible explanation becomes apparent. The members of CSS constantly expose themselves to the types of scenes that most normal people would recoil from. By sheer necessity, they inoculate themselves to the stressors embodied in the horrors they must confront at close quarters, while simultaneously conditioning themselves to notice, analyze, and record each subtle image before them.

Their thought processes, having been strictly disciplined to observe, analyze, record,

and even to initiate physical action (such as pressing the camera's shutter release button at the very moment that the horror is framed perfectly in the view finder) function as conditioned perfectly well in the simulated environment of the House of Horrors.

The result is a human being who functions extremely well working under stress generated by fear and while facing horror; who is able to smoothly initiate a physical action (such as pressing a camera's shutter release button or the pistol's trigger at the very moment the horror is framed perfectly in their view); and who is also able to recall what has been observed even when experiencing various degrees of midbrain override because the inner-puppy has been effectively conditioned to "heel" in the face of horror, leaving the lines of communication between the midbrain and the forebrain open.

Physical Manifestations of Stress

1. Common Physical Manifestations

As with perceptual distortions, many of the common physical manifestations induced by stress (and the powerful chemical cocktail dumped into the system as a result) have also been observed and documented while conducting the House of Horrors program.

Trembling, sweating, hyperventilation, and hyperactivity are the most common. Participants will also occasionally report feelings of dizziness, exhaustion, and even mild nausea.

Though sometimes exhibited during the conduct of the course, most of these physical reactions are usually most apparent *immediately after* the participant has completed the program and been told it was over. For it is *then* that the full effects of the chemical dump are felt.

This too is explained to officers after they complete the program, in an effort to eliminate the common misperception that these effects are simply "the fear catching up with you." For the truth is, the fear has been dealt with one way or another at that point, and what now must be immediately dealt with is the effects of the chemicals coursing through the bloodstream.

In this regard and on a basic level, participants are advised to drink water, stay away from stimulants like caffeine, and to perform mild calisthenics to help burn off the adrenaline.

2. Additional Physical Manifestations

To complete this chapter, I think it important to include a few other observations that have been made. While these also pertain to the stress-induced psychological effects experienced by participants during the House of Horrors course, they are provided in a separate section here because these effects result in actual physical manifestations that have been observed and analyzed to the best of our abilities. They are provided here for consideration.

Hollywood Stylizations

Holding the pistol up next to the head is a well-known Hollywood-inspired practice that is commonly derided in the police firearms training industry. Often referred to as the "High Sabrina" (named for one of the characters on the old "Charlie's Angels" television show), the technique as illustrated in the photo places the officer and those around him in a great deal of danger. For should the officer experience an unintentional discharge while holding the pistol in this manner, there is a very good chance that he may inadvertently shoot himself or someone else in the head. At the least, the officer could easily inflict serious injury to himself or others close to him by exposing their ears, eyes, and faces to the loud report and hot, high-pressure gasses that follow the bullet out of the muzzle.

Knowing this, we would assume that this specific technique would not only be absent

from any viable police firearms training program, but would also be highly discouraged. And so it has been within our department for decades. Yet we still see it occur both in the field and in the House of Horrors. The obvious question is *why?*

For the answer, I believe we need to once again check-in on our "inner puppy."

Picture this: the average American spends an inordinate amount of time relaxing by watching television and movies. As a result, police officers, like most people, have been exposed to uncounted hours of Hollywood violence and mayhem on both the big and small screens.

While watching all this violence unfold, our training-educated forebrains may often scoff at what the Hollywood screwballs do, such as holding the pistol right next to their heads to get that dramatic combination-shot of face and gun in the same frame. The midbrain, however, that inner puppy that learns best by experience, sits deep within our psyche observing through our eyeballs and assimilates what it sees. (Remember the phrase we use to describe the state of mind we allow ourselves to achieve in order to more fully enjoy the entertainment experience the movies provide, "a temporary suspension of disbelief.") And what the puppy sees is people moving through dangerous environments with pistols in their hands, and over and again it observes these people to hold their pistols up next to their heads, and so it learns the apparent lesson: *when moving through dangerous environments with a pistol in your hand, it should be held up next to the face.*

This is, I believe, the main reason police officers employ this technique–often with no conscious awareness or recollection, unless it is pointed out to them in training or the field. (The act of identifying and correcting this safety violation is much better addressed in training. While I have on occasion observed officers holding the pistol in this manner during critical situations in the field, there are usually too many other things going on to allow it to be addressed at the moment it occurs. As for addressing it immediately afterwards, either you, or they, or both will usually be too busy completing the mission, or will simply not recall that it occurred. In addition, there is always that awkwardness experienced when trying to correct another officer's actions, no matter how well intentioned the offering officer may be.)

It must be noted that I while I have observed this technique being employed in the field on occasion, I have rarely, if ever observed this technique while conducting or taking part in standard firearms training sessions. That is why it came as a bit of a surprise to me when I started observing the technique being employed by my fellow officers while taking them through the House of Horrors.

During one such memorable occasion, I observed a veteran officer slowly bring the pistol up to the classic High Sabrina position using a two-hand hold.

"Look where the pistol is!" I cautioned him.

The officer looked to his right and was visibly startled to see his pistol directly next to his face. He quickly returned it to the low ready position and continued to move through the course. Within no more than a few moments the pistol was again raised up next to his face, and again I told him to look at his pistol.

This time, after looking to his right and

The High Sabrina

practically striking the slide with his nose, the officer looked back at me with a confused expression and asked, "Mike! Why am I doing this!?"

"Too much TV!" I responded.

After staring at me for a moment he nodded and understood, again lowering the pistol and continuing the course. He did not raise the pistol again throughout the rest of the program. The reason I believe we were able to correct the problem there and then is 1) I had given his class a briefing prior to commencing the House of Horrors program during which I expressly commented on the Hollywood stylizations we had seen and why it was important to avoid them, and 2) once his conscious mind had been made aware of what his subconscious mind was causing him to do, he was able to take control and perform as we desired him to. This then allowed the puppy to be corrected, and learn how to move safely through a dangerous environment while holding a pistol. "Good job!"

Trigger Affirmation

I first heard this term used while training with Tom Aveni at the Smith & Wesson Academy in Springfield, MA, prior to my being assigned to the State Police Academy.

Tom mentioned that while conducting dynamic simulation training incorporating Simunition® FX Marking Rounds, the staff had observed students placing their fingers on the trigger with no apparent conscious awareness.

During House of Horrors iterations this propensity to unconsciously place the finger on the trigger when facing imminent danger was also often observed. Again, as with the Hollywood stylization phenomena, this activity was rarely observed during standardized firearms training iterations, surfacing primarily when the students were operating while in a true high arousal state.

As with the Hollywood stylizations, this activity can best be corrected on a deep

160

subconscious level while the student's midbrain is actively engaged in dynamic simulation training by making the student aware of where his trigger finger is, having him correct the placement as needed, and reinforcing the correct placement with positive feedback.

The Reassurance Grip

The *reassurance grip* is the term I've come up with to describe an unorthodox two-handed grip we've seen demonstrated enough times by different officers to rate its own moniker.

Never taught by our firearms instructors (or any other that I am aware of), this grip has appeared primarily during dynamic simulation training iterations. The practice of placing the non-dominant hand around the slide as shown in the photograph below, while obviously danger-ous, is performed without conscious awareness just as are the Hollywood stylizations described previously.

My first thought regarding this particular stylization was that it was perhaps a result of prior training and real-world experience with a long gun such as a rifle or carbine. If this had been the case, I theorized, then that might explain the use of the non-dominant hand in this

manner, for with a long gun the non-dominant hand would be held in such a manner, albeit far forward of the working mechanism of the weapon, up along the fore-stock or fore-end.

This theory was dashed, however, as interviews with most of the students who exhibited this stylization revealed they had no such prior training or experience.

Further questioning revealed that these students could provide no rational explanation for the grip, except to mention that it made them "feel better" holding the pistol in that manner. Hence the moniker.

Another interesting theory regarding this grip was offered by Greg Morrison after I described it to him during a telephone conversa-tion. He felt that it could suggest a subconscious desire to hold and employ the pistol as if it was a stick or club. "After all," he observed, "we have had more historical experience using blunt impact weapons than firearms, which are still relatively new tools, evolutionary-wise."

We addressed this physical manifestation of stress by again making the students aware of what they were doing, correcting their behavior, and reinforcing the proper behaviors with positive feedback.

The Reassurance Grip

Countering the Effects of Stress by Breathing

Controlling the breathing cycle to calm and strengthen the mind and body has long been practiced by martial artists.

A common "Zen breathing technique" requires the practitioner to slowly breathe in through the nose, allowing the air to fill the lower part of the lungs as well as the upper. Once the lungs are full, the practitioner then consciously holds the breath deep within the chest cavity for a few moments, usually four seconds or more. Finally, the breath is slowly released through the mouth, using the lips to regulate the flow.

The amount of power that can be developed through this process is incredible. Certain breathing exercises I have been taught over the years, for instance, produce the same physiological results as physical exercise, increasing both strength and stamina.

In regard to the statistically-likely police-involved gunfight, while some proponents of the Old Paradigm style of training still insist on incorporating breath control into the marksmanship-based shooting cycle (usually characterized by an acronym such as *BRASS*, for *Breathe, Relax, Aim, Squeeze, Surprise*), most instructors today will concur that the most important thing an officer should be concerned about in regards to breathing, is that he or she is *still able to do so* after those few terrifying moments are over.

Though I agree with the basic logic of this position, I also know from personal experience that police officers are often involved in stressful activities of longer duration than the typical police-involved gunfight. While these activities may eventually lead up to the gunfight (such as when an officer is searching for a suspect in a building or through a wooded area), they are, in and of themselves inherently stressful.

If this stress is allowed to increase unabated, it can reach levels high enough to drastically impair the officer's judgment, reaction time, and performance.

This is why we have been educating our officers about the proper way to regulate their breathing cycles before, during, and after dangerous and stressful encounters. In addition, we encourage them to practice this technique both when involved in static training on the range and especially during dynamic training in the House of Horrors.

The technique we use, while sometimes described as something fairly new under the title of "Autogenic" or "Combat" breathing, has literally been known and practiced for thousands of years. This in itself would seem to serve as a testament to its effectiveness.

To truly appreciate the stress-harnessing power of controlled breathing, however, you need to try it yourself.

Combat Breathing Cycle:

1) Breathe in deeply through the nose for a 4-count
2) Hold the breath, pushing it down into the lower abdomen for a 4-count
3) Blow the air slowly out of the lungs through the mouth for a 4-count
4) Wait for a 4-count before beginning the next inhalation
5) Repeat

(Left) Paul Wosny demonstrates another Hollywood Stylization seen during the House of Horrors program. We referred to this one as the "Peter Gunn", named for a television detective series popular in the late 1950s, early 1960s. This stylization is characterized by the officer holding the pistol pointed in one direction, while moving toward danger in the opposite direction, usually while moving close to a wall or other vertical surface. This was corrected by reminding the officer to always keep the "muzzle first to danger!"

CHAPTER SEVEN
The New Paradigm In-Service Training Program: One Day *Can* Make a Difference

All who think cannot but see there is a sanction like that of religion which binds us in partnership in the serious work of the world.

– Benjamin Franklin

Time and Money

"Just what do they expect us to accomplish in six hours?!"

This is a common refrain among police firearms trainers, for very often six hours of actual training time is the most an eight-hour training day will yield.

And in many cases, six hours is stretching it.

When faced with the realities of the time constraints, limited funding, and mandatory qualification courses that must be conducted in order to comply with state training requirements, many instructors simply hunker down, focus on the job at hand, and try to get everyone through the training day with as little difficulty as possible. If they are creative and motivated, they may also design an extra course of fire or two to put their people through their paces, increasing the realism a bit to make the day more productive and the training more relevant.

Very often the instructors will be facing a tough crowd, however. Too many officers view firearms training as a necessary evil, something that must be gotten through as quickly as possible. This is especially true in departments where firearms qualifications have been relegated primarily–if not entirely–to the single purpose of having department personnel put enough holes in paper in order to be deemed "qualified" with their weapons.

In many cases department instructors share this feeling, having also been exposed to this approach and sentiment for years, and will try to keep everyone happy by running a quick and efficient course of fire that will rival the fastest dry cleaner in the business–*"In by 9:00, out by 11:00!"*

Occasionally, motivated by haste or, as is more common, a desire to be a "good guy" and help out a fellow officer experiencing difficulty achieving enough hits on the paper target, an instructor may even add a few holes to the piece of paper with the ubiquitous 9mm, .40 or .45 caliber pen or pencil.

Combine all these elements and then add in courses of fire that seem to have little relevance to the officers' actual mission, and you can understand how many police firearms training days can prove to be less than productive.

In addition to time, money is another common obstacle to viable training. For many departments, training funds are often in short supply. Funds to cover personnel shortages created when officers are participating in training may also create additional pressures on police administrators. Very often, training is minimized or canceled altogether as a result of these budgetary pressures.

Another aspect of this problem can occasionally be found when the administrators responsible for disbursing funds throughout a city, municipality, or agency are either partially or totally removed from the realities of police work. Unbelievably, over the years there have been reports of administrators possessing these "bean counting" types of mindsets stating words to the effect that– speaking strictly economically–it is cheaper in the long run to avoid training than to pay for the occasional police funeral or law suit.

Other Considerations

After speaking with many officers and trainers across the United States, I have no doubts that time and money constraints comprise two of the biggest general impediments to viable police firearms training. While the degree to which this is true is dependent upon many variables, one of the more significant would appear to be the area of the country you work in.

Historically, police firearms training has been more of a political priority in some parts of the US than others. Many trainers I have discussed this with have expressed the opinion that there seems to be a direct correlation between the number of officers killed in the line of duty in any particular region and the amount of training time made available or required.

While I do not have enough information to properly analyze this theory, I can state from experience that police firearms training has not typically appeared to have been considered of critical importance politically to many people in the Northeastern United States over the past several decades. Paradoxically, during this same time period, we have experienced (based upon Uniform Crime Reports) fewer numbers of police officers murdered in the line of duty than have many other parts of the country.

While some might wish that this information could be used to indicate that there are fewer police murdered in the line of duty because we *train less* in this part of the country, common sense and logic dictate that the more reasonable conclusion one could deduce from this information is that the lack of emphasis on

training exists because, on average, there are fewer police murders.

One Human Life

In the end, of course, the fact that fewer officers are murdered in one area of the country as opposed to others is completely irrelevant as far as our interests are concerned. The fact that training involves expenditures of both time and money are also irrelevant, for while we must all work within certain bounds and constraints, our ultimate objective, our total focus, can be expressed simply as "one."

"One human life," Lt. Roger A. Ford once asked an administrative type at a hostage barricade situation. "What is it worth?"

The hapless bean-counter, blinded by overtime expenditure concerns, had interrupted Roger who was in charge of resolving the critical situation.

"Roger," the administrator had asked during a quiet moment, tapping his index finger on his wristwatch for effect, "how much longer do you think this will take? We've got a lot of officers here on the big clock (overtime), you know…"

That's when Roger turned, looked him straight in the eye, held his index finger up in front of the startled man's face, and said steadily, "*One.* One human life. What's that worth? How much time, how much money would you spend if it was *your* mother, or *your* sister, or son or daughter in there? How much would you be willing to spend to make sure they got out of there safely?"

A bit stunned by the quiet intensity of Roger's address, the bean counter apologized for bothering him and, as he moved quickly away said, "Of course, Roger, do whatever you have to, don't worry about the costs."

I have tried to apply this simple approach to training as well.

Lieutenant Roger A. Ford
1948-2002

Why One Day *Must* Make a Difference

In order to do our jobs as police firearms trainers, I believe we must first re-phrase the question posed at the beginning of this chapter.

"Just what do they expect us to accomplish in six hours?!" must be turned around so it becomes "Just how much *can* we accomplish in six hours!?"

I have taken this tact for the simple reason that it has been the only logical avenue available to me given the realities of the bigger picture.

My hope was that if we could provide our people–all of our people, from the Colonel to the newest recruit–with training that was self-evidently worthwhile to them all, training that would in fact make them safer while out there doing their jobs, that eventually the mainstream, somewhat negative attitudes toward firearms training would begin to shift. It only made sense to me that our people wanted to feel and be safer out there, just based on the fact that we all carry guns for a living and may be called upon to use them at any time and under any number of circumstances.

To date, the response from those who have attended our one day training program has been overwhelmingly positive. Many of our people have stated verbally and in writing that the training has in fact helped them feel and be safer out in the world while operating with gun in hand, more so than ever before.

That–not punching holes through paper for score–*is the mission*.

And I firmly believe, based on the empirical data we have developed and recorded these past four years, that one day can absolutely make a positive difference in an untold number of people's lives.

THE NEW PARADIGM IN-SERVICE FIREARMS TRAINING PROGRAM

The ultimate overall objective of the in-service program is to prepare each individual police officer as best we can to deal with extreme situations as he is likely to encounter while operating in the field. This includes working in populated and unpopulated environments while properly employing the firearm to control out of control behavior that is being exhibited by an individual or individuals.

According to current statistics, the average police-involved gunfight will occur within 20 feet. In fact, 85% of these gunfights take place within this 20-foot distance. More significant, 73% will occur within a distance of 10 feet, and, most significant, approximately 53% of these engagements will occur while the officer and offender are *five feet or closer* to one another.

The majority of deadly force confrontations will also occur under diminished light conditions.

Our training during the courses of fire is designed to reflect these realities.

The Program

The New Paradigm In-Service Police Firearms Training Program has been formatted using a progressive, building-block approach. Each individual module that comprises the total one-day program is designed to assist the student to accomplish specific goals. Each module is also designed to serve as the foundation for the module that follows.

Once the entire four-tiered program has been completed, the student will have progressed naturally from a static training level (positional marksmanship and skill development), to a dynamic level (moving, thinking and shooting), and finally, to a dynamic interactive level (thinking, moving, and engaging adversaries under realistic conditions).

An outline of each of the four individual modules is provided below. For detailed information please refer to Chapter Six.

Individual Module Outlines

DPTC No. 1 utilizes a series of exercises designed to assist the participants in developing and improving their individual skills with the pistol.

DPTC No. 2 involves firing a specified number of rounds from several different positions at various distances from the target. The distances and the number of rounds fired statistically reflect the realities of police-involved gunfights.

The target itself will serve as a diagnostic tool that will allow the instructor to gauge the ability of the participating officer to successfully deliver rounds to a specified target area.

The incorporation of the various positions, tactics, and techniques that are employed during the course of fire are intended to provide the participating officer with an opportunity to employ them safely under controlled conditions so they may best be learned and assimilated.

Trained and experienced instructors will also be able to evaluate the participant's ability to properly and safely perform these techniques under controlled conditions, and assist the participants in the improvement of marksmanship, safe handling skills, and additional techniques as needed.

DPTC No. 3 is designed to expose the officer to some of the physical (and to a lesser degree, psychological) realities that may be encountered during a dynamic, real-world, police-involved encounter. The scenarios that are used closely replicate police-involved situations that have occurred in the past, and that also have a high likelihood of occurring again.

DPTC No. 4, the final module, is the most intense segment of the program. It is intended to allow the participants to experience extreme force-on-force situations under controlled conditions in a training environment, where trained instructors will be available to provide information, guidance and assistance to them as needed or requested.

In addition, this course will also provide instructors and students with an excellent means of verifying the officer's individual skill retention levels, while allowing for the identification and reinforcement of strengths, the identification and improvement of weaknesses, and for the immediate identification and correction of any observed operating errors.

NEW PARADIGM POLICE FIREARMS IN-SERVICE TRAINING PROGRAM

NOTE: This single-iteration sample schedule is presented for consideration only. Timelines have been based upon one relay consisting of twenty (20) students maximum per iteration. Instructor-to-student ratios of no less than 1 instructor per 6 students are strongly recommended, though a 1-5 instructor to student ratio is preferred. Individual departmental policies and procedures must be taken into account when designing or modifying any use-of-force training program. (Please reference Chapters in Section One and Appendices in Section Two for detailed information where noted).

SAMPLE SCHEDULE

Classroom

0800-0830   **a) INTRODUCTION:** Primary Instructor introduces him/herself and assistant instructors. Explains what the day's training is intended to achieve, and what is expected of the students.

b) BRIEFING ON COURSE: Primary Instructor gives a brief overview of day's training, explaining why the training is formatted as it is, and why each segment is important to the students. A review of the department's Use of Force Policies and Procedures is conducted. (A copy of these policies and procedures is included in the handout/lesson plan.)

c) SAFETY BRIEFING: Safety forms are passed out, briefing is conducted. (App. D) Includes lead safety briefing and determination of master eye. (App. J)

d) ADMINISTRATIVE CONCERNS: Primary Instructor ensures that all paperwork (i.e. sign-in sheets, safety forms) have been completed and collected, and that students possess all required equipment needed for training. Also ensures students have been advised as to location of restrooms, water points, frequency of breaks and training duration. Students are queried regarding any injuries, illnesses, or other concerns that may affect their performance or participation in training.

Cold Range

0830-0915   **a) SAFELY UNLOAD ALL WEAPONS** (App. D)

b) PRESENTATION & RECOVERY EXERCISE: Instructor demonstrates, students perform. (App. K) All weapons must be safe, clear and empty.

c) ONE HAND PISTOL RE-FUNCTION TECHNIQUE: Instructor demonstrates, students perform. (App.G) All weapons must be safe, empty and clear (double-checked!).

d) STOPPAGE CLEARING DRILLS: Instructor demonstrates TIRR CLEAR DRILL. Students practice. Instructor demonstrates DOUBLE-FEED CLEARING DRILL. (App. H) Students practice. All weapons must be safe, clear and empty.

e) SAFELY LOAD MAGAZINES FOR DPTC No. 1: Instructor explains how to load magazines (with dummy and live ammo) & prepare for DPTC #1. (Chapter Six)

Hot Range

0915-1000 **SAFELY LOAD WEAPONS FOR DPTC No. 1:** At instructor's discretion, range may be conducted HOT from this point forward. Students will be expected to keep their magazines full, but will ONLY remove weapons from holster to load or unload chamber, and will chamber a round on-line only at instructor's direction or in designated SAFE DIRECTION. (App. D)

MODULE I: DPTC No. 1, Skill Builder Program: Precision Shooting / Point Shooting / Stoppage Clearing Drills / CQB Drills. NOTE: This course should be conducted one time. (Chapter Six)

1000-1100 **MODULE II: DPTC No. 2, Marksmanship & Safe Firearms Handling Skills Test:** NOTE: This course should be conducted twice; First employing no time limits, second time employing time limits. (Chapter Six)

1100-1145 **MODULE III: DPTC No. 3, Combination Drill:** Use of Cover / Moving Target / Verbalization / Judgment. NOTE: This is a very time-efficient course. It can be administered once or twice, depending upon time / logistics. Weapons can be cleared or students may reload with duty ammunition prior to lunch break depending upon policy / logistics (i.e. will students leave training area?) (Chapter Six)

1145-1245 **LUNCH BREAK**

Classroom

1245-1315 **AFTERNOON BRIEFING** (Chapter Six)

1315-1600 **MULTIPLE TASKS, ROUND ROBIN STYLE**

MODULE IV: DPTC No. 4, Scenario-based, Dynamic Encounter Training Exercises / Diminished Light Training: House of Horror Program (Chapter Six)

FAST TRACK PROGRAM (If needed) (Chapter Six)

WEAPON CLEANING, MAINTENANCE, AND INSPECTION

NEW DUTY AMMUNITION ISSUED

CRITIQUES FILLED OUT (Appendix U)

WELLNESS CHECK & DISMISSAL (Students are again queried as to any injuries or problems they may have had during the training iteration. Any reports of either should be documented and referred to the appropriate personnel / departments.

CHAPTER EIGHT
The New Paradigm Recruit-Level Training Program

The psychological time to arouse and create interest in pistol shooting in the mind of the recruit officer is when he is undergoing his training course and assembling his equipment. If he can at this time be given a course in pistol marksmanship he will be very likely to develop an interest in shooting that will be retained, if the means are provided for future participation in practice. It is quite evident from a study of the trend of police thought at this time that greater attention is being paid to the matter of pistol marksmanship for police officers... The courses of fire prescribed and the methods of teaching should be similar to those used for the military services, with greater attention paid to firing at disappearing silhouette targets under poor illumination. Silhouette practice should also include quick firing at very close range with the time limit per shot such that gun pointing and not aiming will be required to assure getting the shots off within the time allowed.

– Major William D. Frazer
American Pistol Shooting
1929

The Foundation

The importance of the recruit or basic level firearms training program cannot be overstated. Much is riding upon this initial introduction to police-specific weapon's handling and use. While the recruit level program naturally must address the issues of safe weapon handling and basic marksmanship, it must not be allowed to focus upon these facets to the exclusion of the weapon's primary purpose in law enforcement applications–the administration of deadly force when necessary to save the officer or others from death or serious bodily injury.

In a word, *combat*.

Configured and administered properly the recruit program will generally produce a safe, capable, and conscientiously-armed officer who possesses true confidence in his ability to defend himself or others with the duty sidearm should it be necessary.

Producing this specific result must be the goal because the ability to defend oneself and others when needed is the keystone to the foundation upon which an officer can build a solid, lasting and rewarding law enforcement career.

Should, however, the recruit level program be configured with the focus placed not on combat but primarily on the development of safe handling and basic marksmanship skills as is often the case, then the desired result as stated above may not be achieved. In many instances this type of marksmanship-oriented program will only produce an officer capable of safe weapon's handling and the ability to participate in and pass marksmanship-oriented qualification-type courses of fire.

It is imperative we recognize that these types of training programs do not properly prepare officers for the real world–especially since the majority of officers trained in this manner have realized this for years! Recognizing that the training they have received has little or no relevancy for the streets, many officers will have little faith in their actual ability to protect themselves or others with their duty pistol during critical incidents. This lack of confidence can translate into hesitancy, increased stress levels, and tragic mistakes in the world.

In addition, if the qualification-focused, marksmanship-oriented program is administered by instructors employing various "up-range stress" activities as noted in Chapter Four, then the results produced may actually be grossly counter-productive as opposed to simply less than adequate.

Multiple Goals

The recruit level firearms training program must accomplish a number of specific goals simultaneously.

First, it must provide enough information and physical skills training to allow a complete neophyte to develop into a safe, competent pistolero capable of using the handgun during crises situations well enough to save his own life or the life of another.

Second, it must be thoroughly researched and specifically designed to accommodate the needs of those officers in the program who have had prior firearms training experiences in the police, security, or military industries. This means that the instructors must possess a broad base of knowledge of firearms training techniques and approaches, so the rationale used to select the specific methods and approaches included in the program can be explained to these students' satisfaction. In addition, the program must be configured to "pick these students up" quickly during the training/learning curve, providing them with new skills and challenges as well as allowing them to achieve greater levels of proficiency with the duty pistol.

Third, it must establish and enforce reasonable standards of acceptable performance based upon the mission-specific realities of the job being prepared for, while also allowing the best possible opportunity for each individual officer to reach his maximum potential.

Finally, the program must prepare the student psychologically, physically, and emotionally to deal with the types of lethal force situations most likely to be encountered during the officer's career. This includes providing the

Trooper Donna Losardo watches over a member of a Recruit Training Troop (RTT) during the DPTC No. 3 drill. Trooper Losardo was instrumental in ensuring the success of both the FTU and the New Paradigm Program. She would eventually be promoted to the position of Director of the FTU and continue to develop the program during her tenure. She in turn would be succeeded by Trooper Paul Wosny, the current Director. The FTU was designed from inception to continue to evolve based upon the tenets established by the system. It was never intended to be dependent upon any one individual instructor. In this way, we hoped to ensure the unit's longterm survival and avoid the development of the "cult of personality" that arises in units that focus on tactical firearms training.

students with enough legal and procedural information to base their rational judgments upon, as well as interactive dynamic experiential learning segments during which they can begin to understand how the entire process actually meshes together during high-stress encounters when rational judgment is diminished and/or impaired.

Time and Money

Just as with in-service training, the issues of limited time and funding must be dealt with when formatting a recruit level firearms training program.

Too many departments across the country do not provide enough of either.

While this fact might surprise many members of the public, those of us within the police industry realize it to be true.

Any agency that provides its personnel with less than eighty hours of basic police firearms training is remiss. I have been involved with the administration of 40-hour recruit level programs (which is the norm for many departments across the US) and while it is possible to conduct a reasonable basic safe handling and marksmanship course in that amount of time, it is unrealistic to believe that the officers who participate in such programs are fully prepared to enter into society as armed members of civilian law enforcement.

The New Paradigm Recruit Program as currently formatted is comprised of approximately 100 (actual) hours of training.[1]

This includes the administration of a four-hour classroom-based *Mental Preparation for Lethal Force Encounters Course* prior to the start of the two-week long immersion program, and the administration of two days of additional range and classroom work after the immersion program has been successfully completed.

I realize that the amount of firearms-dedicated training time I have outlined here will seem like a luxury to many police training officers throughout the country, and as a minimal amount of time to a few fortunate others.

The New Paradigm Recruit Level Program has been developed to accomplish specific goals in a professional and efficient manner. As always, there have been parameters that we have had to work within. Many factors dictate what these parameters are; the size of the class, capacity of the range, number of trained instructors, amount of ammunition and attendant training equipment available—all must be included in the training matrix equation.

The two-week long immersion segment that is outlined below is the heart of the current program. It is adequate to assisting in the production of better-prepared officers. Yet, even with the positive feedback and results we've documented, I am not satisfied. A three week-long immersion program would be better, with officers participating in in-service training as soon as possible once they have graduated from the academy.

Then, if possible, continuous ongoing training structured along the same lines as the basic program should be administered quarterly (the ideal), biannually, or at the minimum, annually.

New Paradigm Recruit Program Overview

The following overview is provided to give the reader an idea of the type of program we have employed with a great deal of success. The schedule and content of the recruit level program was based upon 30-person classes and the employment of two separate firing relays.

Smaller classes were modified by adding additional courses of fire that allow individual students more exposure to all DPTC levels of training.

Should it be necessary to delete any specific course of fire from the schedule due to equipment failure or other reasons, then another course of the same training level type should be immediately available to be administered in its place. Time cannot be wasted!

Introduction to the Training

All members of the Recruit Class were advised up-front that they must satisfactorily complete the New Paradigm Basic Police Firearms Training Program in order to graduate from the academy.

They were further advised that all members of the firearms training staff would apply themselves fully to the task of properly and

---

[1] The numbers noted in the text reflect actual training hours. Meals and other breaks are not included in the tabulation of training time. Training days often began at 9:00 a.m. and ended at 8:00 p.m. This was possible as the recruits lived on-site at the academy throughout the training week.

thoroughly instructing and training each recruit in this critical discipline and that each recruit would be expected to apply himself fully to the training program as well.

The goal of the training staff was twofold. First, staff members would strive to assist each recruit to perform to the best of his individual abilities in regard to the tasks at hand.

Second, the staff would ensure that each recruit who completed the program had successfully achieved all of the stated performance objectives. This determination was based upon the recruit's ability to demonstrate both the physical ability to handle the issued weapon systems in a safe, proficient, competent and confident manner, and a sound working knowledge of proper law enforcement weapon's applications and justification for use.

Should any recruit fail to meet the stated performance objectives (as noted in the fully-realized lesson plan that each recruit was issued) by the completion of the New Paradigm Basic Police Firearms Training Program, then that recruit would receive additional remedial training, all of which would be thoroughly documented by the members of the training staff.

If, after all reasonable remedial training attempts (as determined by the Director of Training/Rangemaster) had been employed, any recruit still failed to meet the program's stated performance objectives, then that recruit would be subject to discharge from the program and the academy. (To date, we have had a 100% success rate. This does not imply that the program's standards have been compromised in any way. In each class there have been a few students who found themselves facing their final opportunity to meet the training standards. In each instance, to their credit and the credit of the staff instructor's tenacity and teaching ability, they have dug deep into themselves and found the resources to meet the challenge.)

Overall Subject Objectives

The recruits were then advised that the ultimate overall objective of the program was to instill the knowledge and develop the necessary firearms skills and confidence to enable each student officer to deal appropriately with extreme deadly force-type situations as he was likely to encounter while operating in the field as a sworn member of U.S. law enforcement.

This included working in populated and unpopulated environments while properly and reasonably employing the firearm to control any perceived serious life threatening and/or dangerous out of control behavior that was being exhibited by an individual or individuals.

The Program

NOTE: The Recruit-level Program as outlined here is a multiple-iteration, integrated training program. Schedules and training timelines were based upon thirty (30) students maximum per class operating in two separate relays. Instructor-to-student ratios of not less than one instructor to five students were maintained. While this outline can be used for reference by trained, qualified, and experienced police firearms instructors, individual departmental policies and procedures must be taken into account when designing or modifying any use-of-force training program.

The recruit-level program was formatted using a progressive, multi-segment building-block approach to the training. Each individual segment of training was designed to assist the student to accomplish specific goals. Each segment was also designed to serve as the foundation for the one that followed.

Once the entire multi-tiered program was completed the student would have progressed naturally from a basic introduction of the subject matter (safety, armorer's briefing, legal considerations overview), to a static training level (positional marksmanship and skill development), to a dynamic level (moving, thinking and shooting), and finally, to a dynamic interactive level (thinking, moving, and interacting with both threatening and non-threatening subjects under realistic environmental conditions).

An outline of each day of the ten-day, eighty-hour (10/80) training program is provided for informational purposes.

The New Paradigm Basic Police Firearms Training Program: Daily Overview of 80-hour Immersion Segment

Day One

The first day set the tone for the program. I advised the recruits that the firearms training staff were not drill instructors, and would not be performing as such. Rather, the primary mission of the firearms training staff was to ensure that each recruit was given safe, competent instruction that would allow them to excel throughout the course. In order to ensure the maximum potential for achieving these goals, the training cadre would allow the recruits to learn in a more relaxed, less stressful environment than they were required to operate in during other segments of their training.

During this same briefing, the recruits were also advised that while the instructors were not going to be acting like drill instructors, only the highest levels of self-discipline on the part of the recruits would be expected and tolerated.

Duty Pistols were then issued. The department armorer, Sgt. Marty Driggs, then provided a thorough lecture and training block regarding the function, disassembly, cleaning and maintenance of the duty pistol.

The Primary Instructor's lecture was then administered. Lesson plans were issued, performance standards identified and explained. Student Information Sheets were completed, and

each student was requested to provide a brief general oral biography. A written pre-exam was then administered. A review of the department's use of force policy was then conducted, followed by the first *Range Safety Rules & Regulations* briefing. Carry equipment was issued and the recruits were assisted in the proper placement of the equipment on the duty belt. An initial weapon familiarization regarding the disassembly and operation of the duty pistol was conducted, at the conclusion of which students were timed as a group both in disassembly and reassembly. These baseline times were recorded.

The next segment consisted of an introduction to safe weapon handling and operation skills. The Point Shooting Technique, stances, grips, trigger manipulation, presentation, and tactical recovery to the holster were all demonstrated (modeling) and thoroughly explained by the Primary Instructor.

After this two hour block was completed, the weapons were collected and secured for the evening. A copy of the text, *In the Line of Fire: A Working Cop's Guide to Pistolcraft* was then issued to each of the students for use throughout the program, and the class was dismissed.

Day Two

Day Two began with attendance, and then a quick review of the prior day's training. Any questions the students may have had were answered, and they were strongly encouraged to ask for clarification or explanation regarding anything told, demonstrated, or implied by any of the instructors throughout the program.

Weapons were then issued. A daily weapon clearing procedure using body armor to provide a safe direction was then demonstrated and instituted. (Appendix D)

An overview of the day's training was then provided. The *Firearms Safety Rules & Regulations Briefing* was conducted. Also included in this segment was a lead safety briefing, and a user-friendly explanation of the following subjects: how bullets function, point of aim and point of impact, configuration and functioning of both training and duty ammunition, and finally a block of instruction on how to load and unload magazines using dummy rounds.

Next, we continued with weapon familiarization (including disassembly, reassembly, and operation), safe handling and operation skill development. Loading drills (administrative, combat, and tactical) were introduced using dummy ammunition. (App. I) The administrative unloading procedure, stoppage clearing drills, and one-hand pistol refunction technique were introduced and demonstrated. (App's H, G)

After lunch break, we continued safe weapon handling and operation skills training, having the students demonstrate the presentation and police challenge, tactical recovery to the holster, and Point Shooting Technique (one & two hand) with empty weapons (dry-fire).

Trigger manipulation and convulsive grip exercises were then completed, after which the students were introduced to live-fire exercises.

This was a critical point in the training program. The approach I chose was to follow Applegate's recommendation and have the student's fire their first rounds from a close distance to the target while employing the Point Shooting Technique as they had practiced.

The drills consisted of a total of nine rounds fired from three yards. This was accomplished by having the students first load one round in each of their three magazines. Standing in front of the target, the students were instructed to assume the Point Shooting stance they had been shown and had practiced. They were then talked through the administrative loading drill which they had also been shown and had practiced with dummy rounds. Once the pistols were loaded, they decocked the weapons and stood at the Point Shooting low ready position. On the command of "Make ready, up!", they raised the pistol (as they had been shown and practiced earlier with an empty weapon) while staring at the target and fired.

As the first round left the pistol (keep in mind that for many of the students, this was the *first round* they had ever fired), a neural pathway that had been formed within them over two days was crystallized. As the students looked at their targets and observed the hole they had neatly created in the otherwise pristine silhouette, the sense of relief and confidence became immediately evident. They were then again instructed to administratively reload their pistols, and the one-shot drill was repeated twice more.

Magazines were then reloaded with two rounds in each, and the drill was repeated. This time the students fired both rounds on each command of "up".

After completing this drill, the students safely cleared and checked their pistols. This would be the first and last live-fire exercise of the day. The results of this type of introduction fire were both significant and lasting.

The students were able to successfully and safely load and fire their pistols at a man-sized silhouette target and achieve solid hits easily and consistently. Because they did not use their sights for these critical first shots, but rather employed the Point Shooting Technique and the convulsive grip, there were none of the problems normally associated with new shooters such as anticipation or improper trigger manipulation.

Students walked away from the drills with a sense of accomplishment and confidence. *This would be the foundation they would build their skills upon throughout the rest of the training program and their careers.*

After the initial drills students were introduced to the wonderful world of policing up brass and how to remove and replace targets. They then turned-to on weapon cleaning and maintenance, after which the weapons were secured for the evening.

Plastic "Redman" training guns were then issued to the recruits. These would be carried in their holsters when they were not training with their duty pistols. The Redman guns were also secured by the recruits in their lockers at the Academy each night using trigger locks we provided for them. In this way they began to develop essential off-range safe handling habits that would last throughout their careers.

Finally, after the evening meal, the recruits received a two-hour block of instruction regarding the specific legal issues that pertained to firearms and the use of force in Massachusetts. While the primary firearms instructor traditionally delivered this block of instruction to the recruits during past programs, I requested that one of the officers from our Legal Training Section format and deliver the block. Trooper Peter DiDominica, a veteran officer and attorney, reviewed the content of the overall firearms training program before formatting his class to ensure uniformity and validate the legal aspects of the program.

My feelings regarding this matter were simply that Tpr. DiDominica would be better able to answer any questions of a legal nature that might be posed than would I, as he had more training and education in this area than did I or any of the other members of the FTU cadre.

In addition, I believed that the inclusion of a subject-specific specialist such as Tpr. DiDominica (or Sgt. Driggs, the department armorer), increased the professionalism of the program as a whole, offering greater depth and as a result, greater liability-insulation for all involved. It also allowed for some lively discussions, during which many of the subtle nuances and shadings of the law were brought into sharper clarity for students and cadre alike.

At the conclusion of this class (8:00 PM), Day Two came to an end.

Day Three

After morning attendance and a quick review of the prior day's training Day Three commenced. Weapons were issued. Questions answered. *Firearms Safety Rules & Regulations Briefing* conducted. The morning ritual of timed weapon disassembly, reassembly, and function check completed.

Immediately after this, students were selected at random from the class and brought to the front of the room to demonstrate one of the following: loading drills, unloading drill, stoppage clearing drills, and the one hand pistol refunction technique.

This was done to accomplish two goals. First, it gave me a chance to see how the material was being received, interpreted, and assimilated by the students. Second, it put the class on notice that they could be required to demonstrate any of the techniques at any time individually. This, I believed, would prove to be an additional powerful motivator for them all to pay attention and work hard at developing the lifesaving skills we were attempting to impart to them.

The next subject tackled on Day Three was the use of the sights and the introduction of the principles of precision shooting. Wall and Coin Drills were used to assist the students in the development of smooth trigger manipulation. (App. J) Also explained and then practiced during this block was the proper technique for switching the pistol from one hand to the other.

Finally, the students practiced trigger manipulation, holding the pistol in one hand, arm fully extended in a safe direction while pressing the trigger fifty times in fast succession. They then placed the pistol in the other hand and repeated the drill. In addition to allowing the students to get a better feel for manipulating the trigger while holding the pistol in either hand, this drill allowed us to see who in the class needed to develop more hand strength. (Handgrips, rubber balls, and other exercises to increase hand strength had been recommended to the recruits prior to their beginning the program.)

The class then broke for lunch. After

lunch, we again reviewed the principles of precision shooting. The Master-eye Technique was introduced and explained, as were non-dominant hand shooting techniques, and positional shooting from the kneeling and prone. (App. N) The advantages and disadvantages of each position were explained. Next came an introduction to the concepts and techniques of the use and employment of cover.

A series of exercises were then demonstrated to the class, after which the students practiced while being coached by the FTU cadre.

Positional shooting from the holster (dry fire) while standing, kneeling, and prone, using both one and two-hand grips were rehearsed, as was the use of the Low Ready and Body Point Positions. (App. K)

Once all of the students had demonstrated the ability to safely perform each of the exercises (we were striving for baseline proficiency at this point, not perfection), we headed into the range and commenced with a series of live fire drills. These drills are provided on the facing page.

After completing these exercises, the recruits cleared and checked their weapons, policed the range, and secured their pistols for evening chow.

Upon returning from dinner, the recruits were then introduced to DPTC No.1, the Skill Builder Course. (Chapter 6)

The course was administered using slow-fire, each stage being demonstrated and explained to them before they participated. The Close Proximity Drill (CPD) was carefully explained, and the students performed multiple repetitions of this critical drill slowly and by the numbers at first, progressing to the point where they performed the drill at their own cadence at approximately ¾ speed. (App. K)

After completing DPTC No. 1, the students cleaned and secured their weapons, and were released back into the care of the Drill Instructors for the evening.

Day Four

Attendance, review of the prior day's training, and weapons issued. Questions answered. *Firearms Safety Rules & Regulations Briefing* conducted. The morning ritual of timed weapon disassembly, reassembly, and function check completed. Students were observed becoming very proficient at this exercise, all demonstrated positive attitudes toward their individual sidearms. Confidence with their skills continued to grow.

During the overview of the day's activities, students were advised that they would begin participating in both Firearms Simulation Training (FATS) and the House of Horrors Program this day. Eyes widened. Students had been briefed regarding the House of Horrors Program prior to beginning the program, and the curious mixture of fear, anticipation, excitement, and dread was palpable.

This was understandable, as they would all be involved in at least one gunfight before the end of the day.

During the rest of the morning segment, we reviewed safe weapon handling and operation skill development, to include loading, unloading, stoppage clearing, one hand pistol refunction technique, non dominant hand and precision shooting techniques, and positional shooting methods.

After completing the review and answering any questions the students had, we proceeded to the range.

DPTC No. 2, the Marksmanship and Safe Handling Skills Assessment course was then administered. As with DPTC No. 1, this course was conducted slow-fire, step by step, with full demonstrations and thorough explanations given. (Chapter 6)

After the students completed the course, they participated in it a second time. This iteration was completed with fewer demonstrations, and explanations were given only when asked for, or when they were apparently needed.

COURSE OF FIRE: 42 ROUNDS (Originally designed for .40 Cal. SIG P226)

SAMPLE LEVEL ONE DUTY PISTOL TRAINING COURSE (DPTC)
(Skill Development, Individual)

Live Fire Exercises, Point Shooting & Precision (Sighted) Shooting, Reload Drills

Note: Load **one round** in each of three magazines

Distance	Technique	# Rounds	# Reps
5 Yards	**Point Shooting** (one hand) from Low Ready Position	1	3
	Demonstrate **Administrative Reload** between reps		

Note: Load **two rounds** in each of three magazines

5 Yards	**Point Shooting** (one hand) from Holster	1	3
	Demonstrate **Tactical Reload** between repetitions		

Note: Load **six rounds** in each of three magazines

Magazine #1

5 Yards	**Point Shooting** (one hand) from Holster	1	3
5 Yards	**Point Shooting** (two hands) from Holster	1	3

Magazine #2

5 Yards	**Point Shooting** (one hand) from Holster	2	3

Magazine #3

5 Yards	**Point Shooting** (two hands) from Holster	2	3
	Demonstrate **Combat Reload** when changing magazines		

Note: Load **six rounds** in each of three magazines. **Administrative Load** Magazine #1

Magazine #1

4 Yards	**Precision Shooting** (two hands) from Low Ready All six shots fired double-action. **Tactical Reload**	1	6

Magazine #2

4 Yards	**Precision Shooting** (two hands) from Low Ready First shot fired double-action, remaining fired single-action. **Combat Reload**	6	1

Magazine #3

4 Yards	**Precision Shooting** (two hands) from Low Ready First shot fired double-action, remaining fired single-action.	6	1

The student's confidence and smoothness at this point in the program was evident to all. The few students who demonstrated any continued weaknesses in technique or understanding were also identified during this block. They would receive additional one-on-one assistance (Fast Track) during the evening block.

After lunch break, students were introduced to the first "round robin" series of training exercises. Because students participated in the House of Horrors individually, and in small numbers while taking part in FATS training, the afternoon program was broken into three components; 1) *Classroom*: FATS Training, 2) *Range*: Introduction to movement with the pistol, engaging moving targets, and participation in DPTC No. 3 (Combination Drill, dry-fire first, then slow fire at a slowly moving target), and 3) The House of Horrors. (Ch. 6)

Each of these components was run simultaneously until dinner time.

After evening chow, the House of Horrors and FAT'S components were continued. (With so many students, these components usually required two days to complete the first time through.) The Fast Track program was also implemented for those students that required it. (On average, out of thirty students approximately 6 (20%) would require additional individual coaching and attention at this point). Another classroom segment focusing on specific weapon nomenclature was also administered during this block, and weapon cleaning was also conducted. Training continued until 8:00 PM.

Day Five

Friday, end of the first training week. This day's training segment was limited to three hours, 9:00 AM - 12:00 PM. Attendance, review of the prior day's training, and weapons were issued. Questions answered. *Firearms Safety Rules & Regulations Briefing* conducted. Timed weapon disassembly, reassembly, and function check completed.

Morale was extremely high, participation in the House of Horrors Course and FAT'S training having had an enormous positive impact. Students reported having a "totally different perspective" about the training and their weapons after having used both to negotiate the "House."

Many positive comments were offered by the students in this regard, especially by those with prior military or civilian law enforcement firearms training.

"We never did anything like this," was a common refrain, as were glowing commendations about the Point Shooting Technique, most to the effect of "It really works!"

For the rest of the morning the House of Horrors Program and FATS Training were conducted, the remaining students completing these components by early afternoon.

Those students who required additional Fast Track time were also accommodated, the rest of the class spot-cleaning their weapons and studying the course materials and textbook in preparation of the final written exam that would be administered the end of the following week.

Prior to dismissing the class for the long rotten weekend, they were given two homework assignments:
1) They were to review specific chapters in the textbook.
2) They were to prepare a safe weapon storage area in their homes and be prepared to describe it to the class the following week.

Day Six

Back to work. Attendance completed, review of the prior week's training, weapons issued and questions answered. *Firearms Safety Rules & Regulations Briefing* was conducted, as were the timed weapon disassembly, reassembly, and function checks.

Students reported having spent a good portion of their weekend thinking about the

House of Horrors in addition to preparing their uniforms and equipment for the coming week.

Next on the agenda was a brief review of everything that had been covered the previous week including all the safe weapon handling and operation skills that had been learned. In addition to these skills and techniques, a review of the principles of moving with a loaded pistol (no Hollywood techniques, proper trigger finger placement, etc.) were covered, as was a review for the written exam.

The "Poker Chip Drill" (App. K) was also introduced, demonstrated by the instructors and practiced by the students during the morning segment. (Students truly enjoyed this drill, competing with themselves and one-another while simultaneously improving and refining their presentation skills.)

After lunch break, the students proceeded to the range where they participated in DPTC No. 2 (Marksmanship and Safe handling Skills Assessment) three times. During the first iteration the course was conducted un-timed. The following two iterations were conducted using the recommended time limits and turning targets. The results of these three courses of fire were used to determine the student's individual proficiency regarding safe weapon handling and marksmanship skills. This was the first major testing hurdle they had to successfully complete. The vast majority were able to achieve better than the minimum standards required with above average shot groups. Overall speed and smoothness was also clearly evident. A few students who did not meet the standards, or who had but might have exhibited marginal handling skill were identified and earmarked for additional Fast Tracking during this block.

After completing the afternoon courses of fire, the recruits were released for the dinner break after securing their weapons.

A review of legal issues and considerations was conducted upon returning from chow. A review of the concepts of both weapon disarming techniques and weapon retention techniques was then conducted. (This topic was presented only to serve as a review: the actual training of these skills was thoroughly addressed in great detail during the recruit's Defensive Tactics Training Program under the direction of Tpr. Todd McGhee.) Redman guns were used during these hands-on drills. Vulnerable target areas of the human body were also discussed in relation to both defense and offense, and physical demonstrations were provided. Members of the FTU who were cross-trained and certified as Defensive Tactics Instructors administered this block.

The evenings training was concluded after a weapon cleaning session, during which students individually described the firearms storage location they had prepared in their homes over the weekend.

Day Seven

Morning routine of attendance, review of the prior day's training, and weapons issue. Questions answered. *Firearms Safety Rules & Regulations Briefing* conducted. The morning ritual of timed weapon disassembly, reassembly, and function check completed. Morale extremely high. Brief review of safe weapon handling and operation skill development provided as was a review of the preferred stoppage clearing drills.

An introduction to alternative low-light techniques was then provided, with the instructor providing both demonstrations and explanations.

Students were then allowed to practice the Poker Chip Drill for a short time in order to prepare for the day's first live-fire training exercise featuring "Cold Bore Shots."

After loading their weapons, students stood on line facing the targets at the four-yard mark. After explaining the drill, the instructor, equipped with a Competition Electronics Pocket Pro electronic timer, then stood behind each student, and initiated the exercise one-at-a-time.

At the tone, the student would draw his pistol from his secured holster and fire into his target using the proper technique. These were speed and accuracy drills, with the emphasis on accuracy, for to paraphrase Bill Jordan, "No one was ever 'stopped' by a fast sound."

Each student was allowed three attempts at achieving the standard. For this exercise, the standards were 1) achieving two hits (double-tap) within the preferred area of the silhouette target within two seconds using the Point Shooting Technique from four yards (12 feet), and 2) achieving two hits (double-tap) within the preferred area of the silhouette target within two seconds using the Body Point Technique from 1.5 yards (4 ½ feet). Needless to say, competition between the recruits to claim the "fastest and most accurate" title was intense. While the vast majority performed very well during these drills, breaking well under the two-second mark, a few demonstrated speed and skill that was quite impressive to say the least. More than once I expected to see a holster burst into flames when one of these burgeoning pistoleros slapped leather.

Due to the large number of students in the class this exercise generally took us up to lunch break.

After returning from lunch, the students were provided with a review of movement and use of cover techniques. They were also provided with a review of flashlight techniques, as well as an in-depth look at the various types of flashlights and beam configurations available.

The class was then broken into round robin components again. This time the components consisted of:
1) DPTC No. 3A, the Saber Challenge Course (App. P)
2) Poker Chip, Coin, and Wall Drill exercises
3) Fast Track for any personnel who required it, and finally
4) weapon cleaning and study time once all the other components had been completed.

Another component instituted during this

segment was to initiate feedback from the students regarding the training they had participated in to that point. It was clearly explained that we were looking for honest comments, positive or negative, about what they had done (or not done). Due to the climate that had been established between instructors and students from the outset, students felt relaxed and confident enough to offer their opinions professionally and forthrightly, helping us to improve the program for the following classes. (Due to the overall size of the 75th Recruit Training Troop–nearly 150 students–we conducted the 80-hour New Paradigm Recruit Program five consecutive times for this class alone.)

Most of the comments indicated they found the program to be balanced and professionally administered. Most stated they found the various components (especially the House of Horrors and the Saber Challenge course) both exciting to participate in and relevant. A few stated that they wished they could fire more rounds down range (which they would before the program was completed). The majority stated they believed this type of training would prepare them to survive far better than if they had simply been target shooting at paper for the entire two weeks.

After this session the recruits went to the academy for evening chow. When they returned one hour later, they were again issued their pistols. Another class on low-light techniques and operations was then administered. Students were educated on various facets regarding this subject, and provided with demonstrations that illustrated how objects and people appear and may be perceived differently under various lighting conditions.

The class proceeded to the range where they participated in DPTC No. 1B, (the Reduced Light Technique Familiarization and Skill Builder Course). After completing this course, all weapons were cleared. The students were then presented with one final demonstration.

This demonstration, adapted from the OSS program, required the students to stand together twenty-yards downrange in a group facing uprange while the instructor fired a handgun to the sides and above of where they were standing. Please note that the critical difference between the OSS demonstration and ours was that we used safety-blanks while the OSS instructors used live ammunition. (While the use of live rounds may have been justified when training commandoes for military wartime service, I do not believe that there can be any justification for subjecting the members of civilian law enforcement to this extremely dangerous practice.)

We also turned the lights down while this was done so the students could learn what a weapon's muzzle flash looked like from the receiving end. They were further instructed to notice how the muzzle flash appeared depending upon the direction of fire. (Stress Inoculation).

Regardless of the fact that only blanks were fired from a revolver specially-designated for this demonstration, the muzzle was never pointed directly at any of the students.

After the demonstration was completed, the weapons were cleaned and secured for the evening, class dismissed.

Day Eight

Attendance, review of the prior day's training, and weapons issued. Questions answered. *Firearms Safety Rules & Regulations Briefing* conducted. The morning ritual of timed weapon disassembly, reassembly, and function check completed, this time with a twist. Students were required to do it with their eyes covered (bills of the baseball caps pulled down snugly.)

They seemed surprised by how smoothly and efficiently they could perform this exercise. This time-tested weapon's training approach was not employed as a gimmick, but rather as a confidence builder, as well as to assist the students in achieving a clearer image of their

handgun and all its components in their mind's eye. A "bonding" exercise you might call it. It was effective. Best times were recorded.

We then reviewed various principles of strategy and tactics, to include the "Triad of Tactical Thinking," armed entries and vehicle approach techniques.

A review of alternative low-light techniques was then provided, with students being asked for feedback regarding which technique they preferred and why. As always, not everyone agreed as to which was the best technique, validating our approach of providing them with a variety of options instead of "the one way we do it" philosophy.

The class was then introduced to off duty and plainclothes firearms carry and use considerations.[2]

Next on the day's agenda was an introduction to tactical pistol techniques and stoppage clearing practice to reinforce these critical skills utilizing dummy rounds. A review of contact and cover officer responsibilities was then provided, as was an explanation of the psychological conditioning concepts behind the House of Horrors. (As expected, none of the students could clearly recall what it was the instructor said or did immediately after they engaged a threat scenario in the House of Horrors. Expressions of recognition, however, flooded the majority of faces when I demonstrated, pounding on the podium and saying "Good job!" loudly and enthusiastically.)

After lunch break we then proceeded to the range where the students participated first in DPTC No. 2 (Marksmanship and Safe Handling

---

[2] Tpr. Donna Losardo, who succeeded me as FTU director, would introduce an additional DPTC No. 1 (Plainclothes Skill Builder) course of fire when she conducted the 76th RTT program the following year. The administration of this course would mark the first time in the history of the MSP that recruit-level (or in-service level for that matter) students were provided with this type of training. The program has since been expanded and will be offered on an in-service level for the first time in 2004 under the auspices of Tpr. Paul Wosny, the current director of the FTU.

Skills Assessment Course), and then in DPTC No. 1A (Tactical Pistol Skill Builder Course). Included in DPTC No. 1A were the vertical track and busy hands drills, fired from four yards and 1.5 yards, respectively.

Weapons were then cleaned and secured for the evening and the recruits returned to the academy for evening chow. This night they also received an additional hour after dinner to attend to other duties before returning for training. The time was formatted in this manner because this day's training included integrated use-of-force scenarios that would run from 6 PM until 9 PM. These scripted scenarios were conducted in another training area on the academy compound and employed live role players, immediate feedback and critiques. Each student's performance was also individually documented.

During this training segment, students were provided with Simunition-equipped firearms, flashlights, portable radios, batons, and inert pepper spray canisters. They were also given cruisers in which they patrolled an actual neighborhood located on the academy grounds. (This area, known as Circle Drive, included a number of houses that had been converted for use by the academy staff.) Trained instructors were utilized both as role players and also as safety and training officers.

It was while observing the students perform with their pistols during these dynamic encounters that the effectiveness of the Point Shooting Technique became impressively clear.

We documented numerous instances during which the trainees responded to immediate threats not only appropriately, but with accuracy the likes of which we had never witnessed during previous training iterations. During one memorable scenario I watched as a trainee (who had never fired a weapon prior to Day One of the recruit firearms program) reacted to an immediate threat in the form of a handgun being drawn, pointed, and fired at him by running laterally (as he had been trained to do during DPTC No. 3A) to cover while accessing his

weapon. As he completed drawing his pistol while still moving to cover, I watched as he pointed and fired his own weapon at the role-playing suspect (who was then in the process of running, gun still in hand, in the opposite direction). Out of three rounds fired by the trainee, two hit the suspect role player center mass (66.6% hit rate). This while both were moving and under low light conditions! It was remarkable to watch. The trainee, incidentally, was not hit by the role player's gunfire.

Other similar instances of superior pistolcraft were also observed and reported during that and the following night's scenarios. Instructors overwhelmingly commented on the almost uncanny ability of the student officers to draw, fire, and accurately hit what they were shooting at from a variety of distances and positions, all while operating in real world environments and facing the threat of not only performing poorly in training, but also of receiving the potential pain penalty should the role playing instructors find their mark with their own Simunition-equipped weapons.

I freely admit that the student's performances during the scenario training segments validated in my mind and the minds of the other instructors once and for all the training approach we had taken. Over a period of years I had come to believe that Applegate had been right all along. Over a period of two days I realized that we could now prove it–in training anyways.

The real world proof would come shortly afterward. (See Chapter 9).

Day Nine

Attendance, review of the prior day's training, and questions answered. *Firearms Safety Rules & Regulations Briefing* conducted. Pistols were issued this day only to those few officers who had still not met the training standards required of the individual DPTCs.

These officers had been advised that this

would be their final Fast Track session and opportunity to demonstrate proficiency. The pressure was absolutely on them, as was the responsibility for demonstrating their individual proficiency.

This was so because the instructors had worked extensively with these individuals during Fast Track iterations, using no up-range stress and providing all positive reinforcement.

Any physical deficiencies or problems the students may have had had been addressed. (As an example, if the officer's hand had been identified at any stage during the program as being too small or fingers too short for the full-sized .40 Caliber SIG P-226, they were accommodated with a P-226 with a factory short trigger; if the pistol was still too large for their hand, they were then issued a smaller-framed .40 Caliber SIG P-229 with a standard or factory short trigger.)

In addition, instructors had worked tirelessly to assist the recruits in identifying and correcting individual problems and weaknesses with their skills or techniques.

Furthermore, in order to give the recruit the best chance of succeeding and to avoid frustration on the part of the instructors (which generally results in a more nervous recruit) our approach entailed having different instructors work with each recruit on a one-on-one basis in an effort to help "turn on the light" for the recruit. This was done because, ego aside and despite the best of intentions, sometimes, for whatever reason, a person will respond better to one instructor than another.[3]

By Day Nine of the program, however, all reasonable attempts had been made to assist each recruit succeed in the program. The few that remained unqualified, so to speak, had previously demonstrated the ability to perform up to standards, but could not do so consistently or when under pressure–*when it counted.*

In my experience, any recruit who had not satisfied the standards by this point in the program was the victim of internally generated

stress or lack of confidence–especially since the program had been structured in as positive a way as it had been. I further based this opinion on the acceptable-to-exceptional performances of the vast majority of the recruits who had participated in the program.

That is why on Day Nine, the Fast Trackers were calmly and professionally advised that this was their final attempt to demonstrate proficiency. If they failed, the procedure to remove them from the Academy would be initiated, resulting in their termination from the 75th Recruit Training Troop.

Whether it was the final realization of the situation they faced, or if these few individuals simply performed best when under intense pressure, I'll never truly know. But they all passed the final testing phase, demonstrating the ability to perform both up to standards and consistently during multiple skills assessment tests. Regardless of why they required the extra time, the Fast Track experience proved to be a sobering and maturing one for them, allowing them to grow and develop greater inner strength

---

[3] Contrary to those within the police industry who would mock this approach as being politically correct or overly kinder and gentler, I believe that this approach is not only simply the right thing to do, but is also the only approach a professional trainer should consider for the following reasons: 1) you cannot and should not attempt to bully or shame anyone into performing better during training, because it is a nonsensical approach. Even if the performance does improve enough for the student to just get by, the forced proficiency will more than likely only be temporary. This means the approach will have to be repeated during every training session, leading to ever greater levels of frustration and resentment in both the student and trainer; 2) the vast majority of people seeking employment in the law enforcement profession are trainable. Generally, in my experience, if the firearms training program and performance standards are reasonable and you have individuals who cannot meet the standards, the fault can be laid squarely at the feet of the instructor/s; 3) Finally, should you encounter an individual who actually is untrainable for whatever reason, in today's litigious society you will have a much better chance of removing this person from the training program (and the law enforcement profession) if you can demonstrate that every reasonable opportunity to improve was provided in an unmistakably professional manner to that individual. Otherwise, you may find yourself being ordered by a member of the judiciary to readmit an unsuitable–and now *untouchable*–candidate to your training academy/program.

and resources, "saving themselves," in a way, as opposed to having had the instructor provide the strength and motivation externally. Bottom line, they never gave up, and did complete the mission. Good job!

Also on the schedule for Day Nine was a block of instruction dedicated to a basic overview of the ubiquitous police pump-action shotgun. The previous recruit training program had discontinued the practice of including the shotgun briefing and familiarization block for several different reasons, chief among them that shotguns were individually-issued to officers on the department and these officers were required to successfully complete a separate training program prior to issuance.

I had decided to reinstitute the shotgun familiarization block for two primary reasons: 1) worst case scenario, one of the officers is involved in a deadly force situation, and the only weapon option available is another officer's shotgun (such as happened during the infamous FBI Miami shootout). In such a case, simply having a general knowledge of how to load, aim, and fire the shotgun could mean the difference between life and death. 2) Many of the recruits had no experience whatsoever with any type of firearms. Better to provide them with as broad a base of experience, additional knowledge and confidence as possible during the program, so long as it did not detract from the primary mission of pistol training.

This block was conducted as efficiently as possible. The class was presented with a structured overview regarding the weapon's configuration, law enforcement applications, strengths and weaknesses. Each student was then given the opportunity to handle, safely load, fire, and clear the 12 gauge Remington 870 Shotgun.

As usual the big bore blaster proved to be loud, powerful, impressive, and a bit intimidating to the uninitiated. However, after being instructed on how to best mount and fire the gun, most of the students walked away with less fear and greater confidence. Only a few walked away rubbing their shoulders.

After lunch break, pistols were issued and the class reconvened on the range. Since the Fast Trackers had been successful, shotguns had been fired without incident, and afternoon chow had proved less than lethal, the entire group's mood was buoyantly optimistic.

The class then participated in the second session of DPTC 1A, Tactical Pistol Drills. That day's exercises included Seated Drills from 5 yards and the Serpentine / Muzzle-control Drill.

Afterward, we reviewed off duty and plainclothes considerations and equipment and took an in-depth look at one of Hollywood's favorite police show scenarios (and one which unfortunately makes an occasional guest appearance in real life), the hostage situation. Options were discussed, demonstrations provided, and questions answered.

Weapons were then cleaned and secured for the evening, and the recruits returned to the academy proper for the extended dinner break as integrated scenario-based training was conducted that evening as well.

Day Ten

Last day of the immersion training program. Attendance was taken, a review of the past two week's training was conducted, and questions answered. *Firearms Safety Rules & Regulations Briefing* administered. Pistols issued. Textbooks collected.

First topic of the day covered tactical considerations in regard to patrol operations. Integrated use of force approach was continued in this block.

After this block of instruction, the class was recognized as a whole for the good work they had turned in. High performing individuals within the group were then identified and recognized. This included those students who had achieved numerical scores on DPTC No. 2 that placed them in the top 10% of the class.

Other standouts in the various subcategories were also recognized, as were those members who successfully completed the fast Track Program. The class was then advised to always remember that the entire group is only as strong as the weakest link. Since every human being has individual strengths and weaknesses, we owed it to each other to shore up our own weaknesses and help our fellow officers shore up theirs.

A final review for the exam was then conducted, after which the exam was administered. The written exam, like all other components of the program was conducted legitimately. In this way, the integrity of the training program could not be challenged from any angle.

Any final questions the students might have had were then answered. Critique forms were passed out, completed, and collected.

The weapons were given a final cleaning and were then inspected by the armorer before being secured.

Class dismissed at 12 PM.

Additional Training Segments

After each of the five, thirty-person training groups completed both the four-hour mental preparation course and the eighty-hour immersion training segment, they returned to the range for two additional eight hour training blocks.

During these blocks each of the members of the 75th Recruit Training Troop once again participated in the House of Horrors Training Course. This time, however, the course had been altered with different scenarios, and also included live role players as well as the animated mannequins.

Additional live-fire training courses were also conducted, both to reinforce the prior skills and mental conditioning that had been established as well as to verify that both had been retained.

Feedback from the students continued to be overwhelmingly positive. Excellent skill retention was observed and documented.

The seeds had been planted.

The 75th Recruit Training Troop graduated on December 14, 2000. The 75th RTT was the first class to be trained by the MSP's new Firearms Training Unit and to receive the New Paradigm Police Firearms Training Program. (Photo courtesy Massachusetts State Police archives.)

CHAPTER NINE
Monitoring the Results

If the trainee is not interested in target shooting as a sport, he will not show much enthusiasm in developing his target skill with his sidearm once his rookie days are over. He will always question in his own mind the need for increasing his score from 80% or whatever his organization requires, to go to 90 or 95%. He will realize that such an increase in his target shooting ability has little relation to how he will use his gun against an enemy who shoots back. However, the same trainee, who shows little interest in developing himself as a target shot, will readily see the advantages of a training program that will enable him to use his gun in a practical manner in tense situations. Practical combat firing training will enable him to use his gun effectively at close quarters, under conditions which demand skill and accuracy, without recourse to the sighted or aimed shot. Knowing this, he will apply himself accordingly, because he can see the personal benefit to be derived from such a method of shooting.

– Colonel Rex Applegate
Kill or Get Killed
1942

What We've Seen So Far

In the four years since we initiated the new program, we've seen a tremendous increase in training motivation and performance, personal confidence, and real-world performance in those who have participated.

By employing the four-level Kirkpatrick Model of training evaluation, I believe the training benefits can be clearly illustrated.[1]

Level One: Student's Reaction

The feedback to the program was–and continues to be–overwhelmingly positive. One of the methods we have used from the beginning to allow our people to provide us with honest feedback is a simple anonymous critique form that everyone is requested to fill out at the end of the training day.

A few examples of the types of responses we routinely document are provided here to illustrate not how the program is perceived by those who administer it, but by those who receive and participate in it.

Critiques from One-Day In-Service Training Program

- I've got to admit I was a bit skeptical about this program. But after going through it I realize it's an excellent training drill. All true life situations. The instructors were excellent and it was explained in an easy to follow, stress free, trooper-proof manner. Thanks for bringing the training up to speed.

---

[1] Donald Kirkpatrick first presented his four-level model of evaluation in 1975.

- ... Focus of the program is clearly officer safety and skill building...
- Enjoyed everything from instructor attitudes to entire course...
- ...Geared towards reality as opposed to the old course of qualification.
- This was by far the most relevant firearms training I have ever had. This is the training that will save my life and the lives of others...
- Excellent training. This is the type of training I've been waiting for. It's realistic. "Train like you fight".
- Best requal course in 23 years. Moved along very well and I finally felt very comfortable with the weapon.
- I have learned a tremendous amount today. The reality-based approach to the training makes me feel more confident when I go back to my assignment...
- The firearms training was excellent. Not only was the training geared to make you more proficient with the firearm, it also stressed the importance of shoot/don't shoot situations. The training was extremely realistic and useful.
- It was the first time in 24 years that I've enjoyed the range...
- ...Past qualifications were a chore of going through the numbers. This new training is exciting, keeping you alert to the dangers of our job.
- Best firearms training day in 8 years on the job...
- I have been on the job for 28 years and this has been the very best firearms training I have ever had.
- Training was aimed at a more realistic approach. It was very enlightening to see yourself in realistic situations.
- Best qualifying in 19 years...
- Best range qual in 32 years as a police officer
- We have finally arrived. This is a program ahead of its time. A novel approach to firearms training.
- The best firearms course in 15 ½ years of training. To sum it up in one word: fantastic

- ... I've never felt more confident with the weapon.
- This firearms training was by far the best I've gone through in my eight year career. It is very well known that most police related shootings take place up close. This was the best close combat shooting training that any police agency can adopt...
- It's about time! After 30 years it helped me greatly.
- Program deals with a lot more situations of normal course of police duties. Great change from target shooting.
- ...Course was entertaining and rewarding...
- Without a doubt the best firearms training program I have participated in in the past 19 years. Practical exercises designed to protect police and civilians...

Critiques like these are the norm rather than the exception. Considering that this feedback is being given by thousands of individual working police officers–the majority of whom are not in the least bit shy about expressing a negative opinion–you can understand why we believe we are on the right track as far as our in-service training administration approach is concerned.

On the basic, or recruit level, the program has also been extremely well received by those with prior training and experience and those who come into the program never having touched a firearm previously. A few examples are provided below.

Critiques from the Recruit Training Program

- The course is excellent. The flow, the scenarios, the relaxed atmosphere all combined to create a great learning experience...
- The training was done as though it was real life, real incidents, not just shooting at paper from different distances.
- The best firearms training I have ever had. It was very realistic.

- I feel very comfortable carrying a weapon now. The course covered every aspect to make me a safe, effective shooter.

- I think the point and shoot technique is the most important training I could have received. It is something that if ever used is realistic. This was proven in the House of Horrors.

- Point shooting system seemed to be very effective as well as reality-based.

- I thought this program was excellent. I went through the local academy, and we were only trained to shoot with sights. I am impressed with how the point shooting system really relates to real life.

- This trainee never once fired a weapon, but with this program I can honestly say that I was never nervous or unsure of myself. This trainee enjoyed every lesson and will take this knowledge throughout my career...

- Every police officer in Massachusetts should be re-trained using this method. The results would be in saved lives...

Level 2: Learning Results

While increasing the participant's motivation and enjoyment of the training program is very important to the overall process, this aspect would be meaningless if the physical skills we were seeking to assist them in developing were not being administered properly and documented. That is why the performance of each individual officer is thoroughly documented throughout each segment of training, and kept within that officer's individual training file. In this way we can monitor the progress or decline of each officer's basic pistolcraft skills. Obviously, barring any physical impairment, we would expect each officer's demonstrated skills performance to either continue to improve, or plateau at an acceptable level.

As of the time of this writing, we have continued to observe this occurring and have documented both these observations and the demonstrated performance improvements of the vast majority of our people.

In addition, we have conducted surveys of test groups in order to attempt to document the effectiveness (or ineffectiveness, if that were indicated) of the Point Shooting system and the stress inoculation aspects of the House of Horrors Program. It was surmised that this type of training program would enable the officers to develop better mental and physical coping skills in regard to managing the specific stressors commonly present when facing dangerous (or potentially dangerous) situations and environments.

One such survey was conducted by the members of the Firearms Training Unit under the supervision of Trooper Paul Wosny during the Fall of 2003.[2] The test group was selected completely at random during in-service training iterations each day the survey was conducted. The random method was employed in order to ensure both impartiality and that all segments of the department were represented.

The results of this survey also indicated an improvement in both physical performance and stress management, while also documenting some interesting data regarding the viability of the Point Shooting technique. (Reference Appendix B.)

Another example indicating the effectiveness of the system was found in Spring 2002 during the administration of an in-service level, interactive dynamic training iteration conducted by members of the department's tactical team. As part of my duties, I was assigned to evaluate the training, which can best be described as a variation of what has commonly come to be referred to as an "active shooter" course. Simunition® modified duty pistols and FX® Marking Cartridges were used by both students and role-player instructors during multiple scenarios.

---

2 MSP FTU Research Project 01-003: *Combat Stress, Point Shooting & Shots Fired-to-Hits Achieved Ratio Survey.*

To quote from my report:

"The firearms-related performance results of the student officers involved in the scenario-based exercises indicates that the specific type of firearms training they have participated in during the past two years (New Paradigm) is having a positive effect. I base this opinion strictly on their firearms shot-to-hit ratio while engaged in simulated deadly-force encounters at the moment of engagement/ apprehension and the student's responses to questions regarding their performance immediately after the exercises were completed. The data gathered during this program (noted in the above text) indicates that the involved student officers achieved an average shot-to-hit ratio of **approximately 85%** during the encounters while employing the Point-Shooting Technique. The scenarios also reflected other similarities to the average real-world police encounter, including close proximity, low-light, and short duration. Considering that the "old paradigm" of police firearms training has consistently produced an average shot-to-hit ratio of approximately 8-14% over the past thirty years (or an approximate 85% shot-to-MISS ratio) when officers engaged threatening suspects under similar conditions, one could reasonably infer from these training exercises alone that the New Paradigm program more accurately reflects the realities of police engagements and produces a better-prepared officer with more efficient police-specific firearms skills. This in my opinion helps validate the changes the department has made to the firearms training program and adds more evidence to the argument that the changes were both needed and viable. My recommendation would therefore be to continue with the ongoing implementation of the New Paradigm program and to have all officers who perform as firearms instructors on behalf of the department certified as instructors in the department's approved firearms training system. This will help ensure consistency in all firearms training being administered as well as prevent dissemination of conflicting information or training practices". [3]

---

[3] Evaluation of STOP Team Training Program, Active Shooter iteration, April 29, 2002

Level Three: Behavior in the Workplace

All of the feedback to date regarding the effects of the new training program on officer's actual real-world performance has been positive. A number of verbal and written reports have been forwarded to us that indicate the training is not only assisting officers when they are required to shoot a suspect in order to stop an immediate threat, but that it is also assisting them to *better determine if they do indeed need to shoot during high-stress encounters*.

In several of these incidents, officers directly attributed their ability to control their reactions and respond appropriately when faced with what initially appeared to be subjects armed with deadly weapons to the training received while going through the House of Horrors course.

Level Four: Business Results

As noted above, the department has seen a significant return on the investment of time, money and energy required to bring the new program on-line. The quality of both the instruction and individual officer's performance has absolutely improved, as have morale and appreciation for the importance of firearms training.

As for the bottom line regarding benefits gained through the implementation of this type of reality-based training, I believe the most accurate gauge we can and should employ is the Roger A. Ford Unit of Measurement: *One human life*.

And in my opinion, based on the information we have received from the field as well as our observations during training iterations, the number of human lives on both sides of the badge that have been–and will be–saved from death, serious injury, trauma, and stress, would have made Roger proud.

# CHAPTER TEN
The Future

It is not good to settle into a set of opinions. It is a mistake to put forth effort and obtain some understanding and then stop at that. At first putting forth great effort to be sure that you have grasped the basics, then practicing so that they may come to fruition is something that will never stop for your whole lifetime. Do not rely on following the degree of understanding that you have discovered, but simply think, *'This is not enough.'*
— Yamamoto Tsunetomo
Hagakure: The Book of the Samurai
1716

Upon successful completion of the recruit-level program and the in-service courses of instruction outlined on the preceding pages, the students will have participated in a firearms training program that has been developed specifically around the general realities of the environment, duties, and responsibilities of a member of U.S law enforcement.

Furthermore, the use of mission-specific training-track formatted programs (for uniformed and plain clothed officers) will ensure that the individual members of each department will have been exposed to training designed expressly to reflect the realities and environments they operate within on a regular basis.

The New Paradigm Program also establishes a sound methodology for both instructing and evaluating the members of each department in the use and application of all levels of force, up to and including the employment of lethal force.

Ongoing, documented training of this nature will assist each department in ensuring that all sworn members are sufficiently trained and qualified with all issued firearms, and can be reasonably expected to safely carry and employ them while engaged in any and all law enforcement-specific activities.

The Future

Logic would dictate that once a professionally formatted, reality-based police firearms training foundation had been established, it should be built upon and expanded with additional training courses designed in accordance with the methodologies and formatting formulas used to produce the base.

As the department's personnel successfully participated in and completed each training module, they would be allowed and expected to participate in the next, more challenging module. (Refer to Appendix O, Moving Target: Engaging One & Becoming One.)

Once they achieved proficiency in the specific skills that had been identified as mission-relevant and viable, then regular training iterations designed to assist them in maintaining and improving their individual proficiency levels within those disciplines would need to be administered. While similar to what has been expected of officers and departments employing the old marksmanship qualification-based paradigm for decades, the difference with the New Paradigm is that the skills that are taught, reinforced, and improved upon are actually applicable to the officer's day-to-day jobs and professional lives.

As with any type of critical skills training activity, great care and thought must go into ensuring that the programs are both safely run and varied enough to stimulate interest– simultaneously while ensuring that they do not deviate from, or actively work against, the New Paradigm-identified training formula that properly incorporates stress inoculation, operant conditioning and classical conditioning to produce law enforcement-specific, positive results.

Ideally, eventually both of the primary use-of-force disciplines; firearms and defensive tactics as well as emergency vehicle operations training must be integrated into one synthesized training program.

In this way, police officers will finally be able to train as they actually work, and have the best possible chance of performing as they have been trained when operating in what Clausewitz termed *the element of danger*.

The Integrated Use-of-Force Training Model – The Future is Now

We have been working on developing and implementing a model as outlined above.

As a comprehensive integrated use-of-force training program includes and combines elements from at least two of three primary disciplines–firearms, defensive tactics, and emergency vehicle operations–this is where we have been directing our focus and efforts.

Under the Firearm heading, we have included all firearms, including less-lethal firearm-delivered munitions. Under the heading of Defensive Tactics we have included empty hand, impact weapons, chemical agent weapons, edged and improvised weapons.

Emergency Vehicle Operations (EVOC) has also been included because of the nature and

employment of the vehicle in law enforcement activities.

In addition to covering the basic use and employment of each option individually, we have also developed interactive dynamic training courses that require the use (or potential use) of all of the above.

When constructed properly, a streamlined, integrated program designed using this model provides an opportunity for officers to develop the ability to decide upon which options to use (or combine) while operating under conditions and in environments similar to those they actually work in.

To date we have integrated these elements successfully in both the recruit-level program and with a series of experimental programs that have been conducted in conjunction with the basic New Paradigm pistol courses.

A brief outline of two of these programs is provided here for reference.

Undercover Operator Tactical Pistol Course

This course was developed in response to a critical need for training by those members of the police industry who have volunteered to perform what is undoubtedly one of the most dangerous facets of law enforcement work.

All of the exercises and drills included in the course have been specifically formatted to assist those officers whose professional duties require them to carry their weapons concealed on their person in an unconventional manner, and who may need to access and employ their weapons under emergency, mission-specific cir- cumstances while performing in an undercover capacity.

These drills have also been designed to help condition the officer's subconscious mind to handle the mechanics of safe weapon's han- dling and shooting so the officer can concentrate on resolving threatening situations with appro- priate responses and tactics.

In addition, the development of these skills in conjunction with specially selected defensive tactics skills will help increase the officer's confidence level in his ability to defend himself or others during high-stress, lethal force encounters as may be encountered by the undercover operator.

Multiple Integrated Skills Training Course

This one-day course, commonly referred to as the "MISTiC" Program, was first developed and administered in June 2001.

The initial course was custom designed for the members of the MSP, and was based on the progressive, integrated skills training model.

Participating officers were exposed to multiple skills development training blocks during the same course of instruction, rather than the more common single skill development model. After receiving focused blocks of instruction in several of these disciplines, the participants were then given the opportunity to employ all of the skills during the final segment of the course, which included dynamic-interactive scenario training.

MISTiC No. 1 incorporated three distinct disciplines (Firearms, Defensive Tactics, and Emergency Vehicle Operations) into its eight-hour training block. Participants were instructed in mission-specific tactics and techniques by qualified members of the Academy staff in each of these disciplines during a round robin training segment. After successfully completing all three individual training blocks, the participating officers then took part in a series of dynamic exercises during which they used all of these skills while involved in the pursuit and apprehension of role-playing instructor-offenders.

Immediate feedback and debriefings added to the training value of these exercises, as did the ability of the students to observe other participants during the dynamic training segments.

A second iteration, MISTiC No. 2, was developed by Trooper Donna Losardo the following year. This course incorporated several elements including off-duty and plainclothes tactics and techniques.

In regard to funding these programs, members of the State Police Association of Massachusetts (SPAM) went the extra mile and "outside the box" to secure monies to pay for the overtime required to allow officers to attend. In addition, a cooperative effort between SPAM, state police management, and the academy allowed the program to be fully realized.

Preparing for the Terrorist Threat

On the morning of September 11, 2001, I was running an in-service training iteration at the range in New Braintree. While the shooters were on the line preparing for the final morning drill, one of the instructors, Trooper Jay Park, tapped me on the shoulder and said quietly and evenly, "Boss, terrorists just attacked New York City by flying airplanes into the Twin Towers of the World Trade Center."

As I stared into his face my first reaction was to nonchalantly say, "No kidding?" to which he replied, again evenly and without any loss of composure, "No kidding."

Convinced he was simply trying to mess with my mind–something we all continually did to one another as a means of entertainment–I smiled, shook my head and said "Bullshit."

Then Trooper Johanna Lawlor walked up to me and confirmed it was all too real. "What do we do?" one of the instructors asked me.

"We keep training them," I replied, motioning to the officers on the firing line, "until we hear different."

After completing the drill, I advised the officers of what we had heard. They too didn't believe it at first, thinking I was laying out some type of training scenario. After assuring them I wasn't, I told them to contact their duty stations to see if they were needed to report immediately. I also suggested they call their families if they desired to check in and make sure everyone was alright. I then told them that we (the instructors) would do the same, and that my plan was to continue with the day's training program.

"We're at war," I reasoned. "We're going to need as much training as we can get, and we're here now. Unless we're urgently needed elsewhere right this minute, we'll finish here."

And we did. With the exception of a member of the Bomb Squad who was told to report to his station, everyone returned after the break and completed the day's training.

In the ensuing years, as my involvement with training police officers has continued and evolved, the events of September 2001 have had a decided influence on the direction of my focus. On the academy level, we immediately began to include terrorism awareness programs into our curriculum.

A short time later, I was temporarily seconded from the Academy to the Massachusetts State Police Troop "F" at Logan International Airport to assist with the development and training of a new, specialized Anti-Terrorist Unit (ATU).[1]

The ATU would ultimately break much new ground in US Law Enforcement, incorporating such things as an Americanized version of the Israeli-developed Behavioral Pattern Recognition (BPR) approach, and the adoption of MP5 submachine guns for daily use by uniformed members of the patrol force.

We also implemented training scenarios that addressed dealing with the stark and terrifying realities of the suicide/homicide bomber. Simply by designing reality-based scenarios and then allowing our people to deal with them, we have been able to better prepare our officers to face these specific types of threats in addition to

the more familiar threats we have traditionally dealt with in this country.

Much more work needs to be devoted to this specific facet of training on a national level than is currently being done. As always, it is our responsibility as police officers–and more specifically, as police officer-*trainers*–to deal with the realities of these threats directly, reasonably, and with the valor that has always been the hallmark of the members of American Law Enforcement.

Summary

While there are some US police departments that conduct training similar to that I've described in this chapter, I believe that programs such as those outlined above must eventually become the norm for the majority of law enforcement organizations nation-wide. I also believe that this will come to pass only as a result of cooperative efforts between all the various elements involved. That means representatives of management, unions, training, and the individual members of the departments themselves need to put aside individual interests and desires and work together to ensure the greater good is served.

Based on our experiences, I also believe that the impetus for change can come from the top levels of the administration or the lowest levels of the rank and file.

As always, however, it is best when dedicated individuals from both ends of the spectrum and all levels in between share a common vision and desire.

And in that regard, I will always be proud to have belonged to an agency whose members have fostered critical changes in training based upon a shared desire to save lives on both sides of the badge, and whose desire to continue to advance and improve can be expressed through the words, *"This is not enough."*

---

[1] My assignment to Logan Airport would become permanent with my promotion to the rank of sergeant in 2004.

APPENDICES
Formatting and Use

The following appendices have been included to provide a structured source of information the police firearms instructor may reference in order to assist in the development of a New Paradigm-style training program.

Please note: Many of the techniques in this section are shown being demonstrated while the instructor is not wearing protective eye and hearing equipment or the required brimmed cap. No live fire demonstrations were conducted while these photographs were being taken. They are intended for illustrative purposes only.

Proper protective equipment–including body armor–is a <u>MUST</u> when conducting or participating in any type of live fire training exercises.

Proper protective equipment is critical when involved in firearms training. The instructor sets the tone through his own example. Investing in a quality set of personal protective equipment is highly recommended. Examples shown above: **1.** Wiley X Saber wrap-around shooting glasses (www.wileyx.com). **2.** Peltor Tactical 6S hearing protector (www.aosafety.com). **3.** Baseball-type cap with brim (old fashioned type with brim worn to the front) and **4.** Point Blank firearms instructor vest as used by the Massachusetts Law Enforcement Firearms Instructors and Armorers Association (www.mlefiaa.org). Using bright red caps and/or outer vests makes identification of instructors easier for both participants and observers during training iterations.

POLICE PISTOLCRAFT TRIVIA

First US Police Department to Issue Pistols to its Officers

While the Boston, Massachusetts Police Department is often cited as the first civilian law enforcement organization in the nation to have issued pistols to the members of their department (in 1863), that distinction may actually belong to the Baltimore City Police Department in Maryland.

The Baltimore Police Department traces its roots back to 1784 when constables were first appointed, organized, and given police powers.

In 1853, the State Legislature passed a bill "to provide for the better security for the [citizens] and property in the City of Baltimore." It was this statute that allowed for the establishment of a professional police force in Baltimore. Language in the bill stipulated that officers should be armed, as well as issued a badge and commission.

In 1857, the Baltimore City Police Department officially adopted and issued a standardized pistol for duty use. The first US police-issued pistol was the Colt 1849 Pocket Model, a .31 caliber percussion revolver (shown right).

Today, the members of the Baltimore Police Department are armed with .40 Caliber Glock semi-automatic pistols.

APPENDIX A
Selected Firearms Training Course Analysis & Comparisons to Statistical Data

These tables were developed in order to better illustrate the actual training value of each individual program. The aggregate training value can be estimated based upon a comparison of the number of rounds fired, positions, hands, equipment used, distances, etc.

The mental conditioning value can be indicated based upon the type of targets used, initiating stimuli employed, and desired/intended responses to those stimuli.

The comparisons to statistical data was included to verify that the training focus (and as a direct result, police training value) was based on the most statistically probable events and conditions those being trained would encounter.

Both Old Paradigm (OP) and New Paradigm (NP) courses of fire are analyzed in the following pages.

Note: The following abbreviations are used throughout this section:

DPTC ....**Duty Pistol Training Course (New Paradigm)**

DPQC ....**Duty Pistol Qualification Course (Old Paradigm)**

NP ....… **New Paradigm**

OP ....…... **Old Paradigm**

MT ....…...... **Marksmanship Training**

PSD ....…...... **Physical Skills Development**

MC ....…….. **Mental Conditioning**

OC ....…...... **Operant Conditioning**

CC ....…...…. **Classical Conditioning**

JT ....…...... **Judgmental Training**

NS ....…..... **Not Specified**

SC ....…...…. **Student's Choice**

Course Analysis 1: DUTY PISTOL QUALIFICATION COURSE (OLD PARADIGM)   (MT/PSD)

# Rounds	Distance	Position	Hand	# Hands	Time
5 rounds	25 yards	kneeling	dominant	two	20 seconds
5 rounds	17 yards	standing	dominant	two	12 seconds
5 rounds	17 yards	standing	non-dominant	two	15 seconds
RELOAD					
5 rounds	12 yards	kneeling	dominant	two	
5 rounds	12 yards	standing	non-dominant	two	
5 rounds	12 yards	kneeling	non-dominant	two	45 seconds total
RELOAD					
2 rounds	7 yards	standing	dominant	two	2 seconds
2 rounds	7 yards	standing	dominant	two	2 seconds
2 rounds	7 yards	standing	dominant	two	2 seconds
2 rounds	5 yards	standing	dominant	one	2 seconds
2 rounds	5 yards	standing	dominant	one	2 seconds
2 rounds	5 yards	standing	dominant	one	2 seconds
2 rounds	2 yards	standing/hip	dominant	one	2 seconds

Total rounds fired	% Rounds per distance	% Rounds per position	% Hand used	% # Hands used	Average time per shot
44	25 - 11% 17 - 23% 12 - 34% 7 - 14% 5 - 14% 2 - 5%	Stand - 66% Kneel - 34% Prone - 0% Other - 0%	Dom.- 77% Non-Dom.- 23%	one - 18% two - 82%	25 - 4.0 17 - 2.7 12 - 3.0 7 - 1.0 5 - 1.0 2 - 1.0

Total # Presentations (and Recoveries)	# Presentations per distance	# Presentations per position	# Presentations per hand	Total % Pres. requiring shot
10	25 - 1 17 - 1 12 - 1 7 - 3 5 - 3 2 - 1	Stand - 10 Kneel - 0 Prone - 0 Other - 0	Dom. - 10 Non-Dom. - 0	100%

Total # Reloads	Type Reloads %	% Reloads per position	% Reloads per # hands
2	Admin - ? Combat - ? Tactical - ?	Stand - ? Kneel - ? Prone - 0% Other - 0%	one - 0% two - 100% (NOTE: ? = not specified)

Use of Cover per % rounds fired	Type of Cover	% Time cover used per position	Flashlight technique use per % rounds
34%	Barricade (upright)	Stand - 33% Kneel - 67% Other - 0%	0%

Course Analysis 2: COMBAT STRESS PISTOL COURSE (OLD PARADIGM) (MT/PSD/MC)

# Rounds	Distance	Position	Hand	# Hands	Time
6 rounds	15 yards	kneeling	dominant	two	
6 rounds	15 yards	kneeling	non-dominant	two	18 seconds total

TACTICAL RELOAD

6 rounds	10 yards	kneeling	dominant	two	
6 rounds	10 yards	kneeling	non-dominant	two	18 seconds total

COMBAT RELOAD

2 rounds	7 yards	standing	dominant	two	2 sec
2 rounds	7 yards	standing	dominant	two	2 sec
2 rounds	7 yards	standing	dominant	two	2 sec

(NOTE: All rounds fired from the low-ready position from the 7 yard line)

2 rounds	1 yard	standing	dominant	one	2 sec

(NOTE: 2 rounds fired holster to hip from 1 yard line)

Total rounds fired	% Rounds per distance	% Rounds per position	% Hand used	% # Hands used	Average time per shot
32	15 - 38% 10 - 38% 7 - 18% 1 - 6%	Stand - 25% Kneel - 75% Prone - 0% Other - 0%	Dom - 63% Non-Dom.- 37%	one - 6% two - 94%	15 - 1.5 10 - 1.5 7 - 1.0 1 - 1.0

Total # Presentations (and Recoveries)	# Presentations per distance	# Presentations per position	# Presentations per hand	Total % Pres. requiring shot
2	15 - 1 10 - 0 7 - 0 1 - 1	Stand - 10 Kneel - 0 Prone - 0 Other - 0	Dom. - 2 Non-Dom. - 0	100%

Total # Reloads	Type Reloads %	% Reloads per position	% Reloads per # hands
2	Admin - 0% Combat - 50% Tactical - 50%	Stand - 100% Kneel - 0% Prone - 0% Other - 0%	one - 0% two - 100%

Use of Cover per % rounds fired	Type of Cover	% Time cover used per position	Flashlight technique use per % rounds
75%	Barricade (upright)	Stand - 0% Kneel - 100% Other - 0%	0%

Course Analysis 3: FBI STRESS/REACTIVE COURSE (OLD PARADIGM) (MT/PSD/MC)

# Rounds	Distance	Position	Hand	# Hands	Time
30 rounds	12 yards	standing	dominant	two	N/A

TACTICAL RELOAD / COMBAT RELOAD (Optional)

(Note: All rounds fired from ready position)

Total rounds fired	% Rounds per distance	% Rounds per position	% Hand used	% # Hands used	Average time per shot
30	12 - 100%	Stand - 100% Kneel - 0% Prone - 0% Other - 0%	Dom.- 100% Non-Dom.- 0%	two - 100%	N/A

Total # Presentations (and Recoveries)	# Presentations per distance	# Presentations per position	# Presentations per hand	Total % Pres. requiring shot
1	12 - 1	Stand - 1 Kneel - 0 Prone - 0 Other - 0	Dom. - 1 Non-Dom. - 0	N/A

Total # Reloads	Type Reloads %	% Reloads per position	% Reloads per # hands	
2	Admin - 0% Combat - 50% Tactical - 50%	Stand - 100% Kneel - 0% Prone - 0% Other - 0%	one - 0% two - 100% (NOTE: ? = not specified)	

Use of Cover per % rounds fired	Type of Cover	% Time cover used per position	Flashlight technique use per % rounds
50% (Stood behind barrel-upper torso exposed)	Barricade (upright)	Stand - 50%	0%

Course Analysis 4: MOVING TARGET COURSE (OLD PARADIGM) (MT/PSD/MC-OC)

# Rounds	Distance	Position	Hand	# Hands	Time
6-8 rounds	7-10 yards	Not Specified	dominant	two	Not Specified

(Note: All rounds fired from low ready position from behind cover)

Total rounds fired	% Rounds per distance	% Rounds per position	% Hand used	% # Hands used	Average time per shot
6-8	7-10 - 100%	Stand - NS Kneel - NS Prone - NS Other - NS	Dom.- 100% Non-Dom.- 0%	one - NS two - NS	NS

Total # Presentations (and Recoveries)	# Presentations per distance	# Presentations per position	# Presentations per hand	Total % Pres. requiring shot
1	7-10 - 1	Stand - NS Kneel - NS Prone - NS Other - NS	Dom. - 1 Non-Dom. - 0	100%

Total # Reloads	Type Reloads %	% Reloads per position	% Reloads per # hands
0	Admin - 0% Combat - 0% Tactical - 0%	Stand - 0% Kneel - 0% Prone - 0% Other - 0%	one - 0% two - 0% (NOTE: NS = Not Specified)

Use of Cover per % rounds fired	Type of Cover	% Time cover used per position	Flashlight technique use per % rounds
100%	Barricade (upright)	Stand - NS Kneel - NS Other - NS	0%

Challenge / Warning Used?	Type of Challenge / Warning Used
YES	"POLICE - DON'T MOVE!"

Threat Stimulus	Conditioned Response	Viable?
1. When realistic threat (photo target w/gun) moves:	Fire rounds as accurately as possible	YES
2. When realistic threat stops moving:	Stop firing and cover down on threat	NO*

Submission Indicator	Conditioned Response	Viable?
When realistic threat (photo target w/gun) stops:	Cease fire, cover down on target and issue verbal challenge/commands	NO*

(* By employing this method, officers were being (Operant) conditioned to cease firing at a suspect armed with a handgun when he stops, while the suspect still presented an immediate threat. A suspect would be MORE dangerous at this point, for his accuracy would more likely be better firing from a stationary position than while on the move.)

Course Analysis 5: DPTC No. 1 (NEW PARADIGM) (MT/PSD/MC-OC-CC)

# Rounds	Distance	Position	Hand	# Hands	Time
Reset Drill					
3 rounds	3 yards	standing ready	dominant	two	N/A
3 rounds	3 yards	standing ready	dominant	one	N/A
3 rounds	3 yards	standing ready	non-dominant	two	N/A
3 rounds	3 yards	standing ready	non-dominant	one	N/A
COMBAT RELOAD, TACTICAL RECOVERY TO HOLSTER					
Point Shooting Drills					
1 round	3 yards	standing	dominant	one	N/A
1 round	3 yards	standing	dominant	one	N/A
2 rounds	3 yards	standing	dominant	one	N/A
2 rounds	3 yards	standing	dominant	one	N/A
1 round	5 yards	standing ready	dominant	one	N/A
1 round	5 yards	standing ready	dominant	one	N/A
2 rounds	5 yards	standing ready	dominant	one	N/A
2 rounds	5 yards	standing ready	dominant	one	N/A
TACTICAL RELOAD, TACTICAL RECOVERY TO HOLSTER					
Stoppage Clearing Drills					
6 rounds	7 yards	standing ready	dominant	two	N/A
ADMINISTRATIVE SUSTAIN LOAD MAGAZINE FROM POCKET, RECOVER TO HOLSTER					
Reactive Engagement Drill					
2 rounds	1-1.5 yards	stand/hit/move	dominant	one	N/A
2 rounds	1-1.5 yards	stand/hit/move	dominant	one	N/A
2 rounds	1-1.5 yards	stand/hit/move	dominant	one	N/A
Transition Drill to Aerosol Subject Restraint					
0 rounds	3 yards	present/challenge/transition to ASR/challenge			N/A
0 rounds	3 yards	present/challenge/transition to ASR/challenge			N/A
0 rounds	3 yards	present/challenge/transition to ASR/challenge			N/A

Total rounds fired	% Rounds per distance	% Rounds per position	% Hand used	% # Hands used	Average time per shot
36	1.5 - 17%	Stand - 100%	Dom.- 83%	one - 67%	N/A
	3 - 50%	Kneel - 0%	Non-Dom.- 17%	two - 33%	N/A
	5 - 17%	Prone - 0%			N/A
	7 - 17%	Other - 0%			N/A

Total # Presentations (and Recoveries)	# Presentations per distance	# Presentations per position	# Presentations per hand	Total % Pres. requiring shot
13/13	1.5 - 3	Stand - 12	Dom. - 13	77%
	2 - 0	Kneel - 0	Non-Dom. - 0	
	3 - 8	Prone - 0		
	5 - 1	Other - 0		
	7 - 1			

CONTINUED ON FOLLOWING PAGE...

Course Analysis 5: DPTC No. 1 (NEW PARADIGM) (MT/PSD/MC-OC-CC) (Continued)

Total # Reloads	Type Reloads %	% Reloads per position	% Reloads per # hands
3	Admin - 33% Combat - 33% Tactical - 33%	Stand - 100 Kneel - 0% Prone - 0% Other - 0%	one - 25% two - 75%

Use of Cover per % rounds fired	Type of Cover	% Time cover used per position	Flashlight technique use per % rounds
0%	N/A	Stand - 0% Kneel - 0% Other - 0%	0%

Course Analysis 6: DPTC No. 2 (NEW PARADIGM) (MT/PSD)

# Rounds	Distance	Position	# Rounds per Hand	# Hands	Time
3 rounds	25 yards	prone/cover	2 dom/1 non-dom	two	20 seconds
3 rounds	17 yards	kneeling/cover	2 dom/1 non-dom	two	15 seconds
2 rounds	7 yards	standing	2 dominant	two	2 seconds
2 rounds	7 yards	standing	2 dominant	two	2 seconds
2 rounds	7 yards	kneeling	2 non-dominant	two	6 seconds

COMBAT RELOAD, TACTICAL RECOVERY TO HOLSTER

# Rounds	Distance	Position	# Rounds per Hand	# Hands	Time
2 rounds	4 yards	standing	2 dominant	one	2 seconds
2 rounds	4 yards	standing	2 dominant	one	2 seconds
2 rounds	4 yards	standing	2 dominant	one	2 seconds
2 rounds	2 yards	standing ready w/light	2 dominant	one	2 seconds
2 rounds	2 yards	standing ready w/light	2 dominant	one	2 seconds
2 rounds	2 yards	standing ready w/ light	2 dominant	one	2 seconds

TACTICAL RELOAD, TACTICAL RECOVERY TO HOLSTER

# Rounds	Distance	Position	# Rounds per Hand	# Hands	Time
2 rounds	1.5 yards	standing/cpd *	2 dominant	one	2 seconds
2 rounds	1.5 yards	standing/cpd	2 dominant	one	2 seconds
2 rounds	1.5 yards	standing/cpd	2 dominant	one	2 seconds
3 rounds	1.5 - 2 yards	standing/move	3 dom (reactive drill)	one	4 seconds
3 rounds	1.5 - 2 yards	standing/move	3 dom (reactive drill)	one	4 seconds

ADMINISTRATIVE RELOAD

Total rounds fired	% Rounds per distance	% Rounds per position	% Hand used	% # Hands used	Average time per shot
36	25 - 8% 17 - 8% 7 - 17% 4 - 17% 2 - 22% 1.5 - 28%	Stand - 78% Kneel - 14% Prone - 8% Other - 0%	Dom.- 89% Non-Dom.- 11%	one - 67% two - 33%	25 - 6.6 17 - 5.0 7 - 1.6 4 - 1.0 2 - 1.0 1.5 - 1.1

Total # Presentations (and Recoveries)	# Presentations per distance	# Presentations per position	# Presentations per hand	Total % Pres. requiring shot
16 / 16	25 - 1 17 - 1 7 - 4 4 - 3 2 - 2 1.5 - 5	Stand - 15 Kneel - 1 Prone - 0 Other - 0	Dom. - 16 Non-Dom. - 0	100%

Total # Reloads	Type Reloads %	% Reloads per position	% Reloads per # hands
3	Admin - 33.3% Combat - 33.3% Tactical - 33.3%	Standing - 100% Kneel - 0% Prone - 0% Other - 0%	one - 33.3% two - 66.6%

Use of Cover per % rounds fired	Type of Cover	% Time cover used per position	Flashlight technique use per % rounds
17%	Barricade (modified)	Stand - 0% Prone - 100% Kneel - 50% Other - 0%	17%

*(NOTE: CPD = Close Proximity Drill)

Course Analysis 7: DPTC No. 3 (NEW PARADIGM) (MT/PSD/MC-OC-CC-JT)

# Rounds	Distance	Position	# Rounds per Hand	# Hands	Time
0-7 rounds	12 yards	optional	optional	one or two	20 seconds
ADMINISTRATIVE UNLOAD					

Total rounds fired	% Rounds per distance	% Rounds per position	% Hand used	% # Hands used	Average time per shot
0-7	12 - 100%	Stand - SC Kneel - SC Prone - SC Other - SC	Dom.- SC Non-Dom.- SC	one - SC two - SC	N/A

Total # Presentations (and Recoveries)	# Presentations per distance	# Presentations per position	# Presentations per hand	Total % Pres. requiring shot
2	12 - 1	Stand - SC Kneel - SC Prone - SC Other - SC	Dom. - 1 Non-Dom. - 0	Depends on target/stimulus & student's judgement

Total # Reloads	Type Reloads %	% Reloads per position	% Reloads per # hands
0	Admin - 0% Combat - 0% Tactical - 0%	Stand - 0% Kneel - 0% Prone - 0% Other - 0%	one - 0% two - 0% (NOTE: SC = Student's Choice)

Use of Cover per % rounds fired	Type of Cover	% Time cover used per position	Flashlight technique use per % rounds
100%	Vehicle Mock-up	100% All positions	0%

Judgement Required?	Challenge / Warning Used?	Type of Challenge / Warning Used?
YES	Yes, if feasible	i.e. "Police - Don't move!" / "Drop your weapon!" "People get down!"

Threat Stimulus / Non-Threat Stimulus	Conditioned Response	Viable?
1. When realistic threat (photo target w/gun) appears:	Take cover & engage without hitting innocent bystanders	YES
2. When realistic threat (photo target) disappears:	Maintain cover, stop firing, scan area, advise innocents to move to safety	YES

Submission Indicator	Conditioned Response	Viable?
None	Use cover, issue verbal commands, engage without endangering innocents, maintain threat and environmental awareness	YES

Course Analysis 8: DPTC No. 3A SABER CHALLENGE (NEW PARADIGM) (MT/PSD/MC-OC-CC-JT)

# Rounds	Distance	Position	Hand	# Hands	Time
Target dependent	4-6 yards	optional	optional	one or two	NS

(Note: All rounds fired from behind cover. Officer in induced high arousal state)
MODIFIED COMBAT LOAD (Student loads pistol during course from behind cover while maintaining threat/environmental awareness)

Total rounds fired	% Rounds per distance	% Rounds per position	% Hand used	% # Hands used	Average time per shot
Based on threat	If fired - 100% @ 4-6 yards	Stand - SC Kneel - SC Prone - SC Other - SC	Dom.- SC Non-Dom.- SC	one - SC two - SC	N/A

Total # Presentations (and Recoveries)	# Presentations per distance	# Presentations per position	# Presentations per hand	Total % Pres. requiring shot
1 / 1	0	0	Dom. - 0 Non-Dom. - 0	0

Total # Reloads	Type Reloads %	% Reloads per position	% Reloads per # hands	Total Unloads	Type Unloads %	% Unloads per position
1	Admin - 0% Combat - 100% Tactical - 0%	Stand - SC Kneel - SC Prone - SC Other - SC	one - SC two - SC	2	Admin - 100% (NOTE: SC = Student's Choice)	Stand - 100%

Use of Cover per % rounds fired	Type of Cover	% Time cover used per position	Flashlight technique use per % rounds
100%	Various	100% All positions	NS - Adaptable

Judgement Required?	Challenge / Warning Used?	Type of Challenge / Warning Used?
YES	Yes, if feasible	i.e. "Police - Don't move!" / "Drop your weapon!"

Threat Stimulus / Non-Threat Stimulus	Conditioned Response	Viable?
1. When being fired at:	Move to cover & use properly	YES
2. When realistic threat (photo target w/gun) appears:	Take cover & engage / challenge	YES
3. When realistic threat disappears:	Maintain cover, stop firing, scan area	YES
4. When non-threat stimulus appears:	Maintain cover and challenge	YES

Submission Indicator	Conditioned Response	Viable?
None	Use cover, issue verbal commands, engage	YES

Course Analysis 9: DPTC No. 4 HOUSE OF HORRORS (NEW PARADIGM) (MT/PSD/MC-OC-CC-JT)

Distance	Position	# Hands	Total # Rounds	Number Rounds Fired per Hand	Sugg. Time

1) SUBJECT IN MOTORVEHICLE (Threat Stimulus Moving Target)

0-5 Yards	Students choice (SC)	SC	SC	SC	N/A

2) SUBJECT HIDING (No-Threat Stimulus Moving Target w/ Auditory Stimulus)

0-7 Yards	Students choice (SC) Cover available	SC	SC	SC	N/A

3) HOSTAGE-TAKER WITH HOSTAGE (Combined Threat and No-Threat Stimulus Targets)

4-7 Yards	Students choice (SC) Cover available	SC	SC	SC	N/A

4) SUBJECT IN WINDOW (No-Threat Stimulus Target w/ Movement and Auditory Stimulus)

0-5 Yards	Students choice (SC) Cover available	SC	SC	SC	N/A

5) NEGOTIATE NO-THREAT STAIRWAY (Non-Threat Stimulus Target w/ Auditory Stimulus)

0-1 Yard	Students choice (SC) Cover available	SC	SC	SC	N/A

6) SHOOTING MAN (Threat Stimulus Target w/ Auditory Stimulus and Pain Stimulus)

0-5 Yards	Students choice (SC) Cover available	SC	SC	SC	N/A

7) REFLECTED IMAGE (No-Threat Stimulus Target)

0-2 Yards	Students choice (SC)	SC	SC	SC	N/A

8) NEGOTIATE HALLWAY, ENCOUNTER TURNING MAN (No-Threat Stimulus Moving Target)

4 Yards	Students choice (SC)	SC	SC	SC	N/A

9) KNIFING MAN & VICTIM (Threat Stimulus Moving Target w/ Auditory Stimulus and No-Threat Stimulus Target)

6-1 Yards	Students choice (SC)	SC	SC	SC	N/A

ADMINISTRATIVE UNLOAD

NOTE: STUDENT IS RESPONSIBLE TO SAFELY RELOAD PISTOL AND CLEAR STOPPAGES AS NEEDED

COURSE ANALYSIS 9 CONTINUED ON FOLLOWING PAGE

Course Analysis 9: DPTC No. 4 HOUSE OF HORRORS (MT/PSD/MC-OC-CC-JT) (Continued)

Total rounds fired	% Rounds per distance	% Rounds per position	% Hand used	% # Hands used	Average Time per shot
0-24	100% w/i 21 feet	SC	SC	SC	N/A

Total # Presentations (& Recoveries)	# Presentations per distance	# Presentations per position	# Presentations per hand	Total % Pres. requiring shot
SC	SC	SC	SC	Depends on target/stimulus

Total # Reloads	Type Reloads %	% Reloads per position	% Reloads per # hands
0-1	SC	SC	SC

Use of Cover per % rounds	Type of Cover per position	% Time cover used	Flashlight technique use per % rounds
SC	Varies	100% Encouraged	SC

Judgement Required?	Challenge / Warning Used?	Type of Challenge / Warning Used?
YES	Yes, if feasible	"POLICE - DON'T MOVE!" "DROP YOUR WEAPON!" "SHOW ME YOUR HANDS!" etc.

Threat Stimulus / Non-Threat Stimulus	Conditioned Response	Viable?
1. When realistic threat encountered:	Take cover & engage / challenge without injuring innocent bystanders	YES
2. Once realistic threat is stopped/controlled:	Maintain cover, stop firing, scan area, advise innocents to move to safety	YES
3. When realistic non-threat is encountered:	Take cover and challenge / advise	YES
4. If hit by adversary's gunfire:	Move to cover and/or continue to engage until threat has been successfully stopped; THEN move to cover, scan area and call for assistance.	YES

Submission Indicator	Conditioned Response	Viable?
Varies	Use cover, issue verbal commands	YES

Course Evaluation Summaries & Comparisons to Statistical Data (SD)

Course 1: DUTY PISTOL (OLD PARADIGM) QUALIFICATION COURSE (9mm)　(MT/PSD)

% Rounds fired per distance (ft.)	SD Encounter distances (ft.)	% Time flashlight used	SD Encounter Time of day
0-5　-　0% 6-10　-　5% 11-20　-　14% 21-50　-　48% Over 50　-　34%	0-5　-　53% 6-10　-　20% 11-20　-　12% 21-50　-　8% Over 50　-　6%	0%	6 P.M. - 6 A.M. - 62% 6 A.M. - 6 P.M. - 38% (All figures rounded up)

Total # Presentations	Total % Pres. requiring shot	Total % shots requiring judgement	Total % shots fired in high arousal state
10	100%	0%	0%

Total # Reloads/Unloads	Total # Stoppage Drills	Total # positions used	Use of cover per % rounds fired
2 / 0	0	2	34%

Course Evaluation Summaries & Comparisons to Statistical Data (SD)

Course 2: STRESS PISTOL (OLD PARADIGM) COURSE (.40 CAL)　(MT/PSD/MC)

% Rounds fired per distance (ft.)	SD Encounter distances (ft.)	% Time flashlight used	SD Encounter Time of day
0-5　-　6% 6-10　-　0% 11-20　-　0% 21-50　-　94% Over 50　-　0%	0-5　-　53% 6-10　-　20% 11-20　-　12% 21-50　-　8% Over 50　-　6%	0%	6 P.M. - 6 A.M. - 62% 6 A.M. - 6 P.M. - 38% (All figures rounded up)

Total # Presentations	Total % Pres. requiring shot	Total % shots requiring judgement	Total % shots fired in high arousal state
2	100%	0%	0%

Total # Reloads/Unloads	Total # Stoppage Drills	Total # positions used	Use of cover per % rounds fired
2 / 0	0	2	75%

Course Evaluation Summaries & Comparisons to Statistical Data (SD)

Course 3: FBI STRESS/REACTIVE COURSE (OLD PARADIGM) (MT/PSD/MC)

% Rounds fired per distance (ft.)		SD Encounter distances (ft.)		% Time flashlight used	SD Encounter Time of day
0-5	0%	0-5 -	53%	0%	6 P.M. - 6 A.M. - 62%
6-10	0%	6-10 -	20%		6 A.M. - 6 P.M. - 38%
11-20	0%	11-20 -	12%		(All figures rounded up)
21-50	100%	21-50 -	8%		
Over 50	0%	Over 50 -	6%		

Total # Presentations	Total % Pres. requiring shot	Total % shots requiring judgement	Total % shots fired in high arousal state
1	N/A	0% (identification ONLY)	0%

Total # Reloads/Unloads	Total # Stoppage Drills	Total # positions used	Use of cover per % rounds fired
2 / 0 (weapon runs dry)	0 (unless naturally occurs)	1	50% (Upright behind barrel - torso exposed)

Course Evaluation Summaries & Comparisons to Statistical Data (SD)

Course 4: MOVING TARGET COURSE (OLD PARADIGM) (MT/PSD/MC-OC)

% Rounds fired per distance (ft.)		SD Encounter distances (ft.)		% Time flashlight used	SD Encounter Time of day
0-5	0%	0-5 -	53%	0%	6 P.M. - 6 A.M. - 62%
6-10	0%	6-10 -	20%		6 A.M. - 6 P.M. - 38%
11-20	0%	11-20 -	12%		(All figures rounded up)
21-50	100%	21-50 -	8%		
Over 50	0%	Over 50 -	6%		

Total # Presentations	Total % Pres. requiring shot	Total % shots requiring judgement	Total % shots fired in high arousal state
1	100%	100%	0%

Total # Reloads/Unloads	Total # Stoppage Drills	Total # positions used	Use of cover per % rounds fired
0 / 0	0 (unless naturally occurs	NS	100%

Course Evaluation Summaries & Comparisons to Statistical Data (SD)

Course 5: DPTC No. 1 (NEW PARADIGM) (MT/PSD/MC-OC-CC)

% Rounds fired per distance (ft.)	SD Encounter distances (ft.)	% Time flashlight used	SD Encounter Time of day
0-5 - 17% 6-10 - 50% 11-20 - 17% 21-50 - 17% Over 50 - 0%	0-5 - 53% 6-10 - 20% 11-20 - 12% 21-50 - 8% Over 50 - 6%	0%	6 P.M. - 6 A.M. - 62% 6 A.M. - 6 P.M. - 38% (All figures rounded up)

Total # Presentations	Total % Pres. requiring shot	Total % shots requiring judgement	Total % shots fired in high arousal state
13	77%	0%	0%

Total # Reloads/Unloads	Total # Stoppage Drills	Total # positions used	Use of cover per % rounds fired
3 / 0	7	1 (3 variations)	0%

Course Evaluation Summaries & Comparisons to Statistical Data (SD)

Course 6: DPTC No. 2 (NEW PARADIGM) (MT/PSD)

% Rounds fired per distance (ft.)	SD Encounter distances (ft.)	% Time flashlight used	SD Encounter Time of day
0-5 - 28% 6-10 - 22% 11-20 - 17% 21-50 - 17% Over 50 - 16%	0-5 - 53% 6-10 - 20% 11-20 - 12% 21-50 - 8% Over 50 - 6%	17%	6 P.M. - 6 A.M. - 62% 6 A.M. - 6 P.M. - 38% (All figures rounded up)

Total # Presentations	Total % Pres. requiring shot	Total % shots requiring judgement	Total % shots fired in high arousal state
16	87.5%	0%	0%

Total # Reloads/Unloads	Total # Stoppage Drills	Total # positions used	Use of cover per % rounds fired
3 / 0	0 (unless naturally occurs)	3	17%

Course Evaluation Summaries & Comparisons to Statistical Data (SD)

Course 7: DPTC No. 3 (NEW PARADIGM) (MT/PSD/MC-OC-CC-JT)

% Rounds fired per distance (ft.)		SD Encounter distances (ft.)		% Time flashlight used	SD Encounter Time of day
0-5 -	0%	0-5 -	53%	0%	6 P.M. - 6 A.M. - 62%
6-10 -	0%	6-10 -	20%		6 A.M. - 6 P.M. - 38%
11-20 -	0%	11-20 -	12%		(All figures rounded up)
21-50 -	100%	21-50 -	8%		
Over 50 -	0%	Over 50 -	6%		

Total # Presentations	Total % Pres. requiring shot	Total % shots requiring judgement	Total % shots fired in high arousal state
2	Target/stimulus dependent	100%	0%

Total # Reloads/Unloads	Total # Stoppage Drills	Total # positions used	Use of cover per % rounds fired
0 /10	0	SC	100%

Course Evaluation Summaries & Comparisons to Statistical Data (SD)

Course 8: DPTC No. 3A SABER CHALLENGE (NEW PARADIGM) (MT/PSD/MC-OC-CC-JT)

% Rounds fired per distance (ft.)		SD Encounter distances (ft.)		% Time flashlight used	SD Encounter Time of day
0-5 -	0%	0-5 -	53%	May be adapted	6 P.M. - 6 A.M. - 62%
6-10 -	0%	6-10 -	20%		6 A.M. - 6 P.M. - 38%
11-20 -	100%	11-20 -	12%		(All figures rounded up)
21-50 -	0%	21-50 -	8%		
Over 50 -	0%	Over 50 -	6%		

Total # Presentations	Total % Pres. requiring shot	Total % shots requiring judgement	Total % shots fired in high arousal state
1	Target/stimulus dependent	100%	100%

Total # Reloads/Unloads	Total # Stoppage Drills	Total # positions used	Use of cover per % rounds fired
1-2 / 1-2	0 (unless naturally occurs)	SC	100%

Course Evaluation Summaries & Comparisons to Statistical Data (SD)

Course 9: DPTC No. 4 HOUSE OF HORRORS (NEW PARADIGM) (MT/PSD/MC-OC-CC-JT)

% Rounds fired per distance (ft.)		SD Encounter distances (ft.)		% Time flashlight used	SD Encounter Time of day
0-21	- 100%	0-5	- 53%	SC (60% of course conducted in low / dim light)	6 P.M. - 6 A.M. - 62%
		6-10	- 20%		6 A.M. - 6 P.M. - 38%
		11-20	- 12%		(All figures rounded up)
21-50 -	0%	21-50	- 8%		
Over 50 -	0%	Over 50	- 6%		

Total # Presentations	Total % Pres. requiring shot	Total % shots requiring judgement	Total % shots fired in high arousal state
1-9 (SC: student decides when or if)	SC (100% judgement)	100%	100%

Total # Reloads/Unloads	Total # Stoppage Drills	Total # positions used	Use of cover per % rounds fired
0-1 / 0-1	0 (unless naturally occurs)	SC	SC (100% encouraged)

Course Evaluation Summaries & Comparisons to Statistical Data (SD) Sample Worksheet

This sample worksheet is provided as a template. Actual training value of any courses of fire can be illustrated by extrapolating the pertinent data (reference the various course analysis presented in this section), and plugging it in as indicated.

COURSE NAME: _____

COURSE TYPE: (Old Paradigm / New Paradigm) _____

PRIMARY TRAINING ELEMENTS: (MT/PSD/MC-OC-CC-JT) _____

% Rounds fired per distance (ft.)	SD Encounter distances (ft.)	% Time flashlight used	SD Encounter Time of day
0-5 - _____%	0-5 - 53%	_____%	6 P.M. - 6 A.M. - 62%
6-10 - _____%	6-10 - 20%		6 A.M. - 6 P.M. - 38%
11-20 - _____%	11-20 - 12%		(All figures rounded up)
21-50 - _____%	21-50 - 8%		
Over 50 - _____%	Over 50 - 6%		

Total # Presentations	Total % Pres. requiring shot	Total % shots requiring judgement	Total % shots fired in high arousal state
_____	_____%	_____%	_____%

Total # Reloads/Unloads	Total # Stoppage Drills (intentional)	Total # positions used	Use of cover per % rounds fired
_____ / _____	_____	_____	_____%

APPENDIX B

Research Project 01-003: Combat Stress, Point Shooting, and Shots Fired to Hits Achieved Survey Results

This survey was initiated by the author and conducted by members of the Firearms Training Unit in 2003, under the direction of Trooper Paul Wosny.

The intended goal of the project was to assemble a data base of information collected from self report and behavioral observation of law enforcement officers under controlled, mission-specific generated stress.

Ultimately we hoped to be able to measure and assess any reduction in physiological arousal achieved through the stress inoculation process in training, and to evaluate both the viability and effectiveness of the Point Shooting Technique as taught to the officers participating in the program.

The survey was administered during in-service training over a period of three months to ninety-six individual officers immediately after they had participated in the House of Horrors training course.

For the purposes of the study (as well as to increase the effectiveness of the training experience), the House of Horrors course had been slightly modified from the version presented in this book. In addition to reformatting the various mannequin-based stations, a live instructor/role player was used to provide an immediate threat stimulus (shooting man) at Station #6.

The information gathered for the survey was based upon the participant's reactions and performance while dealing with this station only.

All data was recorded by the primary instructor. The participant was questioned first. After the participant answered each question, the primary instructor then recorded the answers provided by the instructor/aggressor (role player). In cases of acute memory gaps, questions were asked of the participant after the scenario was revealed to him/her.

The officers who participated in the survey were chosen completely at random from the overall number of attendees present at each day's in-service iteration. In this way, we were assured of capturing an accurate cross-sectional "snapshot" of the department as a whole, for while all of the officers were sworn members of the department and had participated in the New Paradigm program at least one time previously, each brought a different set of experiences, training, and educational backgrounds to the table.

Both male and female officers participated in the survey. Ages ranged from early twenties to late sixties. White, Black, Hispanic, and Asian ethnic groups were represented. Officer's current assignment job descriptions ranged from patrol, K9 and SWAT to administrative, investigatory, and supervisory positions. All ranks from line officers to staff officers participated.

Both the questions that were asked and the data extrapolated from the survey are presented here.

It is hoped that the information gathered through this and future surveys will help us to better understand the nature of combat and the type of training that is most effective in preparing police officers to deal with it.

INDIVIDUAL SURVEY REPORT QUESTIONNAIRE

Question	Participant	Instructor
1. Do you remember what happened here?	Yes / No	N/A
2. Were shots fired by participant?	Yes / No	Yes / No
3. If Yes, number of shots fired by participant?	_____	_____
4. If Yes, number of hits achieved by participant?	_____	_____
5. Did you say anything to the Instructor/Aggressor?	Yes / No	Yes / No
6. Were shots fired by Instructor/Aggressor?	Yes / No	Yes / No
7. Number of shots fired by Instructor/Aggressor?	_____	_____
8. Did the Instructor/Aggressor say anything?	Yes / No	Yes / No
9. Do you know what the Instructor/Aggressor said?	Yes / No	Threat [1]
10. Time involved (from first to last shot)?	_____	_____
11. Number of hands participant used to control weapon?	One / Two	One / Two
12. Did you see the sights on the weapon?	Yes / No	N/A
13. Was the Point Shooting Technique used by participant?	Yes / No	Yes / No
14. Did you have any intrusive or distracting thoughts?	Yes / No	N/A
15. Was verbal "lock-up" experienced and/or observed?	Yes / No	Yes / No
16. Manifestations of "Hollywood Stylizations" observed?	N/A	Yes / No

Additional Instructor Notes / Comments: _____

[1] The threat presented was consistently similar: Role player armed with pistol, standing approximately 15 feet away from threshold in low light environment. When the participant opened the curtain, the role player, in plain view of the participant, stated clearly and loudly, "I'M GONNA' KILL YOU!" and then brought the pistol up and pointed it at the participant. If the participant fired immediately and hit the role player, the role player would respond appropriately depending upon placement of the shot. Other options available to the participant included taking cover, verbalizing, firing, and doing nothing. If the officer did not take action to get to cover and/or to stop the threat, the role player would fire until such time as he was incapacitated. If participants were hit by the role player's rounds during the encounter, they were required to continue the exercise until they had successfully stopped the immediate threat. If a participant froze or otherwise failed to respond to the threat (something we had observed occasionally when people participated in the House of Horrors course for the first time), he was required to immediately repeat the station and complete it successfully.

RESEARCH PROJECT 01-003: COMPLETED SURVEY RESULTS

The data presented below was extrapolated from ninety-six (96) completed survey forms.

Of the 96 individuals who participated in the survey:

19%   Experienced a *complete* memory gap during which they could not recall anything that had happened during the encounter within five minutes of the event.[2]

68%   Did not verbalize during the encounter. Of this group:
        - 23% believed they had verbalized when they actually had not

16%   Remembered verbalizing but did not [3]

5%   Did not believe they had verbalized when they actually had

32%   Experienced "verbal lock-up", during which they tried to speak but could not

2%   Described experiencing intrusive thoughts. (In both instances, they stated that while engaging the threat subject in the scenario, they had simultaneously vividly recalled a similar real-world incident they had been involved in.) [4]

5%   Exhibited "Hollywood Stylizations", most commonly pistol held up next to face [5]

73%   Experienced auditory exclusion, during which they did not hear, or could not interpret what the instructor-aggressor said to them [6]

(Continued on following page)

---

[2] Our initial data indicated that approximately 85-90% of officers participating in the House of Horrors course would experience at least one *complete* memory gap during the course, remembering absolutely nothing about a particular station, event, or action. This higher figure was based on a debriefing of the entire course, including all nine stations. While only 19% of the participants experienced a complete memory gap at this one station, many, many more experienced partial memory loss during the event.

[3] This number is based upon the overall survey group of 96 individuals.

[4] Reliving similar past experiences is the most commonly reported intrusive thought.

[5] Observations of Hollywood Stylizations have been significantly reduced since the first iteration of the program. Officers commonly stated that they were not aware of their tendency to assume these positions until it was experienced and pointed out to them in the House of Horrors.

[6] Tunnel vision is another very common perceptual distortion we consistently noted in the House of Horrors. Rare is the officer who can describe the face of the assailant at the Shooting Man station when the automated mannequin is used. What is almost always perfectly described however, is the pistol and how it is held. No data was developed in the survey regarding the occurrence of tunnel vision due to the necessity of having the instructor/role player's head and face concealed by a Simunition brand protective face mask, as it was felt that this would unfairly influence the results of the survey. An estimate based on prior iterations would indicate occurrences of tunnel vision are experienced by at least 90-95 percent of participants at this one station alone.

29%   Experienced a *significant sense* of time distortion.[7] Of this group:
- 24% experienced slow motion time
- 5% experienced fast motion time

10%   Did not remember being fired upon when they were

2%   Remembered being fired upon when they were not

6%   Remembered being fired upon by more rounds than were actually fired

24%   Remembered being fired upon by less rounds than were actually fired

8%   Did not remember firing at the threat subject when they actually did

5%   Remembered firing at the threat subject when they actually did not

23%   Remembered firing fewer rounds than they actually had

11%   Remembered firing more rounds than they actually had

98%   Employed the Point Shooting Technique while engaging the threat subject

95%   Fired at the threat while holding the pistol using only one-hand. Of this group:
- 40% believed they had held the pistol using two hands when they had not

2%   Claimed to have seen and/or used the sights during the encounter

98%   Stated they never saw, or even thought about looking for their sights because:
- there was not enough time (consistently the #1 answer)
- their eyes were on the threat subject / area because they *needed to see what was happening*

3   Average number of rounds fired by the officers during the encounter

64%   Average hit rate achieved by officers against the threat subject while operating in a low-light environment and under fire, from a distance of fifteen feet.

---

[7] While I have come to believe that most officers probably experience time distortion to some degree when involved in dangerous or potentially dangerous activities (see Chapter 6), only those who indicated a significant degree of distortion were noted in the survey. (For example, an officer reports that his encounter lasted 15-20 seconds, when in actuality it was over in approximately 2-4 seconds.)

Summary

The data gathered from the sample survey is significant for many reasons. First, it shares many similarities to data gleaned by studies that have been conducted interviewing officers who have been involved in real-world deadly force encounters. The fact that we are able to consistently document that officers experience perceptual narrowing, memory gaps, etc., while participating in the House of Horrors Training Course just as they do in real-world events indicates that we are able to successfully and consistently induce true high arousal states under controlled conditions.

Second, the data presented above validates not only the approach we have taken to achieve one of the primary goals of stress inoculation, but also validates the adoption of the Point Shooting Technique. I base this statement on the following:

The vast majority of officers participating in this survey have received a maximum of just two days training in the Point Shooting Technique during in-service training iterations. Due to logistical constraints, these two days were conducted separately–and about a year apart! Yet not only did 98% of the officers actually employ the technique consistently during the heat of action–unlike the Modern Technique and the rarely-seen (during close quarter battle) "Weaver Stance"–but they also achieved an average hit rate (most impacting in the middle and upper torso) of 64% while doing it. That is quite a jump from the national average (shared by our department prior to the implementation of the New Paradigm) of 8-14%.

And this is just the beginning. As the program progresses and we are able to provide more frequent training iterations to the thousands of men and women we serve, we anticipate that our officer's close quarter proficiency will continue to improve as their skill retention levels are much higher with the more easily learned and retained–not to mention extremely more combat effective–Point Shooting Technique.

APPENDIX C
Professional Experience & Work History Questionnaire

PLEASE NOTE: This form is intended to assist us in providing you with the best training possible. **Completed forms will be included in individual firearms training record jackets and maintained on file.** Future general and specialized programs will be formatted based on the information gathered. **While these forms will be kept private, they are not considered legally confidential.** Please do not write in any comments or information relating to specific incidents or cases. NOTE: YOU ARE NOT REQUIRED TO FILL OUT THIS FORM. IT IS STRICTLY VOLUNTARY.

Name: _____ **ID#:** _____ **Date:** _____

DOB: _____ **SSN:** _____

Dominant Hand: ( )R ( )L ( )CO **Dominant Eye:** ( )R ( )L ( )CO

1. Current assignment: _____

2. Primary function: ( ) PATROL ( ) INVESTIGATOR ( ) OTHER_____

3. Total length of police service (years / months): _____

4. Note prior assignment types: ( ) PATROL ( ) INVESTIGATOR ( ) K9 / SWAT

   OTHER _____

5. How long since you last fired your weapon in a training capacity? _____

6. How would you rate your past firearms proficiency?
   ( ) POOR ( ) FAIR ( ) GOOD ( ) EXCELLENT

7. Have you encountered any significant problems while participating in past firearms training iterations? ( ) NO ( ) YES If YES, what? _____

   _____

8. During your career, have you ever taken your weapon from its holster in the performance of duty in an enforcement capacity? ( ) YES ( ) NO

   If yes, indicate approximate number of times: (circle) 1 2 3 4 5 6-10 10+

9. During your career, have you ever intentionally pointed your weapon at a human being while in the performance of duty in an enforcement capacity? ( ) YES ( ) NO

   If yes, indicate approximate number of times: (circle) 1 2 3 4 5 6-10 10+

10. During your career, have you ever intentionally fired your weapon at a human being while in the performance of duty in an enforcement capacity? ( ) YES ( ) NO

    If yes, indicate approximate number of times: (circle) 1 2 3 4 5 6+ (Turn form over)

11. During your career, have you ever fired your weapon (intentionally or unintentionally) and shot a human being while in the performance of duty in an enforcement capacity?
( ) YES ( ) NO

If yes, indicate approximate number of times: (circle) 1 2 3 4 5   6+

If yes, indicate result of shooting/s: ( ) FATAL   ( ) NON-FATAL

---

12. During your career, have you ever been physically assaulted by another human being while in the performance of duty in an enforcement capacity?   ( ) YES   ( ) NO

If yes, indicate approximate number of times: (circle) 1 2 3 4 5   6-10   10+

13. During your career, have you ever been physically injured by another human being by means OTHER THAN FIREARMS while in the performance of duty in an enforcement capacity?
( ) YES ( ) NO

If yes, indicate approximate number of times: (circle) 1 2 3 4 5   6-10   10+

Also, if yes, indicate means by which injury was inflicted:
( ) BODY PART e.g. hands/feet/head   ( ) IMPACT WEAPON e.g. club/stick/pipe
            ( ) EDGED WEAPON e.g. knife/razor/machete   ( ) VEHICLE
( ) OTHER _____

14. During your career, while in the performance of duty, have you ever been presented with a situation involving a human being armed with a firearm?   ( ) YES   ( ) NO

If yes, indicate approximate number of times: (circle) 1 2 3 4 5   6-10   10+

15. During your career, while in the performance of duty, have you ever had another human being intentionally point a firearm at you?   ( ) YES   ( ) NO

If yes, indicate approximate number of times: (circle) 1 2 3 4 5   6-10   10+

16. During your career, while in the performance of duty, have you ever been intentionally or unintentionally fired upon?   ( ) YES   ( ) NO

If yes, indicate approximate number of times: (circle) 1 2 3 4 5   6-10   10+

17. During your career, have you ever been wounded by gunfire while in the performance of duty?
( ) YES   ( ) NO

If yes, indicate approximate number of times: (circle) 1 2 3 4 5   6-10   10+

Thank you for taking the time to fill out this Questionnaire. Your responses will help us shape and improve future training iterations.

POLICE PISTOLCRAFT TRIVIA

Down in Hogan's Alley

While the FBI's modern "Hogan's Alley" tactical training facility at the Training Academy in Quantico, Virginia, is very well known, the origin of the name "Hogan's Alley" is not.

Often erroneously believed to have been named in honor of an instructor or agent, the name can actually be traced back to the first comic strip to appear on a regular basis in U.S newspapers. Created by Richard Outcault, "Down in Hogan's Alley" was first published in 1895. The series appeared in Joseph Pulitzer's *New York World*. Each installment depicted the lives and adventures of various characters–both human and animal–that found their way to the slums of New York City and the rough and tumble Hogan's Alley.

Approximately 25 years later, the name Hogan's Alley would be connected for the first time with police firearms training at the NRA-sponsored Special Police School conducted at Camp Perry, Ohio.

"Down in Hogan's Alley" by Richard Outcault, circa 1895.

APPENDIX D
Safety On the Range

A man who has never once erred is dangerous.
                        - Yamamoto Tsunetomo
                          Hagakure: The Book of the Samurai
                          1716

As police officers, we all realize that proper firearms handling and storage methods, both while operating in the field or when at home, are critical to ensuring that no one is unintentionally or needlessly injured by gunfire.

As instructors, the idea of safe firearms handling, as well as recommended methods and techniques for carrying it out, is–*or should be*–drilled into us on a more regular basis than the average police officer will ever receive in a typical 25-year career.

And yet, every year in the US, professional police firearms instructors are either injured or killed during training, or they injure or kill other instructors or trainees.

So while you may think that everyone you work with knows about safe firearms handling, or has been taught and should know about it, you must always approach any type or level of firearms training with the knowledge that *anyone* involved in the training *including the instructor* is capable of making a stupid mistake, or experiencing a lapse in attention or judgment at any time, anywhere.

Like many instructors, I know this is true because it has happened to me personally. Fortunately, in these few embarrassing instances, no one was injured, and I have come away from them with a deeper awareness and greater resolve to ensure that it does not happen again.

The fact that any of us can make a mistake is also good to remember should a student or coworker screw up in training. Whenever I'm running a program and someone makes a mistake, I always try to treat them as I'd like to be treated should it happen to me. In my opinion, however, the Golden Rule does not apply to anyone who screws up because they were playing grab-ass or acting boisterously, foolishly or recklessly.

While it's absolutely preferable for the instructor to enjoy training and to try to make it enjoyable for those being taught, the instructor's ultimate responsibility is to ensure the safety of all by neither encouraging nor permitting unsafe, unprofessional behavior.

Safety as a Compulsion

When working with firearms, you must ensure safety at all times: You MUST check and recheck and check again to ensure that the weapon you or anyone else is holding is safe, clear and empty when doing anything other than firing it or preparing to fire it in training.

While I always prefer to use an inert training pistol when demonstrating any tactic or technique in front of a class, occasionally it is necessary to employ a real, unloaded weapon. When this is the case, in addition to never pointing it at anyone *for any reason*, I tend to perform a safe condition check so often it might appear I have obsessive-compulsive disorder–too bad! You cannot check too many times!

All it takes is a single instant, a lone moment when you are distracted or inattentive for tragedy to result. So forget about appearing savoir faire and debonair–keep it real and keep it safe instead.

This fact can never be stressed enough. At the start of any firearms training program, regardless of the age or experience of the members of the class, I always include a quick "reality check" in the following way.

The "One Round" Reality Check

After clearing my pistol and having someone else double-check it to confirm it is indeed safe, clear, and empty, I hold it up sideways to the class, slide locked to the rear, and recite the following spiel:

Today we are going to be working with deadly, deadly weapons. Now usually when I say this, I get a lot of 'no shit' looks, but we always have to be aware of this. We carry this gun day in and day out, bring it into our homes, and after a while we sometimes start to think of it as just another piece of gear. But you must remember, all it takes is *one round*–if just *one round* comes out of the end of that barrel, and goes into your body or someone else's, no matter how much we may want to we can never call it back. And that one round can change or end your life or someone else's life *forever.*

As police officers, most of us have seen the damage bullets do to a body. We understand *forever.*

So stay sharp, stay in control of yourself and your weapon, keep your fingers away from the trigger unless you're in the process of shooting, and keep that muzzle controlled at all times.

We're going to have a good training day today, you're going to enjoy this–but never

forget exactly what it is you will be holding in your hand–*a deadly, deadly weapon.*

Hot Brass

Hot shell casings landing on exposed skin or falling inside clothing is another reality of conducting firearms training with a number of shooters on line at the same time. This should also be addressed in the morning safety briefing.

I usually explain it in the following way:

Today we'll be firing semiautomatic pistols on the line. As you all know, these pistols extract and eject hot shell casings out of the chamber and up in the air. Occasionally, one of these hot shell casings from your weapon or some one else's weapon will go up in the air and come down on you. They may fall right into your shirt collar and down your shirt, and once in there start to burn your skin. Usually what happens is it burns, burns, burns, hotter and hotter, and then just stops as the heat dissipates. In fact, some of these casings are so hot, that they may even hit your neck and just stick there, and start to sizzle. It's excellent when they do that!"

That usually evokes some slightly nervous laughter. Then I perform a physical demonstration. I turn and face the side wall and assume a static-type firing stance in front of the class, arm extended as if holding a pistol, and extend my index finger, forming my "finger gun", and say,

If that happens to you today on the firing line, if a piece of hot brass goes down your shirt or sticks to your neck and starts to burn, this is what you will do...

I then use my non-dominant index finger to trace the arc of a shell casing flying through the air and falling into my shirt collar. Once it is in, I maintain my stance and keep my dominant hand "finger gun" locked onto the side wall and enthusiastically growl, "Yeaaaahhhh!"

224

Then I turn to the class and say,

That's what you do, you stay focused and you suck it up, you maintain your discipline and eat that little bit of pain–it's good for you actually, it's pain inoculation training!

Again, there is usually some laughter, and then I drive the point home.

If, however, the casing comes up and then falls down your collar, or sticks to your neck, and you do *this*...

Again I assume the stance and trace the casing's arc into my shirt, except this time once the casing is in I break my focus from the wall, grab my neck with my non-dominant hand, and wave my finger gun all around the room, pointing it at the class while saying, "Oh, jeese, jeese! Hot! Hot!", usually evoking more laughter.

Then I stop, look soberly at the class, and finish with,

If that happens to you today, then you're out of here. We won't be screaming and yelling at you, you'll just be removed quietly from the firing line and you'll come back another day. For make no mistake about it, ladies and gentlemen, while we do run a more relaxed range, we run an absolutely *safe* range. And the ultimate responsibility for the safe handling of your weapon is right on you, right where it is every day when you're out there operating in the streets, and when you bring that weapon into your homes with your families.

Explaining the possibility of catching hot brass and modeling both the desired and the unacceptable reactions to it as described above works for me. I've found that by taking a chance and putting myself out there, playing the clown a bit, I'm able to grab the attention of all the members of the class and plant a picture in their minds that stays with them. It's no exaggeration to say that at least one or two people catch some hot brass every day we train. Incredibly, the vast majority of them does as instructed, and sucks up the pain, maintaining their focus and control of the weapon. In fact, four years and thousands of people later, we've only had a few instances when the brass got the better of the shooter and caused him or her to significantly break focus, losing momentary control of the muzzle.

Most of them just growl or grit their teeth, and smile through the pain.

Based upon my own experiences catching brass on the line, and from what I've witnessed when others do the same, I believe it *is* pain inoculation, and it is good for us.

I also try and comment on it when it happens, providing both positive reinforcement and an additional operant conditioning reward. "Good job!" [1]

Unloading the Semiautomatic Pistol

Properly unloading or clearing the pistol to make it safe and empty is a basic activity that can be done practically anywhere at anytime if certain precautions are taken.

Acceptable procedures for accomplishing this are usually drilled into officers at the basic academy level.

As basic an activity as it is, however, it should be modeled and explained at the start of each day's training iteration, regardless of the student's level of skill or experience. The method we use is illustrated here.

With rare exception, the first step in the administrative unloading or clearing process requires the operator to remove the magazine from the holstered pistol. The magazine should then be placed in a pocket or otherwise secured to ensure that both hands are free to finish the

---

[1] Operant Conditioning is also present. Stimulus: Unexpected and focused burning pain Response: Ignore it and focus on task Reward: Success and "Good job!"

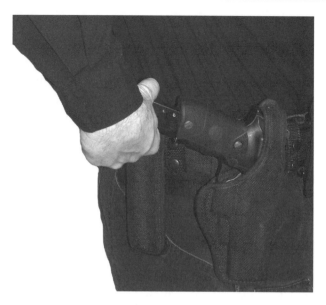

STEP ONE: Remove the magazine.

clearing process. You should explain why this is preferable to the unwieldy–and therefore unsafe–practice of keeping the magazine in your hand while trying to perform the next step of the operation, cycling the slide. (Though the practice of removing the magazine from the pistol while the pistol is still secured in the holster is preferred, the practice of safely removing the magazine from the drawn pistol

STEP TWO: Draw pistol and point the muzzle in a SAFE DIRECTION. Personal body armor placed on a chair is used to provide a safe direction in this illustration.

should also be discussed, demonstrated, and practiced.)

After the magazine has been secured, the pistol is then drawn, finger off the trigger, and the weapon's muzzle is pointed in a safe direction.

When instructing, I usually stop at this point and ask the class to define a safe direction. The most popular answer to this question is, "Down range."

I then ask the next question, "Okay, where is downrange in this classroom? In fact, where is downrange in your home?"

Common, reasonable answers to this include, "Down at the basement floor; in the corner; etc." I've also heard answers that curled my hair such as:

"I point it into the drawer of my bureau"

"I point it up at the ceiling" (turned out this officer lived on the second floor of a three-story building) and, one of my all-time favorites, "I point it out the window."

Believe me, if you want to find out what people are really doing with their firearms, regardless of what you or anyone else has ever told them or taught them, simply ask them point blank. (Just know that the first time you guffaw or berate any of them for telling you the truth, the word will spread and you'll never hear another honest answer. Developing trust with your people is a two way street–the more trust there is between you and those you're trying to help, the better the training experience will be for everyone involved, including you. Relating stories about specific people and identifying them by name for the class without the expressed permission of the involved officer is another way to destroy this trust. Sure, the people present when you relate the embarrassing story will laugh, but they will be silently thinking, "No way I'll ever let this guy know about that mistake I made.")

After listening to the various answers, I then summarize by pointing out that unlike on the range, *there is no downrange in the real world.*

Stray bullets might not be stopped by a floor or wall, but may pass through into another room or even outside. Ricochets are another possibility. "So what can you do?"

Once a problem has been identified, the instructor must provide solutions. One method for doing this is to solicit suggestions from the class, commenting positively on the good ones and redirecting the thinking of the less desirable ideas. If time is short or class participation not forthcoming, then you can simply provide the solutions yourself. (Should the members of the class fail to volunteer answers, or even ask a pertinent or obvious question, you can always employ the old instructor's device of asking yourself the question, and then answering it.)

One common solution for providing a safe direction at home includes designating a specific corner of a room in the house or apartment for this purpose. Any corner chosen should be constructed of surfaces that will not cause ricochets, yet will also not allow a round to penetrate and exit into either another room or outside of the building.

STEP THREE: Cycle the action and clear the chamber using either an overhand grip (shown above) or "slingshot grip" (gripping the rear of the slide between the index finger and thumb of support hand).

> *Safe Direction*: Any direction in which an unintentional discharge would result in no loss of life, no injury, and limited property damage.

Rooms located in basements are preferable. Other options include placing a drum or barrel filled with sand in a designated location at which the muzzle may be directed while loading and unloading the weapon.

The simplest solution, as usual, is right in front of us. (And in back of us, in this case.) Body armor–after you have taken it off and placed it on a floor, chair, couch or bed–provides a portable bullet-trap in any secure room in your home.

Next, while maintaining a safe hold and muzzle direction, demonstrate and explain how to grip the rear of the slide using either an overhand or slingshot type grip, and cycle the slide THREE times before locking it to the rear. (Ensure that the muzzle is kept pointed in the designated safe direction during cycling and while locking the slide to the rear.)

When cycling the action, the slide should be drawn fully rearward each time and then released. Avoid maintaining your grip on the slide as it travels forward, "riding the slide". If you do this in front of the class, some of them will do it later, possibly inducing stoppages.

When demonstrating this I count aloud with each rack of the slide, "One, two, three." If there is a round in the chamber, it should be allowed to eject freely from the weapon, with no attempts by the instructor to catch it or drop it into his hand.

We have adopted the three-cycle rule for a reality-based reason. This reason is explained to the class as the technique is demonstrated:

The reason we have adopted the three-cycle rule is because of the nature of the beast. If you have been out working double-shifts, over time, details, whatever, and you get home tired and worn out, it is possible that you might forget to remove the magazine prior to clearing the weapon. If this happens, you can find yourself ejecting the round in the chamber while unknowingly chambering another round from the magazine. Should this occur, you are now in the doubly-dangerous situation of holding a loaded pistol that you *think* is unloaded. If, however, you do the one-two-three clearing drill religiously, then no matter how tired you are, you will get the message that you've overlooked something when those rounds keep ejecting out of the weapon.

Far from talking down to the class, you are discussing a very real danger that any one of us may face at any time during our careers. This technique in particular has been commented on by many of the people we've taught it to as being "a real good, common sense-based idea."

Finally, while still keeping the muzzle pointed at the vest, first visually and *then physically* inspect the magazine well and chamber to ensure the pistol is absolutely safe, clear and empty. Once you are satisfied it is, have *someone else* CHECK and VERIFY it.

STEP FOUR: Visually and physically check to ensure the magazine well and chamber area are ABSOLUTELY safe, clear and empty of ammunition.

Lead Safety on the Range

While some firearms training facilities are beginning to require the use of clean or lead-free ammunition (a trend I believe will become the norm eventually), most still do not.

Lead, whether contained in the projectile, propellant, or primer, is a hazardous material. Since the instructor is responsible for ensuring the safety of everyone he trains, the hazards of lead exposure during training must be addressed any time you engage in any training activities that employ ammunition that is not 100% lead free.

Airborne lead particles are produced with every round fired when the ammunition contains lead-based components. If precautions are not taken, these hazardous particles can then enter the human body through several methods: inhalation, absorption, and ingestion.

Inhalation: Particles enter through the respiratory system and are absorbed into the bronchial aveoli.

Absorption: Particles are absorbed through the skin and hair follicles.

Ingestion: Particles are ingested through the mouth.

Once lead is introduced into the body through one of these routes, it works its way through the blood stream and soft body tissue and eventually is stored in the bones. The reason this occurs is because the human body cannot differentiate between lead and calcium.

Having been present while countless rounds had been fired on all types of ranges for many years, I was a bit surprised when I first learned how lead actually entered and was stored in the body. In addition to standing in lead-contaminated clouds generated by a line of shooters on windless days, the first thing I thought of were the police calls conducted afterward, and how we would gather the expended shell casings in our hats, dump them into buckets, and then place the hats back on our heads–depositing all those lead particles right onto our hair follicles.

Make no mistake, lead is a poison, and if too much is stored in your body, it will kill you.

Police firearms instructors are extremely susceptible to this because of the nature of the work, and some have indeed succumbed to lead poisoning over the years. That's why establishing baseline lead levels and then checking them periodically is recommended, if you do indeed train with leaded ammunition on a regular basis.

Some other guidelines that should be used to protect you and your family from lead poisoning are:

1. **Don't smoke on the range.** Smoking cigarettes, cigars, or pipes on the range may increase the quantity, and will accelerate the speed of absorption, of inhaled lead into the blood stream.

2. **Don't eat on the range.** Lead particles on your hands and face can be ingested through contact with food.

3. **Don't collect fired brass in hats.** Whenever you collect expended shell casings in your hat, you're simultaneously collecting lead particles as well. If you then dump the casings into a bucket and put your hat back on your head, you've dumped those lead particles on your hair. They can then work their way through the follicles and into the skin.[2] A better idea is simply to collect the casings by hand, place them into containers, and then wash your hands thoroughly.

4. **Decontaminate yourself and your clothing.** Lead particles may attach to all exposed surfaces, including your face, arms, clothing, etc. Wash thoroughly with cold water after training. Use plenty of soap. Pay attention to areas where exposed hair is present, including moustaches and beards. You may want to change your clothing after you complete training and before returning home. At the least, remove or change your shoes before you enter your home, especially if there are little ones or even pets inside, to prevent tracking lead particles onto the floor that may be picked up or ingested. Wash range clothing separately from your family's clothing, and let them air dry as opposed to placing them in the dryer. This will further help prevent contamination.

5. **Avoid contaminating others.** Lead particles can be transferred by casual contact. Family and friends should not be hugged or kissed until you've had a chance to shower and change your clothes.

6. **Minimize risks to pregnant officers.** While studies indicate that the amount and levels of noise experienced during normal firearms training iterations seem to pose little danger to the health of the fetus, the possibility of lead contamination being passed from the mother's body to the fetus is very real.[3] For this reason, it is recommend that only 100% lead-free ammunition be used when training pregnant officers if they are required to participate, and there is no medical necessity that precludes their participating in firearms training. (Many agencies require written consent from the officer's physician prior to allowing them to participate in training.) While other safeguards such as having the officer wear some type of

---

[2] There are some who claim that the type of lead particulates produced during the firing process are not able to enter the body through the hair folicles. Until absolute proof is established verifying this, it is better to err on the side of caution.

[3] The Hospital for Women Medical Center's Reproductive Toxicology Center (RTC) has provided clinical information on both subjects. The RTC advises that "some direct effects of environmental sound on the human fetus...include fetal movements and fetal cardioacceleration." "The diversity of sounds reaching the fetus is relatively large, with sounds with frequencies below 2 khz being attenuated very little. The investigation of possible adverse effects resulting from ambient, aversive sound has not yielded any clear associations." Additional research suggests that amniotic fluid reduces the noise levels by 30db (which is greater than most of the ear protection worn by shooters).

respirator may be employed when training with leaded ammunition, the availability of lead-free ammo and the potential for injury to the child generated from exposure to the lead, in my opinion, make the choice simple.

7. **Participate in lead safety training programs.** Attend all training programs provided by your department or agency to ensure awareness of the hazards of lead.

Safety Rules

After completing the morning briefing, each student should be given a copy of the *Range Safety Rules*. After everyone has a copy in front of them, it is a good idea to have the first student at either end of the class begin by reading the first rule aloud. Each student in turn then reads the next rule aloud, until the entire form has been completed.

Having the students read aloud does three

things. First, it insures that they all read the entire form. Second, it provides the instructor with a sound basis to reasonably and articulately explain why he believed that each student was fully aware of the rules, should that question arise. And third, it serves as another method for getting the students personally involved in the training experience.

During the course of the briefing, I usually interject a few comments and/or demonstrations at key points, expanding upon specific rules for the benefit of the class.

The content of the form we have adopted for use has been drawn from many sources, and can be altered or adapted to suit your department's individual needs.

In the dissected sample provided below, I use asterisks (*) and *italics* to indicate additional material that may be added during the safety briefing, and provide a synopsis of its content.

This additional material would not normally be included on the printed safety form.[4]

(See sample form on page 235.)

FIREARMS SAFETY RULES

A.   CARDINAL RULES OF FIREARMS SAFETY:

1. Treat all firearms as though they were loaded.
2. Keep your finger outside the trigger guard until you are on target and have decided to fire.
3. Point the muzzle in a safe direction at all times. *(* Define a safe direction.)*
4. Be sure of your target and what is beyond it.

REMEMBER THE "LASER RULE": TREAT YOUR FIREARM AS IF IT IS A LASER GUN WITH THE BEAM ALWAYS ON; WHATEVER THE BEAM TOUCHES, IT CUTS THROUGH!

(*Teaching Moment: At this point, the preferred Recovery Method (See Appendix K) is explained and demonstrated. In the past I have employed a laser-equipped pistol for more dramatic effect during this explanation, allowing the laser's beam to provide a visual indication of the dangers of improper muzzle control.)

Continued on next page...

---

[4] The form shown in this section was originally adapted from that used at the SIGARMS Academy in Epping, NH.

B. SPECIFIC RANGE SAFETY RULES:

1. Ear and eye protection are required at all times when firing is being conducted on the range. This includes observers.

(* In addition to ear and wrap-around eye protection, we also require that a hat with a brim be worn on the line. The reason for this is explained to the class as, "We must wear hats with a brim when training on the line to prevent one of those hot extracted shell casings from falling behind your eyegear and getting trapped against your eyeball.")

2. Eye protection is required in the cleaning room.

(* The reason we require protective eye wear be worn in the cleaning room is explained at this point. Brush-flicked particles, solvents being sprayed, etc. can easily induce injury to the eyes. Copies of this requirement are also posted in the cleaning area.)

3. Immediately upon picking up a firearm, visually and physically check to see it is unloaded.
4. Check a second time.

(* After number 4 is read, I usually comment, "You got the easy one!" This comment generally elicits some laughter, simultaneously recognizing and breaking the tension that reading aloud induces in many of the participants. It is easy to forget that for some people, reading aloud in front of their peers will be the most stressful part of the training program.)

5. Never give a firearm to, or take a firearm from anyone, unless the action is opened and the weapon is confirmed to be safe and clear.
6. Load/reload/unload only after position is taken at the firing point and on command unless directed otherwise.
7. Keep the firearm pointed down-range at all times.
8. Never draw a handgun from the holster on the range unless instructed to.
9. Never draw or reholster with your finger in the trigger guard or on the trigger.
10. NEVER holster a cocked weapon. _____(Initials)

(*Note: Number 10 is included in our program because we use a double-action configured, decocking lever-equipped weapon. This rule should be modified depending upon the weapon system employed by your agency.)

Teaching Moment: At this point, I direct the class's attention to me by saying, "Okay, look up here for a moment please." Again turning my body to the side of the room (modeling), I draw my cleared weapon, perform a quick safety check, and say, "Sometime when you are firing on the range or in the world, you may perform your recovery properly, lowering the weapon, scanning with your head in all directions, decocking and recovering to the holster." I then perform these actions as described. When I decock, however, I merely flick the lever so the clicking sound can be heard but do not depress it hard enough to cause it to decock. Once the weapon is holstered, I continue, "Then, after the pistol is holstered, you try to snap the holster, only to find it won't close. You then look down and see that the hammer is still cocked! Now, should this happen to you here today or anytime, I want you to remember two things. First, don't panic! Your pistol will not fire unless you touch that trigger, so just calm down and relax if you see that hammer back when you look down into your holster. The second thing you do when you see this, is simply take the pistol out of the holster, keeping your finger off the trigger and muzzle pointed in a safe direction, decock it, and then re-holster. That's it. Remember it's your pistol, so you just take care of it nice and easy. The only time I've ever seen this be a problem is when the person panics and grabs at the weapon, resulting in BANG!, sometimes redecorating their pants in more ways than one!" Again, some laughter, but it gets the point across. This issue must be addressed with decocking lever-equipped systems, because it can and DOES happen.)

11. Always wash hands before eating and shower and change clothing (including footgear) at the end of a shooting day.
(* This is in regard to lead as discussed earlier.)

12. Never go forward of the firing line unless instructed.
13. Never bend over to retrieve dropped articles on the firing line until instructed to do so by an instructor.

(* Teaching Moment: "If you drop something while working on the line, don't worry about it. Just leave it where it falls. We will take care it. If you bend over to pick something up at the wrong time, you can lose your focus and create a dangerous situation. Just relax.")

14. No talking on the firing line; except by, or with an instructor.
15. Pay strict attention to the instructor.
16. Never anticipate a command.

(* Teaching Moment: "Again, pay attention to the commands, and resist the urge to jump ahead. A few of the exercises we'll be doing today will be conducted by the numbers. If you jump ahead, you can create a dangerous situation.")

17. Never permit the muzzle of a firearm to touch the ground.

(Teaching Moment: *After number 17 is read, I ask the class, "Why don't we want the muzzle to touch the ground?" Someone usually knows, saying that material can be forced into the muzzle, possibly blocking the bore and causing the barrel to bulge or worse when fired. Even though most people are aware of this fact, many are not. Good teaching moment.)

18. Conduct a proper safety check of the weapon before and after a training session.
19. Never dry fire on the range unless instructed to do so.
20. All safety precautions must be adhered to and enforced.
21. REMEMBER: Everyone has the responsibility for range safety.

(*After the last rule has been read, I ask if there are any questions about any of the rules and regulations. If not, they are instructed to sign and date the form and pass it in. The forms are then collected, to be added to each officer's training file. In addition to providing documentation for that day's training, it conveys to the students the seriousness–and permanence–of the form they have filled out.)

SAMPLE FIREARMS SAFETY RULES FORM

A. CARDINAL RULES OF FIREARMS SAFETY:

1. Treat all firearms as though they were loaded.
2. Keep your finger outside the trigger guard until you are on target and have decided to fire.
3. Point the muzzle in a safe direction at all times.
4. Be sure of your target and what is beyond it.

REMEMBER THE "LASER RULE": TREAT YOUR FIREARM AS IF IT IS A LASER GUN WITH THE BEAM ALWAYS ON; WHATEVER THE BEAM TOUCHES, IT CUTS THROUGH!

B. SPECIFIC RANGE SAFETY RULES:

1. Ear and eye protection are required at all times when firing is being conducted on the range. This includes observers.
2. Eye protection is required in the cleaning room.
3. Immediately upon picking up a firearm, visually and physically check to see it is unloaded.
4. Check a second time.
5. Never give a firearm to, or take a firearm from anyone, unless the action is opened and the weapon is confirmed to be safe and clear.
6. Load/reload/unload only after position is taken at the firing point and on command unless directed otherwise.
7. Keep the firearm pointed down-range at all times.
8. Never draw a handgun from the holster on the range unless instructed to.
9. Never draw or reholster with your finger in the trigger guard or on the trigger.
10. NEVER holster a cocked weapon. _____(Initials)
11. Always wash hands before eating and shower and change clothing (including footgear) at the end of a shooting day.
12. Never go forward of the firing line unless instructed.
13. Never bend over to retrieve dropped articles on the firing line until instructed to do so by an instructor.
14. No talking on the firing line; except by, or with an instructor.
15. Pay strict attention to the instructor.
16. Never anticipate a command.
17. Never permit the muzzle of a firearm to touch the ground.
18. Conduct a proper safety check of the weapon before and after a training session.
19. Never dry fire on the range unless instructed to do so.
20. All safety precautions must be adhered to and enforced.
21. REMEMBER: Everyone has the responsibility for range safety.

I HAVE READ AND UNDERSTAND THE RANGE SAFETY RULES AND REGULATIONS.

Print Name: _____

Signature: _____ Date: _____

Portable Safe Direction for Home or Office

The best option for providing a safe direction indoors is found in the proper use of a professionally made, portable bullet trap. Barring that, the employment of personal body armor as shown in the photo on page 226 will ensure that any unintentional discharges that occur while loading or unloading will be contained as safely as possible.

While the purchase of a bullet trap as shown above may appear to be an extravagant expense, it is actually a very worthwhile investment for any professional who carries a firearm on a daily basis. The "Check-it" model shown above is compact (13"x4"x15"), weighs 33 lbs. and costs around $200.00. This one-time investment will last a lifetime, and, should an unintentional discharge occur, prove considerably cheaper than replacing ruined body armor. The Snail Systems models employ a unique deceleration chamber that allows the bullet to safely expend its energy and then drop inside the trap. More information is available at www.snailtraps.com.

APPENDIX E
Safety Off the Range

In addition to discussing the necessity for determining a safe direction in the home as discussed in Appendix D, a viable police firearms training program must also include instruction pertaining to the safe storage of weapons in the home. Not only is this good common sense, but in many states laws have been passed that require firearms to be secured, or at the least, to have their ability to fire disabled by trigger locks or other means.

Options to allow the safe storage of handguns should be identified, and, if possible, examples of these options should be available for officers to see and handle. In this way, questions or confusion relating to their use may be addressed.

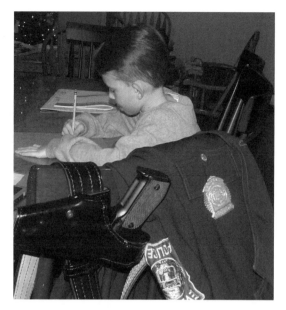

The more accessible a weapon is, the more liable the owner. It is up to each of us to protect those around us from the dangers of a firearm improperly used or in untrained or irresponsible hands.

Safes

Safes are available in a variety of shapes, sizes, and costs. Large floor safes weighing many hundreds of pounds can easily store dozens of pistols and long guns, while small metal wall safes can be used to store only one or two handguns. Many decent safes are available within these two extremes, and should be chosen according to each officer's specific needs.

At the least, some sort of lockable case or compartment should be utilized to store the duty weapon when it's not in use. It is also recommended that the ammunition be kept in a separate locked container.

Other Options

Another option to secure the cleared weapon is a **trigger guard lock**, a device which is secured around the trigger guard and completely covers and prevents any manipulation of the trigger. **Cable-type locks** can also be used to effectively disable the action of most handguns. Many manufactures now include or have available plastic **lockable gun cases** specifically designed to house their particular weapons.

One option some instructors used to recommend for use with revolvers was to employ handcuffs as a firearms disabling device by securing one of the cuffs around the top strap with the cylinder open. Even though this practice is effective at rendering the weapon inoperable, I strongly recommend against it because the metal on metal contact can easily damage the weapons frame, possibly causing problems in operation.

Yet another option for disabling firearms is being made more readily available by many gun

Small metal combination lock box-type safes can be secured to the wall or floor.

manufacturers in response to political pressure from various quarters. This option is designed into the firearm itself, and usually takes the form of an **internal trigger lock** that is activated by some type of key. While some might choose to go this route when selecting duty weapons, in my opinion any firearm intended for self-defense use should not be so equipped. This is especially true in regard to law enforcement weapons, as they are taken out and re-secured on a daily basis in most cases. Should the weapon's internal safety device be used regularly, I believe it would only be a matter of time before an officer was found killed or wounded because he drew his pistol in a critical situation and tried to fire, only to find that the trigger had been inadvertently left disabled. As always, with any

Various handgun securing devices. Clockwise from left; trigger guard lock, lockable plastic gun case, plastic coated cable with padlock.

The Steyr M40 Pistol, .40 S&W. Though superbly crafted, reasonably priced, and possessing an excellent bore-to-grip angle, the M40 is, I believe, unsuitable for law enforcement / combat use in the configuration shown because the manual safety mechanisms have been over-engineered. The ambidextrous manual safety (visible protruding down within the trigger guard in front of the trigger) can be inadvertently activated by a sharp blow to the bottom of the frame. The *"world's first integrated limited access key-lock safety in a semiautomatic pistol"* (Steyr's verbiage) is also a liability. The M40 would be much more desirable if the manufacturer would produce a version without these safeties while still retaining the three passive safeties.

type of weapon designed for combat use, the simplest approach is best.

Home Firearms Safety & The Junior Detective

In addition to discussing home firearms safety with the members of your law enforcement organization, the idea of them discussing firearms safety with their own family members should also be suggested. Everyone in the home where a firearm is kept is effected by its presence, and in my experience, ignorance regarding the realities of keeping a gun in the home is not bliss.

We have all heard the stories of police officer's firearms being picked up by small children in the home, and the resulting tragedies that occur. Too often, when you hear about these incidents, the child has turned the weapon on himself, perhaps looking down the barrel when the weapon was inadvertently discharged. Other times, the weapon is discharged by the child and the round strikes someone else. As I write this, there is a story in the news about a police officer who was shot and killed by his three-year old son while the officer stood in his kitchen talking with his pregnant wife.

Very often tragedies such as these are thought of by police officers (as is common with most people, regardless of profession) as things that *only happen to other people.* We may also dismiss the incident as an aberration, caused by negligence on the part of the officer responsible for the weapon's safe handling and storage. And many times this is true–the officer did fail to properly secure the weapon, and he or his family members will have to live with the result for the rest of their lives. Having talked with people directly involved in situations like these, I can tell you that I would not wish that burden and heartache on anyone.

Having grown up the child of a police officer in a home where weapons were kept,

however, I am also aware of a greater reality, one that has influenced me to not only discuss firearms and their safe handling with my young children, but also to make myself available to them as their own personal firearms instructor, should they desire to learn to shoot. (My daughter took me up on this when she was eight years old, and proved herself not only smart and responsible enough to work with firearms under my supervision, but also to be a crackerjack shot!)

The reality I am referring to is this–most kids, by the time they are old enough to want to snoop and poop throughout the house, pretty much know where all the hidden stuff in the home is kept.

This includes mom's or dad's firearms.

And if these firearms are deemed to be absolutely off limits, and if the children–especially male children, in my experience–are forbidden to see, handle, or get acquainted with these firearms under adult supervision, then these firearms may become a secret, unimaginably fascinating obsession for that child or children.

How do I know? Well, besides the fact that common sense and numerous recorded experiences indicate this occurs, I was one of them. In fact, the first time I held a real pistol was on a fine summer morning when I was three years old. According to my parents, I apparently climbed up on a chair, crawled across a large table, and opened a metal box where my father kept his .38 S&W Model 10 police-issued revolver. (My father, who was new on the force and working midnights at the time, had apparently placed the unloaded pistol into the green lockable box and shut it without locking it before going to bed.) I then playfully terrified my mother with the weapon (so I am told, I do not recall the event), holding her at gunpoint until my father was woken by my mother's incessant calls, calls she tried to make while conveying urgency to him and calm control to me. According to the story, my father got up, unckeremoniously relieved me of the pistol, got yelled at by my mother (even after he explained that it was unloaded), locked the pistol in the box, and then took it with him back to bed.

By the time I was around ten, my parents had divorced, I had graduated to the rank of junior detective, and I now had two houses to snoop and poop through. By the time I was twelve, not only did I know where my father then kept his pistol and the green metal box, but I also knew how to get through the intricate series of locks, alarms, and safes to get to my older brother's pistol collection. Considered too young by my gun-shy mother (who was probably still traumatized by my first pistol-handling exhibition) to be taught about real guns at the time, I surreptitiously taught myself, learning how to disassemble, load, unload, and clean every type of pistol in his collection, from derringers to revolvers and semiautos.

These regular self-training sessions continued until my brother began impromptu lessons about a year later. He was surprised at how quickly I picked it up, and never knew about my covert infiltrations until years later, when the big brother statute of limitations had run out and I was old enough to avoid the beating he surely would have issued me.

Thinking back on those days I count my lucky stars that nothing bad ever happened while handling those guns. I cringe to think of my own kids–or anyone else's–doing the same.

For years I was embarrassed to admit my early proclivity for B&E'ing into areas in my house where I had no business being in order to get to those objects that so fascinated me. Then one day I offhandedly mentioned it to a fellow officer I was working closely with, and he laughed and told me his story.

His father had also been a police officer who worked midnights. Every morning, his dad would come home from work, lock his pistol in a small metal box similar to my father's, place the box high up on a shelf in a cabinet in the kitchen and then go to bed. Starting when he

was around nine-years old, every afternoon my friend and his younger brother would arrive home from school, and immediately perform the same ritual, day after day. My friend would grab a kitchen chair, place it against the counter, step up on the chair and onto the counter, and then reach way up high and check the metal box.

Each day, my friend told me, the box was locked, and he and his brother would close the cabinet, put the chair back, and go on their way.

Then one day, after a few years of performing their routine, my friend reached up and found the box to be unlocked. Excitedly, he reached into the box, grabbed the revolver inside, turned toward his brother, muzzle pointed at the young man's chest and exclaimed, "We got it!" while pressing the trigger, CLICK, CLICK, CLICK.

As he related this story to me his face went a little pale. Then he said, "I pointed it right at my brother and pulled the trigger three times. Every day I thank God that my father was wise enough to always unload that gun before he put it in that box. When I think of what might have happened…"

Years after he told me this, I started to include both our stories when training to illustrate just how curious and determined children can be when it comes to firearms, especially when they see one of their parents wearing that gun day to day. That exposure and parental identification, combined with the media's often irresponsible portrayal of firearms use, can prove to be an irresistible combination for young minds.

It was after I started including these stories that I began to learn that this attraction, and these types of close calls, are much more common than anyone is even aware of, simply because we tend to cover them up when they occur or are discovered. I have now heard more stories along these lines from other officers than I could have imagined.

It is part of the reality we live with. We should not, we must not, choose to ignore it.

Rather, we need to deal with it. The way I have decided to do it with my own children is through education, controlled exposure to the weapons, and straight talk.

Far from a new or unique model, this type of education was once an inherent part of many American children's upbringing, when firearms were still generally thought of as the dangerous, though useful and necessary tools they actually are, rather than simply mechanical incarnations of evil or intrinsic components of violent videogames.

So far, it seems to be working.

TEN COMMON SENSE RULES OF OFF-RANGE SAFETY

1. Treat every gun as if it were loaded.

2. Always keep that muzzle pointed in a safe direction.

3. Never point a gun at anything you are not willing to destroy.

4. Keep your fingers away from the trigger unless firing.

5. Should you need to fire, be aware of your surroundings and the location of all people—friend and foe—around you.

6. Never climb a tree, fence, or ladder, or jump a ditch with a loaded weapon in your hands.

7. Be aware of the possibility of ricochet should you need to fire in areas where there are hard flat surfaces or water.

8. Unless working deep undercover, always have your badge/ID with you whenever you carry a firearm.

9. Unload ammunition from guns and store both securely and separately when not in use.

10. Never drink alcoholic beverages or use any kind of drug when handling weapons.

Safety In The World

When operating as a police officer in uniform, just our presence alone will often have a calming, civilizing affect on members of the public, as people generally tend to modify their behavior when the police are around.

This is both common and normal. A prime example of this is the way most people will alter their driving habits when they spot the cruiser's two-tone paintjob and light bar, uniformed officer at the wheel. Regardless of how they were driving previously, people tend to slow down and often become models of civility and proper road etiquette.

After enough time on patrol, police officers tend to get accustomed to this, and eventually come to take their affect on the driving habits of others for granted. I first became aware of this as a young trooper one afternoon while off-duty, negotiating my personal car around a notoriously treacherous traffic circle in Revere, MA.

As I smoothly entered the rotary, seamlessly merging with traffic, I was suddenly confronted with several angry motorists blasting their horns and signaling their displeasure with a one-finger salute as they aggressively cut me off and jockeyed for position on the congested roadway.

Frankly, I couldn't believe it! Were they crazy? I was a cop for crying out loud! As I reached down to activate my overhead lights and siren, it dawned on me–pulling them over was going to be tougher than I thought, because I wasn't in my cruiser. *That's why* these too-typical screwball drivers had reverted to true form in my presence, because they had *no way of knowing I was a police officer*.

After this, I began to refer to this condition as "cruiser shock" and would constantly remind myself while driving off duty that I wasn't in a marked sled, and couldn't count on the normal civilizing effects generated by the uniform and bluebird.[1]

Another version of cruiser shock is also fairly common in the police industry, though this type often proves more dangerous, occasionally lethal.

This type occurs when a police officer, either off-duty or operating in plainclothes, becomes involved in a situation and takes action as a police officer. The problem here is that should the officer be afflicted with a case of cruiser shock, *he may know he is a cop* and he may be *acting like a cop*, but no one else may know who he is or what his intentions are–including *other cops.*

Too often when this happens, tragedy results. In December 2000, for example, I believe that the effects of cruiser shock played a part when an off-duty Providence Rhode Island Police Officer, Cornel Young, Jr., died after being shot by two of his brother officers while attempting to assist them during the apprehension of an armed suspect.

According to reports, Officer Young came out of a restaurant and moved toward the officers and a suspect armed with a handgun. Officer Young, holding his duty pistol in his hands, was not displaying his badge at the time. The uniformed officers, responding to a report of a fight at the scene, repeatedly ordered both subjects to drop their weapons. From reports based on witness testimony, the armed suspect then threw down his gun, but Officer Young, who apparently either did not hear the uniformed officers ordering him to drop his weapon (perhaps as a result of stress-induced auditory exclusion), or *did not think they were addressing him*, did not drop his weapon and continued to move toward the suspect and officers.

The officers then fired, hitting Officer Young in the chest and head. It wasn't until moments later when other officers arrived at the scene that someone discovered Officer Young's identification in his pocket and announced to the stunned officers, "He's one of *ours.*"

Putting all of the media-driven controversy that surrounded this case aside, this was not the first time that an officer dressed in plainclothes had been mistaken for an armed suspect.[2] In fact, anyone who has ever worked undercover or in a plainclothes capacity can probably relate an instance or two during their career when they have been perceived as suspect rather than police officer.

The reason for this is simple. When our weapons are visible when we are not in uniform or otherwise immediately identifiable as a police officer, *we are perceived only as a man or woman with a gun.*

For again, while *we may know* we are police officers, the uniformed officers we encounter will generally have no way of knowing this unless we make it completely clear to them. (In fact, even if we know the officers personally, the effects of stress on them may preclude them from taking their eyes off our weapons and looking at our faces.)

The uniformed officers, on the other hand, are operating on the assumption that since they are clearly identifiable as police officers, then they must take control of any dangerous or potentially dangerous situation using whatever means are appropriate.

And that is the way it *must* be.

Having worked both in uniform and in plainclothes, I can attest to the truth of this, as I'm sure can many of my colleagues.

So in the name of off-duty and plainclothes survival, the following *Off-Range Firearms Safety Guidelines* are respectfully provided for consideration.

---

[1] "Bluebird" is a term used to describe the two-toned French and Electric Blue marked cruisers used by the MSP.

[2] Officer Young was black, the officers that shot him were not. Many so-called "community leaders" and members of the media contended that Officer Young was shot down simply because of the color of skin. Many published articles describing the incident completely omitted the fact that he was holding a pistol in his hands when shot.

OFF-RANGE FIREARMS SAFETY GUIDELINES

1. Unless absolutely required by the circumstances at hand, do not get directly involved when off-duty in plainclothes. This is especially true if you are with family members or other non-law enforcement personnel. If your direct intervention is not required, you may still assist by observing and collecting information that can be given to responding officers after they have arrived and gained control of the scene.

2. If you must intervene, make sure you clearly identify yourself to ALL parties present. If your weapon is out, you must have your badge out as well. The badge can be held next to the weapon, or even better, while holding the weapon in one hand, hold the badge/ID in the other hand high up and over your head. The badge/ID can then be rotated back and forth for 360-degree visibility. This method is strongly advocated by Jim Cirillo (shown demonstrating this technique at right).

3. If someone present has access to a telephone, order him or her to call the police. Make sure that the person tells the police officer or dispatcher that you are present at the scene, that you are a police officer, that you are armed, and that you are wearing plainclothes. You should also have the caller describe you and your clothing, and insist that responding officers be advised of this information. **Be adamant about this**, and ensure that the caller confirms that the information has been relayed.

4. When uniformed officers arrive at the scene, or should you be challenged by a uniformed officer, remain calm, do not make any sudden moves, *do not turn toward them or point your weapon toward them or directly at anyone else*. Reholster if you can do so without putting yourself or others in jeopardy. Continue to rotate the badge above your head and loudly repeat, "POLICE! I'M A POLICE OFFICER! DON'T SHOOT!"

5. Once uniformed officers arrive on the scene, THEY are in control of the scene. Regardless of your rank, position, or department affiliation, you must follow ALL of their commands instantly and without question. Only after they have gained control of the scene or asked you directly should you attempt to explain the situation to them.

6. USE COMMON SENSE. Remember that criminals will sometime identify themselves as police officers in order to create confusion or doubt when confronted by the police. Remember that most police officers are aware of this, and that *anyone* armed with a weapon must be treated as a potential deadly threat until they have been positively identified otherwise.

7. ASSUME *NOTHING*. It is too easy for mistakes to happen, especially when we are operating under the affects of stress that will be present during any lethal force encounter. And until we have been positively identified, a lethal threat is exactly the profile we present when armed and not readily identifiable as one of the good guys.

Jim Cirillo demonstrates another method that can be used to simultaneously employ the pistol and display the police identification.

Keeping the ID or badge next to the pistol–whether the pistol is in your hand or the holster–is the smart approach since the eyes of onlookers are most always drawn to the weapon. When wearing plain clothes, a clip-on badge holder should be worn on the belt directly in front of the holster to avoid inducing panic or unwanted attention if the weapon is seen.

THE SAFE CONDITION CHECK

Whenever you pick up or hand someone else a weapon, first open the action and render the weapon safe, keeping your trigger finger off the trigger and out of the trigger guard.

Then, have the other person check to confirm that the weapon is indeed, *absolutely* safe, clear and empty.

This action will help identify you as a competent professional to those you work around!

Negligent vs. Unintentional Discharge

A *negligent discharge* occurs when an officer causes a weapon to discharge because of carelessness, negligence, or improper handling of the firearm. The onus of responsibility in these cases is squarely on the operator, though the people responsible for training and/or employing that operator may also be held accountable depending upon the circumstances.

In contrast, an *unintentional discharge* normally occurs while working in the field as the result of an involuntary physiological phenomenon commonly referred to as "sympathetic involuntary muscular contraction."

This phenomenon–which causes the muscles of one or both hands to involuntarily contract–is usually initiated when the person holding the weapon is operating under stress. Often, the trigger finger is on the trigger, or finds its way into the trigger guard during the incident with no intent on the operator's part.

There are three primary recognized types of stimuli that can initiate sympathetic involuntary muscular contraction.

1. **Startle effect:** May be initiated by a loud and/or unexpected noise, or the sudden appearance of someone or something that causes you to flinch while holding the weapon.

2. **"Postural disturbance" or loss of balance:** Contraction may be initiated should you trip or fall while holding a weapon as the hands tend to involuntarily clench around anything being held in these cases.

3. **Exertion of maximum force:** The contraction is initiated in one hand as a result of the actions of the other. Very common among police officers, for we often find ourselves in situations in which we are controlling a weapon in one hand while trying to control something else with our other hand. Common situations include having to exert physical force against a subject with the empty hand, or while trying to aggressively open a door with one hand while holding a weapon in the other.

Education about the phenomenon's existence and proper training are the best methods of prevention.

APPENDIX F
Fitting the Gun to the Shooter

Lt. Colonel Bob Hunt (MSP, Retired), instructing recruits from the 51st RTT on the finer points of properly gripping their S&W 6" M&P Model revolvers. Hunt would later retire from the MSP and become Director of the prestigious Smith & Wesson Academy in Springfield, MA. (Photo courtesy Massachusetts State Police archives, circa 1968.)

If possible, all weapons should be selected so that they fit the individual's hand, whether it be large or small.
- Colonel Rex Applegate
Kill or Get Killed
1943

In the not too distant past, recruits at the Massachusetts State Police Academy were subjected to this simple rule when being introduced to training with their issued duty pistol: "If you are right-handed, you are right-handed. And if you are left-handed, *you are right-handed*!"

That's correct, regardless of whether the individual was naturally right or left hand dominant, they were required to carry their weapons on their right side and trained to employ them as though they were right-hand dominant. This was done ostensibly for two reasons.

First, starting in the early 1920s and continuing for many years, all troopers were instructed in motorcycle operation at the Academy and expected to ride them on patrol. These motorcycles were altered so that the handlebar-mounted grip throttle was located on the left, leaving the right hand free to draw and fire the pistol while in pursuit should it be necessary. The second and more oft-cited reason was uniformity of appearance. Since there are not many recorded incidents of troopers having to engage in gunfights while operating their Harleys at high speed, this means that back then, ensuring that all uniformed troopers looked similar when in formation was deemed to be more important than their ability to defend themselves when faced with a deadly threat.

Of course that was then, and this is now.

Today, thankfully, this perspective is considered ludicrous, and wouldn't be tolerated by rational thinking people.

However, in many police departments throughout the US, another ludicrous perspective regarding the issuance, training, and use of duty pistols is still being enforced. The matter I am referring to is the practice of issuing the same model handgun to every member of a police department, regardless of whether that pistol fits the hand the individual officer.

The sad truth of the matter is that many people in the police industry today still view the duty pistol as more a symbol of the profession than a tool. And as far as they are concerned, if an individual cannot master the particular model handgun that has been selected for general issue, then that individual has no business being a police officer.

While I strongly agree that the police profession is no place for anyone who professes or demonstrates an ardent inability to *use* the weapon to employ deadly force should it be necessary, I also believe that requiring someone to train with and employ a dangerous piece of equipment that they cannot consistently and efficiently control *because it's too big for their hand* is not only ludicrous, but borders on criminal negligence.

Think about it. Right now, across our country, there are police officers carrying pistols that they cannot fully control during training because they cannot adequately fit their hands around the grip, access the trigger, or work the various operating levers. The reason we don't often hear about this is because given enough desire, perseverance, hard work, and assistance, most officers with smaller hands are usually able to squeak by during basic academy training. Many of these officers then spend the rest of their careers dreading annual firearms training, for they invariably become identified as

problem or poor shooters, always achieving minimal scores with great difficulty.

Given these circumstances, it is not hard to understand how some of these people might come to resent, and in some cases even develop a genuine disdain for, their issued pistol, firearms training, and anything associated with either.

These negative feelings toward a potentially life-saving piece of equipment are compounded ten-fold when you add in the emotional toll exacted on a person who is sent out day after day with little or no confidence in their ability to defend themselves or others with that duty pistol. After all, if you are a "poor" or "problem" shooter in training, what possible good will you be should you need to employ the pistol against someone presenting a deadly and immediate threat?!

While discussing the idea of fitting the gun to the individual with other police officers who disagree with this position, I've usually encountered two distinct arguments.

The first can be summed up as, "If these people can't handle the issued pistol then they should be thrown off the job!"

As I stated earlier, this perspective seems to be shared by people who regard the pistol as some sort of unchangeable, mythological talisman or status symbol, rather than the hand tool it actually is. And to these ardent proponents of "one size for all", it is self-evident that the duty pistol has been manufactured to absolute perfect dimensions, because it fits their own individual hand.

I have found that most—but not all—of the people who raise this argument can be made to see the irrationality of this position simply by substituting a cruiser for the pistol, and asking them if it would be reasonable to prohibit officers from adjusting the seats and mirrors so they could safely operate the vehicle.

The second argument I've heard for issuing only one model of the selected duty weapon to all members of the department generally revolves around the possibility of two or more officers becoming involved in an extended gunfight, during which one officer runs out of ammo and can't use either the ammunition or a magazine from the other officer's weapon because it is configured differently.

The first weakness in this argument lies in the fact that most manufacturers produce both standard and compact sized weapons that are chambered for the same caliber ammunition.

The second weakness is found in the fact that the extended gunfight scenario isn't exactly common in the police industry. Statistics consistently indicate that the vast majority of police-involved gunfights involve fewer than three rounds fired and are over in a matter of seconds.

The third weakness is found in the reality check that would most likely occur should you become involved in the rare scenario outlined above, and, after blasting away all your rounds, you turned to the officer next to you and asked for some of his. Good luck to you.

And the final weakness to this argument is the fact that no department operates in a vacuum. Officers from different agencies and departments are constantly intermingling, working together, and assisting one-another, all while armed with different makes and models of handguns.

Solutions

The idea of ensuring that each individual officer is equipped with a pistol he can operate safely and efficiently was incorporated from the beginning into the New Paradigm Firearms Training Program.

The way we addressed it was to ensure that there were reasonable options available that would allow us to best fit the pistol to the operator. These options are implemented strictly on a case-by-case basis, with physical hand size being the only determining factor.

The approach to fitting the gun to the hand is made in a progressive manner. The first option we try

is a standard duty pistol equipped with a factory-produced short trigger. In most cases, this simple solution is all that is needed to vastly improve the operator's ability to establish and maintain a solid grip on the pistol from the holster to full presentation and throughout the firing cycle.

In the few cases where this has not rectified the problem, we employ a smaller framed pistol produced by the same manufacturer and chambered for the same caliber. All other operating characteristics are the same to ensure uniformity in training.

To date, only a handful of officers have required this accommodation.

Results

One of the first (and best) results we have observed is the look of relief on the officer's face when finally fitted with a pistol he can fully control. Once this has been accomplished, we have then consistently seen (and documented) an immediate and substantial improvement in operating efficiency and marksmanship skills in training.

All who have been assisted in this manner also expresses true confidence in their ability to protect themselves and others with the duty pistol, and this confidence absolutely permeates other aspects of the officer's attitudes toward themselves, their profession, and others.

Summary

Most people's hands stop growing upon reaching approximately 18 years of age. During the course of a normal police career, the average officer will be issued and trained with various pistols of different make, model, and caliber.

Bottom line, we can *always* change the pistol to fit our officer's hands, but we can't do the opposite.

It's high time we all came to grips with this reality. [1]

---

[1] Portions of this chapter appeared previously in Guns & Ammo Magazine. Used with permission.

SIZE *DOES* MATTER!

Right: The difference between holding a pistol that doesn't fit your hand (top) and one that does (bottom) is often a matter of mere millimeters. (SIG P226 and SIG P239 shown. Both are chambered for .40 S&W.)

> You should not copy others, but use weapons which you can handle properly.
>
> – Miyamoto Musashi
> *The Book of Five Rings*
> 1645

Below: In addition to making various models available to fit different hand sizes, some manufacturers offer adjustable grip and/or trigger configurations.

Shown below are (from top) the SIG P226 with factory short trigger, SIG P229 with regular trigger and SIG P229 with factory short trigger installed. These pistols are all chambered for .40 S&W.

Beware the man with one gun...
Once you find a reliable pistol that fits your hand and your needs, stick with it and train often.

APPENDIX G
One-Hand Semiauto Pistol Refunction Technique

"All I saw was the huge bore of the barrel of the pistol pointing at me!"

These familiar words are often expressed by people who have had the unenviable experience of looking down the business end of the muzzle of a gun held in someone else's hand.

This reporting of a completely normal reaction indicates a number of things have occurred. It indicates that a true high arousal or fear state has been induced in the person making this statement. It further indicates that as a result of this fear state, naturally-occurring chemicals have been released into the person's blood stream. Along with this chemical dump, perceptual narrowing has occurred, resulting in the person experiencing what is often referred to as the tunnel vision effect, where the eyes' focus is drawn inexorably to a specific object to the exclusion of all else.

Now if this person had a pistol in his own hand at that moment, and if he had fired his weapon at the subject holding that gun with the "huge bore", would it be surprising if his rounds were to hit that offending weapon or the area directly around it?

My short answer to this question is, no.

In fact, based on my training, experience, and research, unless the shooter thrust the gun toward the threat canting the muzzle downward before firing, I'd be surprised if at least a few of the rounds fired didn't hit the gun, the subject's hands, or his arms.

While we normally look at this type of situation solely through the eyes of the police officer, in this case we must step back and take in the bigger picture, recognizing that this type of stress-generated focus upon the adversary's weapon works both ways.

To the criminal, it is the *police officer's pistol* that may become the focal point.

Looking first from the perspective of the police officer, we have observed this pattern repeated numerous times, day after day in training while conducting DPTC No. 3 as outlined in this book (Chapter 6). Officers get out of the cruiser, run down range to cover, and engage a threat-stimulus target (subject armed with handgun) that moves laterally across their line of sight. Officers track and engage the target, firing 1-6 rounds at it while avoiding hitting the non-threat-stimulus targets in the area. Normally the threat-stimulus target makes one pass lasting approximately 4 seconds. After everyone has completed the course, we check the target, and without fail the vast majority of hits are centered on and around the pistol, regardless of the fact that we train our officers to shoot to incapacitate *the operator*, not the weapon.

From the criminal's perspective, there are, unfortunately, numerous examples of real-world incidents during which officers were wounded in the hands or arms during the initial stages of an encounter, leaving them vulnerable to further attack.[1]

One such incident occurred in the town of Colebrook, New Hampshire on August 19, 1997, at approximately three in the afternoon.

---

[1] This is true despite statistics that indicate that suspects that shoot at police generally only achieve hits with approximately 10% of rounds fired.

The Colebrook Incident

It began when New Hampshire State Trooper Scott Phillips, 32, stopped local resident Carl Drega, 67, in a supermarket parking lot. Drega, driving his pickup truck that day, was known to Trooper Phillips. Drega, whose wife had recently died, had been in conflict with town officials for years regarding zoning laws and a number of other issues. Because Drega was known to be confrontational, Trooper Phillips wisely radioed and requested back-up.

Unknown to Trooper Phillips, Drega had a semiautomatic rifle and a handgun in the cab of his pickup truck that day. As soon as he stopped his truck, Drega stepped out with his rifle and began to fire at the Trooper, who exited his cruiser and returned fire with his handgun.

During the initial exchange Drega escaped unharmed, but Trooper Philips's non-dominant arm was disabled.

Just at that moment, another officer, Trooper Leslie Lord, responding to the request for back-up, arrived at the scene.

Drega immediately turned his attention to Trooper Lord, firing into Lord's cruiser through the windshield. As Lord tried to back away from the attack in his cruiser, Drega walked across the parking lot and continued to fire. Standing next to the driver's side window, Drega fired again, murdering the critically wounded officer.

According to witness accounts, Drega then turned his attention back to Trooper Phillips, who, wounded and bleeding, had moved into a field of tall grass behind his cruiser.

As Trooper Philips knelt in the tall grass, undoubtedly in shock and suffering the debilitating effects of what had to be an incredible amount of fear and confusion, his empty pistol remained in his hand, loaded magazines in the pouches on his belt.

As witnesses watched, Carl Drega walked over to Trooper Phillips, the father of two small children. As Trooper Phillips begged for his life, Carl Drega raised his gun and fired, murdering

the young officer.

Drega would continue on with his rampage that day, murdering two more people, Vickie Bunnell and Dennis Joos, and wounding four other officers, until he himself was shot and killed by a US Border Patrol Agent and a New Hampshire State Trooper.

This tragic incident clearly illustrates why police officers must be taught not just how to operate their weapons when both hands are available, but also how to make them work when one of the officer's hands is wounded or otherwise incapacitated.

It for this reason that we have taught all of our officers how to perform the one hand pistol refunction technique, and why it is presented here for consideration.

Notes Regarding Teaching the Technique

The technique can be performed with the slide forward or locked to the rear, as it may be should the weapon have been fired until empty.

We require our officers to perform the technique with the slide forward, which is slightly more difficult than with the slide locked to the rear. There are two reasons we do this:
1) there is a high probability that the slide may indeed be forward during an actual event
2) if the officer can master the technique with the slide forward configuration, then the slide rearward configuration presents no problem.

All weapons must be administratively unloaded and verified to be safe, clear and empty prior to the exercise.

First, officers are given an explanation for the need for the drill, and then given a demonstration by the instructor. We teach the technique with the officers standing on line, facing down range. (Please note that while it is preferable to have the exercises conducted using magazines loaded with dummy rounds, officers may also simulate retrieving fully loaded magazines and inserting them into the weapon. Empty magazines are not recommended for use when practicing the drill when they are equipped with followers that cause the slide to lock to the rear during the chambering phase.)

Second, officers are walked through the drill, step by step, as illustrated in the accompanying photographs. Once they demonstrate the ability to successfully perform the drill using their dominant hand, they are instructed to visualize being engaged by gunfire and sustaining a wound to their non-dominant arm.

They are then instructed to seek cover (if possible), keep scanning the area, and execute the technique. Officers do this on line by using simulated cover (barricade) or taking a knee and visualizing themselves using cover. Once the refunction technique has been completed, the officers are told to simulate re-engaging the assailant. This is repeated several times.

Officers are then given a demonstration on how to perform the technique using their non-dominant hand, in the event that their dominant hand is incapacitated, and the drills are repeated.

In the following series of photographs, Paul Wosny demonstrates one version of the One-Hand Pistol Refunction Technique.

1. Take cover (if possible) and eject the magazine from the pistol. Some pistols not equipped with "free fall" magazines may require the officer to hook the magazine floorplate on something to assist in ejection. Note: The simulated injured arm/hand should not be placed in the pocket or held behind the back, but simply allowed to hang as if it were disabled.

SAFETY NOTICE:

All weapons must be administratively unloaded *and verified* to be safe, clear and empty <u>prior to</u> practicing this technique!

2. After the magazine has been ejected, secure the pistol. The primary recommendation is to keep it simple and just place the pistol in the holster. This is probably the best choice, especially for uniformed officers.

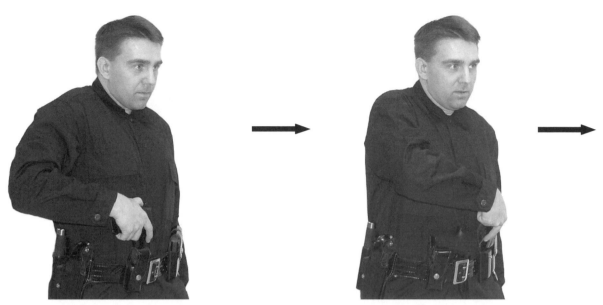

3. The second preferred option is to jam the empty pistol between the belt and the body. This is often the easiest place to secure it when using the non-dominant hand to execute the technique. Using the belt or the holster also keeps the weapon in a more controllable location than behind the knee or similar positions, and can be employed from a number of positions (ie. standing, kneeling, prone).

4. Next, retrieve a fully loaded magazine from your carry location. This must be practiced using both the dominant and non-dominant hand.

7-8. The pistol is then simultaneously pushed **IN** (rear sights against the edge of holster, pocket, heel, etc.), **DOWN** (straight down so contact is maintained between the rear sights and the edge), **and (MUZZLE) AWAY.** Care must be taken to do this aggressively, so the slide is fully retracted before release. Resist the propensity to "ride the slide" slowly, for this can induce stoppages, as well as cause the slide to close around the material of your pants or jacket.

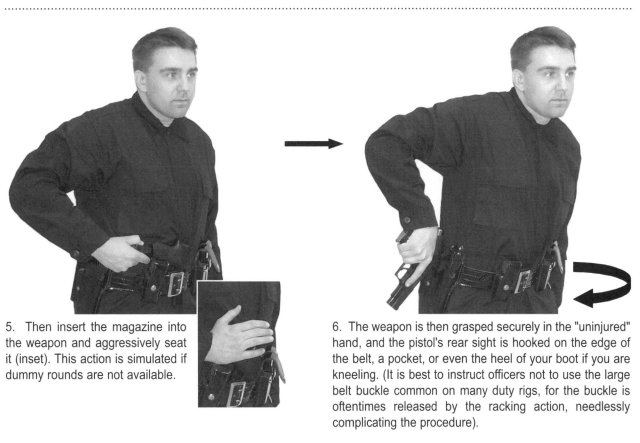

5. Then insert the magazine into the weapon and aggressively seat it (inset). This action is simulated if dummy rounds are not available.

6. The weapon is then grasped securely in the "uninjured" hand, and the pistol's rear sight is hooked on the edge of the belt, a pocket, or even the heel of your boot if you are kneeling. (It is best to instruct officers not to use the large belt buckle common on many duty rigs, for the buckle is oftentimes released by the racking action, needlessly complicating the procedure).

9. The pistol, fully loaded again, is ready for action, as is the injured–but never finished–officer. Just *knowing* how to do this can drastically increase the officer's overall confidence levels and chances for survival.

Above: Detail of the rear sight being hooked on the holster (top) and on the back of the boot heel while kneeling.

COMMITMENT TO WIN

- I am a law enforcement officer.

- I am aware of the dangers of my chosen occupation.

- I know that there is always a very real possibility of my being involved in a shooting or other violent confrontation – *SO I PREPARE.*

- I train as if my life depends upon it – *BECAUSE IT DOES.*

- I stay alert at all times, aware of my surroundings.

- I approach each situation, thinking tactically, giving myself every possible advantage.

- I approach *all people* cautiously, watching for danger signs, anticipating a confrontation regardless of the circumstances. I do this because it is necessary.

- Whenever possible, I will make contact with a violator only from a position of strength; this strength being achieved through proper tactics, positioning, or numerical superiority.

- I will always first CONTROL and *THEN* HANDCUFF suspects – hands behind their backs – *BEFORE searching.*

- I do this for my family.

- I will always search all suspects and prisoners slowly and thoroughly – and request that any officer I turn them over to does the same.

- I do this for my brothers and sisters in blue.

- I will always wear my body armor while working.

- I will use my firearm, should it be necessary, with great willingness, determination, and valor – *I WILL..*

- I do this for myself.

- I will always survive the street and WIN any violent confrontation – *I MUST.*

FAILURE IS NOT AN OPTION!

APPENDIX H
Semiauto Pistol Stoppage Clearing Drills

The following two stoppage clearing drills will clear the vast majority of stoppages that occur when the semiautomatic pistol's firing cycle–*feed, fire, extract, eject*–is interrupted.

The T.I.R.R. Clearing Drill

This variation of the immediate action drill has been adapted for two simple reasons: it is more efficient, and it works better when the operator performing it is engaged in stressful, violent encounters.

As I reported in articles that were published in both *The Firearms Instructor* (1996) and *The Law Enforcement Trainer* (1997), I first stumbled on this variation in 1994 while working on speed shooting drills at the range. After encountering a stoppage that I was in no mood for, and in an effort to clear the stovepipe quickly, I simply tipped the weapon completely upside down (turning it inboard), grabbed the rear of the slide and–operating in an aggressive manner–literally punched the weapon straight out at the target and pressed the trigger.

Not only did it clear the stovepipe successfully, but it also felt right when I did it, and the round hit the target while the pistol was still inverted.

Now over the years I had seen different instructors occasionally clear loose rounds from the chamber/ejection port by tipping the pistol sideways (usually outboard). In some cases, the weapon was completely inverted while the slide was pulled to the rear and held open as the loose rounds or shell casings were shaken from the weapon. In these instances it was performed as an additional, drawn-out movement rather than as an alternate and distinct clearing drill. But this was different, and I felt, warranted further experimentation, because obviously, an effective, simple drill or movement is preferable to a complicated one, or multiple drills, especially when it comes to dealing with the realities of performing the movements under stress in life-threatening situations.

As I experimented with the technique, I also discovered that in addition to clearing stovepipes and the various stoppages normally cleared by the *Tap, Rack, Ready* immediate action drill, (no round chambered, misfire, and failure to feed), the technique also easily cleared stovepipe-type stoppages and some double-feed type stoppages.

The success of the technique when used to clear double-feed type stoppages is variable, however, being dependent upon the weapon system used and the severity of the problem encountered. This fact obviously demands that a second, double-feed specific drill be taught along with the TIRR drill.

The end result, due to the fact that the need for a separate stovepipe clearing drill has been eliminated, is the reduction of the total number of basic required semiauto pistol stoppage clearing drills from three to two–a 33% increase in efficiency!

---

[1] To simplify the description of the drill as well as form an association with the preferred aggressive method of performing it, I refer to it by its acronym–hence the T.I.R.R. Clearing drill. While training, the drill can be initiated by the instructor sounding off with, "TIRR Clear!" (pronounced "tear clear").

[2] *The Firearms Instructor;* the official publication of the International Association of Law Enforcement Firearms Instructors (IALEFI). *The Law Enforcement Trainer;* the official publication of the American Society of Law Enforcement Trainers (ASLET).

How to Perform the TIRR CLEAR DRILL

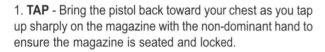

From firing position, first ...

1. **TAP** - Bring the pistol back toward your chest as you tap up sharply on the magazine with the non-dominant hand to ensure the magazine is seated and locked.

2. **INVERT** - Keep the weapon back toward the chest as you completely invert the pistol. The non-dominant hand's forefinger and thumb simultaneously establish a secure "slingshot" type grip on the rear of the slide. You must rotate the pistol *in-board toward the centerline of your body* as shown, not outboard, as some people tend to do.

Author's Note

For those who may have experimented with the original version as illustrated in the publications mentioned above, or the subsequent article that appeared in *Guns & Ammo* (October 2000), or the LETN videotape produced in 2001, please be advised that the drill has been further refined (as illustrated in the accompanying photographs) to improve its effectiveness and efficiency. This refinement requires the shooter to rotate the pistol 180 degrees from the inverted to the upright position *while the chambering stroke is delivered.*

Applicability

Numerous types and sizes of semi-automatic pistols have been experimented with, including SIG Sauers, Smith & Wessons, Glocks, Berettas, and the venerable 1911 Colt. I have also taught this drill to many firearms instructors and police officers and have found the technique to be easily learned and adaptable for use with all of the weapons noted.

How to Perform the TIRR CLEAR DRILL, continued

3 – 4. **RACK** - The dominant hand, trigger finger along the frame, is used to *aggressively* punch the weapon forward (as opposed to the non-dominant hand racking the slide back) toward the threat, literally pulling the slide from the grasp of the non-dominant hand as the slide reaches maximum retraction position (shown left). The sharp action of this movement should cause any loose shell casings or misfed rounds to be dislodged. Gravity will then cause them to fall clear of the weapon through the ejection port. As the pistol is driven forward, the dominant hand simultaneously corkscrews *outboard* (as shown above right), righting the pistol and bringing it into alignment with the threat as show in the photograph below.

5. **READY** - The pistol, once cleared, is immediately ready to be fired if necessary.

Double-Feed Clearing Drill

For double-feed stoppages that will not clear after executing the T.I.R.R. Clear Drill, the standard *LOCK*, (Lock the slide to rear), *RIP*, (Remove magazine), *SHAKE*, (Shake the pistol and magazine to clear them), *TAP*, (Reinsert magazine), *RACK*, (Chamber a round), and *READY* (you are then ready to engage if warranted) drill is taught.

Author's Note

Some instructors who teach this drill advocate that when the magazine is removed from the weapon (RIP) it should be thrown clear and be replaced with another from the pouch.

I believe that this could be problematic, for, as we know, people absolutely do revert to their training when operating under stress. And if they have been conditioned to rip the magazine out of their pistol and throw it aside when clearing a stoppage, then that is probably exactly what they will do in combat.

The problem is, what happens if this is the officer's last or only magazine?

Furthermore, the reason most often offered in support of immediately discarding the magazine–because it may be defective, thereby causing the stoppage–doesn't carry a lot of weight. In my experience, when using quality firearms, the usual causes of double-feed stoppages are a weak or loose grip on the pistol, an improperly cleaned or lubricated pistol, or a combination of all three.

Given these considerations, the choice is to either condition our officers to:
1) automatically respond in a way that may leave them with no ammunition because we fear the magazine lips may somehow have become bent (the least likely cause of the stoppage), or
2) automatically respond in a way that will allow them the best possible chance of quickly getting the gun up and running and themselves back in the fight if the stoppage was caused by a loose grip or fouled weapon (the most likely cause).

For my money, the second method is the more pragmatic choice.

If you encounter a double-feed type stoppage while firing, first take cover (if possible) and perform the T.I.R.R. Clear Drill. If this does not immediately clear the stoppage, then ...

1. **LOCK** - Lock the slide to the rear.

How to Perform the Double-Feed Clearing Drill, continued

2. **RIP** - Remove the magazine and vigorously shake the pistol and magazine. Keep the pistol's *muzzle canted up* to aid in clearing any loose or misfed rounds from the chamber.

3. **TAP** - Reinsert the magazine into the magazine well and drive it forcefully upward using the heel of the palm. Ensure the magazine seats and locks into place. Note: Avoid the Hollywood stylization of inserting the magazine partially into the well, releasing contact with the magazine and then "slapping/slamming" it up into place. In the real world, magazines tend to fall from the magazine well and hit the ground when this is done.

4-5. **RACK** - Release the slide by grasping the rear serrations, pull back and release, allowing the slide to slam home. **IMPORTANT:** Do not maintain your grip on the rear of the slide with your non-dominant hand in an effort to assist or "ride the slide" forward, because this practice will often induce a stoppage. Releasing the slide in this manner is preferable to depressing the slide release lever, for the extra energy generated by fully compressing the recoil spring can mean the difference between the slide closing fully forward into battery or not. This is especially true should the weapon be dry or fouled.

Double-Feed Clearing Drill, continued

5. **READY** - You are then ready to engage, if warranted.

Common Semiauto Pistol Stoppages

Failure to feed (double-feed) type stoppage shown in top photo. Failure to extract/eject (stovepipe) type stoppage shown below it.

Failure to Go Into Battery

The slide fails to go fully forward after loading or during the firing cycle. This usually occurs because the weapon is dry or dirty. In some cases, it occurs because the round's casing is damaged or deformed. The option shown at right–using the heel of the palm to strike the rear or side of the slide (*not* the hammer!) to drive the slide fully forward–is commonly taught to remedy this stoppage. For simplicity's sake, I no longer recommend it.

Should this stoppage occur, the TIRR Clear Drill should be applied for the following reasons:
1.) if the stoppage occurs because the weapon is dry or dirty, the TAP on the magazine will often induce the slide to fully close. If this happens, the rest of the TIRR Clear drill can be omitted.
2.) if the stoppage occurs because the round is dam-

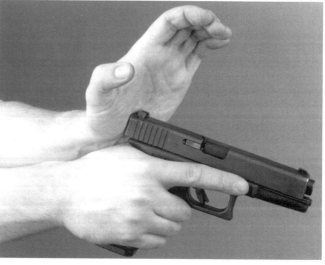

aged or deformed, striking the slide forward as shown at left may only exacerbate the problem, driving the deformed casing further into the chamber making the stoppage more difficult and time consuming to clear. So if the TAP alone does-n't clear it, simply complete the INVERT RACK READY steps as shown on the previous pages. If this still does not clear it, try the force forward technique while moving to cover, or employ the "New York" Reload (accessing your second gun).

APPENDIX I
Semiauto Pistol Reload Drills

Administrative Reload ("Locate, Index, Seat and Tug")

 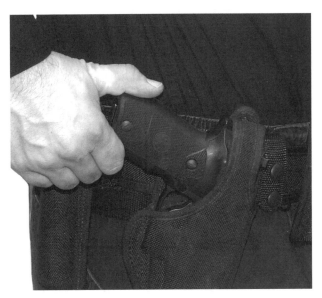

1 - 2. If there is a round in the chamber, remove the empty magazine from the holstered pistol and secure it in a pocket. Locate a fully loaded magazine, index it, and insert it into the holstered pistol (as shown above left). Firmly seat the magazine in the pistol, then give it tug on the floorplate to ensure it is locked in (above right). If the pistol has been fired until empty; after inserting loaded magazine draw the pistol, point it in a safe direction, and chamber a round. Then safely recover the pistol to the holster and secure the retaining snap. Next, remove the magazine and top it off with another round (if desired) and re-insert the magazine (ensuring it is seated and locked), completing the non-emergency, administrative reload.

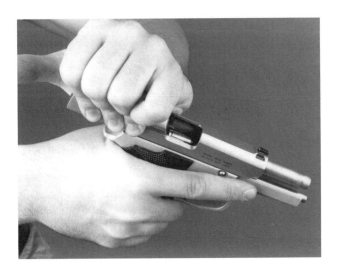 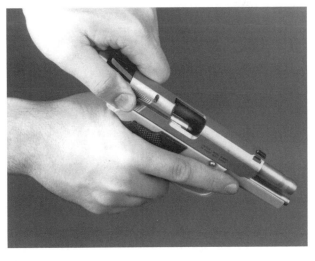

3 - 4. Chambering a round using the overhand method (left) and the slingshot method (right). Either is acceptable. The slide must be cleanly released and allowed to "slam home." Do not maintain the support hand grip on the rear serrated portion of the slide and "ride the slide" forward as this may induce a stoppage. (Bottom photos by Al Pereira)

Combat Reload ("Locate, Index, Drop and Pop")

The Combat or Speed Reload is used when we have expended so much ammunition during an encounter that the pistol has either run out of ammunition or we feel it is about to.

1. **LOCATE** the magazine pouches by placing the loading hand on the center belt-buckle, then sweep the hand along the belt toward the support side. The first item encountered should be the magazine pouch. This movement is incorporated to prevent confusion, for it is not uncommon for an officer to try and load handcuffs, Buck knives, or Mini-Mag lights into the weapon due to failure to properly locate the magazine pouch when performing the reload under stress.

2. Once located, open the *inboard* pouch flap first, then remove and **INDEX** the magazine (index finger placed along front of magazine). These movements should be practiced until they can be accomplished by feel alone. Do not allow your focus to be turned away from the threat target area while performing the reload.

3. (Left) When the loaded and indexed magazine is brought up next to the weapon, the empty magazine is **RELEASED** (**DROP**) and allowed to fall freely from the pistol.

4. (Right) **INSERT** the fully loaded magazine and seat it firmly, driving it upward by using the heel of the open palm. If the slide has locked open as a result of having fired the pistol until empty, it must be released to chamber a round. Use the overhand or slingshot method to accomplish this rather than depressing the slide release lever, as these methods require less fine motor skills and provide more spring tension to assist the slide in fully closing.

Tactical Reload ("Locate, Index, Catch and Seat")

The Tactical Reload is different from the Combat Reload, in that it allows for the only time it is desirable to catch a released magazine when reloading. It is intended to be used during an extended encounter when you realize you have fired multiple rounds and desire to reload, but want to save any ammunition that is in the partially expended magazine.

It is also employed in situations where the sound of an empty magazine hitting the ground could give away your position, and jeopardize any tactical advantage you may have over an armed adversary. One method of performing this reload is provided here.

1. First, *take cover* where possible. Remove the trigger finger from the trigger. Decock if necessary. Then **LOCATE** and draw out a fully loaded magazine, **INDEX** it, and bring it up to the weapon.

2. Press the magazine release and **CATCH** the expended magazine in the same reloading hand. Remove the magazine from the weapon.

3. Rotate the fully loaded magazine up and insert it into the magazine well.

4. **SEAT** the magazine with an upward press, using the meaty portion of the hand or side of the index finger as shown. This should be done in a controlled, deliberate manner.

Tactical Reload, Continued

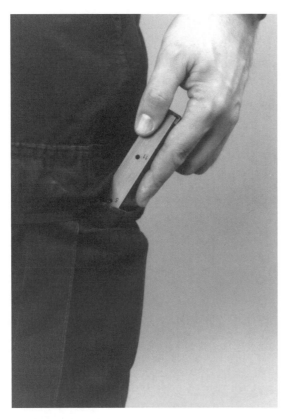

5. Finally, place the empty or partially empty magazine *in a pocket.* Never place an expended magazine back into your magazine pouch, for it could be the one you grab if you must reload again later in the conflict. Always try and observe the suspect and his location while performing the reload.

I hear and I forget. I see and I remember. I do and I understand. – Confucius

Training Note: While it's always best to only demonstrate good techniques (so bad techniques are not seen and remembered) occasionally it's beneficial to demonstrate what you *DON'T* recommend in order to prevent possible injury.

When teaching the Tactical Reload as shown in this section, I find it's worth reinforcing the preferred way to seat the magazine (with an upward press, using the meaty portion of the hand) as opposed to the method shown here.

Otherwise, you may find that people will forcefully slam the top bony-structure of their hand against the magazine floorplate to seat the magazine as shown. When this is done, distracting pain or injury will likely occur.

APPENDIX J
Precision Shooting

The training course must be balanced, with equal emphasis on the aimed shot and on combat type training. The combat phase should not consist of shooting 50 shots every 12 months at silhouettes hanging in the target range, then no further training until another year. After initial familiarization and training on the target range, the shooter should be required to shoot regularly a balanced program of both types of shooting as long as he remains on the active list. This kind of shooting program will enable him to do the most effective job when called on to shoot his weapon. At the same time it will give him the confidence in himself and his sidearm that will carry him through emergencies successfully.

- Colonel Rex Applegate
Kill or Get Killed
1943

First Step: Determining the Master-Eye

Ask most people if they are right or left handed and they will answer instantly. Ask someone if they are right or left *eyed*, however, and they will most likely look at you with an expression similar to that of a hog staring at a wristwatch.

The fact is that one of our eyes *is* usually dominant to the other. Some people–estimated to comprise less than 1% of the population–are *co*-eye dominant, which is similar to being ambidextrous.

It is important to know which eye is dominant before you begin to learn to shoot using the sights, especially in regard to working with long guns. For if you are right-handed and left-eyed–a condition referred to as being "cross-eyed dominant"–then you will have to make an adjustment either in the way you sight or hold the weapon.

This very common situation can cause problems ranging from mild to severe for the average shooter. If you can catch it early enough, you can eliminate a great deal of the complications caused by it, simply by training the individual (or yourself) to mount and shoot the long gun on the dominant-eye side. I took this approach with my left-eye dominant daughter when she turned eight and asked for shooting lessons. Right from the start I trained her to mount, sight, and fire her little .22 caliber "Chipmunk" rifle from the left side, even though she was right-hand dominant. She quickly became a crack shot, and now feels perfectly natural shooting this way.

The alternative was to let her mount the rifle on her right side and try and teach her to close (or half-close) her dominant left eye when shooting, so her non-dominant right eye would take up the slack. Having trained many cross-eyed dominant people over the years, I have come to believe that it is easier to go with the dominant eye-side, if dominant hand-side habits haven't already been deeply ingrained.

Cross-eyed dominant people who have learned to shoot from their dominant hand side can be easily identified, as they will usually try and maneuver their heads over the weapon's receiver far enough to line up the dominant eye with the sights. This creates undue stress, not to mention discomfort, and usually results in frustration and poor marksmanship.

While it's true that most people can learn to overcome this difficulty simply by getting used to sighting with their non-dominant eye, many people experience a great deal of frustration just trying to get their dominant eyelid to close, especially under stress. In addition, when trying to sight and fire under stressful conditions, many find that their brain will try to restore the natural order and employ the strongest weapons in its physical arsenal–in this case the *dominant* eye–which can induce greater confusion and distress on the shooter.

The good news is that in regard to shooting pistols while employing the sights to verify alignment with the target, the difficulties faced by the cross-eyed dominant shooter are minimal, and can be pretty much negated simply by ensuring that the shooter is indeed aware of *which of his eyes is dominant.*

This is true because of the way the pistol, as opposed to the long gun, is held when firing using the sights. With the long gun, when you mount the stock on either the left or right shoulder, the sights will naturally be more easily aligned by the eye on that same side. With the pistol, however, the entire weapon system is held well out in front of your face regardless of whether you use one or two hands to grasp it. This allows you to line up the pistol's sights with either eye, simply by slightly angling the weapon on the horizontal plane to the left or right.

By teaching sighted fire this way, a lot of confusion is immediately dispensed with.

By way of example, for years I was taught that when firing a pistol with my right hand, I was to sight with my right eye, and when firing with my left hand, I was to sight with my left eye. Now while I agree that it is a great idea to be as flexible and efficient as possible in regard to all forms of pistolcraft skills, including being able to sight and fire with either hand and/or eye, logic indicates that under extreme duress, if you can actually get your eyes to focus on the sights at all, your dominant eye will more than likely be the one called into action as a result of the body's survival mechanisms kicking in.

Logic also indicates that should the dominant eye become damaged or disabled, then the brain would automatically shift its resources to the non-dominant eye in order to access the visual information it would find so vital for survival, probably with no conscious awareness on the part of the shooter.

Requiring people to employ the same hand-same eye technique when training therefore, might actually do more to add to their confusion should they need to employ sighted fire during an actual event. The only true possible tactical rationale for even teaching people to shoot in this manner, as far as I can see, is to provide them with an advantage they could exploit should they find themselves in a position where they were trying to line up a sighted shot from behind cover, as less of the face will be exposed to incoming fire if the same-side hand and eye are used as you shoot around that cover. While this absolutely has merit, it is a matter I believe is best addressed after the basic skills have been mastered.

Finally, in regard to our co-eyed dominant pistol shooters, simply having their condition explained to them (after they've been diagnosed) can instantly clear up years of confusion and help them correct a problem many of them didn't consciously realize they had. For with a co-eyed dominant individual, what often happens is that *both* eyes fight for dominance while the shooter tries to focus on his pistol's front sight. This results in one eye sometimes being used for one shot, and the other for a subsequent shot–all without the shooter's conscious determination or awareness.

After conducting the simple test explained on the following pages, I've had co-eyed dominant shooters tell me that for years they had thought that there was something wrong with them, because it seemed like their vision was playing tricks on them as their sight pictures changed from shot to shot. The best solution I'm aware of for a shooter diagnosed with co-eye dominance is to first educate him about the condition, and then assist him to learn to consciously control it to the best of his ability. This can often be aided by having him practice half-closing or squinting one of his eyes just enough to blur the image. The neural systems in the brain then tend to automatically select the unimpeded eye, since both are internally rated as "dominant". As far as deciding which of their dominant eyes they should use, all things being equal–and in this case, I guess they are–it doesn't really matter except in regard to the tactical considerations described above.

Determining Eye Dominance

1. Donna Losardo demonstrates one effective method for determining eye dominance. First, fully extend the arms and form a small opening about the size of a silver dollar with the hands as shown. Both eyes are open.

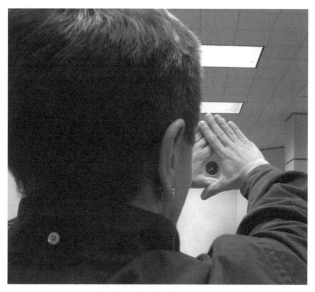

2. **Keeping both eyes wide open** and the arms fully extended, select a distant object (such as the wall clock shown here) and bring the hands up in front of the face. Center the object in the opening formed by the hands.

3. Then bring the hands back slowly toward the face, while keeping both eyes open and the object centered in the opening. Whichever eye is looking through the opening once the hands are against the face is most likely the dominant eye. This can be verified by having the shooter perform the test again. If the hands come back to the same eye consistently, you've determined which is the master. If, however, the opening comes back first to one eye and then the other, you've probably got a co-eye dominant shooter in front of you. NOTE: On rare occasions–I swear it happens–when the hands reach the face the opening will be centered above the eyes on the shooter's forehead. When this occurs, unless the individual has a crystal ball in front of him, you've got a problem. I usually just make a mild joke about it and explain the process again, and then keep my own dominant eye on the person while they're shooting, just in case...

How to Use the Sights (Standard Patridge Front Blade & Rear Notch Configuration)

It's always a good idea to go over the basics, even with experienced shooters. I usually try to keep it short and simple while explaining the re-set drill.

When using typical Patridge-type sights (illustrated at right) to verify that your pistol's bore is aligned with the object you're going to  shoot, place the front sight on the object's center of mass, then align the rear notch with the front sight so the front sight blade is centered in the middle of the notch.

When aligned properly, you should see the same amount of light on either side of the front blade as you look through the notch (equal light).

The top of the front sight blade should also be even with both tops of the rear sight (equal height).

As you look through the sights at the target, your eyes will only be able to bring one of the three objects–rear sight, front sight, or target–into clear focus.

After verifying the identification of your target and ensuring that there is nothing directly around or behind it you are not willing to shoot, you focus intently on the front sight, keeping it both aligned with the rear sight and target as described above and in sharp focus. (Jim Cirillo once mentioned that he sometimes advises shooters to focus on *one edge* of the front sight while maintaining alignment to induce greater concentration.)

The sight picture and the front sight focus should be maintained while pressing the trigger to the rear and continued even after the shot is fired. Often referred to as "follow through", this practice helps to increase accuracy and decrease the amount of time it takes to deliver accurate follow-up shots.

Sights and the "Seasoned" Shooter

When working with older shooters, a few things about sight alignment and sight picture need to be discussed if the instructor intends to be of service to the over-forty crowd (of which the author is a member).

Once the eyes reach the age of forty, the lens-es normally begin to lose flexibility. This results in the gradual loss of ability to focus on near objects. As this loss proceeds incrementally, the "point of accommodation" (or the distance away from the eye at which clear focus is able to be achieved) slowly but surely moves further away from the eye.

One way to monitor this cruel wont of nature, if you're of a mind to do so, is to extend your dominant arm as if holding a pistol, and with your other hand hold a piece of paper with some fine print on it just above your dominant arm. Move the paper back and forth until the print appears sharp and clear. This is your current point of accommodation. Then check it every few months or so, and you'll be able to determine just how much flexibility your lenses are losing as that paper has to be held further and further from your eye so you can read it.

Eventually, that piece of paper will be out in front of where the sights on your pistol are located when the weapon is held at full extension. And when that happens, that means that short of using corrective lenses, for all intents and purposes the whole notion of front-sight focused sight picture has become moot, for all three objects–rear sight, front sight, and target–will appear blurry should the shooter try to focus on the front sight as taught.

When asked for suggestions by officers who've reached this stage and haven't elected to go with special, multi-lensed shooter's glasses (something I don't recommend for active police officers), I usually advise them 1) don't stress out over it, as it's a natural process, and 2) instead of worrying about it, just *go with it*–for even if both of the sights are a little blurry, you still should be able to line them up properly on the target. Just stay true to form, press the trigger smoothly so you don't disturb the sight alignment and you'll do fine.

Of course, if the shooter's eyesight is such that the *target* cannot be clearly identified, *then* we are dealing with an entirely different matter that must be immediately addressed through the proper administrative channels.

***When* to Use the Sights**

Simply stated, you should use the sights to verify alignment with the target whenever possible.

In regard to the realities of police work, there

are certain situations and conditions that may allow an officer to do just that with the handgun.

Some officers–a very, very small percentage of the overall population in my estimation–are naturally hardwired to be able to access the sights under conditions of close quarter spontaneous combat. These are the Jim Cirillo's of the world, a special breed all their own, who in addition to possessing that unique basic ability also devote untold hours to training and practice.

Another small group of officers, most often with extensive military specops backgrounds (in addition to being what Colonel Grossman refers to as "natural soldiers") and who have received extensive amounts of intensive CQB training, may also be able to overcome and control their natural responses to stress, startle and fear and switch their focus from that immediate threat to their front sight at the moment of discharge.

For the vast majority of us, however, the likelihood of being able to use the sights of our handguns when facing an immediate deadly threat at close quarters will usually depend on other considerations.

While many would agree that certain factors such as time, distance and availability of cover contribute heavily in the officer's favor in this regard, what I have come to believe after years of research, debriefings of numerous officers, and my own personal experiences, is this:

> If you perceive that the immediate threat is directed *at you personally*, the chances of you being able to take your eyes from the person presenting that threat and placing your focus on the front sight of your pistol are slim to none.

> If, however, you perceive that the threat is directed *to someone else*, regardless of your distance from the person presenting that threat, then you absolutely may be able to access those sights to verify alignment of the shot.

An example of the type of situation I am referring to was related to me several years ago by an officer in the following way, immediately after we had participated in a meeting during which the relevance of Point Shooting had been discussed.

This officer and his partner had been dispatched to the scene of what was believed to be a domestic disturbance. As soon as they arrived at the location, the officers heard loud screaming and banging coming from the trailer home. The screaming was so intense that the officers immediately drew their handguns and entered the trailer home, yelling out "Police!" as they rushed into the back bedroom from where the sounds were emanating.

In this room the officers were met with a horrific scene.

"A very large male subject," the officer told me, "was straddled over a small female lying on the floor. As we (he and his partner) entered, the male was in the process of stabbing the woman in the chest with a large kitchen knife. There was blood everywhere. As I watched, the knife was aggressively pulled up and out of the victim, spatters of blood flying off the blade and onto the wall.

I was standing directly behind the assailant, my gun drawn and pointed at him," he continued. "My partner was standing 90 degrees to the side, also facing the assailant, and his gun was also drawn and pointed at the big man."

At this point in the story the officer broke his gaze from the mental image he had been replaying in his mind, looked at me and said, "Now understand what I'm saying here, 'cause I love my partner like he was my own brother, but while we're standing there, guns pointed, blood flying, my partner's yelling at me, saying, 'Shoot him! Shoot him!' Meanwhile, in my own mind, I'm thinking, 'I don't want to shoot him, YOU shoot him, YOU shoot him!'

"Finally, as I watched, the knife began to descend again, like in slow motion. I knew I had to shoot to save her, yet I also knew that if I didn't angle the shot correctly, the round could go through him and hit *her*. So what I did was, I lined up my sights as precisely as possible, and stared so hard at them that I could see dust particles on the front sight. The sights, in fact, looked *huge* to me as I fired."

The round entered the back of the assailant's head just as he drove the knife so deep into the victim that it pinned her to the floor. The assailant died at the scene. Unbelievably, the victim survived, owing her life to the officer's actions.

After he finished telling me the story, he said, "So how do you explain that? I was practically right on top of the guy and there's no doubt in my mind as to what I saw."

As I considered this, a thought occurred to me. "Let me ask you this..." I started. "At the moment you fired, did you feel that *you personally* were in any direct danger?"

He considered this for a long moment, then replied, "You know, I never really thought about that before. But actually, no, at that moment I didn't. I mean *she* was the one catching the knife, I just wanted to save *her*."

This and many similar stories I've heard have led me to believe that **the perception of *where the threat is being directed* as opposed to the proximity of the officer in relation to the person presenting the threat, is the key** to understanding the origins of the conflicting accounts of officer's use of the sights during deadly force encounters.

Indeed, when analyzing reports from the field concerning an officer's ability to access and use the sights, this **directed-threat perception** is perhaps a more important factor than are training memories (as explained in Chapter Six), involved officer's desires to appear to have conformed to (Old Paradigm) department training, and the normal stress and confusion experienced during deadly force encounters.

It's All About Control

Before we can we use our pistols to control other people's out of control, life threatening behavior, we must first be able to *control our pistols.*

And before we can control our pistols, we must be able to control *ourselves.*

In regard to delivering bullets to such a target with the handgun, if the sights can be accessed and employed properly, our chances of hitting the threat-presenting suspect precisely where it will do the most good are increased substantially.

---
[1] BRASS: Breathe, Relax, Aim, Squeeze (or Sight), Surprise

In my first book, *In the Line of Fire*, I noted the two-part "secret" formula for achieving great sighted shooting as:
1) properly line up the sights of the weapon on the target, and then
2) cause the weapon to discharge *without disturbing that sight alignment.*

I also offered an acronym that I believed was more accurate than BRASS and its variants in relating the process best used to deliver precision rounds when more than trophies were at stake.[1]

This acronym, **CAPS**, stands for *Control, Aim, Press, Surprise.*

CONTROL includes keeping your mind as focused as possible and your body functioning at near to normal levels as possible. Simply by employing the "combat breathing" technique described in Chapter 6, you will be able to regain and/or maintain a great deal of control and better achieve both of these objectives. Control also refers to maintaining an effective grip on the handgun itself, something that may be harder than you might imagine (again, see Chapter 6).

AIM is described in the *How to Use the Sights* section above. Can be reduced to "Equal Height, Equal Light–Focus on front sight."

PRESS the trigger straight back smoothly as possible. Resist the urge to "stage" the trigger while firing double action. This practice of pressing the trigger so slowly that you can see and hear the separate stages of hammer movement is not desirable. Smoothness and speed are the goals.

SURPRISE doesn't mean we didn't know the pistol was going to fire, because obviously that is the purpose of the exercise. What it means is that the shooter didn't allow his inner puppy to alter his grip, stance, or both to *meet, control, or reflexively flinch in anticipation of the shot being fired* and the attendant recoil. There are several methods that can be used to assist the shooter to avoid and/or overcome problems generated by an inability to achieve this controlled surprise. The Re-Set Drill is one of the best.

The Re-Set Drill

1. Achieve good stance, grip, and sight *alignment*. Choose and aim at a specific spot on the target. Acquire a good sight *picture*, and focus on FRONT SIGHT. Place finger on trigger.

2. Smoothly press trigger to rear in one stroke, firing weapon. Do not "stage the trigger" by pressing slowly. **CONTINUE to HOLD TRIGGER to REAR** through recoil, **CONTINUE TO MAINTAIN FOCUS ON FRONT SIGHT!**

3. Once movement of pistol has stopped, maintain trigger finger contact with trigger and SLOWLY allow trigger to move forward until reset "CLICK" is heard. Then press the trigger *gently* and take up the slack until you feel it re-engage the sear (feels like hitting a "wall") **BUT STOP BEFORE IT DROPS THE HAMMER**... This may take getting used to–*don't give up!*

4. Keeping the trigger held against the sear, realign the sights, using the hole generated by first shot as aiming point for next shot. Then **FRONT SIGHT, PRESS and HOLD!** Repeat process for following shots. (Photos by Katie Conti.)

The Re-Set Drill, continued

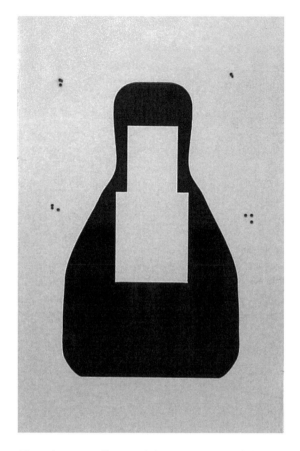

Though you will see tighter groups and looser groups than those shown above, these are typical results of Re-Set Drill after the technique is understood and practiced.

Four, 3-shot groups are visible on the target.

Groups are fired in this sequence during DPTC No. 1 (Skill Builder Course):

1) Top, right of silhouette: two hand-hold dominant, then DECOCK (if pistol is so equipped). Next:

2) Bottom, right of silhouette: one hand-hold dominant, then DECOCK and transfer pistol to non- dominant hand. Then

3) Top, left of silhouette: two hand-hold non-dominant, DECOCK and finally

4) Bottom, left of silhouette: one hand-hold nondominant, DECOCK, reload, and recover to holster.

Classic Blast from the Past!

Please note: Shooting position shown below is *NOT* recommended. Shown purely to illustrate cross-eyed dominance as described in text at beginning of this appendix.

In this photo from the Massachusetts State Police archives, you can clearly see the recruit pictured above holding his .38 Special Smith & Wesson M&P Model duty pistol in his right hand, while sighting with his left eye, indicating this is a classic case of cross-eyed dominance. It's very possible this recruit was unaware he did this. (Other recruits shown in original photograph were not seen to be doing this, indicating this use of opposite eye/hand was not directed or intentional.) Both the M&P (Military & Police) Model revolver and shooting stylizations as shown were employed for decades. This photo is from the late 1960s.

APPENDIX K
Point Shooting

Proper training in combat point shooting achieves quicker expertise, does not necessitate so much retraining to maintain proficiency, saves more police lives, and takes more criminals permanently off the streets. There has been too much concentration on what is called the 'new modern pistol technique' instead of on what has been historically proven in combat.

> - Colonel Rex Applegate
> *The Close-Combat Files of Colonel Rex Applegate*
> 1998

Much has been written and documented about how to perform the Point Shooting Technique. Colonel Applegate's own books on the subject include *Kill or Get Killed*, *Bullseyes Don't Shoot Back* (co-authored with Michael D. Janich), and *The Close-Combat Files of Colonel Rex Applegate* (co-authored with Major Chuck Melson).[1] These titles and others listed in the Bibliography are recommended for study. The photos in this section have been provided to illustrate the technique as employed in the New Paradigm Program.

---

[1] These titles are available from Paladin Press.

Body Point Position From the Holster

1. The commonly taught Interview (or Ready) Position is the preferred starting point during training iterations. The stance is wide and balanced, the body is bladed, gun or dominant side away. Front view shown.

Side View

Detail of the retaining snap being released at the *same moment* the grip is established. People will often improperly perform these as two distinct movements, first releasing the retaining snap with the thumb *and then* establishing the grip. We refer to this as the "Alabama two-step." (No offense intended to our Southern Brothers and Sisters!)

2. Move hand directly to holstered pistol and establish the grip high on the backstrap. **Release retaining snap at the same moment.** Begin to simultaneously assume an *aggressive forward crouching position* as non-dominant arm begins to move to non-dominant side.

3. Draw the pistol up and out of the holster. Note how the trigger finger position along the side of the slide is already established. Keep the elbow pointed back as opposed to sticking out sideways. A smooth draw is achieved by raising the elbow and allowing the wrist to bend as the pistol is removed from the holster.

272

Body Point Position From the Holster, continued

4. Lock the dominant arm elbow against your side as shown. The pistol (gripped securely, wrist locked) is held level and directly in front of the center of your torso. Shooter is in full *forward leaning* combat crouch. Depending upon the distance from, and angle to, the target, you may have to elevate the forearm slightly so the pistol's muzzle points directly where you want it on the vertical plane. This will become automatic with practice. Sometimes referred to as the "third eye" concept, this technique enables you to condition or "calibrate" the muzzle or "third eye" to "look" where the other two eyes are focused.

The non-dominant arm may be extended down and to the side for balance or up next to the head in a defensive position as shown.

5. Opposite side view. While both variations of non-dominant arm positioning–arm held up, and arm held out to the side–should be offered and practiced, the defensive position as shown here is recommended. It must be remembered *what* we are training for. In this case, it's a close-quarter spontaneous threat. For this reason, it makes more sense to use the non-dominant hand and arm to protect the head and neck rather than having it down. Note that the heel of the rearward foot is raised. This assists in promoting an aggressive, balanced, forward-leaning combat stance.

273

Full Extension Position From the Holster
(After completing movements 1-3 as illustrated
in the Body Point position)

1. After clearing the holster, the wrist is locked and the pistol is driven forward, elbow locked at full extension. To avoid muzzle dipping, the arm may first be locked out holding the pistol pointing at an approximate 45 degree angle to the deck (as shown above left). The pistol is held centered on the body's vertical midline, yet the muzzle points directly ahead. In order to achieve this, the pistol must be angled slightly to the dominant side. (This is the same position used when firing from the standing low ready shown on the opposite page).

2. The dominant arm, **wrist and elbow locked**, is then raised like the handle on a pump (pivoting from the shoulder) until it is between the shooter's eyes and the intended target point as shown at right. (This is the "vertical lift"). As the pistol is raised the finger is placed on the trigger. At the moment the pistol is locked on target, the entire hand convulses and the weapon is fired. When training, the pistol should be held at this position for a moment after discharge, and then returned slowly to the low ready prior to performing the Tactical Recovery.

3. Left: When using a two-hand hold, the non-dominant hand supporting grip is established after the pistol is drawn from the holster but prior to it being driven forward to full extension.

The support hand must not be allowed to pass in front of the muzzle!

Both arms may be fully extended, elbows locked (as shown), or the support arm elbow may be kept slightly bent and pointed to the deck as used in the Weaver Stance.

274

Point Shooting From the Low Ready Position

1. The stance is wide and balanced. One foot is placed naturally slightly forward of the other. The body is crouched in an *aggressively forward-leaning posture*. The heel of the rearward foot is raised as shown. The pistol is held in the dominant hand at the low ready position, centered on the shooter's body. The firing arm is extended, the wrist and elbow are locked. The trigger finger is outside of the trigger guard resting against the frame of the pistol.

The non-dominant arm is held to the side for balance.

2. When the decision has been made to fire, the pistol is raised by pivoting the locked-out arm at the shoulder "like the handle of a pump". As the pistol is raised, the trigger finger is placed on the trigger. The hand convulses, like "squeezing an orange" at the moment the weapon is visible between the eyes and the intended target. *The focus remains on the THREAT*. Do not attempt to look at or focus on the pistol's sights!

It is critical that shooters be instructed to raise the pistol until it intersects with the shooter's line of sight from the eyeballs to the intended point of impact as opposed to raising it to "eye level".

It is common for shooters to place rounds high on the target if they have been instructed to bring the weapon to *eye level*, as opposed to **line-of-sight level**.

275

The Close Proximity Drill

This drill is included to provide an example of a close proximity technique as employed in DPTC No. 1. As this drill combines both close quarter defensive physical skills as well as firearms manipulation, it must be fully explained and demonstrated prior to attempting. Students should then be required to perform the drill in three distinct and separate stages as illustrated here using empty weapons. Only when they can perform the drill safely in a step-by-step manner should they be allowed to perform it as one uninterrupted sequence.

Once they can consistently perform the drill safely and fluidly, live ammunition can be introduced and the process should be repeated, students performing the drill slowly, step-by-step, and then in uninterrupted sequence, slowly and fluidly.

Step 1: STRIKE	Step 2: STEP BACK & INTO BODY POINT POSITION	Step 3: ENGAGE

Step 1: STRIKE

While student is standing in front of the target in the *Interview Position*: Instruct student to visualize the target attempting to retrieve a deadly weapon from concealment. On the command of **"Make ready, ...ONE!"** the student aggressively strikes the target in the eyes, throat, or groin.

Forewarn students that if the mannequin begins to tip over as a result of being struck, **they must not attempt to reach out to catch or otherwise prevent it from falling**, as they may move themselves into another student's line of fire.

Target stands designed as shown in Appendix Q usually prevent the mannequins from tipping easily.

Step 2: STEP BACK & INTO BODY POINT POSITION

On the command, **"Ready...Two!"** student takes ONE STEP back and presents weapon, assuming the Body Point Position.

NO SHOTS ARE FIRED AT THIS TIME!

Focus should be on target's center of mass.

It is imperative that the non-dominant arm be held out of the muzzle's line of fire.

Step 3: ENGAGE

On the command, **"Ready... Three!"** Student fires two rounds into the target.

The weapon should then be recovered to the holster following the tactical recovery protocol illustrated on the following pages..

Most people find it slightly disconcerting the first time they participate in the Close Proximity Drill and fire into the clothed mannequin, despite the fact that they visualize it initiating a violent act against them.

The reason the experience is vastly different from firing into a standard paper target is because the mannequin provides a more realistic representation of the actual "target" that will be engaged when necessary–a three-dimensional human being.

The effect is greatly enhanced when the mannequin's face has been painted to appear as real as possible, especially in regard to the eyes.

Due to the natural resistance normal human beings have to performing a severely violent act such as rehearsed during this drill, student's should be advised to pick out a specific spot on the threat mannequin's center-of-mass and stare at it while firing, as opposed to looking at the mannequin's face. This advice, offered by Bill Jordan in *No Second Place Winner*, helps eliminate potential hesitation to deliver rounds and stop the immediate threat, as well as provides a focus point to aid in accurate shot placement.

While this drill may make some people uncomfortable, it must be included. Common sense dictates that the *first time* a police officer is required to fire into a 3-D, threatening human form wearing clothing, should *not* be during a real-world event, but rather during training under controlled conditions.

The Reactive Movement Drill

This drill, incorporated into DPTC No. 2, requires the student to combine the two Point Shooting techniques used in the course. It also requires the student to fire, move, reassess, and fire again, all while maintaining focus on the target and keeping complete control of the weapon using only one hand.

As with the Close Proximity Drill, the Reactive Movement Drill must first be fully

Step 1: MAKE READY

Student stands in front of target in Interview Position. As with all these drills, holsters must be snapped and pistols secured as they are worn on patrol.

explained and demonstrated to the students.

Students should then be required to perform the drill in three distinct and separate stages as illustrated here using empty weapons.

Only when they can perform the drill safely in a step-by-step manner should they be allowed to perform it as one uninterrupted sequence.

Once they can consistently perform the drill safely and fluidly, live ammunition can be introduced and the process repeated, students performing the drill slowly, step-by-step, then in uninterrupted sequence, slowly and fluidly.

Gradually speed is increased to at least ¾ speed. However, the emphasis *must* be kept on performing the drill as *safely, efficiently and accurately as possible.*

In other words, students must not move or fire faster than they can safely and effectively hit the target.

Step 2: EXECUTE BODY POINT AND FIRE TWO ROUNDS CENTER MASS

Step 3: STEP BACK AND INTO FULL EXTENSION POSITION & FIRE ONE ROUND

On the command of **"Make ready...ONE!"** the student draws the pistol and assumes the Body Point Position, firing two rounds into the target's center mass as soon as the position is stabilized.

On the command, **"Ready... Two!"** Student takes **one step back** (*keeping body square to the target*) and fully extends dominant hand/arm as shown, directing his focus and the weapon's muzzle to an alternate target area, preferably the throat or head. One round is then fired into this area. Again, it is imperative that the non-dominant arm be held out of the muzzle's line of fire. Keeping it up and next to the head as shown is recommended.

Spontaneous Improvisations / Stylizations to Watch For and Correct

Instructors should reinforce the idea of keeping the body *square to the target* while stepping backward and extending the arm as shown above. This allows for more control, accurate hits, and efficiency of movement than do some other variations students tend to display when performing this drill.

The "Fred Astaire" position (good naturedly demonstrated by Paul Wosny in the photo at right) is an example of one of these spontaneous variations that should be discouraged.

Don't laugh–you'll see it more often than you'd think!

278

Becoming *One of the Quick*: The Poker Chip Drill

The Poker Chip Drill was reportedly used by American gunfighters of the old West to increase their drawing speed. Bill Jordan used to employ a variation of this drill using ping-pong balls during demonstrations.

Jordan was so fast, he could hold his hand (ping-pong ball balanced on top of it), directly above the holstered pistol and draw with such lightning speed that the ball would drop into the emptied holster.

I have found that this drill, when practiced professionally and safely as illustrated, still provides tremendous benefits to the modern-day pistolero. Presentation speed is increased, physical dexterity is improved and more deeply ingrained, and confidence rises as basic skills are strengthened.

The fact that it is also a lot of fun to perform, especially when in competition with yourself or others, provides another strong reason for using it, for the more people enjoy working with their pistols, the more positive is their attitude toward this potentially life-saving piece of equipment.

IMPORTANT! <u>All pistols</u> must be verified to be safe, clear, and empty prior to performing the Poker Chip Drill.

1. Place the poker chip on top of the dominant hand. The dominant hand is placed directly above the holstered pistol. The holster's retaining strap/ device is secured.

2. Initiate the presentation. The chip (visible in circle) is allowed to fall naturally off the hand, it is not tossed up or thrown.

Note: Sequence shown in real time. Images enhanced to make chip easier to see in photos.

3. The objective of the exercise is to complete the presentation as cleanly as possible before the poker chip (visible in circle still falling) hits the ground. Most officers/trainees should be able to achieve this during the first practice session. Once this can be consistently achieved, try to draw and DRY FIRE on target before the chip hits the ground.

Tactical Recovery

1. Lower the weapon far enough so you can observe the threat area clearly. If the weapon is equipped with a decocking lever that does not disengage the trigger, it should be depressed when the finger is taken off the trigger—regardless of whether the weapon has been fired or not. This ingrained action is performed automatically, providing one more degree of inherent, "built-in" operator weapon's safety.

2. Scan with your head 180 degrees to the right and left, looking for secondary threats. Statistics indicate that there will be at least a 40% chance that the involved officer will be facing more than one potential assailant in any given lethal force encounter. Note that **only the head scans**—the weapon remains stationary. If a threat is detected the weapon is then be pointed at it. This practice is both faster and safer than waving the entire shooting platform back and forth—faster due to economy of motion, and safer, for no innocent bystanders or other officers will be covered by the muzzle during the high-stress incident.

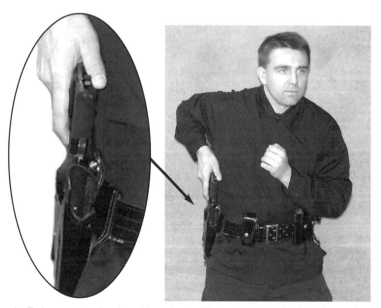

3. Maintain focus on the immediate surrounding area as you bring the weapon back toward the center-line of your body. If the weapon is equipped with a safety, it may be engaged now if policy dictates.

4. Release non-dominant hand grip. The non-dominant hand remains ready to re-establish the support-hand grip should another threat be presented or the initial threat resumed. The dominant hand continues to return the weapon to the holster. INSET: The thumb should be placed against the rear of the slide or the hammer when reholstering.

Tactical Recovery (continued)

5. Return the weapon to the holster as it was removed—using ONE-HAND.

Do *not* re-direct your focus to the holster; instead, maintain focus on the threat / target area!

Note: When returning the pistol to the holster, you may place your index finger along the slide and use it to locate the opening to the holster, as well as manipulate the retaining/safety strap out of the way if necessary. The thumb, placed on the rear of the slide (or back of the hammer), assists as the weapon is securely seated back into the holster by a smooth downward stroke.

6. Once the pistol is seated, the retaining/safety strap is secured, again using only the dominant hand.

Unlike the presentation, the recovery is to be performed *slowly.*

If you rush through the recovery in training, you may find yourself inexplicably holstering after firing at a real threat, only to find that you have not successfully stopped it.

Remember: "*Fast* on the draw, *slow* on the recovery!"

POLICE PISTOLCRAFT RANGE PROP DESIGN

2 Position Portable Barricade Design

1" Plywood - painted / textured

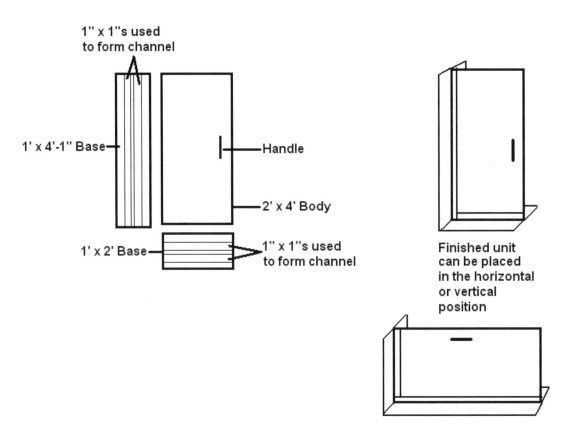

This portable training barricade design is both strong and versatile. It is constructed out of 1" plywood (both the body and the two base components) and 1" x 1" pine (serves as channels for plywood pieces). The structure is glued and screwed together for greatest strength.

When used on the range, the metal handle (if installed) should face DOWN RANGE, to lessen the potential for ricochet.

Most people find picking these barricades up and carrying them by the handles to be quite manageable.

NOTE: Even though it may seem obvious, trainees should be advised that while this training barricade is used to *represent* cover, <u>it does not actually provide cover</u> under real-world conditions. They should be further advised that true cover should always be identified prior to its being needed, and taught the preferred methods of accessing and employing it.

<u>Definition of true cover:</u> **STOPS INCOMING ROUNDS!**

<u>Definition of concealment:</u> **Hides your body and weapon but does not necessarily provide cover for either.**

282

APPENDIX L
Reaction Lag

Action Beats Reaction

Most people are aware on at least a basic level that action generally beats reaction. A simple example could be having two healthy adults facing one-another at close distance, and having one of them–without warning–suddenly slap the other's face. Given no unusual circumstances and having both parties being relatively unexceptional in regard to training and experience, the chances of the slappee being able to block, stop, or otherwise intercept that slap would probably be slim to none.

In regard to police firearms training, while the weapons, circumstances and other contributing factors are more complex, the basic underlying principle remains the same.

Unfortunately, this reality often goes unaddressed in police firearms training iterations. In fact, the vast majority of training efforts in regard to considerations of speed of action have been directed, understandably, toward assisting the officers to develop their own speed presenting and engaging targets with their handguns.

I say unfortunately, for without educating them as to how their own actions may be influenced by the actions of others, we are only partially preparing them to survive on the streets.

Improperly training officers to respond to an assailant pointing a firearm at them as described in Chapter Four is one glaring example of what I am referring to. While there are ways to modify and improve the training programs we administer to our officers, the basic foundation of knowledge regarding the action-reaction principle must be clearly established in each officer's mind if we are to truly prepare them for survival.

How Fast is Fast?

In a recent study conducted by Dr. Bill Lewinski, a professor in the Law Enforcement Program at Minnesota State University, a series of eleven experiments were conducted in order to determine just how quickly a number of typically criminal aggressive movements could be made. The results may surprise you.

Two are synopsized below.[1]

1. Operator of Motor Vehicle: Handgun hidden by right thigh, assailant shoots as officer approaches driver side door post.

Average time: 25/100ths of a second

Fastest time: 15/100ths of a second

---

[1] Dr. Lewinski's study goes on to include an analysis of how fast subjects can fire from a number of positions, as well as while running away from an officer. I highly recommend that police firearms instructors access and study this valuable data, especially in regard to the implications of the research on why suspects often get shot in the back.

According to Dr. Lewinski:

The movement is so fast that is unlikely that a street officer caught in this position would even be able to identify that the subject actually had a weapon in their hand until weapon was at the point of discharge.

2. Standing Suspect: Handgun hidden in waistband, assailant draws and fires from "combat tuck" position.

Average time: 23/100ths of a second

Fastest time: 09/100ths of a second

Again according to Dr. Lewinski:

An officer caught in the open in a 'Dodge City showdown' with even the average subject in this study literally would not stand a chance if the subject has their hand at their waistband, an actual weapon in that waistband, the intent to shoot and any accuracy at all with their weapon.

In regard to the average officer's speed, Dr. Lewinski advises the following:

To fully understand the implications of the research results … it is important to remember that the average officer, with their finger on the trigger and being psychologically set, is able to "react" to a shot timer and pull the trigger of their weapon in about a quarter to a third of a second. I am currently working on research on this topic with a whole police department and the preliminary data indicates it is closer to a third of a second or even longer

for most officers to react, at least with that department. Some officers of course are quicker and others are slower. The reader needs to keep this "average" reaction time in mind as they read about the different motions studied and learn just how really fast the suspect's action can be.

The One Dollar Demo

While explaining the reaction lag phenomenon, I generally employ two demonstrations. The first involves having a volunteer hold an inert toy pistol and pointing it at my face. With my hands raised as if in submission, I first explain exactly what I will do, and then I do it. All this involves is turning my body sideways from the waist while I grab the toy pistol with either of my hands. The volunteer, who has been advised to press the trigger as soon as he detects movement on my part, is invariably unable to make the pistol go "click" in my direction. This demonstration is never conducted using any tricks or unsafe actions. It is simply an effective way to illustrate the reaction lag, while also providing an additional teaching moment regarding options that can be explored when facing a drawn gun.

A second demonstration that also illustrates the reaction lag tends to be less dramatic as well as less disturbing for those not involved in the police industry. The "One Dollar Demo" as I've come to refer to it, provides an opportunity to both entertain and educate. I've found it to be a useful tool in my instructor's toolbox, and offer it here for consideration.

One Dollar Demo

1-2 (right). The Instructor demonstrates what is desired.

The bill, held between two fingers, is released and easily caught between the index and middle finger of the instructor's other hand.

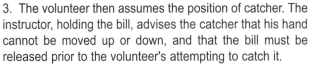

3. The volunteer then assumes the position of catcher. The instructor, holding the bill, advises the catcher that his hand cannot be moved up or down, and that the bill must be released prior to the volunteer's attempting to catch it.

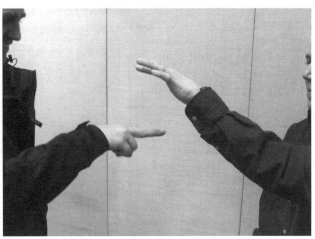

4. Typical Result. The demonstration can be repeated for effect. Then the following explanation is given:

"The reason this happens is because the person *dropping* the bill only has to process one thought-initiated action: *DROP IT!*

The person attempting to *catch* the bill, however, must process two thoughts: 1) *IT'S FALLING* and then 2) *CATCH IT!*"

When instructing police officers, you can then tie it all together by using an example of a suspect with a gun in the waistband or "combat tuck" position.

"The assailant, having decided to draw and fire, simply initiates the action — *ATTACK!.*

The *officer*, however, must first interpret and comprehend what the assailant is doing and *then* respond by whatever means he has been trained or has available to him: 1) *HE'S ATTACKING* and then 2) *RESPOND!*"

Some thoughts on Action vs Reaction, Boyd's OODA Loop, and Mushin

The late Colonel John R. Boyd, USAF (Ret.), was a maverick thinker who had a tremendous impact on the way modern warfare is conducted. In addition to being a legendary fighter pilot, Boyd developed a number of critical tactical theories and helped establish training programs to teach them to others.

Among his many accomplishments, Boyd was instrumental in the creation of the Fighter Weapons School at Nellis AFB, Nevada, the development and design of both the F-15 "Eagle" and the F-16 "Fighting Falcon", was the co-creator of the "Energy Maneuverability Theory", and developed and presented numerous critical briefings on warfare including his 1960 "Aerial Attack Study" that helped change the concept of air-to-air combat.

Despite the enormous amount of work Boyd produced and the far-reaching influence he had, most people who are familiar with his work today know him because of one concept in particular, the "Boyd Cycle" or, as it's more commonly known, the "OODA Loop".

OODA stands for *Observation, Orientation, Decision, Action*. OODA has become a standard description of decision making cycles used in military and business circles. OODA means that in order to survive, you must be able to interact with the environment and those within it appropriately. The way you do this is by continually observing the environment and orienting yourself to it in such a way that you can adapt and overcome by making good decisions and taking action in a timely fashion. One of the tenets of the theory is that if you can "get inside" the adversary's OODA Loop, constantly beating him to the action stage, then you will cause him to continuously "re-set" his OODA Loop, keeping him off balance until he is ultimately defeated.

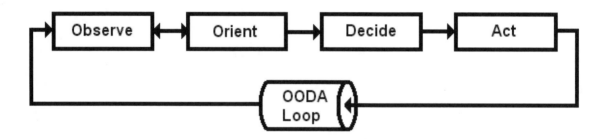

It is easy to see how and why this concept has been adopted by many in law enforcement training circles, as it seems to clearly explain the action-reaction process.

However, while both the OODA Loop model and "Hick's Law" (a theory that states that each available option increases reaction time by 58%) are excellent concepts to be aware of, close combat trainers also need to be aware of another, much older concept known as "mushin".

Mushin was a concept embraced by the Japanese Samurai. It translates into English as "Mind-no-mind". It is a concept that encourages the trained warrior to strive to achieve a state of "*consciousness without thought*". In this state, great speed of action is possible. While those who study the martial arts purposefully train to achieve this state and maintain it for an extended time, many people in various occupations achieve it to lesser degrees over time without realizing it. Examples include the fighter pilot who initiates an instantaneous maneuver to avoid incoming ordnance; a race car driver who reacts automatically to debris on the roadway, steering clear; a firefighter who moves without thinking from one side of a burning structure to another because his training and experience compel him to; or a police officer who reacts appropriately with lightning speed to an unexpected spontaneous threat without pausing to consider the many options available to him.

The ability to achieve mushin comes only through years of hard work, experience, and dedicated skills practice. One of our duties as trainers should be to assist our people in its pursuit. For if they can achieve mushin, even just for one critical moment, then the OODA Loop model could be effectively redrawn to show a straight line from *observe* to *act*. And if we could achieve *that*, very, very few people we will ever encounter would be able to get inside our OODA Loop, and defeat us.

APPENDIX M
Transition Drill

Transitioning immediately from one level of force option to another must be practiced. Only by practicing can we avoid finding ourselves "freezing up" when faced with a serious imminent threat. When transitioning from the ASR or baton to a higher level of force option, the ASR or baton should be immediately released (not thrown–this eats up time!) from the hand and the alternate weapon accessed by the dominant hand.

You must not waste the time required to recover the ASR or baton to the carrier prior to accessing the higher level of force option when necessary!

Transitioning From the ASR to the Baton

1. ASR has been presented from the carrier.

"THREAT!" signal is given.

2. ASR is released (not thrown or tossed away as this eats up time) as...

3. ...primary hand begins presentation of baton. There is no hesitation. Baton is accessed and...

4. ...presentation of baton is completed.

Transitioning From the ASR to the Pistol

ASR has been presented from carrier. "THREAT!" signal is given. ASR is released as...

...primary hand begins presentation of pistol. There is no hesitation. Pistol is accessed and...

...presentation of pistol is completed.

Training drills can be conducted that require the student to transition to the pistol and verbalize a challenge (i.e. "POLICE! Don't move!"), or to transition to the pistol and shoot to stop the immediate threat.

Cover should also be accessed and utilized as appropriate and/or available.

(Transition techniques demonstrated by Paul Damery.)

NOTE!

Transitioning from a higher level of force (pistol) to a lower level of force (ASR, baton, empty hands) should also be practiced.

In these cases, the pistol should be <u>reholstered</u>, *not released*!

This is obvious. However, we will act as we have trained, and if no training has been provided that requires transitioning both to higher *and lower* levels of force, then predicting just how we will react becomes extremely difficult.

TRAIN AS YOU FIGHT!

APPENDIX N
Alternative Shooting Positions

Much has been written about alternative shooting positions over the decades. I am including only two such positions– kneeling and prone–in this book because they are used in the basic program. Several flashlight-assisted shooting techniques are also provided in this section for reference.

Kneeling

The kneeling position provides us with many tactical advantages. Primarily it makes us a smaller target while still allowing us to deliver rounds from a stable platform and preferably, from behind cover.

Kneeling, one knee, unsupported

Kneeling, two knees, unsupported

Kneeling, self-supported

The upper body is rocked back, buttocks lowered onto the rearward foot's heel. The toes of the rearward foot should be pointed forward as illustrated. This will allow for quick movement should it be necessary.

The non-dominant arm (above the elbow) is rested on the support knee, avoiding bone to bone contact. The side of the face may be rested against the inside of the firing arm against the biceps, forming a "cheek-weld," and helping to stabilize the shooting platform. (Al Pereira photo.)

Prone

In regard to assuming the prone position, it must be understood that the method illustrated here was determined based upon the realities of conducting firearms training as safely as possible with groups of individuals possessing diverse training and operational backgrounds and varying physical conditions.

While officers who find it necessary to get down on the ground when operating in the real world will probably get there in great haste as a response to shots fired at them, or as a result of tripping, falling, or being thrown to the ground during a struggle, it is our responsibility to provide all involved with a safe, realistic method that may be used during training and also have applications for real-world employment.

The method, which is in essence a modified version of the "rollover prone", is first demonstrated by the instructor. Students are then talked through the process, step-by-step, until they can perform it safely. Eventually, they are simply instructed to assume the prone position using the preferred technique.

"Old Paradigm" Marksmanship-based Improper Use of Cover

1. Starting from the Interview Position (left), students are instructed to *"Kneel down, both knees on the deck."*

4. Next, students are told, *"Now place your dominant arm on the deck, palm-side facing up, and anchor your arm in position there. The pistol's muzzle should not be turned left or right, but remain pointed down range at all times. Fingers remain off the trigger and alongside the frame".*

(Left) In this photograph from the Massachusetts State Police archives (circa late 1960s), recruits are seen being taught to use cover primarily to stabilize their shooting platform. They are too close to the cover. By bracing their shooting hand against the cover, they expose their position, their weapon, and their bodies. Ricochet or spalling is another hazard they face from incoming rounds.

Closer examination reveals their S&W M&P .38 caliber revolvers are cocked, and they are focusing on the sights of their pistols. This is not a problem if they have enough time and distance from the *positively-identified* threat and make the best use of available cover.

2. Once in the kneeling position, students are instructed to *"Draw your pistols and come to the low ready position."*

3. Students are then instructed, *"Keep the pistol pointed down range, finger off the trigger. Bend forward at the waist and place the palm of your non-dominant hand flat on the deck in front of you."*

5. Finally, the students are instructed, *"Now, simply get down around the pistol. Once on the deck, adjust your position until you are comfortable and able to achieve a good sight picture."* They are further advised to keep their distance from the cover. (A good general rule is to keep back from cover at least an arm's length *plus* the length of the weapon.)

Right: Students should be encouraged to try different variations of the prone position to find the one that works best for them. The proper use of cover in relation to the angle of fire emanating from the adversary must also be explained. This aspect is more fully driven home during the Saber Challenge course of fire (Appendix P).

Flashlight Assisted Shooting Positions

Harries Technique

The dominant hand extends the pistol while the the non-dominant hand grasps the flashlight in an overhand hold. The flashlight is brought up and under the dominant hand. The backs of the hands are "locked" together, creating a stable shooting platform.

Chapman Technique

The light is grasped (palm up) in the non-dominant hand, held by the thumb and index finger. The dominant hand, holding the pistol securely, is pressed against the extended middle, ring, and pinky fingers of the non-dominant hand as shown. Once you get used to it, this technique is very comfortable and effective to shoot with.

Marine Corps Technique

The dominant hand grasps the pistol securely. The non-dominant hand grasps the flashlight securely as shown. The tips of the dominant hand's middle and ring fingers are pressed against the bezel of the flashlight. Slight pressure is exerted against the bezel, stabilizing the platform.

Side / FBI Technique

The light is held to the side and forward of the body. Keeping the light away from the body allows you to direct the beam into darkened areas without placing your torso directly into potential lines of fire. It also may prove beneficial should an assailant shoot at the light.

APPENDIX O
Moving Target: Engaging One & Becoming One

In the great majority of shooting affrays the distance at which firing takes place is not more than four yards. Very frequently it is considerably less. Often the only warning of what is about to take place is a suspicious movement of an opponent's hand. Again, your opponent is quite likely to be on the move. It may happen, too, that you have been running to overtake him.

> – Captain W.E. Fairbairn and Captain E.A. Sykes
> *Shooting to Live With the One-Hand Gun*
> 1942

At the conclusion of my first book, *In the Line of Fire: A Working Cop's Guide to Pistolcraft*, I commented on the need to incorporate moving target training not only from the perspective of police officers engaging one, but in *becoming one* as well.

This aspect of training (along with one-handed, combat pistol techniques) has traditionally been considered by many in modern law enforcement circles as *advanced training* suitable only for tactical team members. Too often, the idea of having rank and file officers moving before, during, or after shooting their pistols in training is dismissed out of hand, considered to be too dangerous and uncontrollable to be performed safely.

In my opinion, this attitude is not only condescending, but borders on negligence. It is condescending in that it denigrates the abilities of the average officer to adapt to increased demands during controlled training iterations. It approaches negligence in that it prevents officers from learning under controlled conditions *what they will most likely be doing during real-world events*–running and gunning.

The New Paradigm Program as presented in this book has been designed to serve as the foundation upon which an evolving training matrix that will benefit *all officers* can be built. Our program has continued to evolve, and we anticipate the next significant phase of training to be fully-implemented very shortly. The plan is to incorporate dynamic movement into the various DPTC level one and two drills. This will allow officers to better develop their abilities to respond appropriately to various threat stimuli while doing what they will actually be doing when the threat is not represented by paper targets, but living, moving, thinking human beings.

An entire series of DPTC's dedicated to this objective has been formatted and successfully administered to several test groups. One of these courses, titled appropriately, T*he Officer as a Moving Target Drill*, is included in this appendix.

More information will be provided about this next phase of training in future publications.

For now, the following information is provided for consideration when administering or participating in training iterations that incorporate the use of movement.

Movement to Cover

When moving to cover, get there as quickly as possible. Remember to check and clear any cover you may be approaching, especially if there is a potential for hidden hazards such as assailants, hazardous devices, etc.

Remember not to crowd your cover, rather, stay back at least an arm's length (plus the length of your weapon) from it so long as you are still protected from incoming fire by it. This will help you avoid ricochet, spalling, or penetration damage, as well as give you a better field of view.

Cover Considerations

Be aware of available cover anytime you are operational. If you suspect that a problem or danger is imminent, start picking out potential sites of cover, as well as escape routes.

Available cover should always be utilized to the best of your ability!

Remember that while some things may provide *concealment* (hiding your body), the best cover *stops bullets*. Also remember to consider what cover may be available to you before you enter any new environment. (E.g., where in a house can you find true cover? Also, what part of an automobile provides the best cover?)

Judgment

For the law enforcement officer, the moment when he is faced with a situation during which he must decide whether to shoot or not may be the most important moment of that individual officer's life. Obviously, it may also be the most important moment of many other people's lives as well, including the officer's family, friends, and co-workers, any injured innocent bystander's, their families, friends, etc., injured suspect's, families, etc., and the list goes on.

Reality demands that we recognize that the rounds fired from the officer's weapon may simultaneously take and save lives.

Reality also demands that we acknowledge that hesitation on the part of the officer at this critical moment may cost or save lives.

This is the most difficult aspect of our profession, for we will often be required to make this decision in a fraction of a moment, based on what we know, see, hear, feel, and believe *at that precise moment.*

The ultimate truth is, there are no easy answers. There are no hard and fast rules that apply to each and every officer, or to each and every situation.

Each human being, including those who may

Does simply being inside a vehicle provide you with sufficient cover against incoming rounds? Absolutely not! Many types of projectiles will easily penetrate the materials most vehicles are constructed with. This car door, shot with various calibers, is used as a display to illustrate this reality.

create situations that require police officers to employ deadly force against them, is responsible for his own actions. That is why we, as law enforcement professionals, must prepare ourselves as best we can to meet this enormous responsibility, and, once prepared, *trust ourselves, our training, and each other* to do the absolute best we can in whatever situation we may find ourselves.

We must also be able to clearly articulate our reasons for employing deadly force at that moment, and be prepared to live with the consequences of our actions.

Verbalization

Verbalization is a key component of officer survival and situational control. Officers often tend to either say nothing during high-stress engagements, or, if more than one officer is present, they tend to all give commands/directions at the same time, creating confusion. This is especially true during dynamic situations when officers and/or suspects are on the move, constantly shifting position and realigning their angles of view and, as a result, influencing their perceptions.

The key to verbalization is simplicity.

If feasible, **give simple commands in a clear, loud voice**. Avoid using profanity no matter how heated the situation. Repeat the commands slowly until compliance is achieved or other means of control are required. If there is more than one officer present, the contact (initiating) officer should be the only one to issue commands.

Verbalization is also highly recommended during any type of entry/search process, as long as the officers are not conducting a stealth search and their presence is obvious to anyone in the area.

Engaging Moving Targets: The Basics

In the real-world a human being can move in many directions. The following guidelines are included to assist the officer in the development of his ability to accurately engage a moving subject who presents an immediate deadly threat justifying the employment of deadly force.

Tracking: Concentrate on the front sight if possible. If not, focus on a specific part of the suspect's anatomy while keeping the pistol pointed and locked on target. Track the moving target while manipulating the trigger as smoothly as possible. *Continue to move the weapon with the target before, during and after firing*. Do not stop the movement to take the shot when tracking, as your rounds will more than likely impact behind the target. In regard to "leading" the target:

• If the target is moving laterally or obliquely toward or away from you at a speed of less than 10 miles per hour, at distances inside 15 yards, move the weapon with the target, concentrating on a specific spot on the target through the sights. There is no lead.

• For distances of 15-20 yards, move the weapon with the target, concentrating on the front leading edge of the target through the sights.

• For distances greater than 20 yards (to 30 yards), lead the forward edge of the target by approximately 4 inches.

Trapping: Trapping is best used from behind cover when the moving suspect presents an immediate threat to others, or is currently moving laterally or obliquely away from you. This is because the trapping technique requires you to focus your vision not directly on the suspect, but at a point slightly ahead of his perceived route of movement. Trapping is also best performed by employing the pistol's

sights, something that may be extremely difficult (if not impossible) to do when facing a threat perceived to be coming directly to you. To perform the technique, as noted above you pick a spot directly in front of the moving suspect's direction of travel and focus at that point. Remaining in a stationary position, you press the trigger when the suspect physically intersects with your aiming point.

Overtaking: This third technique employs elements of the first two. As the target is tracked, the weapon's sights are moved smoothly to a point slightly ahead of the target. The weapon is then held stationary, and fired at the moment the target physically intersects the point of aim.

**Engaging Moving Targets:
Additional Considerations**

a) If the subject is moving *DIRECTLY AWAY FROM YOU*, simply engage as you would a stationary target that is slowly being reduced in size.

b) If the subject is moving *DIRECTLY TOWARD YOU*, you may feel overwhelmed or disoriented. While the subject's weapon will most likely draw your eye, if possible you should try to focus on a specific sighting location on the subject (a button on the shirt, for example) and engage as you would a stationary target. When practicing this technique in training, remember that the goal is not to hit the button, but the shirt and torso behind it! The button (or whatever aiming point is available) just serves to sharpen and narrow the focus.

Officer training with portable moving target system.

Training Officers *to Become* the Moving Target: The Basics

In order to counter the conditioning effects of the overwhelmingly common, static-level training courses of fire, the following suggestions are presented for consideration:

1. Simply requiring officers to step to the right or left (at the instructor's direction) before or after firing on static targets, from static firing positions during marksmanship level training courses of fire, can have a tremendous positive impact. Be advised, however, that years of conditioning officers to stand in front of static targets while they draw, fire, and recover to the holster are not easily overridden. Incorporating a single step to the left or right as described here must be done slowly, calmly, and methodically when training groups of officers.

2. Having officers participate in training courses that require them to turn and move safely in *any direction* with loaded pistols in their hands while on the range is often looked at as an unsafe activity. However, this is precisely what we do when operating in the real world! If we do not believe that we can achieve a safe level of performance on the range under controlled conditions while doing this, how can we possibly justify sending our officers out into the world where they will have do this under extremely stressful conditions!?

3. Having officers participate in training courses that require them to deliver rounds accurately to a static target while the officers are on the move is another activity that can be safely accomplished when conducted properly. Exercises that have officers firing while moving directly toward, or while backing directly away from the target are an excellent first step. Once officers have mastered these exercises, they should be introduced to the "Serpentine Drill". This drill, as taught by Bob Taubert, is perhaps the best overall basic-level "running and gunning" exercise I have encountered. Not only does it help "break" the neural pathways that have been established that often cause officers to stop to take the shot, but is also designed to instill muzzle control discipline and improve threat assessment abilities. It's a simple course to set-up and run and a great confidence builder. It is detailed at the end of this appendix.

Position "Sul" (for "South" or "muzzle down") shown at right. This position may be used to allow safe control of the pistol in 360 degree orientation as long as it's employed properly. **The muzzle must not be allowed to point at your body, including your feet or groin.** While somewhat controversial, I believe Sul provides a reasonable option for safely controlling

the pistol both on the range and in the world when circumstances require the gun in hand and ready though no immediate threat has been identified. (Photo by Kathryn T. Conti)

4. The idea of facing a subject who has the "drop" on the involved officer should be addressed during in-service training. Options for dealing with such a situation should be suggested and discussed. Physical responses to such a scenario should be demonstrated to officers. Various techniques for dealing with an armed subject should be taught and practiced. These techniques should range from close-quarter weapon disarming techniques to creating distance and seeking cover while employing your own weapon. The option of advancing directly and aggressively toward the threat suspect while engaging him with fire should also be discussed, especially in regard to the potentially-unnerving psychological effect that such an action may induce in the suspect.

5. The use of a conditioned threat response can also be integrated into the training drills. A response such as "GUN!", which many departments and agencies currently employ, can be modified to "GUN! MOVE!" In this way, the officer's conditioned physical response can be initiated by his own ingrained verbalized threat response.

6. Finally, distinct courses of fire designed to condition officers to respond to an immediate deadly threat by moving to cover and accessing their own weapons can be employed. One such operant conditioning-based course I've designed and successfully administered is offered for consideration here. A second, "The Saber Challenge", is included in Appendix P.

COURSE OF FIRE: 12-36 ROUNDS (Originally designed for .40 Cal. SIG P226)

THE OFFICER AS A MOVING TARGET DRILL
(Sample Series No. 1 DUTY PISTOL TRAINING COURSE, Skill Development, Individual)

SET-UP: Officers will be standing on the firing line, facing *up-range*, weapons holstered. Cover will be available to their left or right. Threat-stimulus targets will be employed down-range.

INITIATION: Upon signal (i.e. "BEHIND YOU!", "LOOK OUT!", "HE'S GOT A GUN!", or similar non-traditional range firing command), officer will turn and face downrange.

RESPONSE: Upon identification and recognition of threat, officer will sound off with "GUN! MOVE!", while simultaneously moving laterally away from threat target to cover and accessing his own weapon.

OPTIONS: Officer may engage threat while moving to cover.

Officer may verbalize while moving to cover.

Officer may engage threat from behind cover.

Officer may verbalize from behind cover.

RECOVERY: Officer will perform a slow tactical recovery once threat has been engaged and controlled.

OFFICER AS MOVING TARGET / COVER DRILL (Immediate Threat Stimulus Target)

Distance	Position	# Hands	Total # Rounds	Number Rounds Fired per Hand	Suggested Time Limit
7 Yards	Standing / Mobile	1 or 2	2-6 rounds	Shooter's Choice	SLOW
7 Yards	Standing / Mobile	1 or 2	2-6 rounds	Shooter's Choice	SLOW
7 Yards	Standing / Mobile	1 or 2	2-6 rounds	Shooter's Choice	1/2 SPEED
7 Yards	Standing / Mobile	1 or 2	2-6 rounds	Shooter's Choice	1/2 SPEED
7 Yards	Standing / Mobile	1 or 2	2-6 rounds	Shooter's Choice	3/4 SPEED
7 Yards	Standing / Mobile	1 or 2	2-6 rounds	Shooter's Choice	FULL SPEED

(Note: Photographs illustrating this drill are shown on page 300.)

COURSE OF FIRE: 24 ROUNDS

SERPENTINE / MUZZLE CONTROL DRILL
(Sample Series No. 1 DUTY PISTOL TRAINING COURSE, Skill Development, Individual)

SET-UP: Three (3) No-Shoot (NS) Targets set up, IN LANE, at 3-yard intervals facing UPRANGE. Two (2) Threat Stimulus targets will be set up DOWNRANGE on left and right side of No-Shoot lane. Threat Targets facing UPRANGE. Student standing directly in front of first NS Target, pistol drawn and held at low ready position. Instructor stands directly behind student.

INITIATION: Instructor asks student if s/he understands what is expected. Upon affirmative response, instructor says, "Make ready, Up!" and taps student on shoulder.

RESPONSE: Student then moves around NS-target from either direction, keeping pistol depressed until clear of NS-target. As Threat Stimulus target comes into view, pistol is raised and two rounds are delivered *while student continues to move*. Student then weaves in between NS-targets while moving toward the Threat Stimulus targets, depressing muzzle so as not to cover NS- targets, raising pistol to engage Threat Stimulus targets with two rounds each. (Note: Instructor moves with student, staying directly behind him/her throughout drill. Instructor should not interfere unless an unsafe activity is observed.)

RECOVERY: After student emerges from behind the third NS-target and engages the Threat Stimulus target in front of him, the student will issue challenge proto-col such as, "Police! Get down! Arms out! Hands up! Don't move!" Instructor will then advise student that threat has been controlled and the student will perform a slow tactical recovery of pistol to holster.

NOTE: Though students are told and shown (instructor demo's drill first) that they are not to stop while firing, it is very common for them to initially either stop or hesitate noticeably before firing. This is normal and will occur less as new neural pathways are established. Students may also point their weapons at the NS-targets without consciously realizing it the first time through the drill. If either of these activities are observed, the student should be made aware of them immediately after completing the drill for the first time. If the student does either again while participating in the drill, the instructor should then make the student aware of it immediately, correcting the behavior as it happens. The student should participate in the course until the desired behaviors are achieved automatically without instructor assistance.

SCORING: To successfully complete this drill the student must maintain muzzle control and safe handling skills as well as achieve at least 5 hits (83%) on targets.

(Note: Photographs illustrating this drill are shown on page 300.)

SERPENTINE / MUZZLE CONTROL DRILL (Threat Stimulus Targets and No Shoot Targets)

Distance	Position	# Hands	Total # Rounds	Number Rounds Fired per Hand	Suggested Time Limit
10-2 Yards	Walking/Crouch	1 or 2	6 rnds.	6 Dom	SLOW
10-2 Yards	Walking/Crouch	1 or 2	6 rnds.	6 Dom	SLOW
10-2 Yards	Walking/Crouch	1 or 2	6 rnds.	6 Dom	½ - ¾ SPEED
10-2 Yards	Walking/Crouch	1 or 2	6 rnds.	6 Dom	¾ - FULL SPEED

DIAGRAM: SERPENTINE / MUZZLE CONTROL DRILL

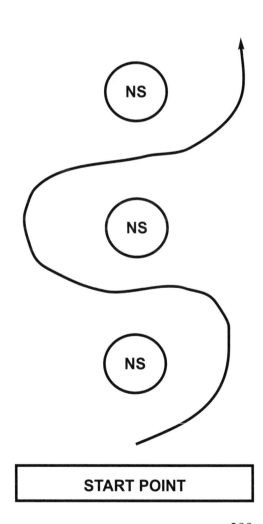

Note: Student is allowed to decide whether to begin course moving toward the left or right side of the first NS target.

Set up as illustrated, if 100% hits are achieved, one threat stimulus target will be shot twice while the other will be shot four times.

A pen/marker is used to clearly confirm hits after each student completes drill.

299

Officer As Moving Target Drill

Officer stands on firing line facing UP RANGE (above left). Upon Instructor's signal of "He's got a gun!" or similar non-traditional range command, officer turns and faces down range, drawing weapon in response to threat stimulus target (center photo). After identifying threat, officer moves to cover while completing presentation and responds appropriately to threat from behind cover (above right). In this case, target #17 provides the threat stimulus. The mannequin represents an uninvolved bystander who must also be dealt with via verbal commands. These photos were taken during an iteration of the *Undercover Operator Tactical Pistol Course*, hence the unconventional appearance and concealed weapon carry. (Photos courtesy Massachusetts State Police archives.)

Serpentine / Muzzle Control Drill

Officer stands in front of No Shoot target with pistol drawn and held at the Low Ready Position (above left). Upon command, officer weaves around and between no-shoot, non-threat stimulus representations, identifying and engaging threat stimulus targets down range (center photo). The muzzle must be depressed so as not to "laser" no-shoot representations. The officer must *keep moving* while engaging threat targets! (Above right) The hits are counted up and noted after each student completes the drill. (Photos courtesy Massachusetts State Police archives.)

APPENDIX P
Saber Challenge Course: A True Stress Inoculation Training Program[1]

The *Saber Challenge Course* being conducted on outdoor range. Instructor #1 (foreground) fires Simunition FX Marking Cartridges from Instructor Point #1 at participant as the participant moves from Point A to Point B. Instructor #2 is visible at Position C at left. Portable target system is set up down-range at left.

Note: This lesson plan, though somewhat unconventional, has been implemented with great success during specialized training iterations, as well as during basic recruit firearms training iterations. It has also been professionally evaluated by several seasoned firearms trainers, a behavioral psychologist, and an attorney. All have found it an efficient model that accomplishes several critical objectives as described in the text.

Introduction

In September 1999, while running a team of law enforcement special operations personnel through an old paradigm style "combat"[2] firearms training program, I observed many of them commit a common tactical error.

The program required the officers to traverse across the range, moving from cover to cover, while engaging various targets with their handguns. The targets included life-size, stationary paper targets that depicted subjects presenting a threat (or no threat) to address judgmental firearms skills training requirements, several pepper poppers, and a moving target.

The error many of the officers committed was found in their improper use of the provided cover.

---

[1] This material has previously appeared in the following publications: *Police Marksman*, *New Jersey Cops*, and the *American Society of Law Enforcement Trainers (ASLET) Journal.*

[2] This terminology will not be used in any New Paradigm programs UNLESS the program incorporates actual combat-type elements (i.e. Simunitions training).

Many of them would not fully employ the cover to their best advantage, leaving themselves exposed to the simulated downrange "adversaries." Some of the officers stopped completely in the open while moving from cover to cover in order to get into a traditional shooting stance and engage the targets.

While obviously neither taught nor desired, this response was understandable, given the fact that most of the officers had been conditioned to stand upright with their feet planted directly in front of the target for years while participating in commonly-encountered, departmental firearms "qualification-type" courses.

It was at this point that I decided it would be worthwhile to try and develop a program that would not only encourage the participants to utilize cover, but would actually condition them to use it to the best of their ability by employing the proven principles of operant conditioning.

As explained in the first section of this book, operant conditioning employs a simple model. First, the subject is presented with a **stimulus** (Discriminative cue). The subject then displays a **response** to the stimulus. If the subject displays *the desired response*, the subject then receives a **reward**.

The first step I took while developing the program was to examine the operant conditioning method that has been used so successfully to condition military personnel to fire at identified enemy targets. This method, which uses pop-up targets, works like this: The soldier is in a fighting position, wearing duty gear and equipped with a personal weapon. The man-shaped pop-up target (**stimulus**) is displayed down range. The soldier fires at the target (**response**). If the soldier hits the target, it falls (immediate **reward**). The immediate reward is later reinforced when the soldier is recognized for his skill with the personal weapon, given marksmanship badges, and held in high regard by his peers.

The second step I took was to turn the

successful model outlined above around in order to achieve the desired result. This was accomplished in the following manner:

The officer, wearing duty gear, is presented with a defined area he must negotiate by traversing on foot.

Various types of cover are provided for the officer to employ as he makes his way across the area.

As the officer makes his way across the area, Simunition FX Marking Rounds are fired at him (**stimulus** [3]).

The officer must think, move, and utilize the provided cover to the best of his ability (**response**) to prevent himself from being hit.

If the officer is successful, he will limit the number of times he is hit, or will not be hit at all (immediate **reward**). The immediate reward is then reinforced when the instructor and his peers recognize the officer as being successful. It can be further reinforced after all participating officers have completed the course, the scores are tallied, and the officers are again praised for what they did right while completing the program.

The third step involved fine tuning the program to make it a more efficient training exercise. This was accomplished by incorporating additional stressors into the program, as well as some specific controls.

The additional stressors included timing each participant as he negotiated the course, as well as requiring the participants to follow simple commands and then deal with a moving target set up to present subjects displaying different threat levels.

The controls included limiting the number of rounds that could be fired at each participant, ensuring that the moving target was set to operate at the same speed for all students, and not allowing participants to observe the other participants negotiate the course until they themselves had gone through it.

---

[3] May also be referred to as the discriminative cue, or conditional stimulus.

Several safety mechanisms were also incorporated into the course. All of these mechanisms are fully described in the lesson plan that follows.

The course, including the moving target, is easy to set up and explain. The principles behind the development of the course should be explained to the students prior to their participating. Students can complete the course (on average), within 3 minutes, which makes the course intense, but time-efficient.

In addition to being conditioned to use cover to a degree that traditional firearms training cannot achieve, each student also accomplished the following:
1) demonstrated a safe administrative unloading procedure
2) experienced a true high-arousal state (the type of which can not be induced simply by having the student physically exert himself by performing pushups or jumping jacks) while negotiating the course
3) been conditioned NOT to freeze or fall down "dead" should they be hit by incoming rounds
4) performed a safe emergency loading drill while in a true high-arousal state
5) had the proper use of cover immediately reinforced while employing their own firearm to deal with a briefly appearing target
6) demonstrated judgmental firearms skills while in a true high-arousal state
7) engaged a moving target (if necessary)

The program has been successfully administered numerous times with great success. No serious injuries have been accrued. Both the students and the instructors learn a great deal from it. Several layers of departmental liability insulation can be attributed to the program content.

With the exception of the initial cost of the moving target system and Simunition equipment, minimum resources are required to administer the program.

Students consistently report that in addi-

tion to getting a lot of value out of it, the program is also challenging and enjoyable to participate in.

This program has also been videotaped and reviewed by students after participating in it. In this way, mistakes can be clearly seen by the participants and learned from. Successes can be analyzed and emulated.

Bottom line–after completing the program, both instructors and students have stated that they believed this course would absolutely help ensure what must be the one true objective of any law enforcement firearms training program–to save lives.

The lesson plan, set-up diagram, and sample score sheet are offered here for consideration and use.

Top photo: View from down-range. Instructor #1 seen in background at Instructor Point #1. Pads are used down-range when course is conducted on hard surfaces. Bottom: Instructor #2 oversees as Student engages moving target at Position C. Bucket used to contain unloaded pistol visible in front of student. (MSP archives.)

COURSE OF FIRE: 0-15 ROUNDS

THE SABER CHALLENGE STRESS INOCULATION TRAINING PROGRAM
(Sample Series No. 4 DUTY PISTOL TRAINING COURSE, Scenario-based, Dynamic Interactive Experiential Learning)

<u>Description:</u>   A dynamic, operant conditioning/stress inoculation training program designed to reinforce proper tactical movement and cover utilization responses by exposing the student to an appropriately realistic stimulus.

The dynamic conditions incorporated into the exercise, combined with inducement of a true high arousal state, will also allow assessment of the student's ability to maintain self-control and employ proper judgmental and tactical firearms skills while engaging a moving target.

<u>Equipment:</u>   *Instructors:* Simunition FX Marking Cartridge-equipped firearm, stop watch, cardboard box, moving target system, cover/barricade items.
Student: Duty carry gear, pistol and ammunition, firearm, Simunition protective equipment.

<u>NOTE!!!</u> This program involves the controlled use of <u>BOTH</u> a SIMUNITION FX Marking Cartridge equipped firearm and a standard, working firearm loaded with penetrating-ammunition. <u>SAFETY IS THE FIRST PRIORITY.</u> Instructors must be knowledgeable and competent. Student must be briefed regarding exercise requirements prior to participation in program. If all safety procedures as outlined in this lesson plan are followed, the risk of firearms injury to any person/s should be extremely limited.

<u>Preparation:</u>   Range is confirmed to be safe and clear. Various barricades/cover items are placed traversing across the range from Point A to Point B. A position of cover will also be in place at Point C directly in front of the moving target system.

Instructor #1 is posted at **Instructor Point #1.** Instructor #1 is equipped **ONLY** with a Simunition-ready weapon and FX Marking Cartridge ammunition. **No other weapons or ammunition are allowed at Instructor Point #1!**

Instructor #2 is the **control/safety officer** and will not participate in the exercise in any other capacity. **Instructor # 2 will be UNARMED.**

Student is equipped with duty handgun and ammunition, protective head gear, eyegear, and throatgear (Simunition Protective Mask is recommended for use.) Additional equipment (**NO ADDITIONAL WEAPONS**) may be added to increase level of difficulty/realism. (i.e. Gas masks, tactical vest, etc.)

THE SABER CHALLENGE STRESS INOCULATION TRAINING PROGRAM, CONTINUED

PHASE 1:   **Instructor #2** instructs Student to conduct a safe administrative unloading drill while facing downrange at **Point A**. After Student completes unloading drill, Instructor #2 checks weapon to ensure it is safe and clear. Instructor then takes control of Student's weapon, magazine, and/or any loose rounds. Student is then asked if he/she has any other weapons on his/her person. **NO OTHER WEAPONS CAN BE CARRIED BY STUDENT DURING THIS DRILL.** (A pat-frisk of the student's outer garments should be conducted at this time.) Instructor #2 then asks if Student is ready / has any questions. Instructor #2 then proceeds to **Point C** with Student's safe and clear weapon and ammunition. **Student stands ready at Point A.**

PHASE 2:   Once **Instructor #2** is clear from fields of fire, Instructor #2 places the Student's weapon, magazine, and/or any loose rounds into a cardboard box, bucket, or other suitable container. The container is then placed behind the cover located at **Point C**. **Instructor #2 then checks to ensure Instructor #1 is ready.** Instructor #2 then begins the drill by signaling to the Student and activating the timer/stopwatch. The Student then traverses across the range moving from **Point A to Point B** using proper movement and cover utilization techniques.

STUDENT'S FOCUS MUST BE UPRANGE AND DIRECTED AT INSTRUCTOR #1 WHO WILL BE STATIONARY AT INSTRUCTOR POINT #1 on opposite side of cover.

While Student traverses the designated area, **Instructor #1** will fire Simunition FX Marking Cartridge rounds downrange at the Student. **No more than 5 Simunition FX Marking Cartridge rounds will be fired at each individual student. No rounds will be fired after Student reaches Point B.** If Student is hit by Simunition FX Marking Cartridge round, Student will continue to traverse range and finish the exercise.

PHASE 3:   Upon completing the traverse and reaching **Point B**, Student will be met by **Instructor #2**. Instructor #2 will ensure Student is not injured and is able to safely continue with the exercise. Once Instructor #2 is satisfied that student is capable of safely continuing the exercise, Instructor #2 will instruct the student to don protective eye and hearing equipment if not already worn. Student will then be directed to take up a stationary position of cover at **Point C,** *FACING DOWN RANGE* toward the moving target system. On the ground in front of the Student will be the container that holds the Student's unloaded weapon (slide locked to the rear / cylinder opened), magazine, and/or any loose rounds.

Instructor #2 will then instruct the Student to make his weapon ready by:
a) Revolvers: inserting rounds into the cylinder's chambers
b) Semiautomatics: inserting the magazine and allowing the slide to go forward while keeping the MUZZLE POINTED DOWNRANGE. Any additional loose rounds are to be left in the box.

As soon as the Student's weapon is ready and the **Student is in a position of cover FACING DOWNRANGE, Instructor #2** will activate the moving target,

THE SABER CHALLENGE STRESS INOCULATION TRAINING PROGRAM, CONTINUED

allowing it to traverse across the student's field of view *ONE TIME ONLY* at a predetermined rate of movement. The moving target will display a reality-type target that depicts either an immediate lethal threat, a less-than-lethal threat, or no threat. **The student will deal with the target using the most appropriate indicated response.**

After the moving target has completed its traverse, the exercise is completed and Instructor #2 stops the timer.

Completion: **HOT RANGE:** The Student will then a) reload and holster the revolver, or b) holster his loaded semiautomatic pistol and top off the magazine.
COLD RANGE: The Student will perform a safe unloading drill at the direction of Instructor #2 at Point C. The Student and Instructor #2 will then check the moving target for hits (if shots have been fired) and review the Student's performance.

The Student will be evaluated on the following:
1) Proper use of movement
2) Proper utilization of available cover
3) Judgmental firearms skills
4) Accuracy in engaging moving target (if appropriate)

Evaluation Form SG-78 may be used to evaluate and record student's performance.

Additional Notes: *Regarding Up-Range Stress...* While the administration of this program may appear to be utilizing "up-range stress", it actually does not. For even though the stressor is being administered by the instructor from up-range, the student is facing the instructor and dealing with the stressor while moving from point to point. Only when the student successfully completes dealing with the stressor being generated from up-range does he turn his attention back down-range, where he must then deal directly with a second stressor.

Regarding a scenario or "back story" for this course... I have used the following to set the stage for this drill, especially when dealing with individuals who believe the course is, at base, unrealistically staged. The scenario is that the student and his partner have been involved in a foot pursuit of a dangerous suspect in a desolate environment. The suspect has taken up a position of concealment and has begun shooting at both officers from this location. The partner, located at POINT C, has been wounded, is bleeding profusely, and requires immediate aid. The student, located at POINT A, discovers that his weapon has fallen from his holster and is lost. In order to save his partner's life he must traverse across the area, using cover as he goes, reach his partner, and employ his partner's disabled weapon to stop the attacker's assault.

Regarding Firing Extra Shots at that "Extra Special" Student... "Lighting up" any particular student during the course for any reason is unprofessional, and will often adversely affect the benefits derived from the program. The rules must be respected by *all* involved.

Regarding the "Running Man Student"... Finally, when administering this course there is usually at least one participant who decides to simply run from POINT A to POINT B. The soundness of this decision is greatly influenced by the pistolcraft skills of the Simunition-equipped instructor.

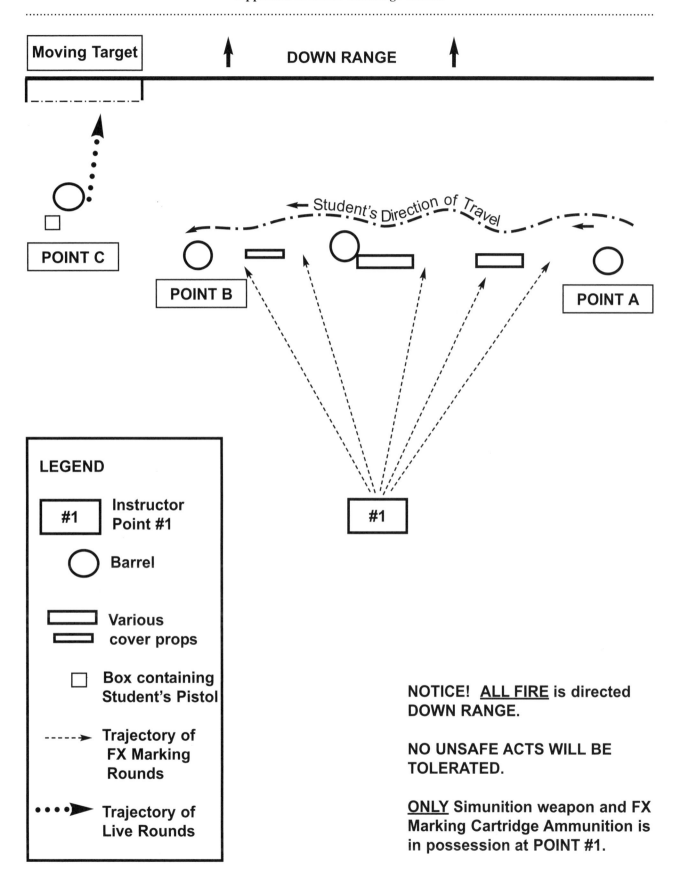

Moving Target

DOWN RANGE

POINT C

Student's Direction of Travel

POINT B

POINT A

#1

LEGEND

#1   Instructor Point #1

Barrel

Various cover props

Box containing Student's Pistol

Trajectory of FX Marking Rounds

Trajectory of Live Rounds

NOTICE! ALL FIRE is directed DOWN RANGE.

NO UNSAFE ACTS WILL BE TOLERATED.

ONLY Simunition weapon and FX Marking Cartridge Ammunition is in possession at POINT #1.

SAMPLE

THE SABER CHALLENGE TRAINING & EVALUATION RECORD

DATE: _____ / _____ / _____   LOCATION: _____

WEAPON TYPE: _____   WEAPON MODEL: _____

INSTRUCTOR/S: _____   PROGRAM ID: _____

WEATHER / COMMENT: _____

NAME / ID#:	MOVEMENT (Rate 1-3)	USE OF COVER (Rate 1-3)	JUDGEMENT (Rate 1-3)	MOVING TARGET (Rate 1-3)	TIME	INSTRUCTOR NOTES, COMMENTS, OR OBSERVATIONS
1._____						
2._____						
3._____						
4._____						
5._____						
6._____						
7._____						
8._____						
9._____						
10._____						

Instructor / evaluator notes: _____

_____

_____

_____

Individual Category Rating Scale: 1 - Needs improvement   2 - Good   3 - Excellent

Suggested format of FORM SG-78.

APPENDIX Q
The House of Horrors–*Back to the Future!*

This sort of thing is not mere play-acting. It is done with the sole purpose of making practice as realistic as possible and of stimulating interest. If the men are kept indefinitely at the same dull routine they will lose interest, and results suffer accordingly. We should add now that the expenses of these productions are negligible if there are available a little imagination, a lot of willing help, some wood battens, old clothes and hessian or old sacking.

> – Captain W.E. Fairbairn and Captain E.A. Sykes
> *Shooting to Live With the One-Hand Gun*
> 1942

This section has been included to provide a glimpse into the modern-day House of Horrors and some of the equipment we have adapted for its use.

All of the information in this section is provided for informational purposes only. No endorsements of particular components, targets or operating mechanisms are intended or inferred. All of the House of Horrors manually-controlled stimulus-response targets shown in this section have been custom-designed and built by me or other FTU instructors based upon specific training objectives and component availability.

As a review of this section will will reveal, only rudimentary construction skills are required to produce the effective, durable training systems needed to run the House of Horrors program. Instructors desiring to create their own version of this program are only limited by their imaginations in regard to the construction of suitable scenario stations.

It is important to remember when constructing the various stations that although the higher the fidelity (realism) of the stimulus to actual persons and environments the better, all that is generally required to evoke a true high arousal response in participants is a realistic "suggestion" of what it is you are attempting to portray. In other words, if the students are psychologically prepped properly during the pre-briefing, you do not need to worry about the hanging wires or plastic faces, for the student's midbrain will perceive the mannequin's movements and features as being 100% genuine during the action.

During the first iteration of the program, only the mannequins illustrated on these pages were employed. I chose to preclude the use of live instructor role-players for the first iteration for the following reasons:

1) We had a limited number of instructors available to conduct the various training segments, so I wanted to create a course that could be run both safely and efficiently by only one instructor.

2) By using only realistic-looking mannequins, I believed that the fidelity levels would actually be higher in some respects since live role-players would need to be outfitted with protective head gear that altered / hid their human facial features significantly.

3) On top of these two primary reasons were my experiences both conducting and participating in scenario-type training programs in the past, during which I came to realize that instructors, being only human, often become bored repeating the same actions in scenario after scenario. As a result, they occasionally deviate from the script. Considering that each station within the course would be repeated literally thousands of times during the year, I could just imagine the toll it would take on the

instructors as well as the consistency of the scenarios.

This last element, consistency, was of particular concern to me, for one of the objectives I wanted to achieve was to develop a database regarding people's normative behaviors/ reactions to the various threat stimuli, and in order to do this I needed to limit the number of variables presented to the individual participants as much as possible.

After tallying up the pros and cons, I decided to go with the all-mannequin cast, much as Fairbairn and Sykes employed in Shanghai when conducting what they called "The Mystery Shoot."

This does not mean that the idea of incorporating live role-players in the House of Horrors is in any way untenable. Applegate interspersed live role-players with the mannequins during 1940's House of Horrors iterations, and we have also done the same,

using a combination of mannequins and live role-players with a great deal of success during both recruit and in-service iterations.

What it does mean is that the creation of these types of mannequin-stimulus targets can provide you with the ability to run consistent, high-yield, reality-based training courses for a minimum investment of time, money, and resources, regardless of whether you have one instructor or twenty available at any given time.

The Preparation

In addition to the pre-briefing as described in Chapter Six, we conspicuously posted notices around the "on-deck" areas and instructed the participants to read them as they waited their turn. Taking my cue from Colonel Applegate, I formatted these notices as shown below.

NOTICE!

NO LIVE FIREARMS, AMMUNITION, KNIVES, OR OC SPRAY ALLOWED IN THIS TRAINING AREA! ALL MUST BE SECURED IN LOCKERS AT LEFT. BATONS MAY BE CARRIED. SEE INSTRUCTOR FOR GUIDANCE.

DO NOT ENTER UNTIL INSTRUCTED TO!

HOUSE OF HORRORS RULES

1. Protective eye equipment must be worn at all times. Hearing protection is not required.
2. Once inside, you will be equipped with a pistol, 24 rounds of ammunition, and an inert OC Spray container. Upon these items your life depends as you travel down our dangerous alley and into the darkness. A police officer is believed to be down somewhere within this area. His last radio transmission was a garbled cry for help. This area is known to harbor violent and desperate types. There may also be other police officers in the area, as well as uninvolved citizens.
3. Any and all threats, situations, and encounters will occur directly to your front, to your left, or to your right. **YOU WILL NEVER FIRE TO YOUR REAR!** A coach will follow immediately behind you to act as your guide and confessor.
4. There are NO booby traps, collapsible stairs, or blood baths to slip on in the darkness. If you come out alive, *please tell no one else the details of what you have been through*.

The Village People

The basic model. These were used to provide simple upper torso props that could be used as threat or no-threat stimuli. The plastic shell bodies are extremely resilient and last for years.

When used for DPTC No. 1, they can be shot repeatedly without losing their effectiveness as long as head shots are not taken. When the center of the chest/torso area is shot to pieces, simply cut out the debris and replace the shirt and its ready for another thousand rounds.

Cutting the wood pieces as shown minimizes the need to replace or repair the stands. This simple design, produced by Tpr. Dana Pullman, provides a great deal of stability.

Village people prior to painting (top) and after. The funky paint jobs were the inspiration for the nickname when someone commented, "Looks like the Village of the Damned!" upon first seeing them grouped together.
Sketch of target stand design shown in inset. (2x4s and 1x2s.)

Threat or No-Threat Subject in Motor Vehicle

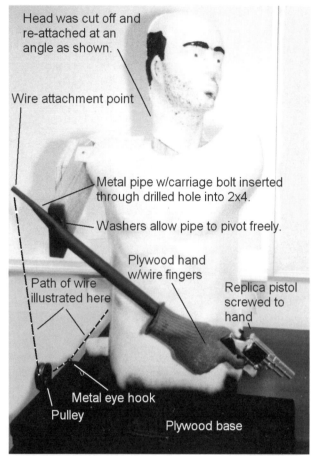

Head was cut off and re-attached at an angle as shown.

Wire attachment point

Metal pipe w/carriage bolt inserted through drilled hole into 2x4.

Washers allow pipe to pivot freely.

Plywood hand w/wire fingers

Replica pistol screwed to hand

Path of wire illustrated here

Metal eye hook
Pulley

Plywood base

Simple design shown here. Can be equipped with a gun, knife, cellphone, wallet, license or badge depending upon desired stimulus. Once placed in car, I ran the wire through the backseat and trunk, drilled a hole in rear of trunk lid and attached a 6" piece of 1" PVC pipe for a pull handle.

Threat or No-Threat Hiding Man

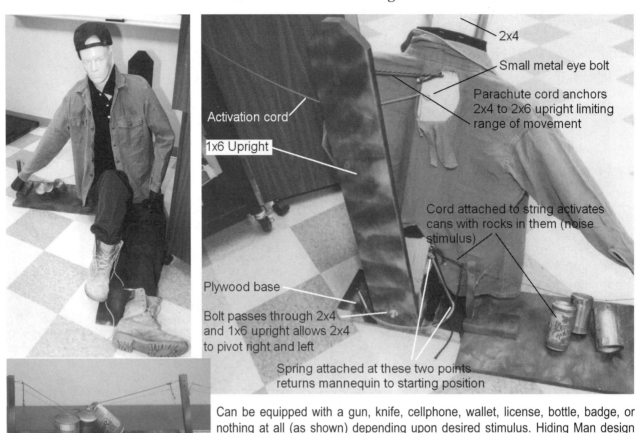

2x4

Small metal eye bolt

Parachute cord anchors 2x4 to 2x6 upright limiting range of movement

Activation cord

1x6 Upright

Cord attached to string activates cans with rocks in them (noise stimulus)

Plywood base

Bolt passes through 2x4 and 1x6 upright allows 2x4 to pivot right and left

Spring attached at these two points returns mannequin to starting position

Weight of cans provides resistance

Nail serves as pivot point

Can be equipped with a gun, knife, cellphone, wallet, license, bottle, badge, or nothing at all (as shown) depending upon desired stimulus. Hiding Man design shown (above right). Keep it robust and simple for years of use. Detail of noise stimulus set up shown at left.

Combined Threat and No-Threat Subjects

Classic hostage scenario construct. These are static displays. Advanced version incorporates Hiding Man pivot-type design to allow display to move for more realism.

Threat or No-Threat Subject Appears in Window

Piece of wood attached to curtain; wire attached to wood & run to activation point.

Spring attachment points (attached on the inside)

Can be configured to present any type of stimulus. Excellent for providing no-threat startle stimulus. A curtain made of strong material is hung over opening. The curtain is attached to a short wood block. A long durable spring is attached to the wooden block and the window frame as shown. A wire is attached to the block and out the side of the box. When the wire is pulled the curtain snaps open, wood hits wall and makes noise. When wire is released spring pulls curtain closed. Simple, durable, and effective.

Entering Doorway into Low-Light Environment

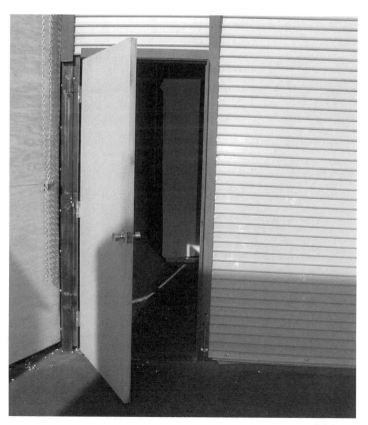

Both doorways and low-light environments are a must for reality-based training. The first version of our House of Horrors utilized the interior portion of a rifle range for the low light training segments. The entrance to this range was originally open to the elements. We closed it in by building a wooden framework at the entrance and covered it with an opaque blue plastic tarp. A pre-hung wooden exterior door was framed into the structure. Though crude, it was effective.

Thanks to support from members within the department, we eventually were able to upgrade the entrance to what is shown here.

Threat or No-Threat Stairway

The stairway is another must-have. Gives students the impression they are entering different rooms and floors, increases stress levels. This stairway can be moved to different areas or turned to reorient the direction of travel in the training area. It's critical to have guardrails in place wherever there is a possibility of someone falling off, down or over the stairway. The stairway is shown from both directions in the two photos above. Keeping control of the student by physically holding onto their belt or vest is always a good idea, but is especially important while negotiating the stairway. This stairway is another Dana Pullman creation.

The Shooting Man

Pin wire

Pipe wire

Blank pistol

Wire attached to weighted pipe is pulled up, lifting weighted pipe. Wire has ring attached at other end. This ring is then suspended by a pin that is stuck into a hole drilled in the rear wall. Pin is attached to wire. When pin wire is pulled, weighted pipe is released.

(Left) The Shooting Man was created in my basement out of miscellaneous parts. Can be equipped with a Simunition FX Marking cartridge-firing pistol, blank-firing pistol, or toy gun/replica firearm.

The Shooting Man, Continued

Simple design. I bought two metal pipes, one slightly larger than the other so it would slide freely over the smaller. I secured the smaller diameter pipe to a block of wood on base as shown at far right. Attached a 2.5 lbs. weight to larger pipe. Attached a wire to top of larger pipe. Secured a ring to end of this wire. The pipe wire is then pulled up lifting weighted pipe. A pin is then stuck through the ring and into a hole in the wall behind Shooting Man. Another wire is attached to the pin. When the pin wire is pulled, the pipe wire is released. Attached to the pipe is a string. When the pipe falls, the string is pulled firing the pistol. The string runs vertically up to a pulley (visible in the photo at far right in front of pipe where the 2x4 sections are joined), is redirected 90 degrees so it runs horizontally through a

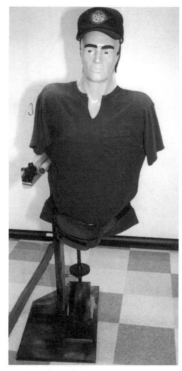

Wood frame
Pipe wire w/ring
1" PVC pipe
Pulley
String
2.5 lbs weight
Sponge cushions impact

piece of PVC pipe and to the trigger of the pistol. The original Shooting Man (shown here) has been fired thousands and thousands of times. Only the string and the metal cap gun needed to be replaced occasionally as they wore out. The cap gun was the primary armament, even though the students were initially advised that threat mannequins would be armed with Simunition-equipped weapons. This was done to better induce a true high arousal state, while also ensuring the highest levels of safety for the participants. It was effective on both counts. (Note: Designs shown on these pages intended only to spark your imagination. Innovation is the key.)

Notes on the Shooting Man

I suppose you could attach a badge to his belt or from a chain around his neck, but I prefer to keep the threats and no threats plain and simple for the purposes of the training objectives–no tricks or playing cute so as to stack the odds against the students.

If a badge was added to the target as shown here, the obvious question from participants would be, "Well why did he keep pointing his gun at me even after I identified myself unless he was a bad guy trying to confuse me with the badge?"

As always, you should try to keep the scenarios and mechanisms simple, straightforward, and reliable.

The Mirror (Reflected Image)

(Right) It's the simple things that get you the easiest!

Common door mirror mounted on a piece of plywood and fitted with 2x4 crosspieces so it is freestanding.

I left myself in the image when I took the photogragh so you can get an idea of the effect when approaching it. When the lights are out it can be very disconcerting to be facing yourself with a gun...

Hallway of Doom

(Top left) Dana Pullman design. This simple but sturdy structure has been improved by the addition of a section of flooring that rocks slightly back and forth when stepped upon. This was another page taken directly from the original House of Horrors. Standard door is installed at opposite end. Structure shown prior to painting outside walls and doors black. (Top right) Open entrance was improved by hanging ribbons from above and flexible foam pieces on sides. This ensures bodily contact with student as he passes into the hallway, increasing sensory input and raising stress and anxiety levels.

Threat or No-Threat Turning Man

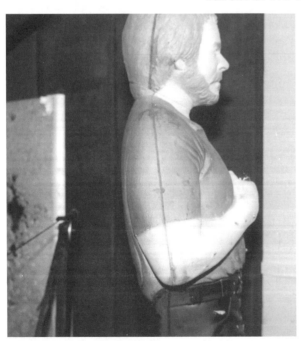
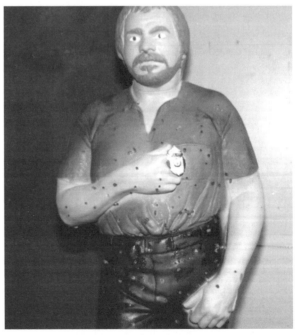

Also built in my basement after a quick trip to the local hardware store for a Lazy-Susan base ring, some pulleys and twine. Different 3-D mannequins can be installed and equipped with a gun, knife, cell phone, wallet, license or badge, depending upon desired stimulus. Unlike the Shooting Man, this target can be used effectively to present a police officer turning toward the student while holding both gun and badge, because the instructor could control and stop the movement in response to a student's verbalization. This mannequin had only a real badge. Note hits on body in photo above.

Threat or No-Threat Turning Man, Continued

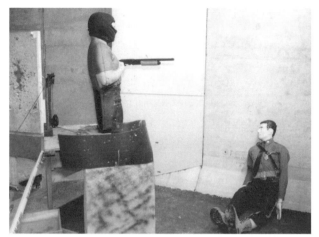

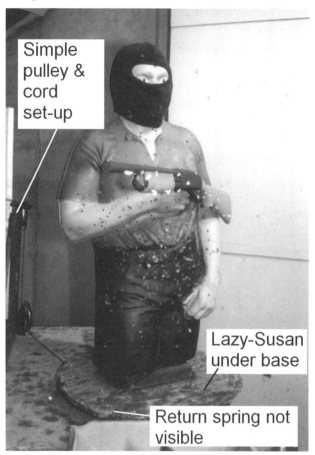

Simple pulley & cord set-up

Lazy-Susan under base

Return spring not visible

(Above and right) Turning Man presented as Threat target. Simple pulley and cord system was used to activate the target. We ran the cord to the side of the Hallway of Doom. A hole was cut in the wall. When the student opened the door from the Hallway, the instructor (behind the student) reached through the hole and pulled the cord while illuminating the target. The cord turned the Lazy-Susan mounted target. The Lazy-Susan had a spring installed to keep the target facing away. When the cord was released, the target returned to original position. This 3-D target lasted more than 3 years and sustained thousands of hits. Repairing the holes with clay is an option that works only so long, then targets must be replaced.

Combination Threat and No-Threat Moving Subject
(Originally designed as the "Knifing Man" station. See Chapter Six.)

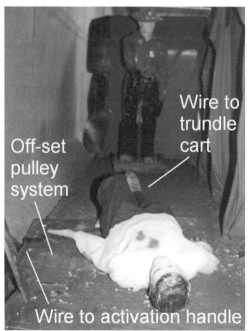

Wire to trundle cart

Off-set pulley system

Wire to activation handle

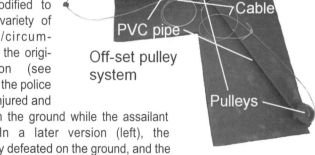

Cable

PVC pipe

Off-set pulley system

Pulleys

Another station that can be modified to present a variety of scenarios/circumstances. In the original version (see Chapter 6), the police officer lay injured and bleeding on the ground while the assailant attacked. In a later version (left), the assailant lay defeated on the ground, and the uniformed officer moved toward the student when the curtain was opened. This station in particular is a heart pounder.

(Above right) A detail of the off-set pulley system is shown above right. The off-set was necessary because the student stood directly in the doorway facing the threat. Activation wire was attached to wall to left and behind student so instructor could pull the trundle cart/mannequin toward the student. A 2x4 anchored into the floor in front of "downed" mannequin stopped the cart. If desired, the instructor could pull the wire hard enough so the moving mannequin fell forward to the deck when it struck the 2x4.

This Old House – of Horrors!

As noted in the Shooting Man section, the designs shown on these pages are not presented as the last word on House of Horrors station construction. Rather, they are presented to show what we have done using easily acquired components and applying a bit of Yankee ingenuity.

From the original models I created in my basement to the new modified designs members of the FTU have created in the years since, the only guiding rules have been to 1) have a clear and articulable goal in mind, 2) make the stations relevant, 3) keep the designs simple, 4) ensure the construction materials are robust, weather resistant, and require little maintenance and 5) make the figures as realistic looking and acting as possible.

A few examples of other stations are included here.

You should let the mission-specific realities facing your own people be your inspiration.

Dumpster Man. Carmichael design. When wire is pulled, counter-weight is released propelling Dumpster Man up and out of dumpster. Dumpster Man's hands are empty and plainly visible in this presentation. A weapon could easily be added to present a different stimulus. Extremely effective, especially when used in combination with the animated Hiding Man shown sitting next to dumpster. Hiding Man moves, student determines he does not present an immediate threat, begins to relax and then out pops the Dumpster Man... startle response like you read about!

Updated Threat or No-Threat Subject in Motor Vehicle. Paluk design. Here a passenger has been added to the scenario. Driver has been modified with a different torso. Torso fidelity has been improved with wig, facial hair and cigarette. In this scenario, driver and passenger are presented as undercover police officers. When wire is pulled, operator presents badge. Passenger officer is stationary but could be easily animated for additional stimulus presentation.

318

This Old House – of Horrors!, Continued

The Upton Police Department Experiment

Officer Michael Lupachini of the Upton, Massachusetts Police Department, designed and conducted his own House of Horrors training course after attending the New Paradigm Instructor Course.

Lupachini, an active member of the Massachusetts Law Enforcement Firearms Instructor and Armorers Association, is also his department's firearms instructor

Shown above and below right with four "range puppets" of his own design. Lupachini put his creativity to work, and the members of his 12-person department through an outstanding, court-defensible training program.

Michael described the station shown above:

"This No-Threat scenario is referred to as 'Moe and Larry'. The officer enters the room and observes a subject standing next to a barrel. The subject, 'Moe' is holding out his arm and his hand is pointing at the officer. While the officer's attention is drawn to Moe, his pal 'Larry' emerges from the barrel. Neither Moe or Larry are armed, and do not pose a threat. This is a no shoot scenario for the officer."

For this station, Lupachini attached a cord to Larry. The cord was then run through an overhead pulley. On the other end of the cord a weight was tied. The weight is held in place on the barrel by a nail. The instructor pulls a cord attached to the nail which causes the weight to fall and Larry pops up from inside the barrel.

The station shown below right is described as "Mack the Knife." Lupachini explains:

"In this scenario the officer enters the room and observes a subject sitting on the floor. While his attention is drawn to that subject, the instructor releases 'Mack' who is hidden behind a black plastic curtain. Mack is on a wheeled platform which is under tension of two door springs. The instructor pulls a cord attached to a steel pin. When the pin is removed, Mack springs forward quickly, holding a large knife. The officer is expected to deal with the lethal threat in an appropriate manner."

Like so many law enforcement trainers, Lupachini took the initiative and went the extra mile for his fellow officers. He designed and built these stations and four others on his own time and at his own expense. He even conducted the training in a barn on his own property.

In a letter Michael wrote:

"Using tarps, plastic sheeting, fishing line, 1"x3" lumber, some plywood, pulleys, weights, caster wheels and plastic torso targets, I was able to construct a six station, *safe*, interactive, dynamic, force on force training and stress inoculation simulator, also known as the House of

Horrors. When officers arrived for the training, they were convinced someone was in the barn who was ready and waiting to get them. Using another concept borrowed from Conti, I purposely shot my ballistic vest with a paint-filled Simunition round. I wore the vest over my shirt for all to see. When asked, I told the officers that I had gone through the House of Horrors. The officer's stress levels were very high at that point, and they had not even gone in yet! Each officer had 3 shoot and 3 no-shoot scenarios to deal with. Most officers responded correctly to the scenarios presented to them. The most common mistake was for an officer to fire upon the movement of an unexpected no-shoot target. I also noticed that officers experienced an increased breathing rate, auditory exclusion, memory loss for parts of each scenario, memory loss for some of their actions, and time distortion. During the debriefing stage for each officer, most had trouble remembering what they had done, seen or heard in the scenarios that took place only minutes before! The actions and the responses from the officers were exactly as Conti had told me they would be."

Lupachini's work is to be commended. He is a good man and a conscientious police officer and trainer. His work also validates the concept that standardized, viable police firearms training programs can be conducted by a 2,000+ member department or a 12 member department and generate similarly beneficial results.

Naturally, the most important result as far as we are concerned is the production of safer, more competent and *confident* police officers.

Racial Profiling in the House of Horrors?

While some people have inquired about the racial and gender attributes of the "village people" and the original House of Horrors mannequins as shown in these photos, posing questions such as "Why are there no black people, or women, or black women, or Asians, or Hispanics for that matter?", most others don't even ask, probably assuming that it's motivated by a desire to be politically correct.

In actuality, the assailants were portrayed as they were primarily so they would fit the description of the subject most likely to present a threat such as depicted in the individual scenarios.

For example, according to the FBI's Uniform Crime Reports, the average assailant who, while acting alone, initiates a violent act against a police officer will most likely be a white male, average age 29 years old.

That is the main reason the mannequins were presented as they were. In addition, the particular torso mannequins we had been using come stock from the factory in the putty Caucasian color. It's both easier and faster to add simple facial features than change the color of the entire torso and then add features.

As for the the village people mannequins used en masse during DPTC No. 1, the final contributing factor for choosing to leave them as they were is simply because I wanted the training environment to be completely professional and uninterrupted by any type of controversy that could be generated should someone make a thoughtless comment in regard to a minority-visaged village person.

Might it happen? Of course. We are all human and sometimes say things in an attempt at humor that don't come out the way we intended. This is especially possible should people be feeling any type of tension, such as when having their proficiency levels tested during training.

It just wasn't worth it, in my estimation.

For those who might not agree, all I can say is that in the end, the range puppet's racial or gender features don't really matter anyway, because all the officers see when facing any of the mannequins in the House of Horrors is simply a person who is either presenting a threat *or not* presenting a threat.

And that is *precisely* what we expect them to see when operating in the world.

APPENDIX R
Simunition® & Airsoft Training Equipment

Simunition® FX® Marking Cartridge ammunition is produced for use in a variety of weapon systems, from revolvers and semiautomatic pistols to shotguns and submachine guns. Conversion kits consisting of replacement barrels, slides, or safety ring inserts allow issued duty pistols to be used with the special training ammunition with no other obvious alterations to the weapon's profile or operation. Installation of the conversion kits is generally accomplished in minutes, and most weapons can likewise be reconfigured for duty use just as quickly.

The ammunition itself is loaded in the duty magazine (or a magazine supplied with the kit), and the cartridges will cycle the actions of conversion kit-equipped semiautomatic pistols and select-fire submachine guns. A 12-gauge shotgun conversion kit containing five unique shotgun shell bodies is also available, allowing the gunner to fire .38 caliber Simunition rounds during interactive dynamic training scenarios.

What this means is that once safely set up, the system allows the officer to train with his actual duty weapons and equipment. It allows him to engage in any number of scenarios that are scripted expressly for him, including the type of work he will be doing, the conditions under which he will be operating, and in an environment similar to the one he faces daily.

When combined with a well-formatted training program, it will also allow him to experience a variety of interactive situations during which he may or may not be required to use force, up to and including an application of deadly force. And he will also experience some of the effects of true stress, for the impact or "pain-penalty" producing ammunition is designed to allow one participant to fire directly at another (at all but very close ranges) when appropriate.

When this occurs, a plastic projectile containing a non-toxic fluorescent red, blue, yellow, green, orange, or white detergent-based, water-soluble compound is catapulted out of the barrel toward the target, in most cases with a muzzle velocity around 400 fps. The telling paint mark (and occasional welt) provides instant verification of who and what was or wasn't hit. A small pistol primer is the only driving force behind the projectile–no propellant is used. Muzzle energy out of a 4 or 5 inch barrel ranges from about 3.8 - 2.7 foot pounds, respectively, making face, eye, throat, and groin protection mandatory. Tactical accuracy can be expected up to 25 feet (7.6 meters).

The fact that officers use the actual weapon they carry on the street not only makes training easier to conduct (guns fit in issued holsters, same operating system, etc.) but provides enormous training value, especially when compared to the paintball gun option many departments have explored.

The conversion kit systems tend to work extremely well, especially after a short break-in period. There is a tendency, however, for the plastic ampules to produce shavings in the bore, especially when the weapons have been fired enough to produce visible fouling in the chamber. This will eventually result in misfires and catastrophic stoppages if a bore brush is not worked through periodically. For this reason we always carry an extra Simunition-equipped pistol for the student's use when conducting House of Horrors iterations, for while students are expected to clear minor stoppages, catastrophic stoppages as described here require disassembly and cleaning of the pistol.

Another negative note regarding the ammunition concerns the shelf-life of the marking solution. After approximately one year, the marking solution can harden up, even though the boxes are foil-sealed in the cases. When this occurs, the ampules become less inclined to break open upon impact. While this tendency generally increases the impact penalty, it also doesn't allow the marking solution to perform its function.

Regardless of these considerations, the Simunition® product line is still the best equipment of its type I have worked with. I would recommend no other.

Heckler & Koch MP5SD3 Submachine Gun converted for use with Simunition® FX® Marking Cartridges. The weapon can be fired in semiautomatic, burst, and automatic modes when using the ammunition.

Glock 17T. Pistol specifically designed to fire Simunition ammunition. Frame and magazine floorplates are bright blue, slide is marked "9mm FX." (www.glock.com)

(Above) A few of the Simunition® conversion kits currently being offered. Shown clockwise from left; 12 Gauge Shotgun kit, Glock 22 & 35 kit, SIG Sauer P226 kit, Beretta 92F kit. Regular ammunition will not feed into the semiautomatic pistol conversion kit barrels.

.38/.357 magnum revolvers may be used for training for only the price of a box of .38 caliber FX® Marking Cartridges, as safety-ring inserts for the cylinder's chambers are included with each box.

Protective equipment produced by Simunition® for use with FX® Marking Cartridge ammunition includes protective mask, throat collar, and vest as shown here. Protective sleeves, pants and gloves are also available.

Simunition also produces another special-purpose ammunition (CQT) that, while designed to be fired through the conversion kits, is NOT intended to be fired at personnel as it will penetrate the body. For this reason instructors must be thoroughly educated and properly trained prior to employing any of the Simunition product line. Training is available from the company. (www.simunition.com)

AirSoft Training Equipment

AirSoft replica firearms have become increasingly popular since first being developed in the US more than 30 years ago. Since then, the 1/1 scale replicas have been extensively refined by Japanese engineers to the point where they are nearly impossible to distinguish simply by appearance from their real firing counterparts.

In basic terms, Airsoft replica models are simply BB guns designed to fire lightweight 6mm plastic ball projectiles at velocities between 200-450 fps. The BBs are projected from the guns by compressed spring, gas, or air pressure–the last being produced by electrically-driven gears and pistons.

They are produced to resemble a large variety of weapon systems, including the more popular models of pistols, subguns, rifles, and shotguns. There are even models that resemble long-range tactical marksman (sniper) rifles, complete with functional telescopic sights.

Hugely popular with the same crowd that enjoys paintball gun matches, the replicas have been extensively used by gamers for years in Italy, Japan and many other parts of Europe and Asia. Enthusiasts often invest a lot of money in their equipment, including customizing the guns with everything from lasers to pellet-spewing grenade launchers. Ancillary tactical equipment is also used to increase the war-gaming realism.

AirSoft products are currently taking the US paintball player market by storm. Many members of law enforcement have also begun employing the AirSoft replicas for interactive dynamic training, and after attending one of the Massachusetts Law Enforcement Firearms Instructors & Armorers Association (MLEFIAA) sponsored AirSoft Instructor classes put on by fellow New England police officer/trainer (and author) Ralph Mroz, I believe that there is a lot to be said for exploring this option.

The better made models look incredibly real, and while many are constructed primarily

According to Mike Pentrack (shown above with Airsoft carbine), Executive Director of the Federation of AirSoft Standards and Training, while there are many high-quality AirSoft replica weapons available, there are also a lot of cheaper models on the market that don't perform or hold-up well under normal use. For this reason, it is best to do some serious research or contact someone familiar with the equipment prior to purchasing. (www.fast-us.org)

of ABS plastic components, metal components are available, adding to their weight and the realism of the training.

Another positive aspect of the AirSoft products is found in their affordability. Most of the top-end gas blow back handgun models can be had for around $100.00 - $150.00.

While some of the Simunition® conversion kits can also be had in this price range, it is in the purchase of ammunition that the AirSoft products prevail economically.

The BBs they fire are extremely inexpensive, costing around $15.00 per bag of 2,000 pellets. Compare this to approximately $450.00 for one case (1,000 rounds) of 9mm Simunition® FX® Marking Cartridges. Additional operating expenses are also incurred when using the gas operated AirSoft models, for you must use a propellant similar to CO2 called "green gas" (HFC134a or HFC22 combined with a silicone lubricant) to launch the projectile and power the semi-automatic action–yes, the pistol slides do cycle when firing.[1]

Depending upon the gun model, your rate of fire and the temperature, one can of green gas costing $12.00 - $15.00 should allow you to fire around 2,000-3,000 pellets.

Clean up is also less of a chore, as all of the BBs are non-toxic, (biodegradable BBs are available), there are no shell casings ejected, and there are no paint marks to wash away. Obviously, these last two aspects can be either positive or negative, depending upon your training objectives and environmental realities.

On the positive side, the BBs allow training to be conducted in a broader range of environments where the use of Simunition® FX® Marking Cartridges would prove problematic.

On a negative note, while the BBs do induce a pain-penalty (thereby increasing train-ing value), none offered at this time are capable of producing any type of mark on clothing to indicate point of impact.

Naturally, full face protection should be required when using the AirSoft products, and throat protection is also strongly recommended. Some people erroneously feel that only eye protection is needed when firing the lightweight BBs at one another in training. I disagree, for I have seen people accrue injuries to the soft tissues of the mouth and tongue, and reports of shattered teeth are not unheard of. The ear canal presents another serious concern, prompting the need for full head coverage. While some laugh at the possibility of one of the little balls finding such a mark, any experienced instructor will tell you, "If it *can* happen, it *will* happen."

Airsoft version of Taurus Millenium Pistol. Metal components, holds 20 "rounds". The magazine capacities are never lower than the real gun. Pistols hold 10-25 rounds, subguns 25-50 rounds. AirSoft guns are quieter than a .22 caliber rifle, but a bit louder than a typical air rifle. Federal law requires the first 5mm of the barrel of any AirSoft gun to be molded in orange plastic or have a blaze orange marking affixed to it. Removal, alteration, or destruction of the orange markings is both dangerous and a violation of federal law. It also voids the manufacturer's warranty. (Photo courtesy Mike Pentrack)

---

[1] Some people contend that "green gas" is simply propane with a lubricant added to it.

Many AirSoft semiautomatic pistols use gas blowback operation. The Green Gas is loaded into the bottom of the magazine along with the BBs. During training, magazine changes are conducted just as with the real weapons. The slides must also be cycled to chamber the first round. Pistols will fire as fast as you can press the trigger. It is worth noting that due to the way the AirSoft models function, the trigger reset may be slightly different from the real pistols. (Photo courtesy Mike Pentrack)

Simunition®, AirSoft, and Safety

The price of freedom is eternal vigilance.
– Thomas Jefferson

Eternal vigilance is the price of safety.
– Rex Applegate

We all know that in regard to training our officers, the higher the realism, the more beneficial the results.

As we continue to refine our approach to law enforcement specific firearms training, moving further and further from the primarily static marksmanship type training so prevalent for so long, and toward the new paradigm of more relevant and viable forms of interactive dynamic, scenario-based training, we must remain aware of the perils that shadow us along the way.

For the reality we face as trainers is this: *since we prepare our people to do dangerous work in often hostile environments while employing deadly weapons, the more we mirror these realities, the more dangerous the training potentially becomes.*

As a result, we, the trainers and guides, must ensure that every possible precaution is taken to ensure that none of us–we or our students–fall prey to negligence, lethargy, or apathy, as sometimes happens.

On the flip side, we must also remember that the closer we take the training to the edge, the greater our student's and our own levels of excitement and adrenaline will be.

Combine these factors with actual deadly weapons that have been converted to fire special training ammunition, or replica firearm models that are exact duplicates of the actual guns our people carry and train with, and you can see the potential for disaster before, during, and especially *immediately after* dynamic training iterations have been conducted, should real or unaltered weapons be on hand.

It is one of the great tragedies of our times that hardly a year goes by without a report of an officer being severely injured or killed while participating in some type of simulation-based training.

Often, it is the instructor who is injured or killed, or the instructor who unintentionally causes the injury or takes the life of one of the students he is teaching.

In addition to the great loss experienced by families, friends and co-workers, and the personal tragedies borne by those involved when such an event occurs, is the potential for a backlash to develop among department administrators, politicians, media, and society itself against the very idea of police officers employing reality-based firearms training methods and equipment. And this would be a true tragedy, for it is this type of training–*responsibly and professionally conducted*–that has and will continue to save many, many lives on both sides of the badge.

That is why it is imperative that force-on-force training be conducted according to rigid rules, recognized and enforced by every participating member.

Chief among these rules is that absolute control must be ensured to keep live weapons and ammunition out of the training areas, and that all weapons used in dynamic interactive training be clearly marked as such. This can be accomplished by applying highly visible paint or tape to multiple areas on the gun so it can be plainly seen by anyone in the vicinity.

All weapons, including those classified as toys or BB guns, must be so marked. They must also be treated with the utmost respect by the instructor and students, and no one should be allowed to use them in an unprofessional or improper way at any time.

It is too easy for a mistake to be made, too easy for one careless moment to change or end your life or someone else's.

> **"Chief among these rules is that absolute control must be ensured to keep live weapons and ammunition out of the training areas, and that all weapons used in dynamic interactive training be clearly marked as such."**

AirSoft and Simunition® altered weapons marked for training use. The markings should be visible from any direction, including when the weapon is being held in the hand. For this reason taping around the grip alone is not good enough, as it will be hidden when the pistol is grasped. Note: Some of the Simunition kits distinctly alter the weapon's appearance, such as the new Glock kit and the Beretta kit shown above. Even so, the tape marking protocol should still be used. Highly visible tape should be wrapped around the grip, front of the trigger guard, and placed on the weapon's sides, top, and any magazines used. It is also critical that ALL such markings be removed once training is completed and the weapons are restored to normal working order.
Remember: SOME MISTAKES CAN ONLY BE MADE *ONCE*!

APPENDIX S
Firearms Training Video Simulation System

FATS System being used

Firearms Training Video Simulation systems such as those produced by FATS or IES (RANGE 2000/RANGE 3000) can be used to provide training that is more psychologically engaging than Level 3 programs, but not quite as intense as Level 4 House of Horror training programs.

We had integrated this type of training into both our one-day in-service program and recruit-level program primarily because we were fortunate enough to have had a simulation system available. (On the in-service level we employed it during the afternoon session, making it part of the round-robin series of activities.)

While this type of training can be very beneficial and should be used if possible, there are many reasons why I believe the House of Horror type of training program is superior. A breakdown allowing a clear comparison of the pros and cons of each training system is provided on the following page.

Video Training Simulation System Guidelines

Any firearms simulation-type training should be conducted in a safe and secure area that has been cleared and checked prior to the commencement of training. A specially designated and secured room that will be used only for simulator training is highly recommended.

No weapons of any kind, other than those specially modified for use with the simulator system, should be allowed in this area. No access to this area without instructor knowledge and control should be possible. It is recommended that individual students participate in a minimum of two scenarios each per training segment. The number of scenarios can be increased depending upon number of personnel present and time availability, but should not be decreased if at all avoidable.

Other students present should also be encouraged to observe the scenarios even when they are not directly participating in them, as long as there are a sufficient number of alternative scenarios

327

SIMULATION SYSTEM

PROS:

High safety margin

Allows individual
training & critique

Provides judgment
training

Allows verbalization
conditioning

Multiple & custom
scenarios possible

CONS:

Limited physical
movement possible

Limited interaction
w/actual environment

No actual (or perceived)
danger to participant:
fails to produce true
high arousal (fear) state

Expensive to purchase
and repair

More information available at:
www.fatsinc.com
www.ies-usa.com

HOUSE OF HORRORS SIMULATION

PROS:

High safety margin

Allows individual
training & critique

Truly interactive

Provides judgment
training

Allows verbalization
conditioning

Multiple & custom
scenarios possible

Environment reflects reality

Realistic movement possible

Consistently produces true high
arousal (fear) state and allows
education of effects, stress
inoculation, & behavior
modification

Easy to construct and maintain,
highly cost-effective

CONS:

Requires initial
instructor training,
dedication, & extreme
vigilance

Requires construction
& maintenance of
interactive targets

Training value may be
slightly negatively
impacted by use of
protective helmets

available so students can each deal with unique situations or variations of those situations.

While everyone involved in the training is responsible for the safety of all, the on-site instructor/s will be ultimately responsible for ensuring that all proper safety precautions and policies are observed.

Signs should be posted on all entrances, clearly stating that:
ABSOLUTELY NO LIVE WEAPONS OF ANY TYPE WILL BE ALLOWED IN THE TRAINING AREA WHILE FIREARMS VIDEO TRAINING SIMULATION SYSTEMS ARE BEING USED!

The on-site instructor is also responsible for maintaining all the video simulator equip-

ment, preparing the students to participate, setting up the scenarios, selecting branching options, and for providing immediate feedback to the participants.

Once the individual student has satisfactorily completed a minimum of two scenarios, (the instructor will make the determination regarding satisfactory performance), the instructor should sign off on the student's Performance Evaluation Form documenting that the training segment had been successfully completed. The specific scenarios the student participated in should be noted on the form. Notes should also be made regarding any problems, discrepancies, or acts of superior judgment and/or physical skills demonstrated by the student.

APPENDIX T
An Eye on Handgun Sight Development

There have been some interesting and significant developments both in the approach to sighting the handgun and in the design of handgun sights since I last wrote about them in *In the Line of Fire* in 1997.

Since a review of the history of handgun sight development reveals there have actually been few significant strides made since the beginning of the Twentieth Century, I believe it's important to revisit the issue and examine some of the more recent developments.

First, a brief look back.

Patridge Sets the Standard

According to Elmer Keith, sights didn't become standard equipment on handguns until after 1836 when the revolver came into general use.[1]

Since then, many different types of sight designs have been developed for the one-hand gun. Like many other aspects of pistolcraft, many of these designs have also been "reborn" and reinvented over the years, with various modifications made to the basic established designs.

For example, the most popular type of sight used on modern handguns is based on a design *more than 100 years old*. The Patridge Sight–often incorrectly referred to as a *partridge* sight–was first developed by Mr. E.E. Patridge in 1892. This sight can be recognized by its simple and efficient design, embodied in a squared front sight and squared rear sight notch.

In A.L.A. Himmelwright's book, *Pistol and Revolver Shooting*, (first published in 1908), Patridge is quoted explaining how to use the sights he had designed *primarily for target shooting*.

Mr. Patridge stated, "In using these sights bring the front sight into the rear notch, making a straight line across the rear bar and the top of the front sight in the notch opening, so the eye will see a black square with two lines of light of equal width on each side."

Today, Patridge Sights are still being produced and used in the same manner, though they have been adapted for purposes other than target shooting over the years.

One of the ways they have been modified for use in low-light environments for both target and combat applications is by the addition of colored paint or luminous inserts. This approach was undertaken as early as the beginning of the Twentieth century, when white and phosphorescent paints were used. Later developments saw the use of Radium and then the drastically safer Tritium. Tritium, a radioactive isotope of hydrogen, is used extensively in the well-known Trijicon® brand of self-luminous sights.

Self-luminous Sights

In *In the Line of Fire,* I recommended the selection of a set of rugged, self-luminous sights that your

(Background photo courtesy Massachusetts State Police archives, circa 1941)

---
[1] *Sixguns by Keith,* 1961 revised edition

eyes can quickly acquire and align while operating in a darkened environment. While I still believe their use can prove beneficial to police officers under certain circumstances and conditions, there are other considerations that need to be examined.

First, under stress, especially in a low light environment during the statistically-likely police-involved gunfight, chances are great that both of an officer's eyes will be wide open and focused on the threat.

If the self-luminous sights were perceived by the officer at all under these conditions, they could possibly impede or distract the shooter's focus *from the threat.*

On the other hand, if the shooter did attempt to consciously access the sights under these conditions, other problems could arise. As Tim Sheehan, inventor of the HexSite™ (covered later) points out, "in stress-fire situations, with both eyes involuntarily open, users of 3-dot night sights may see from four to six dots because of the parallax (apparent displacement of an object seen from two different points) of binocular vision."

Should this occur, it could obviously induce greater stress and confusion on the shooter, especially if the shooter has been extensively trained to close one eye when sighting on the range.

Patridge Sights with Trijicon® Self-luminous inserts.

On the "pro" side of the argument, self-luminous sights *can* provide an officer with a significant advantage should he find himself in a situation during which he was:
1) actually able to access and align the sights on an identified threat while
2) operating in a low-lit environment and/or during the hours of darkness when the statistically-likely gunfight normally occurs.

I experienced another example of a situation that could have been positively-impacted by the presence of a set of illuminated sights one evening years ago while operating in a darkened house during a call out. While moving through the lower level of the building performing a stealth search while exercising complete light discipline, we could hear the suspect we were looking for in a room somewhere above us.

Approaching a staircase, I held my pistol out in front of me, muzzle-first to danger. It was then I realized that even though the top of the staircase was dimly illuminated, from the position I was in, I could see neither my pistol nor my hands as it was so dark. This was prior to our being issued self-luminous sights–never mind night vision goggles–and, regardless of the fact that it "felt" like my pistol was pointing straight and true, the effect was slightly disorienting, apparently causing my "inner puppy" a minor degree of consternation. (I did find myself in a subsequent similar situation after being equipped with a pistol possessing a set of self-luminous sights, and did find it made a positive difference in my confidence level– however, I was not required to fire my weapon during either circumstance, so cannot testify to the positive or negative impact of the sights on close quarter pistol-combat performance.)

Given all of the above considerations, should the decision be made to acquire these types of sights, I would offer the following suggestions, arrived at after much experimentation.

I would suggest the employment of a luminous dot on the front sight in combination with a luminous vertical post or horizontal line for the rear sight, as opposed to the more common three dot configuration. I believe this configuration–reminiscent of another early design and currently being offered in Tritium lamp form by Novak's® –is better because when three dots are used, all emitting the same colored light, it is possible for the muzzle to be grossly misaligned with the target, even when the three little lights appear to be dead-on aligned. This occurs, especially when operating under stress, when the front sight dot is inadvertently lined up to the right or left of the rear sight dots. When this happens, even though the operator sees the three little dots neatly aligned in a row, the muzzle is actually pointing a few degrees port or starboard–a *major* problem, especially at further distances as this misalignment will be greatly magnified.

While some officers opt to install different colored lamps on the rear sight while keeping the green lamp up front to prevent this misalignment from happening, I still prefer the table and ball configuration because nothing is certain when operating under stress, including your abilities to accurately perceive depth and/or colors.

Cirillo Intuitive Sights

The Cirillo "Intuitive" Sights

Many people are not aware that Jim Cirillo, in addition to his unique gun fighting experiences while serving as a member of the NYPD Stakeout Squad, is also an accomplished firearms instructor and world-class competition shooter.

He has also been instrumental in the design and modification of both ammunition and firearms, with several patents to his credit.

As I was preparing this section, Jim happened to mention that he had been working on an improved iron sight design for pistols. Naturally anxious to see what the "Old Gunfighter" had produced, I asked him to send

me the handmade prototype so I could try it out.

The sights, pictured here mounted on a Glock 22, consist of a rear sight with a radius-cut notch. A shallow groove has been cut around the radius and painted white. The front sight, consisting of a standard Patridge blade that has been rounded off, has a self-luminous insert that is also surrounded by a ring of white paint.

When held up to the line of sight, the shooter is presented with a sight picture reminiscent of a Paine Sight, though the rear sight radius cut is more defined, and the white outline does assist the eye to quickly locate and center the Tritium insert. This fast acquisition is aided immeasurably by the thin black outline that surrounds the insert.

When sighting the pistol, Jim recommends that the shooter simply focus on the bright or "high value" front sight. The eye and brain then tend to automatically center the front dot in the rear radius, achieving perfect alignment with the target.

Jim advises that during his experiments to date, this sight configuration has allowed him to fire incredibly accurate groups out to fifty yards. (Keep in mind, however, we are talking about a man who can fire tighter groups while holding the pistol inverted, actuating the trigger with his little finger, than most people can while holding the pistol normally...) He further stated that everyone he has let shoot while using the sights have reported the same effect.

During my own testing with the handmade prototype set, I found that these sights did indeed prove to be extremely user-friendly. In fact, the first groups I fired through my own Glock 22 fitted out with Jim's new sights were tighter than any I had produced when firing it with the factory sights. I also found that the sights were extremely well-suited for use under low light conditions, as they seemed to stand out in a way that most standard sights do not.

Jim anticipates that the production versions will be available shortly. I look forward to purchasing and permanently installing a set on my Glock 22 for further testing and evaluation.

Interestingly, Jim's Intuitive Sights are the last traditional iron-type sights we'll be looking at in this section. For in the area of handgun sight development over the past decade, a definite trend has been observed toward designs that allow the pistol operator to keep both of his eyes open and his focus on the target while he's shooting at it.

Obviously, for law enforcement purposes, this trend may prove extremely beneficial, for sights designed to allow the operator to focus on the target while verifying that the muzzle is aligned properly–either consciously or subconsciously– will eliminate many of the training disparities found when teaching precision and reflexive shooting skills.

Red Dot "Reflex" Sights

Electronic Holographic Diffraction (HDS) and Red Dot-type "Reflex" Sights have become very popular for long guns, and variants of both can be seen on the M-4 service weapons many of our troops currently employ in the Middle East.

The sights are intended to be used keeping both eyes open, while the dominant eye is aligned with the sight's lens aperture or window. The dot or other aiming reticle is then superimposed on the target, indicating the weapon's point of aim.

Contrary to many people's misperception, the eye's focus should be kept on the target, *not* redirected to the dot when using these types of sights.

As for pistols, many competition shooters have been employing similar sights on their highly-modified "race guns" for years, but these sights are normally large bulky affairs that have no business in a duty holster.

A smaller version has been developed, however, that may be worth considering for tactical team or other limited special purpose applications. Referred to as micro-electronic reflex red-dot sight systems, versions have been produced by Tasco (Fire Point™ and Optima

Micro-electronic reflex red-dot sight system.
(Images courtesy JP Enterprises, Inc.)

2000™), JP Enterprises, Inc. (JPoint™), and Docter Sports Optics USA (DOCTERsight™).

These battery-powered sights are installed on top of the slide in place of the rear sight. They can be attached with mounts or "melted in", which requires some machining of the slide and results in a significantly lower profile as well as an easier transition for those accustomed to using iron sights.

The newer JPoint and DOCTERsight models automatically adjust the intensity of the dot to ambient light conditions, allowing acquisition of the dot as long as the environment is bright enough to identify the target. Provided that Mr. Murphy fails to get involved, the sights are always active (lithium batteries reportedly can last up to three years in the units), eliminating potential problems caused by forgetting to turn the unit on prior to work, or having the unit putting itself to "sleep" after a set period of time. Both sights are also waterproof and dustproof.

In terms of weight and durability, the JPoint is lighter, using a polymer frame and acrylic lenses, while the DOCTERsight is hardier, with a stainless steel, brass and anodized aircraft-grade aluminum frame and optical quality glass lenses.

Laser Aiming/Sighting Systems

The concept of laser sighting systems has received a great deal of public exposure, especially since Hollywood fell in love with the image of numerous red dots swarming like angry bees over the chest of the hero or villain during many an action movie's climax.

Much has also been written about the application of these systems for law enforcement handgun purposes since the development of two product lines designed specifically for use with duty pistols. The two companies that produce these products, LaserMax® Inc. and Crimson Trace™ Corporation, have taken innovative yet different approaches to solving

the problem of designing a self-contained laser system that will neither impact negatively on a duty pistol's functioning nor alter its physical profile in any significant way.

I have experimented extensively with both of these products in training and while operational. I have also conducted and attended training courses built around their use, to include participating as an invited member in the 2004 Crimson Trace Master Trainers Summit. I am currently putting the Crimson Trace system through a series of trials, to fully explore the viability of their use for both general and specialized police purposes. I am conducting these trials not on behalf of Crimson Trace or any other commercial entity, but on behalf of my department. I am providing this information in the interests of full disclosure, for some of the opinions I have formed regarding the use of lasers in general and these two premier products specifically, may ruffle some feathers.

Whether you agree with my opinions or not, I wish to make it completely clear that they are mine alone, and have not been dictated or influenced by any parties, private or public.

My *approach* to the subject of laser sighting systems, however, *has* been influenced, primarily by Jim Cirillo, who reminded me to keep an open mind while evaluating the devices. This was necessary–and much appreciated by me–for I had formed a somewhat negative opinion early on regarding the use of lasers for general law enforcement purposes. If not for Jim's encouragement to put aside my initial impressions and re-evaluate the devices with fresh eyes, I might have remained trapped in a foregone conclusion–never a good thing.

Laser Systems, Pros & Cons

Laser sighting systems can provide a number of benefits for the law enforcement officer.

Operationally, they allow an officer to verify muzzle alignment with a threat while keeping his focus *on the threat*. The laser also allows other officers to see which suspects are being covered–and which *are not*–during felony stop or raid/warrant service activities.

This visual indication of muzzle alignment is also very often obvious to the suspect being covered. Numerous instances of suspects being influenced to surrender/discontinue the fight once they observe the red beam flashing from the pistol or find an intensely glowing dot on their chests have been documented. Officers also often report feeling more confident with their laser sight-equipped weapons, especially when operating in low light environments.

In regard to training operations, the lasers can provide an outstanding training aid insofar as officers can "see" what their muzzles are doing by observing the path/movement of the dot. By using the laser in this way, officers can quickly improve the smoothness and speed of their presentation, muzzle alignment, and trigger manipulation.

As for the negative aspects, the one that concerns me most is the potential for officers to hesitate to fire *when it is time to fire* because they are unable to see or find the dot on the threat subject. This first became of concern to me more than 10 years ago while training down in Florida. While there, a local police officer was attacked while off duty by a pistol-armed assailant at close quarters. During the struggle that ensued, the officer succeeded in preventing the assailant from shooting by grasping the assailant's gun hand with his own non-dominant hand. The officer, who was then able to draw his laser sight-equipped pistol, reported experiencing a mental "disconnect", for though he felt he *had* to shoot, his brain was locked onto the fact that he *couldn't see the dot*. And based upon the way he had been trained at that time, *no dot* meant *no "bang"*. (See operant conditioning, Chapter Four). Luckily, the officer was able to overcome this psychological "dissonance" and pressed the trigger, ending the attack.

This possibility for hesitation, especially in regard to close quarter spontaneous attacks, is the single greatest obstacle that must be overcome before a laser sight is provided to an officer. The only way to do this is to conduct a training program specifically designed to limit the possibility of an officer hesitating when it is time to shoot. Simply equipping officers with the devices and putting them through a few courses of fire is not enough.

There are several reasons why an officer might not be able to see or find the dot. While the Class IIIa lasers produce a brilliant beam that is visible at great distances in low light environments and close-in under bright light conditions, the dot tends to be difficult–if not impossible–to discern under daylight conditions at distances greater than 7 yards.

Mechanical or electrical failure is another possibility that may render the laser unavailable.

Though batteries tend to last a long time, routine testing of the lasers and replacement of the batteries before they run down is just good old preventative maintenance.

Again, *proper training* is the key to ensuring that the laser sighting system is used to provide the tremendous advantages it is capable of providing, while minimizing the possibility of catastrophic hesitation on the part of the officer at a critical moment.

While a lot of effort has already been expended in this area, much more is needed to ensure that the tremendous benefits of laser sighting systems can be exploited fully in the future.

LaserMax®

The LaserMax series of laser sights has been designed in the shape of a semiautomatic pistol's recoil guide rod. The laser is installed in the pistol simply by replacing the stock recoil guide rod, recoil spring, and (in the case of SIGs) the takedown lever with those supplied. The takedown lever houses the switch, and the laser can be turned on or off by pressing a small rod from either side. When pressed in halfway between both points, the laser is turned off. Activating the laser can be accomplished by the trigger finger while the weapon is held normally in the hand. Turning it off safely, however, generally requires the use of both hands.

While the aiming point of the laser cannot be adjusted with this model, I have found it to provide suitable accuracy out to 25 yards as it comes out of the box. The pulsing laser dot that is projected is generally clear, bright, and fairly easy to locate (except as noted previously), but will become diffused when the lens is fouled. This tends to occur as a result of firing the weapon, since the laser's lens is situated directly below the muzzle.

The fact that the entire system can be installed in minutes by the operator, and that once installed, does not alter the pistol's profile in any significant way, is rather remarkable. The very idea, however, of replacing any of the duty weapon's internal components bothered me from the outset. After firing less than a thousand rounds through my personal 9mm SIG P226

LaserMax® Combat Laser Sight, shown installed on this Sig P226 and disassembled at left. This unit utilizes a Class IIIa laser and produces a pulsing red dot. Power output is between 3-4mW.

with the LaserMax installed, I encountered a problem that confirmed my fears.

The guide rod tube containing the laser and batteries (shown in the photo) is made of steel and tends to hold up very well against the recoil and action of the spring. The plastic battery cap, however, would occasionally come loose during firing. On two separate occasions, this resulted in a catastrophic malfunction, rendering the pistol completely inoperable. Luckily, these two instances occurred during training, and not in the field.

Though a representative from LaserMax stated that this had not occurred previously to their knowledge, as I noted, I experienced it twice during my testing, the second time after double-checking to ensure that it was assembled properly according to the manufacturer's instructions, and that the unit itself was not damaged in any way.[2]

For this reason alone I could not recommend the LaserMax System as tested for duty use.

Another weakness of this system is found in its switching mechanism, which requires the operator to employ fine motor skills to manually turn the laser on and off, something which could prove to be a distraction (at the least) during a real world, spontaneous encounter.

Crimson Trace Corporation's Lasergrips™

Crimson Trace Corporation's Lasergrips also require the replacement of stock components, though in this case it is the grip panels.

Should this laser system fail, the weapon itself will remain unaffected.

On most models the laser is housed high in the right side panel, running horizontally below

---

[2] After reading the draft copy of this book, Jim Cirillo advised me that he too had experienced this type of failure while working with the LaserMax® system, and had reported his experience to a LaserMax representative.

finger level. Pressure activation switches are located on the grip panels where they can be activated by the fingers of the dominant hand. The positioning of these switches leaves a bit to be desired, however, as some people find their fingers don't fall on the switches when the weapon is gripped naturally. (A single activation switch located in the grip along the front strap is reportedly in the works. Available for some revolver models and the Colt 1911 Government and Commander models, this variation is ergonomically superior.) A second master switch is located on the bottom of the left grip panel. This switch, controlling power to the pressure switches, can be set to "on" or "off". When in the "off" position, the laser will not activate when the momentary pressure switches are depressed.

When the beam is activated while the weapon is held in the right hand with the index finger up along the frame, the beam is usually blocked. When the finger is moved to the trigger or onto the trigger guard, the beam is projected onto the target.

Unlike the LaserMax system, the Crimson Trace system uses a steady, rather than a pulsing

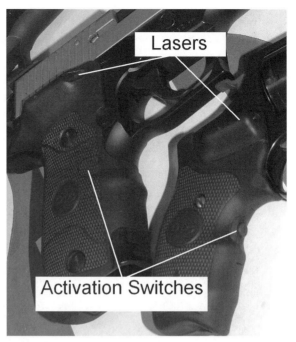

Close-up of the Crimson Trace Lasergrips™ showing laser housings and activation switches. The single activation switch located on the front strap (right) tends to provide surer contact than the side-panel mounted switches for many people. Depending upon hand size, the side panel mounts can be difficult to activate.

beam, and the beam can also be adjusted for windage and elevation to allow zeroing. Due to the positioning of the laser above and off to the right side of the muzzle, vertical and horizontal alignment tends to be less than perfect at any distance other than that at which the weapon is zeroed. At distances from 25 yards and in, this misalignment ranges from negligible to a span of several inches–something which might make a difference when delivering a critical, precision-aimed shot, but won't be much of a factor for the majority of police-involved deadly force encounters when hitting center mass is the objective.

The grips themselves are ergonomically designed, and provide a superior, rubber over-mold surface that is extremely comfortable and provides for positive control of the weapon. Many officers I have trained have stated that they would prefer these grips to the stock panels, even if the lasers weren't included.

We have experienced a few instances

Crimson Trace Lasergrips™ shown installed on (from top) a Colt Combat Commander, SIG P226, and a Smith & Wesson Model 36. The rubber overmold grips are extremely well made and comfortable to shoot with.

where the grips caused a problem when securing the pistol in the duty holster. This was usually corrected simply by making a minor adjustment to the holster, though in several cases the holster had to be replaced–not with a custom holster, but with another standard-issue duty holster.

While the quality control of all the components is plainly evident, several of the units we purchased for use had faulty master switches. Several others that worked fine initially ceased working for unknown reasons after being carried on duty for a period of a few months, including my own. These units were not abused beyond normal handling limits and the batteries tested fine. The customer service provided by the company was exemplary, however, and replacements were shipped immediately.

As I noted, we are currently conducting a series of training tests and evaluations with these particular devices. I am working with a test group comprised of members of the MSP Logan Airport Anti-Terrorist Unit. The equipment has been issued and is being deployed daily.

The feedback thus far has been very positive, and the results of our training approach–based purely on the New Paradigm model–appear to be decidedly positive. My major concern, however, is that we are still seeing a tendency to hesitate firing at the target when the beam is not immediately discerned. Once I have completed testing and gathered the information I seek, I will make my findings available for those with an interest either in an article, on the Internet, or both.

The HexSite™ Sighting Systems

The last sight to be examined in this section is a hybrid produced by Goshen Enterprises, Inc. I use the term hybrid because though at first glance it may appear to be a variation of a set of standard front post and rear ghost ring aperture sights, it is actually something quite different.

For the patented HexSite has been con-

ceived, designed, and created to "solve the problem of conventional sights especially well in circumstances requiring a 'startled response' from a defender," according to Tim Sheehan, the sight's inventor.

Tim, an experienced defensive firearms instructor based in Sedona, Arizona, has expended a considerable amount of time, energy, and money pursuing his vision of a sight that would fit a specific set of requirements (Table 1). Tim based these requirements on a specific set of circumstances likely present during a typical close quarter gunfight (Table 2).

Unlike conventional iron sights, the HexSite has been designed to allow the operator to focus on the target, not on the sights, while keeping both eyes open. Due to the unique design of the HexSite, the operator is able to do just that while still benefiting from the presence of the sights. That is because the HexSite has been designed to be looked *through*, not at, while the operator is engaged in combat.

This is in direct contrast to the approach E.E. Patridge took over 100 years ago when he first created the sights that would become the standard model for handguns, for his intent was to create a set of sights that could be easily accessed and *focused upon* while firing. That was because Patridge–who took a scientific approach to his project, even consulting with an optometrist during the design phase–was trying to produce sights for *target shooting, not combat.*

I first became interested in Tim's work several years back when he contacted me after reading an article I had written for *Guns & Ammo* in which I described some of the training we had been conducting at the FTU. After introducing himself, he described in great and enthusiastic detail all of the experiments, research, and testing he had conducted while pursuing his vision of a usable combat pistol sight.

Later, he provided me with a sample for testing and evaluation. After working with the

Sight Requirements Based Upon Typical Gunfight Circumstances
1. Reasonable size 2. Rugged construction & Fail Safe operation 3. Lowest "value" (darkest) in any ambient environment 4. Allows full, unobstructed visual target perception 5. Allows for effortless natural target alignment without need for subjective thought 6. Allows consistent target alignment in any lighting conditions

Table 1

Circumstances Present During Typical Gunfight
1. Fluid situation (in motion) 2. Focus on threat 3. Shooter's perspective can be adversely impacted by distraction caused by colored or luminous sights 4. Both eyes will be wide open 5. Because the shooter feels a great need to see the threat target, he will tend to stop short when raising his firearm to eye level and look over the sights, depressing the muzzle resulting in shots fired low

Table 2

sights for just a short time, I began to see what he had accomplished. It is an extremely interesting concept, based on a unique blend of science, superior craftsmanship, physiology, and more than just a little dash of Zen. Interestingly, as Patridge had one-hundred years before, Tim also sought out the advice of professionals outside the firearms industry, most notably in the medical and behavioral sciences fields.

One of the core concepts of the HexSite System is that when used correctly by a shooter in a stress-fire situation, the sights actually disappear as they effectively assist the shooter to focus on the target. While it takes a little time to adjust to this idea, especially if you've been using Patridge type sights for any length of time, the validity of the concept can be easily demonstrated while dry firing. Simply stare at an object with pistol in hand, and then quickly and aggressively raise the pistol to eye level while maintaining your focus on the object. After just a short time of exposure to the HexSite system, what you will repetitively and consistently observe when you refocus your vision from the object to the sight is that the top of the front sight blade has been aligned perfectly in the center of the rear sight aperture and

directly on target–all without conscious determination. (This refocusing on the sight is done only to demonstrate that the concept works, and would not be done at all when using the sights for shooting purposes.)

Basically, Tim's design consists of a rear hexagonal-shaped aperture and a specially-machined front blade sight. The front sight has been designed to collect light from any direction and produce a subtle glint at its top.

The extensively-machined rear aperture offers 16 angular reference points that, according to Tim–and experienced by me, for one–are subconsciously accessed when the pistol's sights are aligned with the eye. As a result of the recessed concavity at the rear of the aperture, a truly dark shadow that does not reflect light is produced, resulting in the desired lowest "value". Because this shadow is so much darker than the surrounding environment, maximum contrast with the target in every lighting condition is achieved. The effect for the eyes is to perceive the target through the sight as being brighter or of higher value, resulting in better focus on the target. As for operating in extremely low-lit environments, according to Tim, "If lighting conditions are too dark for the

HexSite™ shown installed on a Glock 9mm.

HexSite, it is too dark to identify the target, and too unclear to shoot at with any sight, at least without flashlight illumination."

Tim goes on to explain:

The HexSite presents six implied equilateral triangles which involuntarily draw the eye to an exquisitely refined convergence at the center of the hexagonal aperture. The angles are reflexively congenial with the eye's inherent physiological makeup, so that the eye effortlessly locates and perceives the sight's precise center. One user commented that it was 'like using invisible scope crosshairs.' The shooter's eye simply cannot dismiss the hexagonal structure's unconscious demand to place the unfocused-upon front-post-top at the center of the sight–which also places it right on the target the shooter is focusing upon. While the shooter is seeing the target, the subconscious is 'seeing' the sight."

Now, having been in the police industry for nearly twenty years, and working professionally as a writer/consultant for more than a dozen, I've had a lot of people try to sell me one brand of snake oil or another from a number of angles, triangular and otherwise. And I'll admit that my BS radar was up and running strong as I first listened to Tim and then read the volumes of information he's produced about his sights.

But right from the start the man's sincerity rang loud and true, as did his approach and methodology. In addition, after working with both the pistol and shotgun versions of the HexSite, I have been so impressed that I felt I had to include what is probably the culmination of his life's work in this book, which for better or worse, is probably the culmination of my own.

I would also like to state for the record that neither I, nor anyone involved with me or Saber Group, Inc., has any type of business relationship with Tim or his company.

He is simply a good man who has developed an exquisitely thought-out and designed iron sight that I believe may bridge the gap between the two primary methods used to aim the pistol during real world engagements.

And I have been fortunate enough to have had the privilege to introduce it here, in *Police Pistolcraft*.

View through the HexSite™ as installed on the Glock pistol shown above.

Sight Systems Resources
(As cited in this section)

www.aimpoint.com

www.crimsontrace.com

www.docteropticsusa.com

www.eotech-inc.com

www.goshen-hexsite.com

www.jprifles.com

www.lasermax.com

www.novaksights.com

www.tasco.com

www.trijicon.com

Another Blast from the Past!

The battery-powered WESPI electric searchlight sight, shown mounted on a Mauser Siderlatch Special. The long tube projects a beam of light at the center of which is a dark focused spot, or dot. The sight is adjusted so the dot and the pistol's point of impact intersect. Sort of a reverse laser/red dot scope concept. Don't look for it at your local gunshop though–it was developed and produced during the early 1900s! (Image courtesy of Paul L. Regnier)

APPENDIX U
The Paper Trail

It is said the warrior's is the twofold Way of pen and sword, and he should have a taste for both Ways.
— Miyamoto Musashi
The Book of Five Rings
1645

If it isn't documented, it didn't happen

"If it isn't documented, it didn't happen." These words sum up the basic reason all training programs must not only be designed and administered properly, but also documented sufficiently so they will survive being scrutinized and evaluated in a courtroom.

For as far as the courts, the Occupational Safety and Health Administration (OSHA), or any other evaluating entity are concerned, if there is no paperwork to support the claims of training, *then the training did not occur*, and can have no impact on the outcome of the evaluation of any subsequent actions taken.

This lack of evidence can leave irreparable gaps in the armor that shields the officers, trainers, administration, and department from the often damaging claims of vicarious liability.

Lesson Plans

A professional lesson plan should be formatted so that any qualified, competent instructor could teach the entire course of instruction from the plan. The days of the one or two page bulleted outline satisfying the criteria of a fully-realized, professional police firearms training lesson plan are gone. The higher levels of police training and standards represented by the professionally formatted and produced lesson plan are not only expected, but mandated by the courts in today's litigious society. The lesson plan is, in effect, the first link in the armor protecting everyone in the agency in regard to training issues.

In addition to producing fully-realized lesson plans for instructor use and departmental records, it is recommended that a copy of the plan or a handout detailing the salient points of the training be provided to the students. If this is not done, it could prove problematic for several reasons. First, the student is not provided with a reference source relating to the material covered. Second, the student is not provided with a written record documenting the training received. And third, the student is not provided with information regarding the source material used to develop the program, or the administering instructor's experience and background.

The major problem with this lack of documentation would be encountered should one of the student officers become engaged in a real world situation and make decisions and/or take action based

---

[1] The vicarious administrative liability "umbrella" includes negligent assignment, negligent entrustment, failure to direct, failure to supervise, negligent retention, negligent hiring, and failure to train.

upon this training and experience. Should the student officer have misinterpreted any of the instructions or training given during the iteration and not had a written reference source to clarify it subsequent to the training, then he would be relying expressly on this mistaken memory when operating in an actual situation. In addition to the types of serious mistakes and consequences that could result, the trainers, training section, and department could be exposed to the perils of vicarious liability.[1]

All training records and other related documents would be subject to review by the courts should such an incident occur.

Instructor Vita

For too many years, police firearms instructors were often widely regarded within departments as individuals who were either "gun nuts", or whose "elevators didn't quite reach the top floor", or worse.

Today, the modern police firearms instructor must not only be extremely capable, technically competent, and dedicated, but also possess high degrees of skill, knowledge, experience, and judgment.

OSHA's *Instructor Qualifications Criteria* provides us with an example of the types of subject matter expertise, training, and delivery skills that the courts expect professional, legitimate instructors to possess:

> Instructors should be deemed competent on the basis of previous documented experience in their area of instruction, successful completion of a 'train-the-trainer' program specific to the topics they will teach, and an evaluation of instructional competence by the Training Director.

> Instructors should be required to maintain professional competency by participating in continuing education or professional development programs or by completing successfully

an annual refresher course and having an annual review by the Training Director.

We can break these paragraphs down into the following elements:

Instructors should:

1. be deemed competent
2. possess previous *documented* experience in their area of instruction
3. successfully complete a train-the-trainer (instructor-level) program
4. undergo an evaluation of instructional competence by a higher certifying authority i.e. the Training Director
5. maintain professional competency by participating in:
   - continuing education
   - professional development programs
   - completing successfully an annual refresher course
   - having an annual review by the Training Director

Any training the police firearms instructor receives, as well as any relevant experience he has gained that can be applied to training, must be documented in a professional manner, preferably in resume or "vita" form.

As for being deemed competent to instruct a specific subject, OSHA also makes the valid point that:

> Instructors should be deemed competent on the basis of *previous documented experience* in their area of instruction. 'Area of Instruction' in this case means *a specific topic or task, not a general category*.

What this means for the modern, professional police firearms instructor can be broken down to this:

The possession of a single certificate that declares the completion of a Basic Firearms Instructor Certification course does *not* mean that the person named on that certificate is now qualified and/or competent to teach anything and everything related to police firearms use!

Unfortunately, this blanket approach to training and instructor certification has been taken by many departments for decades. Fortunately, it is finally beginning to change as more people come to the realization that the accruing of knowledge, skills, experience, and competence in *all facets* of training must be an ongoing, never ending process for the professional police firearms instructor.

The instructor's experience is another critical facet looked at by the courts. Again, as OSHA points out:

> This 'experience' can only result from actually performing the tasks the instructor is teaching. This 'experience' must come from hands on experience in the application of the principles of the specific topic or task..."

> It is not necessary that this experience be in actual circumstances. It may, instead, be under simulated circumstances (training) under the review of a qualified person.

In regard to noting the instructor's experience on the professional vita, a listing of the various police, military, and/or other positions involving the use of firearms held by the instructor along with a brief official job description of each position will suffice. Naturally, if the credibility of any such claims were challenged, they would also need to be verified through documentation, preferably from a third party, i.e. the listed employer or certifying entity.

That is why training programs that do not offer documentation and/or certification should be avoided, for again, if this documentation does not exist, for all legal intents and purposes <u>the training never happened</u>.

In regard to the statement regarding instructor qualification requiring an "evaluation of instructional competence by the Training Director", OSHA suggests:

> The Training Director should preferably be someone certified to that level...In the absence of a certified Training Director, this requirement should be met by having someone with superior qualifications to your own, evaluate your training technique annually. The evaluation should include written documentation and a discussion of strengths and weaknesses with the evaluator. A copy of this documentation should then be forwarded … for inclusion in your file.

Instructors should also be required to maintain professional competency by:

1. **Participating in continuing education:** This may be training of any type that is relevant to the courses taught by the trainer.

2. **Participating in professional development programs:** These may be any training programs that improve your instructional skills.

3. **Completing successfully an annual refresher course:** Most accredited courses are valid for three years and then must be repeated or the appropriate refresher course attended.

4. **Having an annual review by the Training Director:** The evaluation should include written documentation and a discussion of strengths and weaknesses with the evaluator.

Copies of the documentation of all of the above such training should become a part of each instructor's permanent training file.

Additional Required Documentation

In addition to lesson plans and handouts, each

Recommended Instructor Qualification Criteria *

1. Trainers shall have an appropriate level of technical knowledge, skills, or abilities in the subjects they teach.

2. Trainers shall be competent in delivery techniques and methods appropriate to adult learning.

3. Trainers shall maintain their training skills by participating in continuing education, development programs, or experience related to their subject matter expertise & delivery skills.

4. The trainer shall apply adult learning principles appropriate to the target audience and the learning objectives.

Source: American National Standards Institute (ANSI)

---

training iteration must include the following documentation:

• **Daily Attendance Form:** For all training segments. Absences must be noted.

• **Individual Student Performance Record:** For performance-based training segments. Not necessary for seminar-style programs unless tests are administered.

• **Critique Forms:** Should be used to allow students to provide uninhibited feedback. Anonymous format is recommended. Critique form should be kept simple. Responses should be elicited regarding the following:
1) Course relevancy (did course meet expectations?)

2) Instructor performance and teaching technique
3) Course duration (too long, too short, about right)
4) What was liked most and least
5) Would the student recommend the course to others?
6) An additional space should be provided for other comments or suggestions.

• **Certificates:** Certificates (suitable for framing) should be provided whenever possible. Professionally appearing certificates can be easily created by anyone with even rudimentary computer skills and some basic software. In addition to providing documentation that the student may keep in his own files, it is part of the overall "reward" for having successfully completed the training (token economy; see Chapter 4).

Program Revisions

All programs should be routinely updated and revised. The name of the person revising the plan and the last revision date should be noted somewhere on the lesson plan, preferably the cover. Notation should be made even if the instructor simply reviews the lesson plan to ensure it is still relevant and accurately conforms with department policy.

End of the Trail - The Courtroom

If a member of your department is involved in a deadly force situation and ends up in a courtroom on the receiving end of a lawsuit or civil rights action as the defendant, then two things are fairly certain:

1) The primary objective, ensuring the officer survives and wins any deadly force encounter he becomes involved in, has been achieved.

344

2) In order to achieve the second objective and prevail in any attendant civil litigation, the officer will need the assistance and support of the department that selected, equipped, and trained him.

It is important to remember that the department's trainers, regardless of rank, represent the department when conducting training operations. The trainers, therefore, will most likely be the people the courts will look to to provide information regarding how the officer was trained, and *why* the officer was trained in that manner.

The existence, completeness, accuracy and detail of all training records will naturally play a pivotal role in establishing both the credibility of the training the officers have received, as well as the professionalism of the department itself.

In regard to how long training records should be maintained, there are two answers: 1) forever, and 2) at least for as long as the officers who received the training are still working in any law enforcement capacity.

This is because *any training* that an officer has received can be subject to review, especially if the officer has made a critical decision and taken action based on that training. Should that happen, the chain of responsibility (and liability) extends from that officer, through the trainers and to the administration—as it should.

For if the training is both viable and documented, this is a positive thing and will assist the officer in prevailing over any civil litigation while making the entire agency look both competent and professional.

If, on the other hand, training has not been conducted professionally, or has not been documented as thoroughly as it should be, both the trainers and the training provided by the department may appear less than competent.

This in turn would surely taint the officer and department as a whole, and is, therefore, both undesirable and unacceptable.

What the U.S. Courts are Mandating in Regard to Police Firearms Training

1. More frequent training

2. Moving targets

3. Reduced light training

4. Judgmental / decisional training

5. Use of cover

6. Realistic environments

7. Policy reinforcement

8. Force level integration and transition

9. Relevance to assignment

Relevant Court Cases Cited for Reference

1. **Allen v. Muskogee,** 119 F.3rd, 837, (10 Cir. 1997)

2. **Board of County Commissioners of Bryon County, Oklahoma v. Brown,** 520 U.S. 397. (1997)

3. **Brown v. Gray,** 227 F. 3rd, 1278 (10 Cir 2000)

4. **City of Canton v. Harris,** 489 U.S. 378 (1989)

5. **Cornfield v. Consolidated High School District No. 230,** 991 F.2nd 1316 (1993)

6. **Graham v. Connor,** 109 S. Ct. 1865(1989)

7. **Leatherman v. Tarrant County Narcotics and Intelligence and Coordination Unit,** 113 S.Ct. 1160 (1993)

8. **Oklahoma v. Tuttle,** 471 U.S. 808 (1985)

9. **Popow v. City of Margate,** 476 F. Supp. 1237 (DNJ. 1979)

10. **Tennessee v. Garner,** 471 US 1 (1985)

11. **Votour v. Vitale,** 761 F. 2nd 812 (1985)

12. **Walker v. City of New York,** 974 F.2nd 292 (2nd Cir 1992)

13. **Zuchel v. City and County of Denver,** 997 F.2nd 730 (10 Cir. 1993)

APPENDIX V
Dynamic Encounter Training: An Analysis of Contemporary Firearms Training Methods and Their Task Suitability for High Stress Combat Scenarios [1]

– William E. Burroughs

Introduction

Since the inception of structured firearms training in the late 1920's, officers and instructors alike have been taught to believe that stylized techniques for shooting were required in order to score well in qualification and shoot well in combat. These techniques have often focused on complex motor skills and have demonstrated for many that they can be difficult to learn and even more difficult to apply. Add to this that most officers are not adequately prepared through their training to effectively deal with spontaneous life threatening circumstances without significant risk to themselves and are completely unaware of the affects of survival stress on motor skill performance and you have a recipe for disaster.

William E. "Bill" Burroughs

The purpose of this research is to aid in the design and implementation of training programs that are based on human performance limitations as affected by the intensity of the stimuli encountered during combat stress. The research domain for this project relates to both cognitive/perceptual awareness and motor skill development and specifically impacts upon the current paradigm in training with the application of firearms. Core to this research is the analysis of contemporary training standards and their task utility in spontaneous life threatening events.

The data from this research will have significant impact upon the law enforcement community generally and firearms training and high liability interdiction specifically. The focus was to determine, through observation and survey, the innate or natural response to a spontaneous "life threatening" event generated by simulation in a dynamic training environment. The research identifies responses characterized by shooting position preference and "hit" potential and determines whether stylized shooting performance is reproducible during periods of high stress.

Law enforcement professionals face an operational dilemma each time they begin a tour of duty. Often without the benefit of relevant and practical physical skills, they must effectively manage life threatening spontaneous occurrences. Those who have been properly trained for real world need by recognizing human performance limitations are prepared.

---

[1] *Dynamic Encounter Training: An Analysis of Contemporary Firearms Training Methods and Their Task Suitability for High Stress Combat Scenarios* was first published in 1998. Re-printed with permission of the author.

Those who have not had that positive training experience will face their life threatening challenges without the essential tools necessary to succeed. Invariably, this leads to increased personal risk for the officer and costly civil litigation for the agency.

The current paradigm in use throughout the criminal justice system to train officers in subject control procedures, particularly with firearms, is representative of an approach to training that I will refer to as "activity". This approach stems from a managerial view of the training function as one of only conducting mandatory training programs and not one of assisting field operatives in the performance of their mental and physical duties. This value statement clearly demonstrates a serious shortage of collaborative organizational and operational objectives and commits training efforts to unacceptable financial expense for poorly calculated outcomes. Logistically, training often becomes a numbers game where documentation that everyone has "qualified" on paper and "looks" the same on the range is superior to their demonstrated competency in the field.

Regardless of ideologies, egos or money, the data in this study directs that the focus of firearms training change from its static, highly structured marksmanship environment to an interactive, dynamic environment where reality based training is employed. It is obvious that the incidence of field related failure is correlated with the officer's inability to adequately respond using contemporary training methods.

It is the intent of this research to provide hard data on the physiological reactions to survival stress using simulated, spontaneous scenarios and subsequently recommend a defensible direction for future training with firearms applications designed to control violent subject behavior. Specifically, this research analyzed:

1. The physiological reactions to survival stress as they relate to shooting stance preference.

2. Whether traditional sighted fire is employed when the events are spontaneous in nature.

3. Changes in visual efficiency and preference for the objects in focus.

Methodology

This research focused on the question, "What are the effects of induced stress on physical performance with handguns?"

Although there are many effects, only stance preference and visual performance are within the scope of this project. A survey instrument entitled, *Comprehensive Training Survey: The Effects of Induced Stress on Physical Performance with Handguns in a Simulated Combat Environment* was developed to quantify the collected data and provide a platform for the debriefing of incidents. The data was then organized according to theme to determine existing trends.

The research model used for the collection and assimilation of data is an "action research" model presented in *Action Research and Organizational Development* written by J. Barton Cunningham (1993). This model was introduced in 1946 to denote an approach to research combining theory building with research on practical problems. It analyzes the process of systemic change and identifies the practical problem of how to enter an organization or culture effectively and facilitate that change. A basic assumption of action research is that learning within the group through the development of new attitudes is a basic resource for the research (Cunningham).

Operating under the premise of "do the client no harm" and "work for the betterment of the whole", the intent was to first determine who the client was and to what end might they be helped.

The client turned out to be the individual officer as it is that officer who affects the system. How that officer might be helped concentrated upon improving survival skills for risk reduction which also provided a by-product of liability reduction for the agency. The desired end state for the change effort incorporates enhanced skill competency and personal confidence to more effectively deal with spontaneous occurrences of violence directed at the officer personally.

Utilizing the *Comprehensive Training Survey*, data was collected regarding the training backgrounds of all participants to determine what, if any, influence their demographic background or training had on their performance in the simulated spontaneous incidents. All of the incidents were scripted and involved violent physical attack on the officer with an instrument of lethal force. All of the firearms involved were equipped to fire Simunition™ dye marking ammunition which gave feedback on accuracy and provided an impetus to avoid the pain of being hit by making a mistake.

Additionally, the survey served to redefine the problem once again to determine if, in fact, contemporary training methodologies were core to observed diminished performance capacities.

Finally, it provided the instrument that documented the performance of all participants and codified their responses. This required searching for commonality in their responses to determine underlying themes influencing individual performance.

Once data collection and analysis was complete, a diagnosis was made of the current state of firearms training to "get a picture of what is going on." The "picture" of diminished performance provided a broader understanding of the true nature of the problem and helped to establish what the desired end state should be.

Results and Findings

The learning that has taken place since project inception begins to answer the research question

posed. With regard to that postulated, note:

• Physiological reactions to survival stress (sympathetic nervous system activation) demonstrate crouching, squaring the body to the threat and locking the arms at full extension. This favors symmetrical body positioning and not asymmetrical configurations common to "stylized" shooting methods. Further, the sympathetic nervous system prioritizes the visual sense forcing binocularity and causing farsightedness. This eliminates the use of the weapon's sights as previously trained.

• Competency based training to provide a system of instruction relevant to performance expectations of the job is required. This relevance must correlate with the practical nature of the techniques as they are to be applied in a real world environment. Current instructional methodology is designed around a weapon handling, marksmanship, combat progression. Data collected shows that the highest percentage of training time focuses on marksmanship development, with simulated combat experience a rarity. Unfortunately, marksmanship skills are closed motor skills which are not reproducible under conditions of survival stress. One can therefore state that during a life threatening occurrence, the tools provided to shoot accurately are no longer available.

• The findings postulate a new training design methodology of weapon handling, combat, then marksmanship. The emphasis shifts from a scored measure of effectiveness to a demonstrated ability to apply lethal force in a simulated, relevant real world encounter. This focus on combat orientation establishes a framework for reproducible skills, builds confidence and makes the subsequent task of marksmanship development much easier.

The composite results of physical performance

for all respondents during the execution of the *Comprehensive Training Survey* statistically represent:

• Squaring the body to the threat 59%

• Focused vision on the threat 93%

• Used binocular vision 88%

These three items favor the symmetrical Isosceles stance and not the asymmetrical Weaver which is a bladed approach.

Contemporary instructional methods continue to stylize shooting stances and attempt to control the officer's response through periods of high repetition training. Statistically, however, data compiled from this research demonstrates that officers categorically respond to a spontaneous, life threatening occurrence with their survival instincts and not their parasympathetic motor skills training.

This postulates a design methodology more in line with instinctive behavior, that is, combat before refined marksmanship and gross motor skills before fine or complex. This is the venue of combat training. The emphasis must shift from a scored measure of effectiveness to a demonstrated ability to apply lethal force without hesitation when required in simulated, relevant real world encounters. This focus on combat orientation provides reproducible skills training during periods of extraordinary stress, builds confidence and ultimately makes the task of marksmanship development much easier.

Conclusions

It is necessary to develop a new training paradigm to use as the vehicle of facilitation for the new research. Dynamic Encounter Training (DET) has been designed to provide the tools that enable trainers and administrators to work together as partners and achieve specific goals.

This approach requires that trainers develop skills beyond the competencies they currently possess to design and administer training.

In the application of lethal force, law enforcement officers practice a high art. Historically, the Samurai provided a law enforcement function in their application of lethal force, but were arguably more competent in doing so. Was it practice that made them so, or the intangible duty to task? We may never know that answer, but one thing is for certain–if the focus of training does not move from the controlled, static environment to an experiential one, the results of that training will remain where they are today. That finality, with each passing court case, underscores a demonstrated lack of skill.

The expected end result of firearms training for the law enforcement community has remained constant since the earliest records of structured learning. Simply stated, you must hit that at which you are shooting. Officers regularly demonstrate static skill competency each time they report to the range for qualification. Unfortunately, this sterile competency is adulterated in the field to a level of serious concern for personal safety as the skills previously learned do not make the jump to an emotionally charged, violent environment.

Perhaps the answer rests with the next generation of instructors who, while they might have a specialty in one or more aspects of the use of force, are generalists in that they understand the operational needs of officers at all levels within their accepted use of force matrix.

Law enforcement use of force training needs an ongoing assessment framework for everything taught in subject control in order to continue the evolutionary process of moving from the overly complicated to the easily reproduced. The military has not been wrong over the years in presenting material in the "keep it simple" paradigm. So it should be in law enforcement. This requires work, however, and a dedication to the process of research and learning.

To dedicate oneself to improve upon human performance potential with a firearm is a multi-dimensional task with far reaching consequences. The work involved will affect individuals as well as organizations and will bring the desired end state into alignment with training philosophies.

The training determinants of cognitive processing and biomechanical ability will combine to produce a more competent officer of the future.

The challenge is to remain focused and look to the past to provide a window for the future.

About the Author

Mr. Burroughs' experience in the law enforcement community spans 30 years as an officer and personal trainer. Internationally published and recognized as a use of force expert, he conducts training worldwide as President of *TALON International. (Email: taloninternational@yahoo.com)*

Bibliography

Antal, Laslo and Skanaker, Ragnar (1985), *Pistol Shooting*, Antal & Skanaker.

Applegate, Colonel Rex (1943), *Kill or Get Killed*, Paladin Press.

Applegate, Colonel Rex and Janich, Michael D (1998), *Bullseyes Don't Shoot Back*, Paladin Press.

Ashton, Doug (1998), *Dynamic Firearms Training Research*, Peel Regional Police.

Cassidy, William L. (1978), *Quick or Dead*, Paladin Press.

Cunningham, J. Barton (1993), *Action Research and Organizational Development*, Praeger.

Fairbairn, W.E. and Sykes, E.A. (1942), *Shooting To Live*, Paladin Press.

Schmidt, Richard (1975), *Motor Skills*, Human Kinetics.

Siddle, Bruce (1998), *Scientific and Test Data Validating the Isosceks and Single-Hand Point Shooting Techniques*, PPCT Research Review.

Suarez, Gabriel (1996), *The Evolutions of Reactive Shooting*, The Tactical Edge (Fall 1996).

Vila, B. and Morrison, G. (1994), *Biological Limits of Police Combat Handgun Shooting Accuracy*, American Journal of Police, Volume 13, No. 1.

Westmorland, H. (1989), *Isosceles vs. Weaver Shooting Stances: The Selection of a Shooting Stance Under Stress*, PPCT Research Publications.

POLICE PISTOLCRAFT TRIVIA

Delf "Jelly" Bryce
1906-1974

U.S. Lawman and One of the Most Deadly Gunfighters in American History

The November 12, 1945, issue of Life Magazine contains a story about one of the fastest and most deadly gunslingers U.S. law enforcement has ever known. Fortunately, he was one of our own, beginning his career as a member of the Oklahoma City Police Department and eventually being recruited into the FBI where he spent 24 storied years.

Born in 1906 in Mt. View, Oklahoma, Delf Albert Bryce was raised with firearms and displayed an unusually high level of skill with them from an early age. He was, in fact, known as "a perfect shot."

Just a few days after joining the Oklahoma City Police Department in 1927, Bryce would prove that he was a perfect shot when facing armed adversaries as well. Opening the door of a car that contained a suspicious man who resembled a photograph on a wanted poster, Bryce confronted the man and identified himself as a police officer. The man, a known gangster, went for his gun. The young Bryce–just out of high school but already unbelievably fast and accurate–drew his own pistol and fired, instantly killing the gangster. This would be the first of a number of close quarter gunfights that Bryce would be involved in throughout his years of service. In fact, his nickname, "Jelly" was given to him by a dying gangster shortly after Bryce shot it out with him. In front of a crowd of witnesses, the criminal incredulously exclaimed, "I can't believe I was killed by a jelly bean like you." The term jelly bean was used at the time to describe a fancy dresser, which Bryce usually was. The nickname stuck, and soon Delf was known as D.A. "Jelly" Bryce.

Jelly Bryce was believed to have been involved in at least 19 shootings during his career. As noted above, he never missed his mark. His opponents were invariably hardened gangsters and desperados, and Jelly always made sure that he was the first through the door when confronting them.

Unbelievably, this man who had such a high profile, stellar, almost mythical career is relatively unknown to most people, especially in comparison to the criminal gunslingers of his day. Yet Jelly Bryce was undoubtedly braver, faster, and a better pistolero than any of them. And best of all, he was one of the good guys. (Read the full story of Jelly in the book, *Jelly Bryce: Legendary Lawman*, by retired Oklahoma City police officer Ron Owens. Published by Turner Publishing. Image used with permission.)

BIBLIOGRAPHY

Adams, Ronald J., McTernan, Thomas M. and Remsberg, Charles. Street Survival: Tactics for Armed Encounters. Northbrook, Illinois: Calibre Press, Inc., 1980.

Antal, Laslo and Skanaker, Ragnar. Pistol Shooting. Antal & Skanaker, 1985.

Applegate, Colonel Rex. Bullseyes and Silhouettes Don't Shoot Back: Police Handgun Training Without the Use of Sights. Law and Order Magazine, Wilmette, Illinois, 1994.

Applegate, Colonel Rex and Janich, Michael D. Bullseyes Don't Shoot Back. Boulder, Colorado: Paladin Press, 1998.

Applegate, Colonel Rex. Kill or Get Killed. Paladin Press, 1943.

Applegate, Colonel Rex. The Close Combat Files of Colonel Rex Applegate. Boulder, Colorado: Paladin Press, 1998

Artwohl, Dr. Alexis and Christensen, Loren W. Deadly Force Encounters. Boulder, Colorado: Paladin Press, 1997.

Artwohl, Dr. Alexis. No Recall of Weapon Discharge. Law Enforcement Executive Forum, Volume 3, Number 2, Macomb, IL, 2003.

Ashton, Doug. Dynamic Firearms Training Research. Peel Regional Police, 1998.

Askins, Captain Charles Jr. The Art of Handgun Shooting. New York: A.S. Barnes & Company, 1939.

Bennett, Wayne W. and Hess, Karen M. Management and Supervision in Law Enforcement. Thomson/Wadsworth, 2004.

Cassidy, William L. Quick or Dead. Boulder, Colorado: Paladin Press, 1978.

Cirillo, Jim. Guns, Bullets, and Gunfights: Lessons and Tales from a Modern-Day Gunfighter. Boulder, Colorado: Paladin Press, 1996.

Clapp, Wiley M. Modern Law Enforcement Weapons & Tactics. Northfield, Illinois: DBI Books, Inc.

Clausewitz, Carl von. On War. New York: Penguin Books, 1968.

Combat Pistol. John Shaw. Videocassette. L.O.T.I. Group Productions, 1996.

Combative Pistol: Jim Grover's Guide to Extreme Close-Quarters Shooting. Jim Grover. Videocassette. Paladin Press, 2002.

Conti, Michael E. Beyond Pepper Spray: The Complete Guide to Chemical Agents, Delivery Systems, and Protective Masks. Boulder, Colorado: Paladin Press, 2002.

Conti, Michael E. If the Gun Fits. Police and Security News, Days Communications, Inc., Kulpsville, PA, July/August 1999.

Conti, Michael E. In the Line of Fire: A Working Cop's Guide to Pistolcraft. Boulder, Colorado: Paladin Press, 1997.

Conti, Michael E. In the Line of Fire: A Refocus on the "Front Sight" Concept. Guns & Ammo, Los Angeles, California, December 2000.

Conti, Michael E. In the Line of Fire: A Refocus on the "Front Sight" Concept, Part II. Guns & Ammo, Los Angeles, California, February 2001.

Conti, Michael E. In the Line of Fire: A Refocus on the "Front Sight" Concept, Part III. Guns & Ammo, Los Angeles, California, May 2001.

Conti, Michael E. In the Line of Fire: A Refocus on the "Front Sight" Concept, Part IV. Guns & Ammo, Los Angeles, California, August 2001.

Conti, Michael E. Massachusetts State Police Firearms Training Program: The New Paradigm. New Braintree, Massachusetts: Massachusetts State Police Academy Firearms Training Unit, 2000.

Conti, Michael E. Massachusetts State Police Mental Preparation for Lethal Force Encounters Instructor Manual. New Braintree, Massachusetts: Massachusetts State Police Academy Firearms Training Unit, 2002.

Conti, Michael E. The T.I.R.R. Clearing Drill. The Law Enforcement Trainer: The Official Publication of the American Society of Law Enforcement Trainers, Lewes, DE, November/December 1997.

Conti, Michael E. The Tap Invert Rack Ready Clearing Drill. The Firearms Instructor: The Official Publication of the International Association of Law Enforcement Firearms Instructors, Varro Press, Shawnee Mission, KS, Issue 20, November 1996.

Cunningham, Eugene. Triggernometry: A Gallery of Gunfighters. Caldwell, Idaho: The Caxtan Printers, Ltd., 1941

Cunningham, J. Barton. Action Research and Organizational Development. Praeger, 1993.

Damery, Paul. Massachusetts State Police Basic Police Firearms Instructor Manual. New Braintree, Massachusetts: Massachusetts State Police Academy, 1996.

Fairbairn, Major W.E. Get Tough!. D. Appleton-Century Company, 1942.

Fairbairn, W.E. and Sykes, E.A. Shooting To Live. Boulder, Colorado: Paladin Press, 1942.

Farnam, John S. The Farnam Method of Defensive Handgunning. Boulder, Colorado: DTI Publications, 2000.

Fast and Fancy Shooters. Presentation by Colonel Rex Applegate. Videocassette. 1989.

FBI Academy. <u>Combat Shooting at Close Range is Good Training</u>. FBI Law Enforcement Bulletin, November 1961.

FitzGerald, J. Henry. <u>Shooting</u>. Hartford, Connecticut: The G.F. Book Company, 1930.

Frazer, Major William D. <u>American Pistol Shooting: A Manual of Instruction in Modern Pistol Marksmanship</u>. New York: E.P. Dutton & Co., 1929.

<u>Fundamentals of Double-Action Revolver Shooting</u>. FBI Training Academy. Videocassette. National Archives, unknown.

Grossman, Lt. Colonel Dave. <u>On Killing: The Psychological Cost of Learning to Kill in War and Society</u>. Little, Brown and Company, 1995.

Himmelwright, A.L.A. <u>Pistol and Revolver Shooting</u>. New York: The Macmillan Company, 1930.

<u>Jim Cirillo: Modern-Day Gunfighter</u>. Jim Cirillo. Videocassette. Paladin Press, 1996.

Jordan, Bill. <u>No Second Place Winner</u>. Concord, New Hampshire: Police Bookshelf, 1989.

Karwan, Chuck. <u>The Gun Digest Book of Combat Handgunnery, 2nd Edition</u>. Northfield, Illinois: DBI Books, Inc.

Kieth, Elmer. <u>Sixguns By Keith</u>. New York: R&R Books, 1961

Lewis, Jack and Mitchell, Jack. <u>The Gun Digest Book of Combat Handgunnery</u>. Northfield, Illinois: DBI Books, Inc.

Marshall, Colonel S.L.A. <u>Men Against Fire: The Problem of Battle Command in Future War</u>. Gloucester, Massachusetts: Peter Smith, 1978.

Marshall, Colonel S.L.A. <u>Pork Chop Hill</u>. Battery Press, 1956.

McGivern, Ed. <u>Ed McGivern's Book on Fast and Fancy Revolver Shooting and Police Training</u>. Lewistown, Montana, 1938.

Meany, Dan. <u>Carry On, Colonel Applegate</u>. SWAT Magazine, Prescott Valley, Arizona, May 1999.

Miller, Nyle H. and Snell, Joseph W. <u>Great Gunfighters of the Kansas Cowtowns, 1867-1886</u>. University of Nebraska Press, 1963

Morrison, Gregory Boyce. <u>The Modern Technique of the Pistol</u>. Pauldin, Arizona: Gunsite Press, 1991.

Morrison, Gregory B. <u>Police handgun qualification: practical measure or aimless activity?</u> Policing. An International Journal of Police Strategies & Management, Vol. 21 No. 3, 1998.

Musashi, Miyamoto. <u>The Book of Five Rings.</u> Translated by Cleary, Thomas. Shambhala, 2003.

Mroz, Ralph. Defensive Shooting for Real-Life Encounters: A Critical Look at Current Training Methods. Boulder, Colorado: Paladin Press, 2000.

Nofi, Dr. Albert A. A Civil War Treasury. Conshohocken, PA: Combined Book, Inc. 1992.

NRA. Law Enforcement Firearms Instructor Manual. Washington, DC, 1991.

Only Hits Count: Practical Firearms Training for Personal Defense. Louis Awerbuck. Videocassette Tape. Paladin Press, 2001.

OSS Training Group. Office of Strategic Services, Field Photographic Branch. Videocassette Tape. Traditions Military Video, 2000.

Owens, Ron. Jelly Bryce: Legendary Lawman. Paducah, Kentucky: Turner Publishing Company, 2003.

Picariello, Joseph. Massachusetts Law Enforcement Firearms Instructors' & Armorers' Association Firearms Instructors' Course Manual. Holliston, Massachusetts, 2000.

Powers, William F. French and Electric Blue: The Massachusetts State Police, A History. Powers, 1979.

Remsberg, Charles. The Tactical Edge: Surviving High Risk Patrol. Northbrook, Illinois: Calibre Press, Inc., 1986.

Schade, Thomas V., Bruns, Gilbert H. and Morrison, Gregory. Armed Confrontations: Police Shooting Performance in Threatening Environments. American Journal of Police, Volume 13, No. 1, 1994.

Schmidt, Richard. Motor Skills. Human Kinetics, 1975.

Secrets of a Master Gunfighter. Jim Cirillo. Videocassette. Paladin Press, 1998.

Shaw, John. You Can't Miss. Memphis, Tenn.: Shaw/Bane, 1982.

Shooting for Keeps: Point Shooting for Close-Quarter Combat. Narr. Colonel Rex Applegate. Videocassette Tape. Paladin Press, 1996.

Shots in the Dark: A Complete Guide to the Tactical Use of Laser Sights. Clyde Caceres. Videocassette Tape. Paladin Press, 2000.

Siddle, Bruce. Scientific and Test Data Validating the Isosceks and Single-Hand Point Shooting Techniques. PPCT Research Review, 1998.

Siddle, Bruce. Sharpening the Warrior's Edge. Milstadt, Illinois: PPCT Research Publications, 1995.

Sigarms Academy. Firearms Program Development and Defensibility. Exeter, NH, 1992.

Sigarms Academy. Firearms Safety Course. Exeter, NH, 1992.

Sigarms Academy. Instructor's Pistol Course. Exeter, NH, 1992.

Sigarms Academy. Rangemaster Course. Epping, NH, 2000.

Sigarms Academy. Training Administration and Control. Exeter, NH, 1992.

Smith, R. Harris. OSS: The Secret History of America's First Central Intelligence Agency. London, England: University of California Press, Ltd., 1972.

Smith & Wesson Academy. Firearms Instructor Manual. Springfield, Massachusetts, 1997.

Smith & Wesson Academy. Reduced Light Training Instructor Manual. Springfield, Massachusetts, 1999.

Smith & Wesson Academy. Tactical Handgun for the Protective Specialist Course. Springfield, Massachusetts, 1994.

Stanford, Andy. Surgical Speed Shooting: How to Achieve High-Speed Marksmanship in a Gunfight. Boulder, Colorado: Paladin Press, 2001.

Taubert, Robert K. CQB Pistol Course. Springfield, Massachusetts: Smith & Wesson Academy, 1999.

Taylor, Major Grant. The Palestine Police Force Close Quarter Battle (Revolvers, automatics, and submachine guns). Jewish National and University Library, Jerusalem, 1943.

Tracy, Captain Charles D. Revolver Shooting in War. Stoney Creek, Ontario: Fortress Publications, Inc., 1916.

Tsu, Lao, Tao Te Ching. New York, New York: Vintage Books, 1972.

Tsunetomo, Yamamoto. Hagakure: The Book of the Samurai. Bunkyo-ku, Tokyo: Kodansha International Ltd., 1983 .

Tzu, Sun. The Art of War. New York, New York: Delacorte Press, 1983

Unknown author. The Pistol as a Weapon of Defence in the House and on the Road. Boulder, Colorado: Paladin Press, 2004.

U.S. Department of Justice, Office of Justice Programs, Bureau of Justice Statistics. Police Use of Force: Collection of National Data. November 1997, NCJ-165040.

U.S. Department of Justice, Federal Bureau of Investigation. Killed in the Line of Duty: A Study of Selected Felonious Killings of Law Enforcement Officers. Uniform Crime Reports Section, September 1992.

U.S. Department of Justice, Federal Bureau of Investigation. Law Enforcement Officers Killed and Assaulted. Uniform Crime Reports Section, 1992.

Vila, B. and Morrison, G. Biological Limits of Police Combat Handgun Shooting Accuracy, American Journal of Police, Volume 13, No. 1, 1994.

Westmorland, H. Isosceles vs. Weaver Shooting Stances: The Selection of a Shooting Stance Under Stress. PPCT Research Publications, 1989.

Every man owes some of his time
to the upbuilding of the profession to which he belongs.

– Theodore Roosevelt

ABOUT THE AUTHOR

Mike Conti has been a proud member of the Massachusetts State Police (MSP) since 1986. During his career he has been fortunate to have worked with some of the finest police officers in the US while performing in functions ranging from uniformed patrol, high-crime area community policing, SWAT, and special security details to undercover narcotics and death investigations. He has been involved as a professional trainer since 1991 and holds numerous instructor certifications in various use of force disciplines.

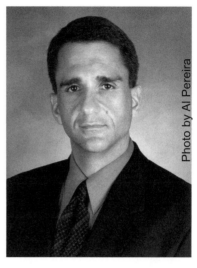

Photo by Al Pereira

In January 2000, Conti was tasked by then Superintendent of the MSP, Colonel John DiFava, to organize, staff, and train the first fulltime Firearms Training Unit (FTU) for the department. During the creation of the FTU, Conti developed a firearms training program specifically geared to preparing police officers for the realities of the lethal force encounter. This successful program, dubbed *The New Paradigm of Police Firearms Training*, has received nation-wide attention and been profiled by the Law Enforcement Training Network (LETN). The New Paradigm was also the subject of a series of articles written by Conti that appeared in his column in *Guns & Ammo* magazine while he served as Law Enforcement Contributing Editor. Response to those articles from law enforcement officers all across the United States inspired the creation of this book.

In 2001, Colonel DiFava presented Conti with the *MSP Medal of Merit* for the creation of the New Paradigm Training Program. In 2003, Conti was awarded the prestigious *Commonwealth of Massachusetts Citation for Outstanding Performance* for work performed during the development and administration of training programs for both the FTU and the MSP Logan International Airport Anti-Terrorist Unit (ATU).

In addition to his work for the MSP, Conti has written two other books, *In the Line of Fire: A Working Cop's Guide to Pistolcraft* (1997), and *Beyond Pepper Spray: The Complete Guide to Chemical Agents, Delivery Systems, and Protective Masks* (2002), both published by Paladin Press. He has also had more than 100 articles published in various local and national publications.

A member of IALEFI, MLEFIAA, and the NRA, Conti currently holds the rank of sergeant and serves as the Director of Aviation Security Policy and Training for the Massachusetts State Police at Logan International Airport. He also continues to serve as the Director of Saber Group, Inc., a private training and consulting services company he founded in 1997.

Quick Order Form

Postal Orders: Saber Press
                                    268 Main Street
                                    PMB 138
                                    North Reading, MA 01864

Website Orders: www.sabergroup.com

Contact us: Telephone: 978-749-3731
                            Fax: 978-475-5420
                            Email: Booksales@sabergroup.com

Please send me _____ copies of:

☑ *POLICE PISTOLCRAFT: The Reality-Based New Paradigm of Police Firearms Training* by Michael E. Conti

Price: $29.95 (+ $4.00 Shipping) Total cost: **$33.95**

Ship-to Massachusetts addresses ONLY add 5.00% Sales Tax: $1.49

for total cost of: **$35.44**

I have enclosed a cheque or money order for $ _____

Please note: Copies of this book are available at special discounts for bulk purchase. Special editions or book excerpts can also be created to specifications.

Ship to:

Name: _____

Address: _____

City: _____ State: _____ Zip:_____

Telephone: _____

email address: _____

Shipping Costs
U.S.: $4.00 for first book and $2.00 for each additional book.
International: $9.00 for first book and $5.00 for each additional book.

Postal Orders: Please send only cheque or money order made out to Saber Press.